China's Regional Relations in Comparative Perspective

China's relations with its neighbors have evolved since 1949, and in the 21st century, many scholars argue that China's rising power has led it to be increasingly domineering over those smaller countries in Northeast, Southeast, Central, and South Asia. The evolution of China's regional relations needs to be examined comprehensively, since China counts twenty-seven countries as its "neighbors," large and small. While China's official policy toward all of these countries is to treat them as "good neighbors" and "partners," some of these relationships have been spectacularly deteriorating, while others have been quietly improving over the last two decades.

Jackson takes a comparative foreign policy approach and compares China's status as a regional hegemon with the United States, Russia, India, Brazil, South Africa, and Nigeria. The result is a broader theory as to why regional powers are sometimes intimidating and at other times accommodating.

An important contribution to studies on China, this book will prove useful to scholars and students in Chinese and Asian foreign policy, comparative foreign policy, and international relations.

Steven F. Jackson is a professor of political science. After receiving his bachelor's degree in International Relations from Stanford University in 1981, he taught English in Xi'an China from 1981–83. He received his Ph.D. from the University of Michigan and joined the faculty at Indiana University of Pennsylvania in 1994. His area of specialization is in Chinese foreign relations, and in particular China's regional relationships, such as with East Asia and Africa.

Rethinking Asia and International Relations
Series Editor – Emilian Kavalski
Australian Catholic University (Sydney)

This series seeks to provide thoughtful consideration both of the growing prominence of Asian actors on the global stage and the changes in the study and practice of world affairs that they provoke. It intends to offer a comprehensive parallel assessment of the full spectrum of Asian states, organizations, and regions and their impact on the dynamics of global politics.

The series seeks to encourage conversation on:

- what rules, norms, and strategic cultures are likely to dominate international life in the "Asian Century";
- how global problems will be reframed and addressed by a "rising Asia";
- which institutions, actors, and states are likely to provide leadership during such "shifts to the East";
- whether there is something distinctly "Asian" about the emerging patterns of global politics.

Such comprehensive engagement not only aims to offer a critical assessment of the actual and prospective roles of Asian actors, but also seeks to rethink the concepts, practices, and frameworks of analysis of world politics.

This series invites proposals for interdisciplinary research monographs undertaking comparative studies of Asian actors and their impact on the current patterns and likely future trajectories of international relations. Furthermore, it offers a platform for pioneering explorations of the ongoing transformations in global politics as a result of Asia's increasing centrality to the patterns and practices of world affairs.

For a full list of titles in this series, please visit www.routledge.com/Rethinking-Asia-and-International-Relations/book-series/ASHSER1384

Titles

The Guanxi of Relational International Theory
Emilian Kavalski

China's Regional Relations in Comparative Perspective
From Harmonious Neighbors to Strategic Partners
Steven F. Jackson

China's Regional Relations in Comparative Perspective

From Harmonious Neighbors to Strategic Partners

Steven F. Jackson

Routledge
Taylor & Francis Group
LONDON AND NEW YORK

First published 2018
by Routledge
2 Park Square, Milton Park, Abingdon, Oxon OX14 4RN

and by Routledge
711 Third Avenue, New York, NY 10017

Routledge is an imprint of the Taylor & Francis Group, an informa business

© 2018 Steven F. Jackson

The right of Steven F. Jackson to be identified as author of this work has been asserted by him in accordance with sections 77 and 78 of the Copyright, Designs and Patents Act 1988.

All rights reserved. No part of this book may be reprinted or reproduced or utilized in any form or by any electronic, mechanical, or other means, now known or hereafter invented, including photocopying and recording, or in any information storage or retrieval system, without permission in writing from the publishers.

Trademark notice: Product or corporate names may be trademarks or registered trademarks, and are used only for identification and explanation without intent to infringe.

British Library Cataloguing-in-Publication Data
A catalogue record for this book is available from the British Library

Library of Congress Cataloging-in-Publication Data
A catalog record for this book has been requested

ISBN: 978-1-409-45589-9 (hbk)
ISBN: 978-1-315-57165-2 (ebk)

Typeset in Times New Roman
by Apex CoVantage, LLC

To my wife, Dr. Andrea M. Lopez, who had to listen to all of this, repeatedly.

Contents

List of figures		viii
List of tables		ix
Preface		xi
1	Introduction	1
2	Regional hegemons and their behavior	14
3	Legacies of China's regional relations	69
4	Restructuring of relations: the "Good Neighbor" 1988–2004	88
5	"Friendly Elephant" or assertive Dragon? 2004–present	138
6	China and Northeast Asia in the 21st century	157
7	China and Southeast Asia in the 21st century	182
8	China and Central Asia in the 21st century	229
9	China and South Asia in the 21st century	254
10	Conclusion	280
	Index	289

Figures

2.1	China: regional population ratios, 1960–2015	18
2.2	China: regional military personnel ratios, 1989–2015	18
2.3	China: regional GDP ratios, 1960–2015 (current US$)	19
2.4	China: regional military expenditure ratios, 1989–2015	20
2.5	Evolution of China's neighboring relations	61
7.1	Map of South China Sea claims	183

Tables

1.1	China's neighboring regions and neighbors	11
2.1	Regional hegemons and their regions	16
2.2	Regional hegemons' dominance ratios in 2000	17
2.3	Regional hegemons' behavior	22
2.4	Regional hegemons' reasons for behavioral change	57
4.1	China: total trade with Northeast Asia, 1988–2003	100
4.2	China: total trade with Southeast Asia, 1988–2003	114
4.3	China: total trade with Central Asia, 1992–2003	123
4.4	China: total trade with South Asia, 1988–2003	128
5.1	Hierarchy of Chinese partnership designations	144
6.1	China: total trade with Northeast Asia, 2004–2015	169
6.2	China and Japan: mutual trade dependency, 2004–2015	170
6.3	China and South Korea: mutual trade dependency, 2004–2015	171
6.4	Mongolia: trade dependency on China and Russia, 2004–2015	172
6.5	China: foreign direct investment in Northeast Asia, 2004–2014	173
7.1	East Asian Coast Guard and maritime enforcement units	190
7.2	China's "partners" and "strategic relations" in Southeast Asia, 2004–2014	195
7.3	China: total trade with Southeast Asia, 2004–2015	211
7.4	Southeast Asia: trade dependency on China, 2004–2015	212
7.5	China: foreign direct investment flows in Southeast Asia, 2004–2014	215
7.6	Chinese tourist arrivals in Southeast Asia, 2004–2012	216
8.1	China's "partners" and "strategic relations" in Central Asia, 2004–2014	234
8.2	Central Asian natural gas reserves, 2015	246
8.3	China: total trade with Central Asia, 2004–2015	246
8.4	China and Russia: mutual trade dependency, 2004–2015	247
8.5	China: foreign direct investment flows in Central Asia, 2004–2014	249
9.1	China's "partners" and "strategic relations" in South Asia, 2004–2014	259

9.2	China: total trade with South Asia, 2004–2015	270
9.3	China and India: mutual trade dependency, 2004–2015	271
9.4	China: foreign direct investment in South Asia, 2003–2014	274
9.5	Chinese tourist arrivals in South Asia, 2008–2012	275
10.1	Summary of China's neighboring relations, 2017	282
10.2	Asia public concern over China's territorial disputes	286

Preface

This book represents a project that has been a very, very long time in development. It began in 1995 with a conference organized at the East-West Center in Honolulu on "The Modernization of China's Diplomacy," organized by Lin Zhimin and my good friend Wang Jianwei. I was assigned to examine China's "Good Neighbor Policy" and wound up also writing a theoretical piece on the modernization of diplomacy as well. Sadly, that volume never came together, but I did not give up on the idea of examining China's "Good Neighbor Policy." The pressures of teaching, tenure, promotion, then serving as a department chair may have put the project on hiatus, but it remained an area of interest, reading and research.

Research for this book was conducted at the Library of Congress and was facilitated by the staff of the Asian Reading Room. Additional research for this book has been in quite a few libraries around the world, including the University of Pittsburgh, Stanford University, and the University of Hawai'i at Manoa.

Portions of this book have been presented over the years, primarily at the Annual Meetings of the International Studies Association, and I thank all of the discussants and fellow panelists whose comments have greatly improved this modest work. Portions of Chapter 7 were previously published as "Does China Have A Monroe Doctrine?" in *Strategic Studies Quarterly*, Winter 2016. Indiana University of Pennsylvania granted me a sabbatical in Spring 2017, which was critical to finishing the manuscript. Most of all, I thank my wife, Dr. Andrea M. Lopez, who has been supportive throughout the project and whose ideas and reactions have served as a first forum for consideration. Errors of interpretation are, of course, my fault.

A note on names

Chinese and Japanese names in this book are rendered in traditional order: surname, then given name. Chinese, Russian, and Hindi words and phrases that are particularly important are also rendered in original characters/scripts and appropriate Romanization. The citations for English-language works of authors with Chinese names uses the surname only. Works in Chinese or translated from Chinese use the full name for clarification.

Some place names carry political implications. In the case of disputed territories, a neutral term such as "Spratlys" or "Paracels" is used where available and commonly known. In other cases, both are referenced: "Senkaku/Diaoyu," without any significance of the order. "Burma" versus "Myanmar" became an issue in 1989 when the military government there changed the official English name for the country. The issue is less distinct in that country, where the two terms are linguistically related, but the United States and several other countries continue to use the term "Burma" even though the government now dominated by Aung San Suu Kyi finds either term acceptable. This study will use "Burma" until 1989 and then "Myanmar," just as it uses "Siam" until 1939, and then "Thailand." The status of the Republic of China/Taiwan is not a major focus of this book, but occasionally, it is necessary for clarity to use "mainland China" and "Taiwan" to distinguish the two, without prejudice to their legal relationship. In discussing most of the post-Soviet republics of Central Asia, the terms "Uzbekistani," "Kyrgyzstani," "Tajikistani," and "Kazakhstani" are all used to denote the adjectival form of these states and their citizens. The ethnic groups associated with these regions are "Uzbeks," "Kyrgyz," "Tajiks," etc. The choice between "Uyghur" and "Uighur" for the ethnic group in Xinjiang divides scholars, and this book will use the much more common "Uighur" because readers are more likely to be familiar with it.

1 Introduction

Four episodes between China and Vietnam

A pall hung over the Vietnamese provincial capital of Lang Son on March 3, 1979. After days of fierce fighting, Chinese and Vietnamese bodies littered Highway One, the main road into the city. After a short siege and heavy artillery bombardment, Chinese troops finally and at great cost took the hills overlooking Lang Son, and then the city itself, the final act in China's punitive "lesson" to Vietnam for invading China's ally, Cambodia the previous December. China's relations with its neighbors reached a nadir in February-March 1979, as global Cold War divisions combined with old Asian animosities. The oily black smoke that hung over Lang Son in March 1979 hung over the international relations of East Asia in general, a future that seemed cloudy at best, and at worst on the brink of great power war, an atmosphere marked by accusations, recriminations, military buildup, and a diplomatic chill as East and Southeast Asia found itself divided into its reorganized Cold War camps.

Lang Son and other border towns in northern Vietnam looked very different in 1995. Lang Son, like Lao Cai and other towns captured by the Chinese in 1979, had rebuilt and became a bustling provincial town, its shops which had been wrecked by Chinese artillery two decades before featured Chinese shirts and toys, knick-knacks, and cigarettes. The streets, once choked with burned-out Chinese tanks and APCs, were choked with Chinese-made bicycles and motorcycles. Chinese and Vietnamese leaders who described each other in vituperative terms fifteen years previously began to regularly visit each other's capitals, and not only normalized their diplomatic relations, they normalized their communist party relations as well. Chinese President Jiang Zemin's visit to Vietnam in February 2002 saw him kissing Vietnamese babies almost like an American politician, with both sides expressing satisfaction with the state of mutual relations. Jiang's successor, Hu Jintao, visited in 2005 and again in 2006. Trade and investment between the two countries boomed, and the border demarcation agreement including the Beibu Gulf area was concluded, remarkable given the seemingly intractable territorial dispute. At sea, China also indicated its approval for the Code of Conduct in the South China Sea in November 2002 at the 8th ASEAN Summit in Cambodia, which did not resolve the ownership dispute with Vietnam and other states in Southeast Asia but which

2 Introduction

did represent a major step forward to improving China's relations with its neighbors over clashes in the disputed islets, reefs, and tiny islands of the South China Sea.

Northern Vietnam erupted in protests and riots in the Spring of 2014 directed against Chinese firms and individuals. A Chinese oil exploration drilling rig had been parked near the disputed Paracel islands, and the government of Vietnam protested diplomatically, dispatched its equivalent of the coast guard to harass Chinese ships, and seemingly allowed public protests against the Chinese actions to spin out of control. The ensuing riots damaged Chinese-owned and invested factories and businesses in northern Vietnam, resulting in injuries and deaths, and an evacuation of Chinese workers during the tense stand-off in the South China Sea. But the conflict never rose beyond words, and, unlike the Spring of 1979, there was no military "lesson" used by China.

The weather and the setting of the Yanqi Lake International Convention Center could not have been better for Chinese President Xi Jinping's Belt and Road International Forum in May 2017. The conference had been a great triumph for Xi's signature policy: the combination of the Silk Road Economic Belt and the 21st Century Maritime Silk Road, grandly labeled the One Belt One Road initiative, a proposal to spend billions of dollars to build the infrastructure for a network of trade and exchange from Asia to Europe and Africa. The meeting was a success: well-planned, tightly scripted, and elaborately stage-managed. The group photo was telling and symbolic: center stage in the front row were the heads of state, President Xi towering in the middle and, next to him, the much shorter Russian Federation President Vladimir Putin. Next to Putin was Trần Đại Quang, the President of Vietnam, no longer just a neighbor of China but rather a "Strategic Partner of Cooperation."

The puzzle: changing foreign policy behavior

Four different episodes between the same neighbors: what accounts for these four very different Chinese approaches to its neighbors, in this instance Vietnam? Chinese policy have gone from aggressive, to cooperative to provocative, to cooperative again across the space of thirty-five years; why did it change? And the episodes seen in Sino-Vietnamese relations can also be seen in China's relations with many – but not all – of its neighbors: Japan, the Philippines, India, and others: a period of mutual hostility from the 1960s to the 1980s gave way to much more harmonious relations in the 1990s and the first few years of the 21st century, only to deteriorate as China appears to have become (in the words of too many journalists) "newly assertive toward its neighbors."

What we know: the debate over the "Rise of China" and China's foreign relations

The "Rise of China" (中国崛起 *Zhongguo jueqi*) literature in international relations now fills a small aircraft hangar, right next to the warehouse full of books on the "East Asian economic miracle" that were written in the 1980s, to use Robert Wade's phrase. Many of the books are written from a popular or even sensationalist perspective, with "Dragon" in the title and dire predictions in the pages. Holslag's *The Coming War with China* (2015) is among the most recent among this genre. They sound vaguely similar to the "Rise of Japan" books that were produced in the 1980s and which now seem amusingly antiquated. There are, however, quite a few serious, scholarly volumes on the subject of China's foreign relations in the second decade of the 21st century, monographs that are much more considered in their analysis but which also examine Chinese foreign policy with care and concern.

Amidst the impressive rise of China both as a regional and a world actor, one might imagine that a coalition of countries in the region would arise to balance against its growing power; realist international relations literature would expect this to happen, but by almost any measure – military expenditures, personnel, alliance treaties – this has not (yet) happened. This lack of "balancing" behavior is a paradox scholars have devoted a significant amount of research to (ably summarized by Steve Chan (2010, 2012). Several alternative explanations have arisen: first, that China's neighbors have begun to engage in a "soft balancing" act against it, nothing overt, and subtle enough that they do not show up in some of the statistical measures international relations scholars use to measure balancing and band-wagoning behavior. Kang (2010) points out that historically, China did not engage in the sort of international behavior that European countries did and which make up so much of the data of the scientific study of international relations. He further proposes (2007) that most countries in East Asia see as much opportunity in China's rise as threat. Second, and closely related, is the proposition that China's neighbors are engaged in "hedging" behavior, neither joining with China – band-wagoning behavior – nor openly opposing it (Tan 2012). The third possibility is that China's neighbors are simply waiting for the United States to reinsert its power into Asia, and they will largely become free-riders on American security. A fourth possibility exists, though it is not as often discussed in the scholarly literature (and never in the popular media), namely that most of China's neighbors are not deeply threatened by its rise; to be sure, Japan, Vietnam, and the Philippines since 2012 are the incessantly mentioned instances in which China's rise and foreign behavior very much antagonize its neighbors. But there are twenty-four other neighbors of China whose opinions may not be as extreme.

Much of the approach to Chinese foreign relations explicitly looks at the US-China relations from a rising-power-challenging-the-established power perspective, which in formal international relations theory is often described as power transition theory. The theory posits that when one great power which is dissatisfied with the international status quo overtakes the established power because of higher rates of economic growth, a major war becomes more likely (Organski 1958; Organski and Kugler 1980; Tammen et al. 2000; Lemke 2002; Walton and Kavalski 2017). To be sure, the formal power transition theorists are careful to point out that their theory only examines great power wars and great power transitions, with much less reference to regional power transitions (Lemke 2002). Many other analysts, both Western and Chinese, use this informal power transition

4 *Introduction*

characterization of Sino-American relations in the 21st century, often with dire predictions based upon previous great power wars. Whether Germany or Japan, the clash of the rising power with the established power seems almost inevitable, known as the "Thucydides Trap." The essays in Rosecrance and Miller (2015) deal with that depressing prospect.

A key point made in many of these works is that an acid test of China's "newly assertive" foreign policy will be in its regional relations, the way China interacts with its neighbors. This question, of course, has given rise to several fine books in this sub-field of Chinese foreign relations. David Shambaugh's *China Goes Global* (2013), its title notwithstanding, deals substantially with China's regional relations and with US rivalry and with the substantial change for the worse in 2009–10. Denny Roy's *Return of the Dragon* (2013) sees China's rise within the region from a neo-realist perspective and sees ". . . ultimately China's expectation of a sphere of influence will create or worsen dangers for China's neighbors. On balance, the rise of an extraordinarily strong China will decrease security for the region" (2). Beeson and Li (2014) are similarly concerned about the rise of China within the regional context of Asia, and Rozman (2010) sees a clear and consistent strategy toward Asia: "China's goals are relatively explicit, steadfast, and overarching. They include boosting comprehensive national power, limiting the influence of rival contenders, and establish itself, in stages, as the 'central state' of Asia" (5). Many other excellent treatments of the subject exist, monographs and conference volumes, and probably several will appear between the time this sentence was written and when it appeared in print.

A different approach

Why then, do we need another book on a subject that has already been well-examined? It is because there is a perspective that is largely missing in much of the treatments of a "rising China asserting itself against its neighbors," namely a *comparative regional* foreign policy perspective. How have other large, powerful states behaved toward their smaller neighbors? Or more simply, do regional hegemons become regional bullies? This approach does not treat China as a unique actor in a unique time and in a unique region, as much as Chinese leaders might want it to be seen that way, but rather as a state type with analogs in other regions and at other times. By examining those other regional hegemons, and their policies and behaviors, we might discern patterns of behavior that China either follows or deviates from. Thus, the fact that the United States had a "Good Neighbor Policy" vis-à-vis Latin America in the 1930s and 1940s and China began a "Good Neighbor Policy" toward its Southeast Asian neighbors in the 1990s is not seen as a mere linguistic coincidence; it is the common approach that regional hegemons adopt during the evolution of their regional foreign relations.

The argument advanced here is that China behaves, much as other regional hegemons behave, in different ways at different times. Its policies and behavior vary between an inactive detachment from its neighbors, to an active engagement of its neighbors as equals, to a more disagreeable, dominating form. China has spent much of the 1990s and early 21st century trying to be an active neighbor; whether its current behavior is moving toward what is described as a "hyperactive" phase is difficult to say, but some of the answers can be found in the behavior of similar regional hegemons in the post-war world. An examination of other regional hegemons also can let us evaluate Chinese foreign behavior; compared to modern Brazil's relations with its South American neighbors, China does indeed look highly assertive and militaristic; compared to Russia in recent years, it seems a bit more measured. All evaluative statements contain a stated or implicit comparative element. This book will make that comparison explicit.

This book also seeks to examine the issue of China's relations with its neighbors systematically. Much of what is written about the rise of China and its relations with its neighbors focuses on the "hot topics" of the day, such as the island disputes in the East China Sea and the South China Sea. And because books such as *China's Coming War with Asia* focus on those disputes, they come to the conclusion that all of China's relations with its neighbors are conflictual. That conclusion may be justified only if all of China's relations with its neighbors are examined, not just the exciting ones that occupy headlines.

A note on the language of neighbors and partners

We begin with the word "neighbor." Words and their meanings influence our thoughts and from our thoughts our policies and actions, and the word "neighbor" has deep roots in English and other languages. As a word meaning a person or household dwelling nearby, the word goes back to Old English *nehgeburas* and Middle English *nychtbur*. Originally, the meaning was "the man who tills the next piece of ground to mine" (Cockayne 2012: 4). The meaning of a country adjacent to another is just as old, going back to Old English as well (Oxford English Dictionary (OED) 1989, s.v., "Neighbourhood"). The concept of a neighbor is a shared piece of knowledge across multiple cultures and languages, frequently invoked. Furthermore, by examining proverbs, we can see that many of the implications of this and related words cross cultural boundaries. The term "neighbor" is common in international relations because it taps into something very old and basic in human interaction. When we use the term, it evokes certain expectations and norms of behavior, and, as we will see below, those norms and expectations have been transferred from inter-personal relations of people in proximate dwellings to sovereign states.

The term "neighbor" in English and many other languages contains both an objective and two subjective elements. The objective one is contiguity or actually bordering. It is used frequently in English because it is short, clear, and infinitely more elegant than "contiguous entity" or "bordering property." The first subjective one is proximity, which many languages include in their definitions of "neighbor" but which is difficult to define. How far away does a household cease to be a "neighbor"? The second subjective aspect of the word is the social role or normative expectation of behavior and most often expressed as "good neighbor."

6 *Introduction*

The study of proverbs or paremiology is one approach to discovering the common accepted wisdom of different cultures (Mieder 2004: xiii–xv); extensive collections of cross-cultural proverbs exist and can be used in this case to look at how different cultures regard neighbors. Cordry's *Multicultural Dictionary of Proverbs* (1997) records 40 proverbs about neighbors, and Stone's *Routledge Book of World Proverbs* (2006) has 36. Most develop six themes or truisms:

1. Good neighbors are important to happiness (and converse proverbs)
2. A near neighbor is better than a distant relative
3. Be friendly with neighbors but respect limits/boundaries
4. Neighbors are observant/gossipy
5. People are jealous of their neighbors
6. Consider the quality of the neighbors before settling down

The relationship expressed is important, but it is distinguished from other human relations in a number of key respects. First, good neighbors are vital to happiness and contentment, and bad neighbors are vexatious. Second, neighbors are not relatives. Third, there is a boundary, border or limit which marks the proper relationship with a neighbor. Fourth, the relationship is distinguished from others in that it is largely unavoidable. Unlike friends – and partners – in which the relationship can be terminated, the relationship with one's neighbor is not easily changed; there are several proverbs that indicate that the choice lies solely in the initial selection of a residence, and there are no proverbs listed in the two collections that contain references to moving away to terminate the relationship with a neighbor. But unlike family or kin with whom one has a relationship whether near or far, the relationship with a neighbor is mandated by the contiguity or proximity of residence.

One of the most extensive discussions of exactly what constitutes "neighborliness" comes from Wrightson's (1982) study of Elizabethan England, a time when modern English had recently become a standard and when the standards of sovereignty in international relations were being established as a result of the Thirty Years' War. Wrightson points out the practicality and equality implicit in the relationship of neighbors:

> ... further characteristics of neighbourliness were that it involved a mutual recognition of reciprocal obligations of a practical kind and a degree of normative consensus as to the nature of proper behavior between neighbours. Finally, and crucially, it was essentially a horizontal relationship, one which implied a degree of equality and mutuality between partners to the relationship, irrespective of distinctions of wealth or social standing. The reciprocity of neighbourliness was a reciprocity in equal obligations, the exchange of comparable services between effective, in not actual, equals. It is this aspect above all which distinguished neighbourliness from those other types of relationship between inhabitants in which the

element of social identification was overlaid and qualified by the realities of inequality.

(51)

An additional proverb closely related to third truism above is "Good fences make good neighbors," popularized by Robert Frost's 1914 poem "Mending Wall." The proverb in that exact formulation first appeared in print in 1850 but similar ideas are expressed in proverbs going back to the 17th century. Mieder (2003: 156–162) traces the evolution of the proverb prior to Frost's poem. Robert Frost has often been (falsely) attributed as the author of the proverb, but there is little doubt that his poem helped contribute to its widespread use. The poem is ambiguous and Frost meant it to be so, a tension between the speaker and the neighbor about why they are repairing a stone wall that separates their properties. One of the most important aspects of the poem is that the act of mending the wall is a mutual one, a community activity (116).

China's idea of neighbors

Beginning in the early 1990s, China adopted a "Good Neighbor Policy" (睦邻友好关系 *mulin youhao guanxi*). China substantially improved its relations with all of its sovereign neighbors, relations which a little over a decade previously had been characterized by fortified borders, diplomatic chills, and armed clashes. This improvement, though easily exaggerated, not only represents an aspect of the modernization of China's diplomacy, it also formed an integral element of Chinese international strategy.

What exactly do the Chinese mean when they speak of "good neighbor," either as a policy or a reference to the people living next door? Here a brief excursion into Chinese language and conceptualization is necessary. The term used in Chinese policy for "good neighbor relations" is 睦 邻 友 好 关 系 (*mulin youhao guanxi*). The first character 睦 (*mu*) can be better translated as "harmonious" instead of simply "good." The distinction is important: "good" implies an inherent quality of the person living next door, as opposed to "bad" or "evil," which may or may not manifest itself outside. 睦 (*mu*) or "harmonious" is a relationship which may not have any connection to the inherent qualities of the two or more individuals. The Chinese word 邻 (*lin*) can be translated as "adjacent" or "bordering" or "neighboring" and the original sense of "neighbor" or a person who lives nearby. By the Han dynasty, the term soon was used to refer to neighboring countries as recorded in Sima Qian's use of the term 邻国 (*linguo*, "neighboring countries") (*Hanyu da cidian*, s.v., *linguo*, vol. 10: 687).

In modern times, the term "neighbor" is frequently recorded in the Xinhua News Agency. China obviously considers its bordering countries its neighbors, and uses the term 邻国 (*linguo*) often. How far China goes in describing a country as a "neighbor" is fairly broad: Chen Xiangyang, a vice section chief at the China Institutes of Contemporary International Relations, explicitly lists the countries in his appendix (2004: 311). China has fourteen contiguous neighbors: Afghanistan,

Bhutan, India, Kazakhstan, North Korea, Kyrgyzstan, Laos, Mongolia, Myanmar, Nepal, Pakistan, Russia, Tajikistan, and Vietnam. In addition, Chen lists the Republic of Korea, Japan, Thailand, Cambodia, Malaysia, Singapore, Indonesia, the Philippines, Brunei, Timor Leste, Bangladesh, the Maldives, Uzbekistan, Turkmenistan among its "neighbors."

In contrast, "neighborhood" is a term with less cultural and religious baggage but more research devoted to it, primarily in sociology and urban planning where it has its own controversies. The word is first constructed in English around 1425 in the meaning of people living near to a certain place or within a certain range (OED 1989, s.v., "Neighbourhood"). (Its sixth definition, that of "friendly relations between neighbours" is now considered rare, though we see it used in Chinese translations).

The Chinese terms for "neighborhood," on the other hand, is quite different, 附近 (*fujin*) or sometimes 邻里 (*linli*), and do not appear in writing on international regions. Although the Sacred Edict of the Kangxi Emperor (1670) (圣谕十六条) does contain a translated term of "neighborhood" in the most common translations of its third edict, 3. 和鄉黨以息爭訟/和乡党以息争讼 "Cultivate peace within the neighborhood to prevent quarrels and lawsuits." the meaning here is closer to "village" in modern Chinese language. When the term "neighborhood" does appear in English language translations of Chinese foreign policy statements, it is usually a translation of *mulin* ("neighborly") or a common phrase in Chinese policy toward other countries in Asia "与邻为善, 以邻为伴" (*yi lin wei shan, yi lin wei ban*). The translation is awkward in English: "With the neighbors act neighborly, with the neighbors act as a partner." In a few cases, the term 周边 (*zhoubian*) is translated as "neighborhood," though this is also not exactly accurate, either. *Zhoubian* is literally "all around, on all sides" or possibly "periphery," "rim" or "region" but not exactly a bounded space of dwelling and belonging. The term does, however, show up increasingly in Chinese descriptions of their regional policies, sometimes translated into English as "periphery" and sometimes as "neighborhood." Finally, former Premier Wen Jiabao often used the term 本地区 (*ben diqu*) in statements that were translated as "neighborhood," and this comes closer to the English language meaning than the other terms ("region of origin" would be the exact translation). The term has been used in this sense by the authoritative *Zhongguo waijiao gailan*.[1] Thus, it is an interesting and significant aspect of the Chinese conceptualization of its region that there is a term for adjacent countries that is evocative of the relationship of people who live in nearby houses, but seldom a reference to the collective. China has a good neighbor policy, but no *neighborhood* policy. That distinction is in turn important, since neighborhood policies in international relations tend to be exclusionary ones. India, as we will see in the next chapter, for instance, has a "Extended Neighbourhood Policy" that essentially amounts to a claim of exclusive dominance to the South Asian subcontinent (Scott 2009).

Partners

There is another term that appears with increasing frequency in international relations, namely "partners." It is not quite as old in English as "neighbor" and comes from Middle English, probably around 1300, and has two closely related meanings: "1. A person with a joint share in or use of something; a person who is party *to* something. . . . 2. A person who takes part with another or others in doing something, esp. either of a pair of people engaged together in the same activity, occupation, etc." (OED 1989, s.v., "Partner"). The term is thus decidedly transactional in its implications: partners *do* something *together*. They have common interests. Whereas neighbors may or may not interact, partners by definition must act.

The Chinese term for "partner" is 伙伴 *huoban* in the simplified version of the characters. The term is first recorded in the Northern Wei dynasty (386–535 CE), and referenced ten soldiers who would share a cooking fire (*Hanyu dai cidian*, vol. 1 pt 2: 1214–1215). From this it acquired the meaning of "companion." The first character depicts a person standing by a fire; the second is a person and the word for half, as if two people were sharing half a fire. That might be a bit of false etymology, however, since the old form of the character (i.e., prior to 1956) is 夥伴, the second character (person and half) is the same, but the first is a compound of the characters for "fruit" and "many," so a possible implication of this form of "partner" is to share many fruits. There are far fewer proverbs about "partners" than about neighbors, and they tend to be cautionary, warning against uneven advantages, cheating, and the like.

By the 21st century, the term "partner" in international relations had taken on an important if vague meaning, something between an "ally," which is a formal and legal contractual obligation, and "friend," which is a nice and utterly meaningless term in international relations (Wilkins 2012). Many countries use the term "partner" when they do not wish to be explicit in the strategic relationship, either because they do not wish to commit themselves to an alliance, or they cannot because of previous policies of non-alignment, such as Singapore in its relations with the United States (Parameswaran 2014).

Approach of the book

The plan of the book is as follows: Chapter 2 examines six regional hegemons, defined here as states which have capabilities roughly equal to those of the rest of its defined region combined. The policies and behavior of each of the regional hegemons is then briefly outlined in three areas: ideational (policies, pronouncements and doctrines), security-related areas (territory and threats), and economic behavior. In each of these categories, regional hegemons' policies and behaviors tend to fall into three types or phases: "inactive," meaning the regional hegemon does not particularly engage its region, "active" meaning that the regional hegemon engages but does not seek to dominate its region, and "hyperactive" a phase in which the regional hegemon does seek to dominate its region. Regional hegemons' policies and behavior evolve over time, sometimes gradually and sometimes quite abruptly, moving from one phase to another, and not always in a normatively positive direction. Causes for these changes are discussed at the end of Chapter 2, setting up what might be called a theory of regional hegemonic behavior. Thus, we will have some criteria for judging China's past and current behavior with its region against other similar states and their regions. The chapter then turns to the relative dominance of these six regional hegemons in statistical terms and adds China and its four regions (explained below) and sees how China compares.

Chapters 3 and 4 then break Chinese regional foreign relations into rough periods to examine the evolution of policy and behavior, from the relatively inactive phase during the late Qing and Republic, to the hyperactive policies of the Maoist and Cold War Period, and then to the "Good Neighbor Policy" phase of the 1990s and early 2000s, an active phase (Chapter 4) and then to five chapters which look at current policy beginning roughly in 2004, in which activity appears to begin moving toward hyperactivity. Chapter 10 concludes with some cautious generalizations not only about China as a regional power, but some broader lessons for the study of regional hegemons in general.

Asia: one region or four regions?

In dealing with China's regional relations, an immediate problem is the geographic definition. China has fourteen contiguous neighbors, plus three entities it would not consider "neighbors": Taiwan, Hong Kong, and Macao are Chinese territory (if not administration) and would not be considered a "neighbor" since that implies they are not part of the "family." China has the distinction of having the longest contiguous land borders of any nation, over 23,000 kilometers. But China has more neighbors than these, by its own account, ranging into the island nations of South and Southeast Asia, among others. And the definition has changed: the Republic of the Maldives was not described as a "neighbor" of China in the official yearbook of China's Foreign Ministry until 2004. Timor Leste, which became independent in 1999 was not described as a "neighbor" by China until 2014, and has not been included in this analysis. Papua New Guinea still is not described as such, even though it abuts Indonesia, which China does describe as a neighbor.

Does China exist in one regional context or more than one? China is geographically similar to the Soviet Union (now Russia) and Brazil, countries which have many neighbors and span multiple regions or sub-regions of continents. Just as Russia has a border with East Asia, China has a border on South Asia, and Brazil borders the Caribbean, though none of these are central to these countries' foreign relations. This issue is one that many scholars have struggled with, and Womack (2009) defines three regions which China is part of: Northeast, Southeast, and Central Asia (10–11). Yet this is a book about China's *neighbors*, those countries which are contiguous, and those that China itself considers and designates as "neighbors" and that includes South Asia. Thus, for purposes of this study, China has four regions with which it has twenty-seven neighbors. This list is similar to that of Chen Xiangyang (2004), except that he includes Sikkim, which India annexed in 1975, but does not include Timor Leste. Table 1.1 shows the breakdown used:

Table 1.1 China's neighboring regions and neighbors

Region	Members
China's neighboring regions and neighbors	
Northeast Asia	Japan
	North Korea*
	South Korea
	Mongolia*
Southeast Asia	Vietnam*
	Laos*
	Myanmar*
	Cambodia
	Thailand
	Malaysia
	Singapore
	Indonesia
	Philippines
	Timor Leste
Central Asia	Russian Federation*
	Kazakhstan*
	Kyrgyzstan*
	Tajikistan*
	Uzbekistan
	Turkmenistan
South Asia	India*
	Pakistan*
	Afghanistan*
	Nepal*
	Bhutan*
	Sri Lanka
	Maldives

*Indicates a contiguous neighbor.

This breakdown is not without its challenges: Russia could equally belong to Northeast Asia, with its port and naval base at Vladivostok; Australia might be included in Southeast Asia, and Mongolia could also belong to either Northeast or Central Asia. Afghanistan forms a "pivot" between South Asia and Central Asia, and Myanmar (Burma) forms a pivot between South Asia and Southeast Asia, a point that has been recognized by specialists in regional international relations going back to 1967 (Russett 1967). It also results in uneven chapters, with Northeast Asia covering only four neighbors, Southeast Asia with ten, Central Asia with six, and South Asia with eight. Much of this division is for a statistical purpose, determining China's relative power capacity vis-à-vis either the leading rival in that region or the region as a whole, which will be examined at the end of Chapter 2. Russia, for instance, has a finite amount of power, and though it might bring it to bear in either Northeast or Central Asia, to engage one diminishes the capacity to act in the other. The alternative organization would be to create a single group,

"East Asia," which would include Northeast Asian and Southeast Asian actors and ignore Central and South Asia. This is a tempting simplification, since these are China's primary regions of interaction. But this is a book about China's *neighbors*, all of them, and how it treats those countries, not only the large and contentious but also the small and inactive. The four-fold division also adheres to contemporary Chinese divisions in official foreign policy and Foreign Ministry organization.

Regions, however, are more than geographical groupings, they are also social constructions: they are perceived by humans. As Acharya (2007: 651) puts it, ". . . regionalist ideas and discourses do determine who is included and who is excluded from regions. . . . In other words, regions, like, nation-states, are to some extent imagined communities. They can be constructed through both discourses and socialization processes." By the 1990s, regional international organizations were playing an increasingly important role in "constructing" the definitions of individual regions. "Europe" most clearly is being defined by the European Community, a body with an extensive application process and membership criteria. Increasingly, organizations such as ASEAN define what it means to be "Southeast Asian," and the South Asian Association for Regional Cooperation (SAARC) is instrumental to the definition of what it means to be "South Asian" as a regional identity. These regional international organizations will be used to define the regions with which hegemons interact and their relative capabilities, to which we turn in the next chapter.

Note

1 This is the official yearbook of the Ministry of Foreign Affairs of the People's Republic of China. Beginning its publication in 1987 as 中国外交概览 *China's foreign affairs review*, it is hereafter ZGWJGL, and after 1995 中国外交 *Zhongguo waijiao*, hereafter ZGWJ for the Chinese language version and *China's Foreign Affairs* or CFA for the English-language version, which began publication in 2003.

Works cited

Acharya, Amitav. 2007. The emerging regional architecture of world politics. *World Politics*, 59(4), 629–652.

Beeson, Mark, and Li, Fujian. 2014. *China's Regional Relations: Evolving Foreign Policy Dynamics*. Boulder, CO: Lynne Rienner.

Chan, Steve. 2010. An odd things happened on the way to balancing: East Asian states' reactions to China's rise. *International Studies Review*, 12(September), 387–412.

Chan, Steve. 2012. *Looking for Balance: China, the United States, and Power Balancing in East Asia*. Stanford: Stanford University Press.

Chen Xiangyang. 2004. *Zhongguo mulin waijiao: sixiang, shijian, qianzhang* [China's good-neighbour diplomacy: Though, practice, prospect]. Beijing: Shishi chubanshe.

Cockayne, Emily. 2012. *Cheek by Jowl: A History of Neighbours*. London: The Bodley Head.

Cordry, Harold V. 1997. *The Multicultural Dictionary of Proverbs: Over 20,000 Adages from More Than 120 Languages, Nationalities and Ethnic Groups*. Jefferson, NC: McFarland.

Hanyu da cidian [Chinese Big Dictionary]. 1986–1994. Ed. Luo Zhufeng. Shanghai: Shanghai ci shu chubanshe.

Holslag, Jonathan. 2015. *China's Coming War with Asia*. Cambridge: Polity Press.

Kang, David C. 2007. *China Rising: Peace, Power, and Order in East Asia*. New York: Columbia University Press.

Kang, David C. 2010. *East Asia before the West: Five Centuries of Trade and Tribute*. New York: Columbia University Press.

Lemke, Douglas. 2002. *Regions of War and Peace*. Cambridge: Cambridge University Press.

Mieder, Wolfgang. 2003. "Good fences make good neighbour": History and significance of an ambiguous proverb. *Folklore*, 114, 155–179.

Mieder, Wolfgang. 2004. *Proverbs: A Handbook*. Westport, CT: Greenwood Press.

OED [Oxford English Dictionary]. 1989. 2nd ed. Prepared by J.A. Simpson and E.S.C. Weiner. Oxford: Oxford University Press.

Organski, A.F.K. 1958. *World Politics*. New York: Alfred A. Knopf.

Organski, A.F.K., and Kugler, Jacek. 1980. *The War Ledger*. Chicago: University of Chicago Press.

Parameswaran, Prashanth. 2014. Explaining US strategic partnerships in the Asia-Pacific region: Origins, development and prospects. *Contemporary Southeast Asia: A Journal of International and Strategic Affairs*, 36(2), 262–289.

Rosecrance, Richard N., and Miller, Steven E. 2015. *The Next Great War? The Roots of World War I and the Risk of U.S.-China Conflict*. Cambridge, MA: MIT Press.

Roy, Denny. 2013. *Return of the Dragon: Rising China and Regional Security*. New York: Columbia University Press.

Rozman, Gilbert. 2010. *Chinese Strategic Thought toward Asia*. New York: Palgrave Macmillan.

Russett, Bruce M. 1967. *International Regions and the International System: A Study in Political Ecology*. Chicago: Rand-McNally.

Scott, David. 2009. India's "extended neighborhood" concept: Power projection for a rising power. *India Review*, 8(2), 107–143.

Shambaugh, David. 2013. *China Goes Global: The Partial Power*. Oxford: Oxford University Press.

Stone, Jon R. 2006. *The Routledge Book of World Proverbs*. London: Routledge.

Tammen, Ronald et al. 2000. *Power Transitions*. Chatham, NJ: Chatham House.

Tan, Alexander C. 2012. China and its neighbors: Too close for comfort?, in *Beyond Great Powers and Hegemons: Why Secondary States Support, Follow, or Challenge*, edited by Kristen P. Williams, Steven E. Lobell, and Neal G. Jesse. Stanford: Stanford Security Studies, 193–206.

Walton, David, and Kavalski, Emilian, eds. 2017. *The Power Transition in Asia*. Abington: Routledge.

Wilkins, Thomas S. 2012. "Alignment", not "alliance" – the shifting paradigm of international security cooperation: Toward a conceptual taxonomy of alignment. *Review of International Studies*, 38, 53–76.

Womack, Brantly. 2009. China between region and world. *The China Journal*, 61, 1–20.

Wrightson, Keith. 1982. *English Society 1580–1680*. New Brunswick: Rutgers University Press.

2 Regional hegemons and their behavior

"Europe's Reluctant Hegemon" was *The Economist's* prominent description of Germany in its Special Report on June 15, 2013. The article, and its accompanying editorial of the same name, portrayed Germany as an overwhelming power within its region of Europe, yet hesitant to assert itself. But the article assumes a status that it does not define: *what exactly is a regional hegemon?* Journalists often use the jargon of *Pax Sinica* and describe China as a regional hegemon, but again, they do not define the term (see, e.g. Ziegler 2017: 8). The definition employed here will be operationalized comparatively by examining a number of states which have been specifically mentioned in scholarly literature as regional hegemons, establishing a simple but clear set of criteria for determining that status, and developing a matrix of behaviors associated with that status. The argument here is that regional hegemons exhibit different types of behavior toward their regions, not a single "bullying" behavior. This behavior ranges from uninvolved (inactive), to cooperatively involved (active) to dominating (hyperactive). Furthermore, most regional hegemons change their behavior over time, moving from one type or phase to another. That in turn will be used in later chapters to analyze China's role as a regional hegemon.

Regional hegemons defined

In the post-Cold War scholarship on security and international relations, a small but important trend began to emerge at the beginning of the 21st century: regional security studies. Beginning with Buzan and Wæver's *Regions and Powers* (2003), this literature looks at the parts of the world instead of the whole that dominated earlier structural theories of international relations and security such as Waltz (1979). Many of the authors are Europeans, and the London School of Economics and in particular the German Institute for Global and Area Studies in Hamburg (GIGA/Leibniz-Institut für Globale und Regionale Studien) have a number of scholars who have focused on one particular aspect of regional security studies, namely, the behavior of the largest and most powerful states within their regions. It is for this reason that one might describe this approach as "The Hamburg School." The terms used by these scholars to describe these dominant states, however, vary. Nolte (2010) calls them "regional great powers"; Destradi calls them "regional powers" (2008); and Pereira (2014) calls them "regional (great) powers" to indicate the contingent nature of such actors. One of the oldest pieces in the regional security literature (Myers 1991) uses the term "regional hegemon" and Williams et al. (2012) use the term "hegemon," but still other scholars eschew the use of the term "hegemon" outside of its Gramscian sense of *hegemony*. Prys (2012) and others subdivide the concept depending on the behavior of the actor: "regional dominator," "regional hegemon," "regional detached power," etc.

This study uses the term "Regional Hegemon" as the generic term for the concept of a powerful state that is much larger or more capable than its neighboring region, further defined below. It does not imply any sort of behavior or ideology; it only implies that the state in question has overwhelming capabilities vis-à-vis its defined region. To be a regional hegemon has two initial minimal requirements: 1) a defined region in which the regional hegemon is physically located or adjacent to, and 2) overwhelming capabilities vis-à-vis the rest of the region combined. This study uses Gross Domestic Product ratios as of 2000 as a first cut to determine regional dominance; if a potential regional hegemon (as identified in the scholarly literature) has a GDP equal to the rest of the identified region combined, it is included. Thus, six regional hegemons are examined: 1) the United States within Latin America and the Caribbean, 2) the Soviet Union and Eastern Europe and its successor, the Russian Federation, within the "Near Abroad" of former Soviet states, 3) India within South Asia, 4) South Africa within southern Africa, 5) Nigeria within West Africa, and 6) Brazil within South America. These states are the most frequently cited in the literature on regional powers (Triska 1986; Mares 1988; Ihonvbere 1991; Turner 1991; Ayoob 1991; Myers 1991; Williams 1991; Roy 1994; Lapp 2012; Horowitz and Tyburski 2012; Sitaraman 2012; Tan 2012; Burgess 2012. For a good literature review on this field, see Pereira 2014). One country that is frequently mentioned as a regional hegemon is the post-war Federal Republic of Germany (Sperling 2001). This is included in Table 2.2 below for comparison purposes, and its ratios are illustrative: Germany does not dominate Europe in anywhere near the ratios that the other regional hegemons do.

Each of the regions is defined by a formal regional organization, even if that regional organization did not exist or had the same extent as it does today. This definition is not, however, limiting; all of the regional hegemons examined below exist in ambiguous regions, such as Nigeria which often talks about its influence in the entire continent of Africa, or 19th century United States which saw the entire Western Hemisphere as its bailiwick. Four major statistics are examined for measuring capabilities: total population, Gross Domestic Product (GDP), military personnel, and military expenditures.

16 *Regional hegemons*

Table 2.1 Regional hegemons and their regions

Regional hegemons and their regions

Hegemon	Region	Regional Int'l Organization	Regional Rival	External Power
USA	Latin America	Organization of American States (OAS)	Mexico	Germany/ Soviet Union
USSR/ Russia	Eastern Europe/ Former Soviet Union	Warsaw Pact (WP) Commonwealth of Independent States (CIS)	–	USA
India	South Asia	South Asian Association for Regional Cooperation (SAARC)	Pakistan	USA, China
South Africa	Southern Africa	Southern African Development Community (SADC)	–	Soviet Union/ Nigeria
Nigeria	West Africa	Economic Community of West African States (ECOWAS)	Ghana	South Africa, France
Brazil	South America	Mercosul/ Union of South American Nations (UNASUL)	Argentina	USA
China	Northeast Asia	–	Japan	USA
	Southeast Asia	ASEAN +3	Vietnam	USA
	Central Asia	Shanghai Cooperation Organization (SCO)	Russia	USA
	South Asia	SAARC (observer)	India	USA

These regional hegemons are much larger than any other state within their region. Table 2.2 shows the ratio of the regional hegemon to the combined capabilities of the rest of its region. Thus, Germany in 2000 had a GDP that was 28.5% of the rest of the EU, 16.8% of its population, and about 24.7% of the military expenditures. As noted, this does not make Germany much of a regional hegemon compared to the other regional hegemons examined.

China's regional dominance

China exists in the context of multiple regions, as set forth in Chapter 1. Table 2.2 shows the degree of regional hegemons dominance over their respective regions, using three ratios: the GDP (using current US$-based calculations),[1] total population, and military expenditures, based on constant 2011 US dollars. This is, however, just a snapshot; a dynamic portrait is also needed since China's economic growth in the 21st century has been quite dramatic.

Table 2.2 Regional hegemons' dominance ratios in 2000

Regional hegemons' dominance ratios in 2000

Hegemon	Region	GDP	Population	Military Expenditures
Germany	Europe	0.29	0.16	0.24
USA	Latin America/ Caribbean	4.61	0.64	8.16
USSR/	Eastern Europe	1.01 (E. Europe 1990)	3.20 (E. Europe 1990)	9.69 (E. Europe 1990)
Russia	Former Soviet Union	2.20 (Former Soviet Union 2000)	1.04	7.24 (Russia: Frmr SU 2000)
India	South Asia	3.20	3.25	0.790
South Africa	Southern Africa	2.63	0.28	0.97
Nigeria	West Africa	1.26	1.23	1.57
Brazil	South America	1.18	1.00	1.41
China	Northeast Asia	0.22	6.34	0.63
	Southeast Asia	1.98	2.42	2.22
	Central Asia	2.12	6.26	1.47
	South Asia	1.93	0.91	1.22

Source: GDP and Population: World Bank, World Development Indicators. Military expenditures: SIPRI, based upon constant 2011 dollars.

Figure 2.1 shows what is well known: China has a huge population, and that is bigger than any of its four neighboring regions. Its population advantage over Northeast Asia (Japan, the Koreas, and Mongolia) is over six times, and vis-à-vis Central Asia (the USSR prior to 1992) is almost as large. As we will see in Chapter 8, that will become a latent foreign policy issue. But China's southern neighboring regions – Southeast Asia and South Asia – have been growing faster than China, and South Asia now has more people than China, and India by itself will soon take over as the most populous country in the world.

That population gives China a potential to recruit an immense number of military personnel without serious damage to economic production or social function. Figure 2.2 shows that although the Chinese military has a large number of personnel, its dominance ratio in that respect has been going down. China has in fact been shrinking its military, especially its ground forces. China's President Xi Jinping announced the demobilization of 300,000 soldiers in September 2015, bringing China's military well below three million (Wong et al. 2015). It is still larger than Central and Northeast Asia, equal to Southeast Asia, and now smaller than South Asia and its population of 1.73 billion people.

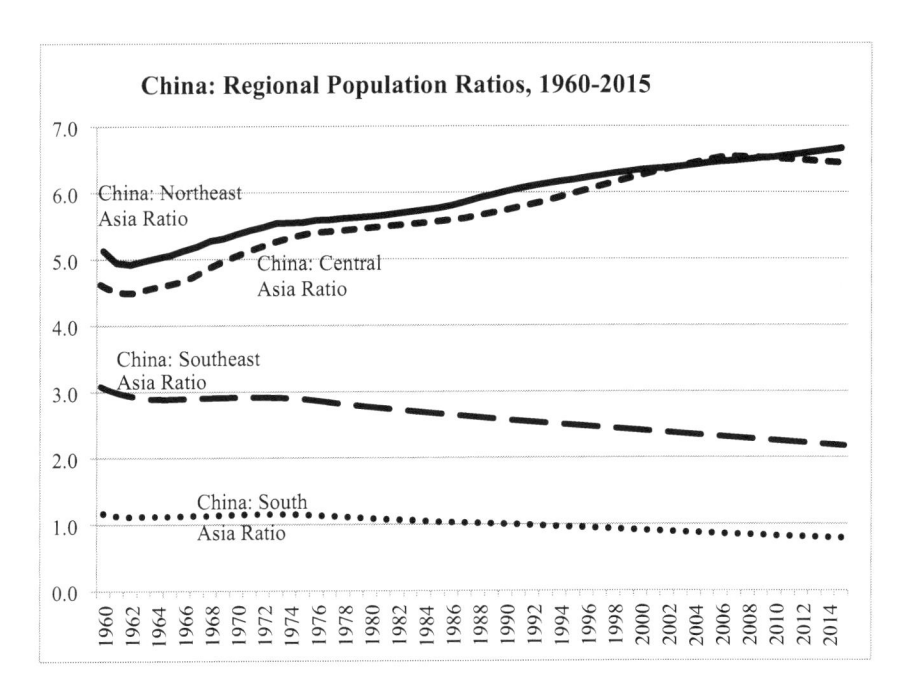

Figure 2.1 China: regional population ratios, 1960–2015
Source: World Bank, World Development Indicators.

Figure 2.2 China: regional military personnel ratios, 1989–2015
Source: IISS Military Balance/World Bank, World Development Indicators.

China: Regional GDP Ratios, 1960–2015 (current US$)

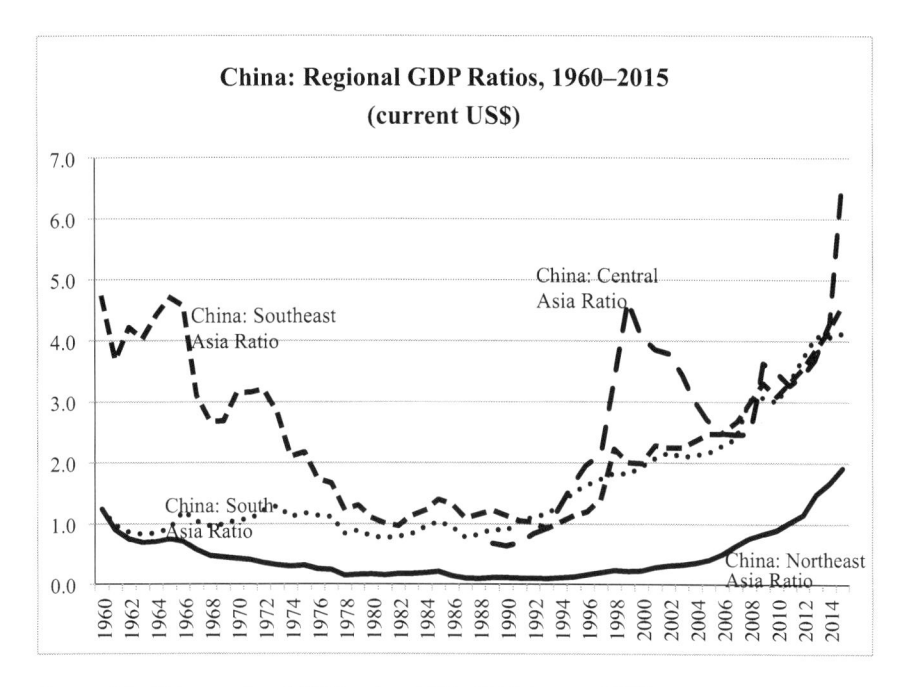

Figure 2.3 China: regional GDP ratios, 1960–2015 (current US$)
Source: World Bank, World Development Indicators.

The real change over time has been China's economic growth, especially in the 21st century. Figure 2.3 shows the regional Gross Domestic Product ratios as measured in the current (i.e., non-inflation-adjusted) Market Exchange Rate (MER) US dollars. In Northeast and Southeast Asia, the relative economic losses of the Maoist era in China are abundantly clear: China began in 1960 with a GDP slightly larger than Northeast and South Asia, and over four times that of Southeast Asia. Twenty years later, Southeast Asia had equalized its ratio with China, and Northeast Asia was experiencing an economic boom such that China's economy (so measured) was only 17% of it. South Asia also experienced a long period of relatively slow economic growth, barely out-performing China. Central Asia as a region does not come into existence until 1992, and the economic disaster of the former Soviet Union shows in the 1994–1999 "peak" in which the region's economy slipped to less than a quarter of China's size before beginning to recover in the 21st century.[2]

But China's growth in the 21st century left all four regions behind by this measurement. China now has roughly twice the GDP of Northeast Asia, over four times South and Southeast Asia, and even more for Central Asia. China achieved a 1:1 ratio with the rest of Northeast Asia (Japan and South Korea being the only other significant economies) in MER dollars in 2011/12. This represents an unusual change, the "leapfrogging" of a one regionally dominant power over another, a change of hegemons. No other regional hegemon examined in this comparison has made such a change, although if we consider Sub-Saharan Africa altogether, Nigeria may have surpassed

20 Regional hegemons

South Africa recently. Thus, the asymmetry that was deeply felt elsewhere in China's neighbors going all the way back to 1949 is now being felt in Japan for the first time; Japanese leaders have always been aware of China's greater population, but were confident beginning in 1895 with their ability to use their superior economy to their advantage; that changed in the 21st century, and Japan now has a smaller population (less than a tenth of China's, though a substantial one nonetheless) and total economic size, though its per capita economy is still nearly six times that of China.

That of course leads China to be able to spend much more money on its military and still spend less than 2% of its total GDP on the sector (the United States spends about 3.3%). Figure 2.4 shows the ratios of China's military spending with estimates of military spending by the countries in these regions. China is now spending between 2.3 and 5 times what the other regional members are.

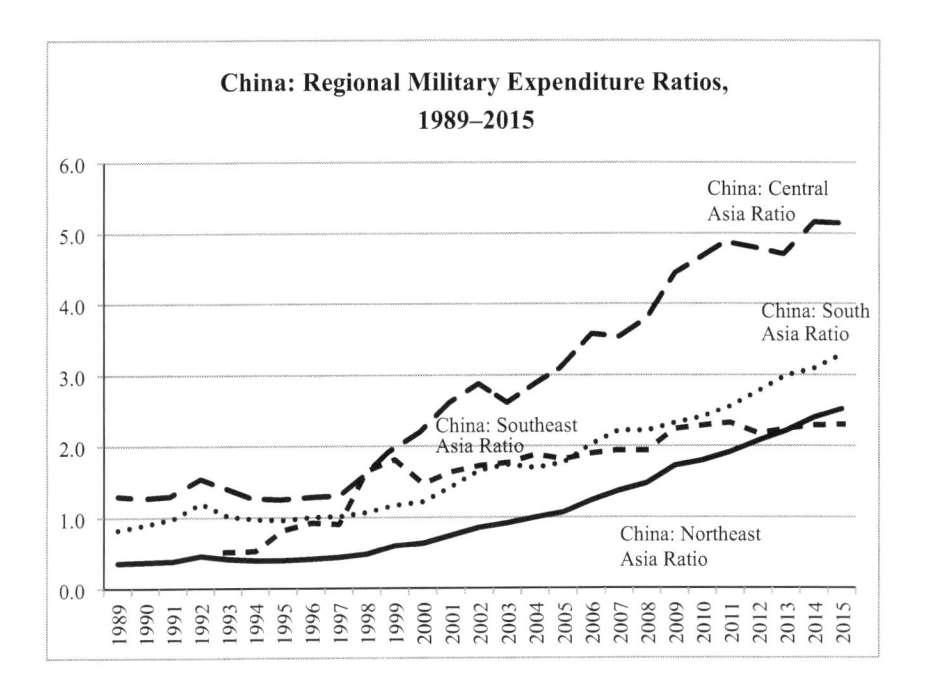

Figure 2.4 China: regional military expenditure ratios, 1989–2015
Source: SIPRI MilEx Database (2017).

Regional hegemonic behavior

What all of this shows is a simple but profound fact: regional hegemons are larger than their respective regional neighbors – much larger. This leads to *asymmetric relations*, an important contribution of Brantly Womack (2010: chap. 5). Womack notes that,

> The disparity in capacities between partners creates an asymmetric relationship, one in which the smaller side is more exposed to interactions than the

larger side . . . leads to a difference in relative attention. . . . Differences in perspective lead to differences in perception. Because the larger side has other concerns of equal or greater importance, it will tend to be less attentive to the smaller side, or, in times of crisis, associate the smaller side with grander regional or global issues . . . from the point of view of the smaller side, the larger side looms very large, and even when the larger side is not threatening the smaller side, the smaller side feels at risk in the relationship because of the disparity of capabilities. Therefore the smaller side will tend to be too anxious and too suspicious of the larger side.

(Womack 2010: 82–83)

This sensitivity or hypersensitivity is a theme we will return to frequently in examining the behavior of regional hegemons in general and China in particular.

Regional hegemons, though they are always much larger than their neighbors, both individually and collectively, do not always behave the same way. There is both variation between regional hegemons' behavior and variation across time. Based upon the above cases, Table 2.3 summarizes the three major general types or phases of hegemonic behavior, from inactive to active to hyperactive, and in three areas: ideational, security, and economic. This approach owes much to the approach of the Hamburg School and primarily to Prys (2010, 2012) and Destradi (2008), though the terms used here are different, and, most importantly, their analyses imply a largely static nature of the regional hegemon's behavior, whereas this study very much focuses on the question of when and why regional hegemons and specifically China change their approach to their regions.

The term "activity" is only loosely defined here as a willingness to devote state resources to interactions with regional actors. An "inactive" regional hegemon is a state which, though possessing the capabilities of a dominant state nevertheless does not interact strongly with its region, for a number of reasons and does not provide public goods, which corresponds roughly with Prys's "regional detached power" concept. A "hyperactive" regional hegemon is one that seeks to use its capabilities to dominate "its" region, controlling the foreign and at times domestic politics of its neighbors, with relatively little provision of public goods to the region beyond what benefits the hegemon, corresponding with Prys's "regional dominator." An "active" regional hegemon's behavior stands between these two tendencies, interacting with its region but not dominating it, and providing public goods (Prys calls this a "regional hegemon"). Of course, these are all tendencies along a continuum, and there are often inconsistencies in the ideational, security, and economic aspects of the regional relationship. Finally, there is a "globalist" phase in which a regional hegemon ceases to focus on its region and largely focuses on global issues. Lemke describes this behavioral tendency of great powers as "regional snobs": "In a sense . . . states are snobs. If they have the resources to be active in the overall global hierarchy, they will do so with more interest than they pay to the local hierarchy from which they emerge and within which most of their past international activity has been carried out" (Lemke 2002: 52). This is not strictly exclusive of the other phases.

Table 2.3 Regional hegemons' behavior

	Aspect	Inactive	Active	Hyper-active
Ideational	Regional Policy/ Doctrine	No specific policy	Good Neighbor Policy	Doctrines of exclusion, intervention; "Monroe Doctrine"
	Imposed Domestic Political System	none	Stable political system	Specific political system of hegemon
	Rhetoric	Little mention; "Other"	"Neighbor" "Partner"	"Brother/ Family"
Security	Territorial Disputes	Disputes not resolved	Disputes resolved legally	Annexation/ Disputes resolved by force, intimidation
	Military intervention	Infrequent	Multi-lateral/PKO	Unilateral/Frequent regime change; creation of new states
	External major powers	Often present (bases, colonies, alliances)	Absent or marginal involvement; delegated responsibility to hegemon by external power	Invited by regional actors; seen as provocative by hegemon
	Diplomatic relations with Regional States	Lack of relations with many regional states	Recognition of all states; multilateralism; regular state visits and summits	Mixed regional reactions to hegemon; Counter-balancing coalitions against hegemon
	Regional Int'l Organizations	Little, no role by hegemon	Provision of security public goods; major role in security issues, used by hegemon to legitimate its role	Hegemonic Bilateralism ("Hub-and-Spokes"); rival organizations form
	Hegemon's Expatriates/ Co-Ethnics	Not seen as a policy issue	Seen as connectors/ intermediaries/ integrated	Seen as compatriots by hegemon, security risk by regional states
Economic	Trade	Not seen as a policy issue	High levels of trade; bilateral and RTAs	Forced, exclusionary or asymmetric bilateral agreements
	Investment	Not seen as a policy issue	High levels of FDI by hegemon in regional states	Asymmetric investment, generally low
	Provision of Collective Economic Goods	Little/None	Provision of Collective Economic Goods by Hegemon	Taking of Collective Economic Goods by Hegemon

Globalist

Naturally, one thinks of the Superpowers and Great Powers in this status: the United States seldom thinks of "North America," for example. It is possible, however, for some regional hegemons to set their horizons well beyond their own region, and, at times, Nigeria, Brazil, and India have done so. Shambaugh (2013) deals extensively with China's attempts to be "global," though he concludes these have not been particularly successful.

Ideational and security foundations of regional hegemons

The stated policies, leadership speeches, and articulated justifications for neighborhood behavior are the first element in determining the type of regional behavior a hegemonic state is engaging in. In short, a hegemon is as a hegemon says. A regional hegemon that is seeking to dominate "its" area invariably articulates a reason for that dominance. Ideational aspects of regional hegemon's behavior are often the best clues as to what it would do if it were to have greater relative capabilities vis-à-vis its region.

Inactive phase

Inaction does not require much justification or thought; not surprisingly, in the "Inactive" phase of regional hegemons, there is not much ideational justification. Regional hegemons often start in an inactive phase for historical reasons: its neighbors are not yet independent, or it has not yet established diplomatic relations. Early independence often requires the regional hegemon to establish its borders against the centrifugal forces of ethnic groups at the margin of the core state, and thus the initial outlook is one of consolidation of the state instead of relations with neighboring states (though the perspective of the bordering areas obviously differs). The maintenance of formal diplomatic relations between regional hegemons and all of its neighbors is a simple measure of relations, but an important one. It is a sign of an inactive phase when regional hegemons do not recognize or have diplomatic relations with their regional neighbors, or maintain a minimal relationship. Apartheid-era South Africa is possibly the best example of this, which had no formal relations with most of its black African neighbors in order to avoid dealing with their ambassadors as equals.

USA

The United States regional policy during much of the 19th century may have been based upon the Monroe Doctrine (discussed below), but in practical terms, the policy was nominal. As one scholar recently summarized, "Following the initial stir, the Monroe Doctrine receded into the background for most Americans during the remainder of the nineteenth century. Indeed, except for Mexico, Cuba, and Central America, Latin America passed out of vogue as a compelling interest" (Gilderhus 2006: 8–9). Once Mexico had been defeated in 1848 and much of its

24 *Regional hegemons*

territory stripped to allow the USA an unimpeded swath of land to the Pacific, that country no longer stood as a serious rival on the North American continent. Until the late 19th century, US attitudes toward its southern neighbors were dismissive and derisive, collectively known as "Spanish America" until the beginning of the 20th century, when the term "Latin America" crept into the vocabulary. Even as late as 1901, Theodore Roosevelt told a German diplomat that "[i]f any South American state misbehaves toward any European country, let the European country spank it" (Morris 2002: 75).

USSR

The Soviet Union from its beginning had an ideological vision of a world revolution, and the official pronouncement never completely died. The idea was, moreover, not regional or neighboring but universal. By the early 1920s, however, it was clear this was not going to happen and the Soviets consolidated most of the former territory of Tsarist Russia (except the Baltic Republics), established diplomatic relations with their neighbors and the great powers, and generally focused on domestic economic reconstruction. The ideational element continued to be active, if not emphasized. In the words of Adam Ulam,

> ... in November 1917 and for some times afterward the world revolution was a constant expectation; during the Civil War it became a more distant but still sustaining vision ... during the 1920's, it was gradually to become something in the nature of an advertising slogan, propounded not cynically but without any of the earlier urgency and enthusiasm.
>
> (Ulam 1974: 129)

After the collapse of the USSR at the end of 1991, the Russian Federation spent much of the mid-1990s focused on itself, mired in a deep economic contraction, the vicissitudes of establishing a democratic political system, and redefining its relationship with the West. The relationship with former Soviet republics, formally organized into the Commonwealth of Independent States (CIS, less the Baltics) and which soon became dubbed, "the Near Abroad" (ближнее зарубежье, *blizhneye zarubezhye*) went through several phases, but lack of Russian capabilities limited its reach, though as will be seen below, the Russian Federation remained very active within its smaller region.

India

Unlike the other regional hegemons examined here, India from the beginning in 1947 had an intense and usually conflictual relationship with the other states within the South Asian region; all became independent within a year of each other, and all had been British colonies or protectorates, and India and Pakistan (East and West) had been part of British India. Thus, India has always been either in an active or hyperactive phase of its regional relations.

South Africa

The ideology of apartheid South Africa was probably the least active of any regional hegemon examined here. At its beginning, since South Africa had no independent neighbors, its inactivity is unsurprising. South Africa's white leaders saw themselves as part of "Western European Christian Civilization," seeking an identity outside of its region. A later prime minister B. J. Vorster admitted this focus: ". . . if we look at our development, it strikes us that at that time [1948] the emphasis fell on our identification with Europe. . . . With colonial Africa we had more or less no connections or alliances; neither in its early history nor in its process of evolution nor in its rise against colonialism" (Vorster 1975a). The ideology of apartheid was also extraordinarily inward-looking, in contrast to the internationalism of the previous dominant leader Prime Minister Jan Smuts (1939–1948). Early Prime Ministers such as D. F. Malan (1948–54), J. G. Strijdom (1954–58), and H. F. Verwoerd (1958–66) made few foreign visits and were mostly concerned about domestic politics, and in particular the Afrikaners' views (Geldenhuys 1994: 249–268). Needless to say, after the independence of Sub-Saharan African states in the 1960s, apartheid South Africa was hardly an inspiration to its neighbors.

Nigeria

The ideas of Nigerian foreign policy have almost always exceeded the resources needed to achieve them and the stability to implement them. The rhetoric of the First Republic (1960–66) echoed the non-alignment of India and other newly independent developing states, though was generally thought to have been mildly pro-Western (Gambari 2008: 62–63). The Second Republic (1979–83) was also undecided and indifferent to foreign relations with its neighbors, burned by its interventions in Chad (see below) and undecided on key issues of Africa (Gambari 2008: 66–67). Nigeria's relations with many of its neighbors are characterized as "benign neglect" (Osuntokun 2008: 147).

Brazil

As the lone Lusophone state of South America, Brazil's relations with its neighbors have often tended toward a degree of separation. Brazil was also the only monarchy of the Western Hemisphere and one of the few countries (along with Cuba and the United States) to practice slavery well into the 19th century. Following the War of the Triple Alliance (1864–70), Brazil's relations with its neighbors were correct, but its ideational focus was on itself and Europe, especially France, which was the source of much of the intellectual movement of Positivism that led to the abolition of slavery in 1888. Only in the 20th century did the government in Rio de Janeiro turn its focus back to its neighborhood.

Hyperactive phase

Most discussions of regional hegemons focus on their "hyperactive" behavior, and a key answer to the question of whether China's current actions are an indication of it becoming a regional "bully" lies in the degree to which it resembles other regional hegemons in their hyperactive behavior, as seen in their ideational, security, and regional organizational and economic behavior.

Regional exclusion doctrines

"China's Monroe Doctrine" is a phrase that has been cropping up with increasing frequency in the popular and academic media. Yet there is no clear sense among these authors as to what exactly a "Chinese Monroe Doctrine" might look like, and the term is used more to provoke than to illuminate. We will examine the evidence for that idea in Chapter 5. Here we will examine just what "Monroe Doctrines" of regional hegemons are, a keystone in the ideational construction of the hyperactive phase of regional hegemons. To begin with, there are actually two policies that are implied by much of the discussion of a "Monroe Doctrine": a policy of regional *exclusion*, and a policy of *intervention* in the states of the identified region. The two policies are also conflated, but the behavioral implications are distinct.

A "Monroe Doctrine" is also not a desire for territorial aggrandizement or conquest, just as "Manifest Destiny" was not the same idea as the Monroe Doctrine in the early 19th-century United States. Conquering or annexing land to the regional power or hegemon's formal control may be part of a regional exclusion doctrine, but in all of the doctrines examined below, most state members of the regional or functional system over which the regional hegemon is claiming exclusivity retain at least nominal sovereignty; it is domination, not annexation (annexation will be dealt with under "territorial disputes").

A regional exclusion doctrine, a more precise term for the concept under discussion, is somewhat closer but still distinct from the idea of a sphere of influence. Defined as ". . . an area into which is projected the power and influence of a country primarily for political, military-strategic, or economic purposes. . . . States within the area are usually nominally independent. . . . [a] sphere may be more or less exclusive . . ." (Vloyantes 1970: 2). Spheres of influence tend to be much less formal than regional exclusion doctrines and indeed were often pre-20th century *sub rosa* divisions of a region or country between two great powers, or the quiet understanding that if an area were to be formally annexed, a particular power had the first rights to it. Rutherford (1926) is one of the few formal discussions of the international legal nuances of spheres of influence. Hast (2012: 57–87) has an extensive discussion of the origins of the concept. Siam (Thailand) was informally divided by the French and British during the late 19th century, for example, as was Persia (Iran), which was divided between Britain and Russia in 1907. To the extent that a sphere of influence area is not explicit, exclusion of other great powers activity is seen as "devious" (Rutherford 1926: 301) and does not bind third parties legally, but does often lead to formal annexation (304).

A regional exclusion doctrine was best summarized as "hands off": an explicit and unilateral foreign policy announcement by the regional hegemon that powers external to the region are not welcome. Unlike spheres of influence, a regional exclusion doctrine must be clearly articulated; a "Keep Out" sign does no good if it is hidden. They are also unilateral. Regional exclusion doctrines usually involve a specific region, or sometimes a functional grouping of states or colonies. These are most frequently the immediate neighbors of the regional hegemon, and an area beyond. The limits of the regional exclusion doctrine's zone depend on a variety of factors, geography being the most important; some regions have clear terminal boundaries that are both objectively and subjectively recognized. Other zones are more difficult to define precisely and "blend off" into other regions and other zones. The Eurasian continent is perhaps the best example of this.

Perhaps the most pertinent aspect of a regional exclusion doctrine is the self-asserted rights adhering to the hegemon. The most prominent of these is the right to determine the foreign relations of member states within the zone. These span a fair degree of control by the regional hegemon, from "suggesting" that states within the region of exclusion consult with the hegemon, to placing treaty controls on the regional states' third party foreign relations. Of the third parties, great powers are the most concerning to the regional hegemons. Formal military alliances with extra-regional powers, purchase or acquisition of arms beyond a hegemon-defined "minimum," diplomatic recognition of governments hostile to the hegemon, are all examples of foreign policies which regional exclusion doctrines seek to deny, mitigate or veto. As we will see in several – but not all – cases below, the introduction or re-introduction of external great powers into the affairs of a region that is dominated by a hegemon can often be the most provocative. As John Mearsheimer opined in a 2015 *New York Times* Op-Ed column,

> Great powers react harshly when distant rivals project military power into their neighborhood. . . . This is why the United States has the Monroe Doctrine, and today no American leader would ever tolerate Canada or Mexico joining a military alliance headed by another great power.
> (Mearsheimer 2015)

Some regional hegemons' application of the doctrines varies substantially over time (broken down in this discussion into "inactive," "active" and "hyperactive" phases) and in some cases between neighboring states; the Soviet Union applied the Brezhnev Doctrine to fellow socialist states but not to Finland, for example.

UNITED STATES OF AMERICA: THE MONROE DOCTRINE

Several regional powers have announced regional exclusion doctrines, and since the United States Monroe Doctrine was one of the first, it is often used as a handy term for the idea. The invocation of the historical "Monroe Doctrine" is also a useful reminder to the United States that it has often treated its own neighborhood in an imperious manner, a contemporary counter to United States criticism of other regional hegemons' exclusive behavior. The Monroe Doctrine *per se* was also one of the most expansive geographically and ambitious in scope. Announced by President James Monroe in 1823, it was actually the work of Secretary of State John Quincy Adams. Geographically, the policy applied to the entire Western

Hemisphere, a region which has clear geographical boundaries set by the very large Atlantic and Pacific Oceans. The policy defined the region as distinct from European politics, republican as opposed to monarchical, a political status the United States had pioneered, though the policy itself did not lay any ownership claim by the USA to the hemisphere. The policy held that no *new* European colonization should occur in this hemisphere, though the United States would tolerate the existing colonies.

The behavior of two European powers prompted Adams to act, Russia and Spain. Russian fur traders of the Russia-American Company had been establishing bases in what is now Alaska at the beginning of the 19th century and in 1822 after Tsar Alexander I issued a *ukaze* (imperial edit) which not only claimed exclusive commercial rights in the area of Fort Ross in what is now California, but furthermore claimed rights to maritime control and commerce 115 miles from the Northwest coast of North America (Borgens 2004: 58–59). This impelled Adams to protest the Russian actions and, with the activities of the Spanish in the Caribbean, created the basis for a hemispherical doctrine.

The colonies of Spain had fought for their independence in the early decades of the 19th century after the King Ferdinand VII of Spain had been displaced by Napoleon, and there was a concern that Madrid might be seeking to re-establish its control, a well-founded concern given the attempt to retake Venezuela and Mexico in the late 1820s, and as the French had tried in Haiti in 1803 and again in 1825. In this regard, it touches on a key aspect of regional hegemon's behavior in the hyperactive phase of regional relations: it is the introduction or *re-introduction* of external powers in the defined region that often provokes a hyperactive policy response. The doctrine had been developed in coordination with Britain, which was looking for commercial advantages in newly independent Latin American states, though the USA acted alone in its declaration, Adams famously saying that he feared the United States appearing to be "a cockboat in the wake of a British man-of-war" (quoted in Gilderhus 2006: 7). The doctrine would be cited as recently as the Cuban Missile Crisis in 1962 as justification for American policy actions meant to keep external actors out of the hemisphere. But as noted above, the ideology of American regional policy during most of the 19th century was largely inactive. Nor did the Monroe Doctrine dictate the regime types or domestic politics of the newly-independent states of the Western Hemisphere, only that they not be new colonies. Subsequent US efforts at excluding extra-regional states, such as the 1945 Act of Chapultepec and the 1947 Rio Treaty, have been multi-lateral, not unilateral pronouncements, and much less explicit about exclusion.

Interventionist doctrines

There is a distinction between a regional exclusion doctrine and an interventionist doctrine: the former is when the regional hegemon simply seeks to keep other powers out of its region, and with an interventionist doctrine, the regional hegemon seeks to shape the internal politics and policies of its neighbors, usually by force or threat thereof (see Huang and Shih 2014: chap. 2, about the distinctions).

The distinction can be a fine one, and regional hegemons often find themselves "compelled" to intervene because of perceived influence of other powers, or the prospect that the instability, insolvency, or incompetence of smaller neighbors. In other cases, most notably the Brezhnev Doctrine, the neighboring ideological regime type was a critical element determining intervention. These general tendencies of regional exclusion doctrines have substantial variation between different regional hegemons, as seen below. In general, a key distinction in types of intervention are unilateral versus those sponsored by international organizations.

USA: ROOSEVELT COROLLARY AND INTERVENTIONISM

As noted, US relations with its neighbors were minimal during most of the 19th century, the Monroe Doctrine notwithstanding. The Monroe Doctrine was exclusionary but did not mandate domestic policies or politics in the Western Hemisphere, only that they not be an expansion of colonialism. That policy underwent a change, known as the "Roosevelt Corollary" in the early 20th century that justified not just exclusion but active intervention into the affairs of Central American and Caribbean states. US interpretation of the Monroe Doctrine had expanded during a border dispute between Venezuela and Great Britain's colony of Guyana in 1895 when President Grover Cleveland's Secretary of State said that, ". . . today the United States is practically sovereign on this continent, and its fiat is law upon the subjects to which it considers its interposition" (quoted in Gilderhus 2006: 10). When the latest military leader in Venezuela, Cipriano Castro, defaulted on the nation's European debts, it provoked a joint intervention by Britain, Germany and Italy in 1902–03. Those navies blockaded Caracas, seized the Venezuelan navy, and German ships shelled a fort before Castro's government agreed to arbitration. That arbitration award gave preference to the European states which had blockaded Venezuela over other creditors and thus the United States government feared that a perverse incentive had been created: defaulting states could be blockaded, and the blockaders would go to the front of the creditors' line, adding to the incentive to intervene by European states in the Western Hemisphere. In addition, the USA feared that European states might annex territory in lieu of cash payment. President Theodore Roosevelt announced it in December 1904 as a "corollary" to the existing Monroe Doctrine. As described by one historian,

> . . . TR's corollary . . . affirmed US responsibility for warding off threats of European intervention in the Western Hemisphere and for taking corrective action whenever Latin Americans reneged on international debts . . . when, in his words, 'chronic wrongdoing' or 'impotence' caused breakdowns in 'the ties of civilized society'.
>
> (Gilderhus 2006: 11)

The main focus of American fears of European intervention at the beginning of the 20th century were increasingly focused on Germany. German ambitions in the Caribbean were the prime focus of American fears prior to World War I, and with its rapidly growing economy, expanding navy and mercurial kaiser, the possibility of Germany establishing naval bases in "America's lake" was not entirely unfounded (Morris 2002: 75–76).

The Spanish-American War in 1898 was not formally justified by the Monroe Doctrine but was obviously an intervention in the Cuban War of Independence. The USA then passed the Platt Amendment (1901) in which the new Cuban government agreed to allow the USA to intervene in its affairs as the USA saw fit, which it did from 1906 to 1909. Other interventions followed. US support of a rebellion in the Colombian region of Panama helped that area become its own state which signed an agreement with the USA to finish the French-initiated canal and created a US sovereign zone around it.

US interventions in Central America and the Caribbean during the early 20th century usually had four elements prompting them: 1) bogus or rigged elections, often leading to 2) a breakdown of law and order, rebellions, revolutions, civil wars, coups d'état, and other threats to stability, which led to 3) physical threats to US citizens and their property, and 4) real or potential financial default on US and other foreign loans (Langley 2002). The list of American armed intervention in the Caribbean area from 1898 to 1934 is long: Haiti 1915–34; Dominican Republic 1916–1922; Cuba 1898, 1906–09; 1912; Nicaragua 1912–33; Mexico 1916; Colombia 1903; etc. The protection of American citizens abroad was a frequently-stated objective of these interventions, such as the small communities along the Caribbean coast of Central America and, most dramatically, when Mexican troops under Pancho Villa attacked an American town in 1916, leading US General John Pershing on a long and fruitless search for Villa (Langley 2002: 108). The United States had no fewer than 47 Militarized Interstate Disputes from 1895 to 1933, many of them regional. After WWII, the total number of MIDs the USA engaged in was 245, the greatest number of any power (Jones et al. 1996). Interventions in Guatemala (1954), Cuba (1961, failed), the Dominican Republic (1965), Grenada (1983), and Panama (1989) were among the most prominent ones in the Cold War period. In other instances, US intervention was only barely clandestine, such as the Nicaraguan war in the 1980s, and the US support for the 1964 coup d'état in Brazil, tellingly named "Operation Brother Sam." In all cases, the influence of (Soviet) communist ideology was a justification for the action.

USSR/RUSSIA: "LIMITED SOVEREIGNTY" AND THE "NEAR ABROAD"

The regional exclusion doctrine most often compared to the Monroe Doctrine was the Brezhnev Doctrine (Доктрина Брежнева/*Doktrina Brezhneva*), formally expounded in November 1968 as a justification of the Soviet invasion of Czechoslovakia in August 1968 to crush the "Prague Spring" reform movement. The analogy between the USA and Latin America and Soviet Union and Eastern Europe, the frequency of intervention, and the formal articulation of exclusion all made for a variety of policy comparisons (see Jones 1990: 162; Triska, ed. 1986). One of its primary elements was interventionist, articulating the "internationalist duty" of the Soviet Union to preserve socialism in wavering countries. As a regional exclusionary doctrine, the Soviets articulated their "keep out" much earlier in 1947/48 in eastern Europe in response to the proposed Marshall Plan, drawing a sharp line between the "People's Democracies" of Eastern Europe and the Western forces of capitalism, imperialism, revanchism, etc. The Soviet government made it quite clear to Czechoslovakia and Poland that they were not to participate in the Marshall Plan, despite the latter countries' initial interest.

As a regional doctrine of limited sovereignty (Доктрина ограниченного суверенитета/*Doktrina ogranichennogo suvereniteta*) there were origins going back to Lenin and the Bolshevik era (Jones 1990: 31–38). After World War II, the Soviets did not formally annex Poland, Hungary, Czechoslovakia, Romania, and Bulgaria.[3] The Soviet doctrine of limiting those countries' sovereignty was justified primarily on ideological grounds, giving the USSR a primary role in those socialist countries' affairs, as head of the socialist camp and thus not strictly speaking a regional doctrine, since it would include Mongolia, the Soviet Union's oldest ally, among others. For practical purposes, the policies were most relevant to eastern Europe, and indeed the Soviets at times further justified by an appeal to "Slavic Solidarity," though this would not appeal to the Hungarians, Romanians or East Germans (Jones 1990: 61–71).

The Russian Federation's policy toward the newly-independent states of the former Soviet Union was quickly dubbed the "Near Abroad," (ближнего зарубежья, *blizhnego zarubezh'ya*), a term attributed to Russian Foreign Minister Andrei Kozyrev in early 1992. The policy implications of the term were recognized quickly, as one analyst said, "Rightly or wrongly, Russia's political classes have difficulty viewing the republics on its periphery as fully sovereign entities; use of the term near abroad, in addition to qualifying their independence, signifies to the 'far abroad' that Russia claims certain rights in the region that transcend traditional conventions" (quoted in Safire 1994). In recent years, official Russian statements have avoided the term. Russian President Vladimir Putin instead used the term "New Russia" in reference to parts of Ukraine after invading and annexing Crimea in 2014, and cited (unilateral) Russian legislation granting Moscow the right to use armed force in Ukraine (Herszenhorn 2014). The rhetoric used is telling. Russian Federation President Vladimir Putin said of Ukraine:

> ... we have always considered Ukraine not only a neighbour, but also a brotherly neighbouring republic, and will continue to do so ... I am certain that the Ukrainian military and the Russian military will not be facing each other, they will be on the same side in a fight.
>
> (Putin 2014)

Of course, this was just before annexing the Crimean area of Ukraine. Brothers can be like that.

Two factors have made Russian policy toward the "Near Abroad" the most hyperactive and aggressive of any of the regional hegemons examined in the post-Cold War era. First is the concern about 25 million ethnic Russians and Russian-speakers who live in neighboring countries of the former Soviet Union. Although many ethnic Russians returned to the Russian Federation in the 21st century, Ukraine, Estonia, Latvia, and Kazakhstan have nearly a quarter of their populations who are Russians or speak Russian as their primary language. This has, of course, been most noted recently in the dispute between the Russian Federation and Ukraine beginning with the Orange Revolution in 2004 and the Maidan movement in 2014.

The second factor has been the Russian perception of Western influence in its former territories. In this case, the Russian accusation of Western and specifically US involvement in the pro-EU popular movement in Kyiv figured prominently in the harsh responses. What is particularly important in this instance is that the Russian policy toward Ukraine is decidedly exclusionary: the Russian government wanted Ukraine to sign a customs agreement with Russia, Belarus and Kazakhstan, whereas the prospect of Ukraine signing an Association Agreement (essentially an elaborate trade deal) with the EU was enough for Moscow pressure Ukraine's leaders against the idea, setting into motion the Maidan protests, the fall of the Yushchenko government, the seizure of Crimea and the war in the east. This is not, however, new policy, though it is easily the most dramatic manifestation of a Russian policy seeking to exclude European Union and NATO expansion into the "Near Abroad." The August 2008 Russo-Georgian war saw Russian troops intervene when Georgia sought to assert control over Abkhazia and South Ossetia, two of its own regions, and following a NATO summit in which the USA sought NATO membership for both Georgia and Ukraine. As one analyst summarized, "Even respectable political circles in Moscow continue to attribute the Rose and Orange Revolutions to US-led machinations, while more extremist politicians have voiced concern that events in Tbilisi and Kyiv were merely a rehearsal for US plans to implant a pro-American regime in Moscow itself" (Mankoff 2012: 127). Only in the case of the Baltic states admission to NATO has a significant strategic shift not resulted in the Russian Federation using force, though it did protest the expansion into former Soviet territory (Mankoff 2012: 50–51).

SOVIET INTERVENTIONISM

Of the regional hegemons examined here, the USSR was doubtlessly the most concerned about managing the domestic politics of its neighbors. The most notable interventions were by the Soviet military which put down revolts in East Berlin (1953), Hungary and Poland (1956), and Czechoslovakia (1968). The suppression of the independent labor movement Solidarity in Poland in 1981 was left to the communist government of Poland under the explicit threat of Soviet intervention. Other Soviet intrusions into eastern European politics were the sponsoring or suppressing of particular leaders within the communist parties of those countries. The Soviet doctrines justifying intervention, the Pomelov Doctrine and later Brezhnev Doctrine not only were exclusionary doctrines, they mandated an ideological and political system affinity as a core element. In only one case, Finland, did the Soviet Regional Exclusion Doctrine allow for a democratic capitalist system, albeit with limits on its foreign policy, what became known as "Finlandization."

In contrast, when the Czechoslovakian government in 1968 experimented with domestic political liberalization, it nevertheless made it quite clear in its meetings with the Eastern Bloc leaders that its membership in the Warsaw Treaty Organization and the Council for Mutual Economic Assistance were not in question and that its foreign relations would not change (Valenta 1991). Romanian foreign policy also diverged noticeably from Soviet policy, though its domestic politics were quite similar. Fear of external influence seeping into Eastern Europe and the theory that such influence was the source of reform in Czechoslovakia were a central part of the Soviet intelligence reporting in the spring and summer of 1968; the "evidence" was largely manufactured by the KGB, to be sure, but paradoxically, the Soviets firmly believed that foreign agencies were behind the Prague Spring and suppressed any intelligence to the contrary (Ouimet 2003: 27). Thus, the Soviet regional exclusion doctrine during its hyperactive period was integrally linked to its intervention doctrine and was much more focused on the domestic political systems of its functional group, the socialist camp. The Militarized Interstate Dispute database shows the USSR involved in 159 incidents (worldwide) between 1945 and 1992.

The Russian Federation has maintained a highly interventionist tendency within the "Near Abroad" of the former Soviet states. The conflict in the Ukraine is the most prominent and most recent instance of Moscow attempting to not only dictate neighbors' foreign policies but also their trade and domestic politics as well. Opposition to the Rose (Georgia), Tulip (Kyrgyzstan), and Orange (Ukraine) Revolutions in 2003–2005 and the implied democratization of formerly stable but undemocratic regimes was a key element of Russian foreign relations (Mankoff 2012: 206–207). These were not isolated instances. Russian troops have been in Kyrgyzstan, Tajikistan, Belarus, Armenia, among others. Measured quantitatively, the Militarized Interstate Dispute database shows the Russian Federation engaged in sixty incidents between 1992 and 2009 (Jones et al. 1996).

INDIA: THE INDIRA DOCTRINE

Other regional hegemons have developed their own regional exclusion doctrines. During Prime Minister Jawaharlal Nehru's terms from 1947 to 1962, India's stated foreign policy was primarily concerned with non-alignment and global issues. At the regional level, however, this translated into a policy of trying to exclude larger powers from the region and an unspoken policy of maintaining Indian dominance over the subcontinent (Malone 2011: 104). Nehru in fact was fairly explicit in the analogy to the Monroe Doctrine and the principle of excluding external great powers:

> I shall go a step further [than the Monroe Doctrine] and say that any interference by any other power [with the annexation of Goa] would also be an interference with the political system of India today ... any attempt by a foreign power to interfere in any way with India is a thing which India cannot tolerate.
> (quoted in Holmes and Yoshihara 2009: 334)

In one important respect, India was unable to prevent extra-regional connections in the subcontinent: Pakistan signed a military pact with the USA in 1954 and maintained close ties during much of the Cold War, though the USA did not come to Pakistan's aid in the 1965 or 1971 wars. China was also closely linked to Pakistan though not a treaty ally.

Nehru's daughter Indira Gandhi was much more explicit with her "Indira Doctrine." One Indian journalist summarized the doctrine aptly: "Therefore, no South Asian government should ask for outside assistance from any country; rather, if a South Asian nation genuinely needs external assistance, it should seek it from India. A failure to do so will be considered anti-Indian" (quoted in Hagerty 1991: 351–352). In response to a refugee crisis originating in East Pakistan in 1971, India invaded, defeated the West Pakistani forces, and helped create Bangladesh. India vigorously opposed US support for Pakistan in the crisis, fearing American involvement in the broader region, and began to apply Nehru's sub-continental doctrine to the broader Indian Ocean area. When a US aircraft carrier group led by the *USS Enterprise* sailed into the Indian Ocean in December 1971, India reacted negatively: "The episode underlined Indian fears about the dangers of major-power intervention. Hence New Delhi demanded that the United Nations declare the Indian Ocean a zone of peace, that the United States vacate its base at Diego Garcia, and that foreign ships leave the ocean's waters" (Basrur 2014: 173–174). Indira Gandhi was especially sensitive to the involvement of other great powers in East Pakistan and Sri Lanka (Shanmugasundaram 2012: 28).

Following Indira's assassination in 1984, her son and subsequent Prime Minister Rajiv Gandhi continued the policies toward India's South Asian neighbors, intervening (unsuccessfully) in the Sri Lankan civil war, embargoing Nepal when it became too close to China, and seizing the Maldives after an attempted coup d'état there (Hagerty 1991: 353–361). The motive for the policy was clearly to ensure the exclusion of other powers' influence in the region, as Hagerty summarizes:

> ... successive Indian governments have systematically pursued an active policy of denial in South Asia similar to that applied to the Western Hemisphere by the United States in the nineteenth century. A true security doctrine outlasts its originators, thrives under different leadership, and survives shifting political tides.
>
> (363)

India's primary regional rival, Pakistan, responded by further cementing its relations with China and the United States. Other, smaller states in South Asia have been much more cautious in their approach to India, though as we will see in subsequent chapters, they have been approached by China.

The next Indian government led by the Hindu nationalist Bharatiya Janata Party (BJP) expanded the concept of "neighborhood." Indeed, beginning in 1998, the India government began to articulate a policy of "Extended Neighborhood" reaching beyond South Asia and into Southeast Asia, Central Asia, and the Middle East (Scott 2009: 108). Part of the policy was the recognition that India's interests had grown with trade and energy security becoming two particular aspects of India's interests that stretched beyond the sub-continent. When the BJP government fell in 2004, the Congress-led successor government took up the idea. Defense Secretary Shekhar Dutt put it in geographic terms: "India's security environment extends from the Persian Gulf to the Straits of Malacca across the Indian Ocean, including the Central Asian region in the North West, China in the North East and South East Asia" (Dutt quoted in Scott 2009: 112). This has encompassed resource diplomacy in the Gulf, naval connections from Africa to Japan, diplomatic approaches to ASEAN, and feelers into Central Asian republics where China and Russia have largely organized the region under the Shanghai Cooperation Organization, of which India became a member in June 2017.

INDIAN INTERVENTIONISM

India has also intervened in its neighbors' domestic politics, largely in search of stability after an initial phase of territorial consolidation, but also to promote democratic forms of government. In the case of Sikkim, it annexed the kingdom outright in 1975, though it had been a protectorate of British India, a status that carried over into the post-independence period. It invaded Portuguese colonies in India (Goa) in 1961, though it did not regard these as legitimate "neighbors," and similarly pressured the tiny French colonies in India to agree to be absorbed in the 1960s as well. And the independence of Bangladesh in 1971 was unmistakably an intervention in Pakistani politics, but prompted by a refugee crisis sparked by West Pakistani army's actions in East Pakistan. The situation in Sri Lanka was more complex; the government and individuals in the Indian state of Tamil Nadu secretly supported ethnic Tamil rebels in northern and eastern Sri Lanka in what became a bloody civil war. As part of an Indian-sponsored peace initiative, the Indian military intervened in Sri Lanka in 1987–90 to disarm Tamil guerrillas, but the LTTE (Tamil Tigers) faction did not accept the peace accord, and the Indian army was involved in a long, bloody counter-insurgency, withdrawing in 1990.

In the Maldives in 1988 ("Operation Cactus"), on the other hand, the Indian army was quite successful in quashing a coup attempt, using paratroopers to restore the president to office. Nepal, moreover, found itself under an economic blockade from India in 1989 (repeated in 2015) following commercial disputes and when Katmandu had been too friendly with China, purchasing consumer goods and weapons (Crossette 1989). Nonetheless, there is little evidence that Indian interventions in South Asia have had much concern with the ideology or domestic policies of the governments involved, accepting ". . . a variety of domestic political systems in neighboring states, ranging from near-absolute monarchies, military regimes, and authoritarian Islamic states to parliamentary governments of the democratic Indian pattern. . . . Reports that India has covertly funded its favorites may well be true; nevertheless, India has accepted the results of various elections and coups alike" (Schaffer and Schaffer 1998: 114). This is not to say that New Delhi does not have preferences, and in Nepal in particular it has been openly against the monarchy and behind the Nepali Congress Party, and a number of South Asian political parties have developed reputations, fairly or unfairly, in the Indian media as "pro-India" or "anti-India" parties. India was involved in 104 interstate disputes between its independence in 1947 and 2009, many with Pakistan.

SOUTH AFRICA: FROM APARTHEID TO THE MANDELA/MBEKI DOCTRINE

Apartheid South Africa's policy during its early years is difficult to characterize as one of regional exclusion, since its neighbors were European colonies and not wholly sovereign; moreover, Pretoria sought to annex its immediate neighbors. Early South African foreign policy toward southern Africa held out the hope that South Africa would acquire the other British colonies and protectorates in the region, the High Commission Territories now known as Lesotho, Swaziland, Botswana, and Namibia. The British, on the other hand, were not interested in allowing South Africa to annex the High Commission Territories in southern Africa, and as the apartheid policies were promoted by the South African government after 1948, the United Nations and much of the world increasingly shunned South Africa (Hentz 2005: 20–23). By the 1960s, the European great powers had decolonized Africa and much of sub-Saharan African became independent, and South Africa's hopes of annexing its neighbors were crushed. Nevertheless, South Africa's independent neighbors (Botswana, Lesotho, Swaziland) were largely surrounded by South African territory, small and weak, and its other neighbors, Mozambique and Rhodesia, remained friendly, white-ruled regimes, for a while.

South Africa's early relations with neighboring entities was also influenced by a sense of identity with expatriate white minorities in other African countries, most notably Rhodesia, but also Southwest Africa/Namibia's German white minority, Kenya's British minority, and to a lesser extent the white Portuguese in Angola and Mozambique. In the case of Namibia, South African authorities exported its formal apartheid regime to that protectorate (including Bantustans) and advocated vaguely similar policies of white dominance in those colonies such as Kenya, in which there was a small ruling minority prior to independence. Rhodesia's unilaterally declared independence in 1965 eventually led to the introduction of South African security forces there in 1967, which lasted into the mid-1970s (Geldenhuys 1994: 264–269).

Post-apartheid South Africa has continued to play a major role in its region; the obnoxious ideology that justified racial hierarchy disappeared but the power politics of an asymmetrical regional relationship remained. There was also a hint of continental exclusion by Nelson Mandela once he was president of South Africa:

> South Africa's growing diplomatic reach unsettled some superpowers that have traditionally regarded Africa as falling into their sphere of influence. In 1996 Mandela told European and American diplomats to leave a Nairobi meeting, saying that African heads of state would do a better job without having to factor in a myriad of foreign agendas.
>
> (Legum 2002: B735)

Prys (2012) characterizes contemporary South Africa as a "genuinely African state that opposes external interferences in African or Southern African affairs" (78).

SOUTH AFRICAN INTERVENTIONISM

South Africa's relations with its black African neighbors was minimal when those countries became independent in the 1960s and became increasingly hostile during the 1970s and 1980s, when South Africa's *cordon sanitaire* of white-dominated neighbors (Angola, Mozambique, Rhodesia) became majority-ruled. Following a brief and unsuccessful attempt at détente with its black neighbors in the mid-1970s (discussed below), the white regime in Pretoria began to use its military power to intervene in its neighbors. Angola was the most prominent instance of this from 1975 through the 1990s when South Africa backed the guerrilla group UNITA against the MPLA government in Luanda. South Africa even went so far as to send its military into the three-sided Angolan civil war in 1975, largely because of the presence of Soviet-equipped and supplied Cuban troops. Pretoria also sponsored RENAMO, a guerrilla group in Mozambique fighting the government of Frelimo, a guerrilla movement cum government, forcing the latter to sign the Nkomati Accord in which Mozambique expelled the ANC from its territory. South African commandos and aircraft struck at Lesotho, Zambia, Zimbabwe, Mozambique, and other neighbors during the early 1980s, targeting ANC facilities and clearly intimidating those host countries. The vigorous South African intervention into its neighbors was justified because of the connection of the leftist governments in those countries with the Soviet Union. Pretoria also used economic coercion against independent Zimbabwe and Mozambique (Hentz 2005: 37–40). Thus, the external great power provoked, or at least justified, the extreme intervention by South Africa. The Militarized Interstate Dispute database shows twenty-seven incidents between the end of WWII and the end of apartheid involving South Africa (Jones et al. 1996).

Post-apartheid South Africa has also intervened in its neighbors' politics. Mandela's failed attempt to solve the political instability in neighboring Lesotho diplomatically in 1997 led to the military intervention of troops from South Africa and Botswana (Operation Boleas) following a disputed election, both to bring stability and restore democracy. Although the prime ministers of Lesotho had asked for outside assistance, the legal mandate for the South African intervention was thin. As Prys concludes,

> ... South Africa seemed to act under the conviction that it had a right and a duty to intervene in Lesotho, even if this meant it had to bend some of the regional, and also national, rules about the use of military force. Overall, both the intervention and the way it had been effected can, therefore, be said to indicate that a sense of responsibility and a sense of exceptionalism are apparent in South Africa's self-perception.
>
> (Prys 2012: 113)

38 *Regional hegemons*

These two incidents were, however, the only Militarized Interstate Disputes between 1994 and 2009 involving South Africa (Jones et al. 1996).

The attempt by President Nelson Mandela and his successor, Thabo Mbeki to promote democracy and human rights has been dubbed the "Mandela-Mbeki Doctrine" (Landsberg 2000). Mandela's emphasis on human rights was clear from his speeches in both Africa and the West, taken up especially in Africa. His Foreign Minister stated that, "human rights are the cornerstone of our government policy and we shall not hesitate to carry the message to the far corners of the world. We have suffered too much ourselves not to do so" (quoted in Landsberg 2000: 108). The South African promotion of democracy and better governance in the continent was not always popular or effective, and the Jacob Zuma government has been much quieter about its approach to the issue. It is noteworthy that a state having undergone a substantial change in its political system would seek to bring that same ideology to other countries, its neighbors being most proximate.

NIGERIA: *PAX NIGERIANA* AND CONTINENTAL JURISDICTION

Nigerian leaders have long seen themselves as the leader of Africa. "Nigeria has long maintained a self-perception of its preeminence in West African and pan-African affairs, to the extent that the pursuit of *Pax-Nigeriana* has been an undergirding principle, to varying degrees, of every Nigerian administration in the postcolonial period" (Werner 2017: 641). In Africa during the 1976–79 period, Nigeria extended this idea with a formally articulated a doctrine of "Continental Jurisdiction," which functioned very similarly to the Monroe Doctrine of the United States: ". . . Nigeria's belief in the philosophy of continental jurisdiction was intended to exclude any non-African nations from exercising influence on or interfering in the African continent" (Abegunrin 2003: 69). Some Nigerian leaders have been quite forthright in this ideology, explicitly using the analogy to the Monroe Doctrine of the United States (Adebajo 2008: 13). This complemented Nigeria's existing sense of "manifest destiny" to lead Africa as its most populous state (Ihonvbere 1991: 512). It was, quite simply, the height of Nigeria's influence in Africa in general:

> [Nigeria] . . . emerged as the most important, most prominent, and most influential power in Africa. The West courted it, liberation movements relied on its diplomatic and financial support, African countries counted on it for financial assistance, and international organizations touted it as the most credible and solvent country in Africa.
>
> (Ihonvbere 1991: 521)

The change of government to the Second Republic in 1979 led to a retreat from this policy, but Nigerians continue to assert a major role in the continent of Africa. One former Nigerian ambassador to Washington, D.C. said, "We have to be recognised as a regional power in West Africa. This is our region and we have a right to go to war. It is a Monroe doctrine of a sort" (Adebajo 2008: 13). The Babangida regime

(1985–92) again revived its concept of regional jurisdiction, asserting its leadership in the region and continent, announcing the "Akinyemi Doctrine" which demanded reciprocal consultation, namely that other African states consult with Nigeria before undertaking new initiatives. It was not well-received: "Not surprisingly, this pronouncement . . . only served to widen the gulf between Nigeria and other African countries, many of whom already perceived Nigeria as a bully" (Ihonvbere 1991: 528). For Nigerians, the terms used for their regional relations are familial, seeing themselves as a "big brother" to the smaller states next door: "Pax Nigeriana is reflected in the utterances of those of Nigeria's soldiers, diplomats, politicians, journalists and students who share a common belief in Nigeria's 'manifest destiny' with special responsibilities to be a regional 'big brother.'[4] The metaphor of a benevolent older brother who is more experienced and thus responsible for protecting his younger siblings has often been employed in Nigeria's diplomatic and popular parlance. This 'big brother syndrome' has afflicted Nigeria's leaders since independence, and smacks of a paternalism that has often irritated its neighbors" (Adebajo 2008: 13). One of the few states in Nigeria's primary region, West Africa, that could argue for an "elder" status is English-speaking Ghana, which is smaller but had gained independence three years before Nigeria and rivaled Nigeria in its Pan-African influence and personal antipathy of their leaders (Abegunrin 2003: 104–106).

Nigeria's other rival for influence in West Africa is France, an external power. Although France granted its African colonies independence in 1960, it remained strongly involved in the security, economic, cultural, and trade affairs of what became known as *Françafrique*. Nigerian leaders saw this as a challenge to its own dominance over West Africa: "For geo-political reasons, France appeared to Nigerians to be the natural rival of Nigeria in Africa. For both camps, this rivalry was self-evident. Nigeria is located at the heart of the French 'sphere of influence' in Africa, and is surrounded by four francophone countries" (Médard 2008: 325). France had tested nuclear weapons in the Saharan Desert north of Nigeria in the 1960s, supported the Biafran rebels in Nigeria, supported Cameroon in the territorial dispute over the Bakassi peninsula with Nigeria, and sponsored a number of international institutions that rivaled ECOWAS but purely for French-speaking states. France has maintained troops in Senegal, Côte d'Ivoire, Djibouti, and Gabon in Africa and has often used them in operations. Yet in at least two of France's military interventions in the region, Nigeria was an active partner: in the 1979 intervention in the Chadian civil war in which Nigeria replaced the French as a unilateral (and ultimately unsuccessful) peacekeeper, and more recently in Mali, where Nigerian troops under ECOWAS auspices supported French troops in 2012 against Islamist rebels ("African leaders agree to send troops to Mali" 2012). Although Franco-Nigerian economic relations have blossomed, France has returned to its security role in Africa (Schmitt 2015). Nigeria remains suspicious of France's renewed efforts in Africa but is entirely too focused on its own domestic problems to do much about it.

Nigerian foreign policy has broader sights than just West Africa, however. During the apartheid era in South Africa, Nigeria was naturally strongly opposed to

40 *Regional hegemons*

the white minority state and spent a great deal of time, effort, and money trying to oppose Pretoria and described itself as a "Front-Line State" in the struggle against white minority rule. Closer to home, Nigeria saw South African influence in nearby Equatorial Guinea to be a substantial threat in the 1980s and used a variety of coercive diplomatic maneuvers to get the leaders of that small state to enter into agreements with Nigeria which were very much in the latter's favor (Adebajo 2008: 151–152). After the end of apartheid, however, majority-ruled South Africa has become Nigeria's rival in continental influence. And under Nelson Mandela's leadership, Pretoria easily became the more respected continental leader. In discussions about UN Security Council expansion to include a permanent seat for Africa, it is usually South Africa that is considered, not Nigeria, and South Africa that joined IBSA and later the BRICS, as well as the G-20 group of nations. However, Nigeria's economy has now eclipsed that of South Africa to become the largest in sub-Saharan Africa ("Nigeria set to become . . ." 2014), and with democratically elected presidents since 1999, Nigeria continues to seek continental prestige.

NIGERIAN INTERVENTIONISM

The interventions Nigeria has been involved in, as noted above, have generally been internationally sanctioned and multilateral. To be sure, Nigeria did have a strong doctrine concerning the governance of countries in Africa, namely that they should be majority-ruled and independent, and thus opposed the colonial regimes such as Mozambique and Angola and the white-minority regimes of Rhodesia and South Africa. Once those states became independent and majority-ruled, Nigeria has generally taken no position on the status of other African governments, unlike post-apartheid South Africa. The Militarized Interstate Dispute database records only fourteen incidents between 1960 and 2009 (Jones et al. 1996).

BRAZIL: NO EXCLUSIONARY DOCTRINE

Not all regional hegemons, however, have developed and maintained regional exclusion doctrines, either implicit or explicit. Brazil did not develop a regional security doctrine that excluded other powers. The history of Brazil has kept it somewhat apart from its Spanish-speaking neighbors: it was the only independent monarchy of South America until 1889, relatively stable, prosperous, and so much larger that it saw itself from the beginning as a "giant" among "pygmies" (Seckinger 1984: 28). Its traditional rival in the continent is Argentina, against whom it fought the Cisplatine War (1825–1828) and the Platine War (1851–52). The former cost Brazil what became the independent state of Uruguay, but the latter established Brazilian dominance over the Platine sub-region (Rio de la Plata states: Brazil, Argentina, Uruguay, Paraguay and Bolivia). A long and bloody war fought against Paraguay in the War of the Triple Alliance (Uruguay, Brazil and Argentina, 1864–1870) was the last that Brazil fought in South America, and thereafter it turned to diplomacy and the United States in maintaining its relations with its neighbors. José Maria da Silva Paranhos, Jr., Baron of Rio Branco, considered the father of Brazilian diplomacy, accomplished the remarkable job of settling Brazil's undefined borders at the beginning of the 20th century through skillful use of arbitration and meticulously researched legal arguments to win favorable – but not too favorable – border settlements. Brazil has never fought a war with its neighbors since.

Indeed, by the early 20th century, one of the hallmarks of Rio Branco was his close attachment to the United States, his policy of approximation. Rio Branco saw the growing economic connection between the USA and Brazil to be the underlying element behind a political understanding as well, an "Unwritten Alliance" (Burns 1966). The two American republics exchanged ambassadors in 1905 as a sign of mutual respect, during an era when only great powers exchanged ambassadors rather than ministers. Rio Branco embraced the Monroe Doctrine and its exclusion of European powers and supported the Roosevelt Corollary with its interventionist policy, which he reasoned did not threaten large South American republics such as Brazil, only small and unstable Caribbean states (Burns 1966: 151). In this regard, Brazil might be thought of as a "delegate" for the United States. Its subsequent leadership role in the UN Peacekeeping force in Haiti (MINUSTAH), which began in 2004, following US military intervention may be regarded as a similar episode.

Contemporary discussions of Brazilian external relations have noted its less-than-prominent articulation of a coherent regional strategy. A *New York Times* editorial summed it as, ". . . Brazil's voice in the international arena barely registers above a whisper" (New York Times Editorial Board 2015). An *Economist* editorial stated that "Brazil's underlying problem in South America is its ambivalence about exercising real leadership" ("Bello: the bets that failed" 2014: 38). The contrast between an expansive global vision and a limited regional appeal has also been frequently mentioned, as one observer appropriately summarized, "While Brazil's global prominence is now universally recognized, it's less certain how it intends to wield its newfound power. . . . That is especially true among its neighbors in Latin America, where it has only reluctantly embraced the role as a bulwark of regional stability" (Goodman 2009: 4). And Burges (2009) summarizes this as the whole thrust of Brazilian foreign policy: ". . . Brazil's diplomatic history is marked by consistent efforts to avoid any suggestion that the country was seeking a leadership role in the region" (43). Although the Lula presidency sought to be a little more prominent in its leadership, a failure to provide public goods has been much of the problem for Brazil's efforts (Burges 2015: 194). Very aware of the asymmetry between itself and the other smaller states in its region, Brazil's efforts to lead the region are subtle at best, unsuccessful at worst, and unarticulated as a doctrine.

This is not to say that Brazil lacks a foreign policy vision; its global vision and foreign policy have often been quite expansive. During the 1961–64 presidencies of Jânio Quadros and João Goulart, Brazil's foreign policy horizons went well beyond the Southern Cone, moving toward a "neutralist" position in the Cold War, promoting the anti-colonial movement in Africa, establishing trade relations with the USSR and China, and taking steps to curtail foreign (read: USA) investment in the Brazilian economy. This relatively radical phase, however, did not yield a strong regional impact, though the criticism of the US Bay of Pigs invasion of Cuba in 1961 had an element of an effort to lead Latin America in a different direction (Burns 1980: 485–486). The pro-US coup d'état that overthrew Goulart would itself be succeeded by a military government in the later 1970s that also promoted an active foreign policy in Africa, terminated its security pact with the USA, and sought a more independent orientation in its policy (Burges 2009: 24–26). In recent years, a change in the world's trading regime, a permanent seat on the UN Security Council, a position as one of several spokesmen for the developing world (in association with Russia, India, China and South Africa in the BRICS), are all part of a global vision of Brazilian foreign relations that can be dated at least to the 1980s and the beginning of the democratization of Brazil (Vigevani and Cepaluni 2009), and particularly since the election of Lula (Brands 2010).

BRAZILIAN INTERVENTIONISM

As noted above, Brazil did not develop a formal doctrine of exclusion, nor of intervention as other regional hegemons did, but did intervene informally in some of its neighbors' affairs in the 19th century. Uruguay, which had been part of Brazil from 1816 to 1828, was a primary focus of Brazilian intervention, given the instability of its politics and the presence of a large number of Brazilian residents.

> The Brazilians . . . continued to meddle clandestinely in partisan politics throughout the region, occasionally funneling money to select Argentines and Uruguayans. This policy was reflexive, with Brazilian diplomats seeking to perpetuate a divided Argentina over which the empire could have maximum influence, which opened the door to renewed Brazilian penetration in the Plata. Much of this was commercial and financial. The baron of Mauá, for instance, actively underwrote scores of Platine ventures throughout this period; indeed, the finances of Montevideo became dependent on the baron's bank. A Brazilian diplomatic campaign was also part of the picture. The empire's representatives wanted both Argentina and Paraguay to grant free access via the rivers to Brazil's Mato Grosso provinces. And the Brazilians wanted to control Uruguay short of outright annexation.
> (Whigham 2002: 123)

The Brazilian military intervention on behalf of a Uruguayan liberal faction in 1851 did not yield a more stable government in Montevideo and only provoked a military buildup in Paraguay, and when Brazil threatened Uruguay again in 1864, Paraguay attacked both Brazil and Argentina. Although the latter two states won the long, bloody war that followed, Brazilian relations with its neighbors never again showed the previous kind of interventionism in what became the two buffer states between Argentina and Brazil (Burns 1980: 229–236). The Militarized Interstate Dispute data show only seven incidents after WWII involving Brazil (Jones et al. 1996). Brazil's current foreign policy shows no strong ideological preference for regime type, having good relations with countries as different as democratic republics, a communist single-party state in Cuba, and a chaotic "Bolivarian Republic" in Venezuela.

Active phase: the "Good Neighbor Policy"

The hyperactive phase examined above is common – but not universal – in regional hegemons' relations with their neighbors. Hegemons assert their power, prerogatives, and dominion and articulate explicit policies to announce and justify this behavior. It is what is normally associated with the terms "regional dominant power," "regional hegemon," "great power," etc. It is also an expensive and alienating approach, one which may inspire fear but little loyalty. Thus, most – but not all – regional hegemons periodically adopt a policy that is much more moderate, one that treats adjacent states as *neighbors*.

USA: "Good Neighbor Policy"

"In the field of world policy, I would dedicate this nation to the policy of the good neighbor – the neighbor who resolutely respects himself and, because he does so, respects the rights of others – the neighbor who respects his obligations and respects the sanctity of his agreements in and with a world of neighbors." Thus did Franklin D. Roosevelt address the issue of foreign relations in his first inaugural address in March 1933, giving rise to the term "Good Neighbor Policy" (Henrikson 2004: 350).[5]

The world of 1933 was not the world of today, and liberal democracy was very much under threat by two competing ideologies which were finding appeal around a desperate world, including Latin America: communism and fascism. The proper approach to Latin America became a substantial issue between the Republican and Democratic parties in the late 1920s and early 1930s, but in contrast with earlier debates, the policies advocated in the early 1930s were much more measured in the type and process of intervention advocated (Benjamin 1974: 76–79). The result, articulated in Franklin Roosevelt's inaugural address, was termed the "Good Neighbor Policy." The phrase was turned into policy at the Montevideo Conference in 1933 when Secretary of State Cordell Hull signed the Convention on Rights and Duties of States, article eight of which stated that "No state has the right to intervene in the internal or external affairs of another." This position was reaffirmed at the Buenos Aires Conference in 1936 where the last American reservations about the right to intervene in its neighbors' affairs were eliminated (Wood 1961: 118–119).

The real test of any such policy lies not in policy pronouncements and conference speeches, however, but rather what a regional hegemon does when its interests really are threatened. That occurred for FDR's administration first in Cuba in 1933, when a leftist regime came to power only to be unseated in an US-endorsed coup d'état led by Fulgencio Batista, and though the temptation to use direct military force to intervene was strong indeed in such a close neighbor and extreme situation, the United States did not. A similar strain came in 1938 when Mexico expropriated American petroleum holdings, and though Republicans charged that the FDR administration was too soft on Cárdenas's government in Mexico, a rupture was avoided (Raat 1992: 142–145). The Good Neighbor Policy did result in generally better relations between the United States and Latin America in the late 1930s and early 1940s when FDR's administration was worried about rising German influence in Brazil and Argentina (Pike 1995: 231–233). US trade with Latin America grew from its depression-era nadir of $975 million to over $5 billion at the end of the war. The real pay-off for the policy, however, was in a boom in post-war trade with Latin America. Trade with Latin America also grew as a percentage of overall American foreign trade, though during the war, America ran a considerable balance of trade deficit with Latin America.

Several factors gave rise to the Good Neighbor Policy of the United States. First, the interventionism of the Roosevelt Corollary in the first two decades of the 20th century had become increasingly costly; US Secretary of State Philander Knox estimated in 1911 that it cost $1 million a year to maintain a naval and Marine force in the Caribbean, ready to ". . . afford adequate protection to foreign life and property" (Knox quoted in Gantenbein 1971: 77), and that was before the much more expensive interventions in Mexico a few years later. Second, intervention continued to be unpopular among Latin American states, and a source of constant criticism; the US Marine Corps had just departed Nicaragua when FDR was inaugurated, and were still in Haiti. Third, the economic milieu of the United States had changed radically and with it a degree of self-confidence. Frederick Pike suitably summarized the shift: "People who make a habit of intervening in the affairs of foreign countries, in order to improve and develop and uplift those countries, must have supreme confidence in their own political, social, and economic wisdom and virtue. By 1930, the Great Depression had delivered a staggering blow to American self-confidence, and thereby ended the mood out of which crusades to uplift benighted foreigners had issued" (Pike 1995: 165).

USSR: Gorbachev's renunciation of the Brezhnev Doctrine

The Soviet Union maintained a tight grip on its Eastern European satellites, as noted above. There were periodic slight moderations of this regime, often following an intervention. The economic relationship evolved and eventually shifted to a net transfer of resources from the Soviet Union to the Eastern European economies (Chafetz 1993: 22–28). The basics of Soviet domination remained clear, however, such as in Poland in 1981, when the imposition of martial law by the Polish communist government was clearly demanded by the Soviet leadership; the alternative was invasion.

A major change in policy occurred during the Gorbachev era, one that resembles the "Good Neighbor Policy" seen in other countries. The net transfer of resources from the Soviet Union to its eastern European neighbors represented an economic drain on an already struggling Soviet economy, and was among the reasons for economic reforms there: "The loss that Moscow suffered on its East European investment was a factor in Soviet internal change and ultimately, Gorbachev's decision to discontinue interference in East European domestic politics" (Chafetz 1993: 14). By late 1987, Gorbachev announced to the Eastern Europeans that the Soviet Union would no longer dictate policy or conformity. The Brezhnev Doctrine was explicitly nullified, and Eastern Europe began to transition to democracy, capitalism, and orientation toward the West (Chafetz 1993: 72–79). Whether the Soviet Union might have enjoyed better relations with its former satellites is impossible to say, since the Soviet Union collapsed at the end of 1991.

India: Gujral Doctrine

As noted, the government of India under the Nehru-Gandhi family and the Congress Party has been explicitly assertive of its privileges in South Asia, but there have been several periods in which political tides have brought other parties to power. After Indira Gandhi lost power following the 1975–77 Emergency, her successor M. Desai fostered better relations with India's smaller neighbors before his coalition was unseated by Mrs. Gandhi in 1980. Those political tides shifted again for a short while under the United Front coalition government in the 1996–98 period and associated with Foreign Minister and briefly Prime Minister I. K. Gujral. Dubbed the "Gujral Doctrine," it was explicitly meant to mend fences with India's small South Asian neighbors (not China or Pakistan, however). In a speech in Sri Lanka, Gujral summarizes the approach: "The 'Gujral Doctrine, if I may call it so, states that, first, with its neighbors like Bangladesh, Bhutan, Maldives, Nepal and Sri Lanka, India does not ask for reciprocity, but gives and accommodates what it can in good faith and trust" (Gujral 1997). Gujral continues in his speech to urge against interference in neighbors' affairs, using territory against one another, and respecting territorial integrity and sovereignty, and peaceful resolution of disputes. Gujral's earlier speeches had articulated the new approach to foreign policy, and his negotiation of water-related issues with Bangladesh and Bhutan both pointed to results from this more "neighborly" approach (Gujral uses the term "neighbor" eight times in this short speech, and "neighborhood" three times).[6]

Finally, there is some discussion of whether the most recently-elected Prime Minister of India, Narendra Modi, has begun a more active engagement with India's neighbors. The new administrations in both Pakistan and India sought to improve their relations during the first days of Modi's administration. Modi's invitation of SAARC leaders to his swearing-in ceremony in New Delhi in May 2014 was seen as a major symbol of a new regional policy, and his visit to Nepal in August 2014 (the first by any Indian Prime Minister) seemed to confirm the trend. As one journalist summarized, ". . . [Modi] has unequivocally underlined that Nepal is sovereign to take its decisions; that Nepal should decide the pace at which and issues for which it needs India's support" (Jha 2014). That lasted a few months before India began a fuel embargo on Nepal, and the "tough India" re-emerged.

South Africa: outward policy and "détente" 1969–1975

Apartheid era South Africa, despite its domestic racial policies, did periodically attempt to smooth its relations with its independent black neighbors. Under the leadership of Prime Minister John Vorster, this "outward policy" of South Africa renegotiated its customs union with its immediate neighbors in 1969, slightly to the advantage of Botswana, Lesotho, and Swaziland, and in 1970 reached out to the conservative francophone states of West Africa for dialog (Hentz 2005: 30–31).

The April 1974 coup d'état in Lisbon changed South Africa's security position radically. The Portuguese military, discouraged by years of fruitless counter-insurgency in Guinea-Bissau, Mozambique, and Angola, overthrew the Caetano regime, leading to the rapid decolonization of those territories, and raised the specter of new fronts in the guerrilla wars in Namibia and Rhodesia and South Africa itself. This breaching of the *cordon sanitaire* of South Africa led Prime Minister Vorster to attempt a "détente policy" toward black African states. Needless to say, the term "détente" was chosen precisely because it was meant to reduce tensions between two seemingly implacable blocs. Vorster's speeches during the 1970s frequently reference "our neighbors" (Vorster 1975a, 1975b) and did achieve some success at the Victoria Falls Conference in August 1975 when Vorster and Kenneth Kaunda of Zambia brought Rhodesian Prime Minister Ian Smith to the table with rebel groups (Geldenhuys 1994: 271).

The Angolan Civil War destroyed détente: both Vorster's brief period of an active South African engagement with its neighbors, and the more famous US-Soviet détente policy. South Africa, however, was primarily responsible for its own failure. Disturbed by the rise of what it saw as Soviet-supported Marxist parties in both Angola (the MPLA) and Mozambique (Frelimo), the South African military launched an invasion of Angola from its bases in Namibia in October 1975 in support of two of the Angolan parties, the FNLA and Unita. The intervention discredited these two parties and embarrassed their other backers, namely the United States, Zaire (now the DRC) and China (Jackson 1995: 413). South African became even more of a pariah in Africa and the world with the Soweto riots in 1976, and after the elections in 1978, the government of P. W. Botha (1978–89) entered into a particularly aggressive phase, despite nominal "reforms" of apartheid during the mid-1980s.

Nigeria

Of the regional hegemons examined here, Nigeria is the most difficult to characterize by period; the rhetorical aspect of the foreign policy greatly exceeded the capabilities of the Nigerian state, linked as they were to a single export commodity. But at least three periods of Nigerian foreign policy resemble (to a degree) an attempt by a regional hegemon to adjust its relations with its neighbors after a period of acrimony, if not hyperactivity. After the end of the Nigerian civil war in 1970, President Yakubu Gowon undertook a fence-mending trip, visiting those African states which had explicitly or implicitly supported the Biafran rebels: Côte d'Ivoire, Gabon, Tanzania, and Zambia, as well as establishing relations with the

Soviet Union and China (Gambari 2008: 64). The government also offered (though they were declined) troops to help protect Guinea against Portuguese invasion in 1971 and then intervened between Benin and Niger on dispute over Lete island in the Niger river, both instances of public security goods (Abegunrin 2003: 43–44). Gowon was overthrown in a coup in July 1975, and Nigerian foreign policy then leaned toward the hyperactive. Ibrahim Babanginda, who overthrew Muhammedu Buhari in 1985, also eased Nigeria's regional relations while attempting to deal with an economy moribund due to the collapse of world oil prices (Adebajo 2008; Abegunrin 2003: 134–138). Finally, the Abacha regime, though largely anathema to the rest of Africa, did participate in West African peacekeeping operations, partly to remain in the (relatively) good graces of the permanent members of the UN Security Council.

Brazil

Brazilian foreign relations with its neighbors in the 20th century have been generally quite good, comparatively speaking. Only in the case of Argentina has there been a long-standing coolness, and even that was substantially ameliorated by the 1980s. Relations with the United States have had their periods of closeness (1902–1950s, 1964–67) and distance (1961–64, 1969–1970s), but these have not strongly correlated with Brazil's regional relations. For much of its history, Brazil's regional relations with its neighbors have been a counterpoint to its rival, Argentina; in this respect it has parallels to India and Pakistan. Efforts at improving relations with the other states of the Southern Cone such as during World War II, and again in the 1970s, when Brazil began building the giant Itaipu Dam along the border with Paraguay, had an undeniably chilling effect on its relations with Buenos Aires. The rivalry reached its 20th-century peak in the 1970s when both sides began research into nuclear weapons, but both renounced their programs by 1991 and have since improved their bilateral relations. On a purely bilateral basis, the capabilities gap between Brazil and Argentina has grown to the point that the rivalry is now largely historical. In more recent years, Venezuela, Chile, and Colombia have demonstrated some degree of rivalry to Brazil, but Brazilian responses have been remarkably limited and conciliatory (Schenoni 2015: 10). If anything, Brazilian regional policy may be that of a good neighbor, but it simply fails to attract many followers in the region (Malamud 2011).

Security behavior of regional hegemons

In addition to the ideational and doctrinal points above, a few other behavioral characteristics of regional hegemons in security matters should be noted because they are significant indicators of the tendencies toward inactive, active, or hyperactive phases. Several have been dealt with above, such as the tendency to impose specific types of political regimes during hyperactive phases, or the negative reaction to external great powers in regional affairs. Three others should be noted:

Territorial disputes

Regional hegemons, like many countries, have territorial disputes. Many are small, long-standing, and inoffensive and thus are a low priority to resolve. The cost to maintain a claim is minimal; the cost to resolve a territorial issue can be high. In inactive phases, it is not uncommon to "let sleeping dogs lie" and leave borders unresolved, not delimited and not demarcated. And in active phases, borders are generally resolved by negotiation and legal processes. Perhaps the best example of that was Brazil at the turn of the 20th century, when Baron Rio Branco's careful preparation and legal approach yielded sound borders for Brazil without firing a shot. Nigeria also ceded the Bakassi Peninsula to Cameroon in 2008 after an International Court of Justice awarded it to Cameroon in 2002 (ICJ 2002). One of the legacies of the late 20th century bequeathed to the world is the rise of maritime disputes; just when terrestrial borders have been mostly resolved, the oceans have become the latest scene of competition. The United Nations Conference on Law of the Sea was supposed to help resolve these issues, but as we will see in the South China Sea, it only takes one side to make the problems severe. Still, India and Bangladesh resolved their maritime border dispute through the UNCLOS-sanctioned Permanent Court of Arbitration in 2014 (after 40 years of negotiations) (PCA 2014).

In hyperactive phases, however, regional hegemons often seek to resolve disputes by force or intimidation, or to adopt intransigent approaches to negotiations. Territorial annexation is sometimes the hegemon's goal, sometimes the threat/tool to intimidate neighbors, and sometimes a bit of both. American expansion in the 19th century at the expense of Mexico and Canada is well known, and the use of the territorial claim of the Nueces Strip was a key *casus belli* in the 1846 Mexican-American War. The Soviet Union pressed territorial claims against Turkey in eastern Anatolia in 1945–53 to recover Tsarist lands for the Georgian and Armenian SSRs, though it dropped the demands after Stalin's death in 1953.

The difference between annexation and the splitting off of new independent states by regional hegemons is a very fine one, and one sometimes is a transition to the other. Americans split the Republic of Texas from Mexico in 1836, but it would be almost ten years before it was annexed to the USA, and in 1893, the Hawaiian monarchy was overthrown by American forces leading to the Republic of Hawaii before it was annexed in 1898. Tannu Tuva was nominally independent from 1921 to 1944 before the Soviet Union incorporated it. Sikkim was likewise independent, though under Indian "guidance" from 1947 to 1975 when it, too, was annexed.

In other cases, the regional hegemon helps create a new country. India helped create Bangladesh out of East Pakistan in 1971, the United States assisted in the creation of Panama in 1903, though it annexed the Canal Zone itself. Apartheid era South Africa was unusual in that its Bantustans – nominally independent black African states meant to be separate countries – were formed out of its own territory in the 1970s, though out of the most marginal land in Natal and Transvaal. The Russian Federation has also maintained three small breakaway sections of former Soviet Republics: the Trans-Dniestr area in Moldova, South Ossetia, and Abkhazia in Georgia, fighting a brief war in 2008 against Georgia to maintain these "states" which only Moscow recognizes (Mankoff 2012: 221). It also has set up the Donetsk and Luhansk People's Republics in eastern Ukraine (Cooley 2017).

Diplomatic relations

Although hardly a precise test, the extent of formal diplomatic relations between regional hegemons and their neighbors does show a degree of interaction. Visits of heads of government, ministers, delegations, military exchanges, and most importantly state visits all show a more cooperative relationship. When relations are suspended, downgraded or broken outright, or when dissident groups or "governments-in-exile" are hosted, it is usually a sign of hostility and hyperactivity.

Expatriates and co-ethnics

The role played by overseas communities or expatriates in regional relations, particularly when the hegemon's citizens or co-ethnics are involved, deserves to be highlighted. In a hyperactive phase, even minor attacks or affronts can become major affairs, particularly when the hegemon wants there to be a major affair, leading to intervention. For the United States in the late 19th and early 20th centuries, threats to American entrepreneurs in Central America and the Caribbean was a frequent justification for intervention. The treatment of ethnic Russians in 21st-century Ukraine and the Baltics is another example. And those ethnic Russians in turn have a far more favorable opinion of Russian Federation foreign policy than do their fellow citizens (Diamant 2017).

But during active phases, incidents can be dealt with at the consular level if both sides are interested in preserving the relationship and show good faith at the resolution of the problem. Furthermore, expatriate and overseas communities can often become a very useful bridge for commercial and cultural purposes. We will see this in the role in which overseas Chinese communities play in Southeast Asia in the 21st century. India's diaspora community has played a similar role in Southeast Asia, as well as the Middle East, Central Asia, and Africa (Xavier 2017). Brazilian commercial farmers are present in Paraguay and elsewhere in South America, and South African commercial farmers have been invited to the DRC ("Boers moving north" 2011). But the presence of hegemons' citizens or co-ethnics can be a very sensitive or hypersensitive issue when there is both a power and a population differential, and the phrase "Fifth Column" is a term still whispered in parts of the world.

Economic and organizational behavior of regional hegemons

How do regional hegemons interact with their regions economically and organizationally? The two issues are closely intertwined because regional organizations broadly have economic origins that lead to policy and then to political functions, but in some cases such as SADC, regional economic organizations begin to take on security functions. Table 2.3 shows some of the organizational and economic characteristics of the three phases of regional hegemons. In general, regional hegemons tend to be indifferent to regional organizations that they do not create and control in inactive phases, hostile toward them in hyperactive phases, and accommodating in active phases.

The economic relationships of hegemons and regions are far more of a continuum than the more discrete policies and doctrines examined above. Trade and investment by regional hegemons in their respective regions can be relatively apolitical and innocuous for two basic reasons: either it is not very large, not imbalanced, or is not seen as a political issue.

Trade is politically sensitive in almost all states, and bilateral deficits are (according to economists) unfairly targeted, whereas overall account balances ought to be the focus of attention. That may be true for economists, but political leaders think differently, and they tend to focus laser-like on trade deficits and market domination, and those will be two key indicators this study will use. Market dominance is the degree to which the regional hegemons' exports to its neighbors dominate their overall imports. Note here that regional hegemons' imports from neighbors is not systematically examined here because those are simply less sensitive, unless they threaten to become monopsonistic, such as American purchases of pre-revolutionary Cuban sugar or China's purchases of Mongolian raw materials today.

Foreign direct investment (FDI) is an important part of economic interaction, though it is more difficult to track statistically than merchandise trade. Although at times unpopular locally, this study will proceed on the assumption that the central governments of all countries welcome foreign direct investment. Exceptions will be treated narratively.

Provision of collective economic goods is one of the characteristics of an active regional hegemon. In practical terms, this often means foreign aid. All regional hegemons examined here gave at least some foreign aid, either humanitarian assistance, economic development assistance, or military assistance (though the latter is considered under security behavior). Numbers, however, can be imprecise for all but OECD DAC countries. In broader terms, actions such as China's lending of hard currency to Thailand, Malaysia and Indonesia during the 1997–97 Asian financial crisis is also the provision of a public good, as was Beijing's decision not to devalue the Renminbi at that time.

USA

The Organization of American States (OAS) is headquartered in Washington, D.C., not far from the White House. The proximity is quite symbolic: the OAS and its antecedents have been strongly connected to American foreign policy since the Good Neighbor Policy of the FDR administration. Thus, the United States had the benefit of generally inclusive and agreeable regional organizations with which to deal. Although Simon Bolivar had envisioned a Latin American international organization in 1822, it was the United States which helped to create the Pan-American Conference, the predecessor of the OAS in 1890, and thus included itself in the regional organization. The obvious geographical division of the hemispheres and the bifurcated rhetoric of the day helped create a regional organization to which the United States belonged and which excluded European influences, grouping a "New World" of republics against an "Old World" of monarchies. Secretary of State James G. Blaine, the organization's initial American sponsor, was particularly concerned about the rise of European commercial penetration of the Western Hemisphere (Thomas and Thomas 1963: 12). The only difficulty the USA found with the organization was that by 1923, the American interventions in a number of neighboring countries and the reaffirmation of the unilateral nature of the Monroe Doctrine had led to a number of criticisms of American foreign policy, especially at the Havana Conference in 1928 (Fenwick 1963: 54). By the Montevideo Conference in 1933, the renunciation of the right of intervention (albeit with caveats) enormously improved American relations with Latin America. The organization's name was changed to OAS in 1948, and its goal was to oppose communism, linked to the Rio Pact. Aside from a minor challenge to US leadership of the hemisphere from Argentina in the late 1930s, the only other major dissident from America's pre-eminent position in the OAS was Cuba under Fidel Castro. The United States solved that problem by simply suspending Cuba's OAS membership in 1962. Its economic arm is the Inter-American Development Bank, established in 1959. The OAS as an organization remains quiet but active, with an annual budget of $84 million in 2014.

Since the 21st century, however, a number of regional organizations and attempted regional organizations have emerged in the Western Hemisphere that have challenged the role of the OAS and the USA. The ALADI (Latin American Integration Association) was founded as a trading group in 1980. The Rio Group was a non-institutional dialog forum established in 1986 and led to the Community of Latin American and Caribbean States (CELAC) in 2010, a body that explicitly excludes the USA and Canada. A smaller but even more explicitly anti-American group is the Bolivarian Alliance for the Peoples of Our Americas (ALBA), formed by Venezuela and Cuba in 2004. The Union of South American Nations is another body that is only South American and so excludes Mexico, Central America, and much of the Caribbean, and has a strong Brazilian influence (to be discussed below).

The North American Free Trade Agreement (NAFTA) was a US response to the growing trend of Regional Trade Agreements (RTAs) which began in the 1980s, most notably with the implementation of the Single European Act in 1992. It may also be the only time American foreign policymakers have thought of "North America" as its own region. Ratified in 1994, it drew Mexico away from the rest of Latin America economically, and the USA began to consider a Free Trade Area of the Americas (FTAA) in 1994 following the success of NAFTA and began open discussions at the Summits of the Americas in 2001 and 2003, but the formal talks broke down after 2005, and US focus on trade pacts shifted to the Pacific Rim with the Trans-Pacific Partnership (TPP) and the EU with the Trans-Atlantic Trade and Investment Partnership (TTIP). The former had its main proponent, the United States, withdraw from it in 2017 in one of the more spectacular disavowals of global hegemonic leadership.

The trade dominance of the USA in Central America and the Caribbean has a long history, and has seldom been challenged. US goods averaged over 60% of Cuban imports during the 1920s and 1930s, and over 75% in the 1940s and 1950s. Similar figures can be seen for Haiti, the Dominican Republic, and Mexico from 1895–1913, and during the 1990s was over 70% (Barbieri and Keshk 2012).

USSR/Russia

The Soviet Union's economic sphere was defined by the Council for Mutual Economic Assistance (CMEA or COMECON). Founded in 1949 as a counter to the US-backed Marshall Plan aid, it had no charter or formal structures until the mid-1950s. Its initial purpose was exclusion of western capitalist economic influence, redirection of trade ties away from the West, and the extraction of capital out of eastern European countries (Ulam 1974: 436–437). After Stalin's death and the rise of Khrushchev, COMECON began to solidify as an organization, though it remained dominated by the USSR's economic size. From 1959 to 1963, there were a number of initiatives to coordinate economic activity in the Eastern Bloc, including central plans, economic division of labor, and communications. The exploitative nature of Soviet extraction from the eastern European economies largely ended by the 1960s, but the economic difficulties of the economic bloc led to disagreements about how to work a socialist group of economies.

After each revolt in Eastern Europe, the Soviet leadership allowed an economic change, at cost to itself:

> Once implemented, Soviet implicit subsidies became a permanent feature of the relationship because subsidies were less costly than the loss of East European stability caused by mass unrest, and Soviet contributions to bloc growth moderated competition for scarce resources within regimes as well.
> (Chafetz 1993: 24)

The economic system also suffered from irrational prices for intra-bloc trade. Roughly speaking, the Soviets exported petroleum and other raw materials to Eastern Europe, which exported semi-finished goods (e.g., steel) and machinery back. By the 1960s, it became clear that the prices set for the transfer of Soviet raw materials for Eastern European finished goods heavily favored the eastern Europeans. The CMEA also sponsored the provision of no-cost intellectual property to its members, primarily in the form of blueprints, the Sofia Principle, though this was largely at the expense of East Germany and Czechoslovakia and was changed in the late 1960s as Soviet intellectual property became more valuable. Attempts to set up a division of labor within the bloc were passively resisted by most member states, since the CMEA worked on an unanimity principle with an "opt-out" provision that was adopted later.

Trade in the Soviet Bloc is difficult to track because it often involved barter trade, which is not listed in official data because there is no standard currency of denomination, and much of the available dataset is incomplete. Still, during the 1970s-1984 period, Poland purchased about 31% of its products from the USSR and dropped to less than 7% after the collapse of the Soviet Union. The German Democratic Republic imported about 40% of its goods from the USSR.

The security organization of the USSR was the Warsaw Treaty Organization, better known as the Warsaw Pact. Formalized in 1955, it was also dominated by the Soviets. From 1945–55 the Soviets used bilateral treaties to legalize their occupation of Eastern European states. The Warsaw Pact and the CMEA both dissolved in July and September 1991, followed by the end of the USSR.

The breakup of the USSR has led to a plethora of regional organizations dominated by the Russian Federation and including a variety of former Soviet states and other countries. All are exclusionary and most are dominated by the Russian Federation. The Commonwealth of Independent States (CIS) was the first, which included twelve out of the fifteen republics of the USSR (the Baltic states pointedly did not join). In contrast, the GUAM Organization for Democracy and Economic Development, headquartered in Kyiv and comprising *G*eorgia, *U*kraine, *A*zerbaijan, and *M*oldova, initially formed in 1997, is something of a competitive organization, which has become much more anti-Russian since the war in Ukraine. The Collective Security Treaty Organization (CSTO) has become a security organization, and gives Russia leased bases, and a veto over its members' ability to grant bases to other powers on their soil and virtually monopolizes weapons sales to its members (Armenia, Belarus, Kazakhstan, Kyrgyzstan, Tajikistan). (Cooley 2017). The Eurasian Union is a trade pact that currently includes Russia, Belarus and Kazakhstan and which preliminarily lowered trade barriers when signed in 2011, to the latter two states' greater benefit; despite Russian interest in making it something more, its two other partners have not followed Moscow's lead ("The other EU" 2014: 50). The Eurasian Union became the Eurasian Economic Union (EEU), established in 2015 and is a customs union, common market, investment pact, all involving former Soviet territories: Armenia, Belarus, Kazakhstan, Kyrgyzstan, and Russia. Trade with Russia remains high in parts of the former Soviet republics: 33% of Kazakhstan imports came from Russian in 2015, 21% of Uzbekistan's imports, and 18% of Tajikistan's imports. Over half of Belarus's imports came from Russia in 2015 (IMF DOTS 2017). Those percentages, however, have declined in recent years as Moscow's economic grip has loosened by cheaper Chinese imports.

India

Unlike other regional hegemons, India did not pioneer regional international organizations for South Asia. SAARC was largely a proposal that came out of the smaller South Asian states (Bangladesh and Nepal) and was treated with a certain amount of suspicion by both Pakistan and India, the latter because it would provide the smaller states of the region with a forum to collectively address India, which preferred to deal bilaterally with them, a "hub-and-spokes" approach to regional relations common to regional hegemons. The initial call for a regional organization was made in 1977 but SAARC was not founded until 1985. Headquartered in Kathmandu, it is primarily a forum for summits of the leaders of South Asia.

The organization did sponsor the creation of the South Asian Free Trade Area (SAFTA) in 2006, though the goal of reducing tariffs among the members has been delayed by the creation of "sensitive lists" by member states on products they wish to protect. In two respects, India has accepted inequitable terms in the trade deal, allowing the poorer countries longer to reduce tariffs and more "sensitive lists," i.e., protected sectors (Chaturvedi et al., eds. 2006: 36–37). In this regard, India is providing economic public goods to the region. In general, India has managed to maintain a moderate level of market dominance in its South Asian region, with over 60% of Nepal's imports (when India allows them in), around 28% of Sri Lanka's imports, 14% of Bangladesh's, levels that have shrunk in the 21st century due to Chinese imports (IMF DOTS 2017).

In general, SAARC has not been a particularly prominent or successful organization. As summarized by the *SAARC Yearbook*, "During the 20 years of it's [*sic*] existence, it has made limited progress towards its objective of 'accelerating economic growth, social progress and cultural development in the region.' Moreover, there is a yawning gap between the decisions adopted by it and their implementation. The reasons for this not-so-satisfactory performance are myriad- historical, political, financial and socio-cultural" (Chaturvedi et al., eds. 2006: 189).

South Africa

Post-apartheid South African economic dominance has been reinforced by its neighbors' willingness to openly engage in trade, whereas previously economic embargos meant that trade was limited or surreptitious. Since South Africa is the only industrial country in the region, it dominates exports to all of its neighbors. Trade with the Southern African Customs Union (SACU) countries is difficult to calculate precisely because it is a customs union, and trade is cumulated in a single figure. It is safe to say that South Africa dominates the trade of Botswana, Lesotho, Namibia, and Swaziland, each doing about 80% of their trade with South Africa (SACU 2009: 2). Malawi, which maintained open trade with South Africa even during the apartheid regime, has grown even more dependent on South African imports than ever: in 1988 under 30% of its imports came from South Africa, but by 2001 the figure was over 50%, before declining to the 35–40% range.

South Africa is also a major investor in other African countries, and dominates southern African banking in particular. South Africa invested over $16 billion abroad since 1994, much of it in Africa (UNCTAD WIR 2012). It has not always been popular, as FDI often involves a love-hate relationship, as Landsberg (2000) points out that South African corporations are not popular: "South Africa's white-dominated private-sector companies have been quick to capitalize on new opportunities in the postapartheid African environment, but they are often seen as agents of a new South African imperialism, determined to dominate Africa" (116).

Nigeria

Despite its size and power, Nigeria does not trade much with its neighbors, a pattern typical of post-colonial coastal states whose economic ties were with the colonial state and not with their next door neighbors which flew different flags. And despite efforts to diversify its economy, Nigeria remains heavily dependent on the export of petroleum. Exports to other Sub-Saharan African countries has risen gradually as Nigeria sells oil to other states, but the total remains about 10% of its total official exports. Imports from sub-Saharan Africa are even less of Nigeria's total trade profile, around 5%. From the perspective of Nigeria's neighbors, Niger is the most linked to its giant southern neighbor, sending 20–40% of its total exports south, and around 10% of its imports from Nigeria. Côte d'Ivoire is also heavily dependent on Nigerian exports, Senegal slightly less so. The smaller states of West Africa trade less with Nigeria, or less consistently. In the 2008–2012 period, Côte d'Ivoire depended on Nigeria for 25% of its imported goods, Ghana depended 12.6% on Nigerian goods, and Senegal 11.2%. The rest of ECOWAS was much lower (IMF DOTS).[7]

Nigeria sought to establish ECOWAS as an economic community, though this was not accomplished until 1975 (Abegunrin 2003: 46). Nigerian leaders from Gowon on saw ECOWAS as a tool to wean francophone states away from their former colonizer, though often without success (Obi 2008: 189). From the 1979 to mid-1980s, however, Nigeria neglected its own creation, ECOWAS, though in 1985 Babangida did put effort into reviving ECOWAS which had been neglected by Shagari and Buhari (Abegunrin 2003: 137), but the money was no longer available: "ECOWAS lost ground in the 1980s. . . . It could not pay its rents, its cheques bounced, and its francophone members redirected their interest and commitment to the French-sponsored CEAO" [La Communauté économique de l'Afrique de l'Ouest] (Ihonvbere 1991: 526–527).

Brazil

With the strategic rivalry with Argentina generally resolved by the 1980s, Brazilian regional policy has generally turned toward economic integration of the continent, an economic integration which will doubtlessly benefit the most industrialized countries in South America, Brazil, and Chile. Brazilian leadership has been fairly quiet, however:

> . . . although understanding and acknowledging its great weight on the continent, Brazil has always refrained from displaying high-profile attitudes of leadership and . . . has been done by building up Mercosul . . . the attempt to

unite nations in a single economic block and has assumed special importance in Brazil's global foreign economic policy.

(Bandeira 2006: 20–21)

Mercosul ("Mercosur" in Spanish) has been a Brazilian project, but a long and slow one to integrate first the southern cone and then all of South America. With Mexico joining NAFTA, Brazilian focus has been on South America per se and less on Latin America (Burges 2009: 38–39). To a substantial extent, Mercosul competed with the American proposal for a Free Trade Area of the Americas (FTAA), which died in 2006, and the Andean Community of Nations (CAN: Bolivia, Colombia, Ecuador and Peru), but the current nascent Union of South American Nations (UNASUR), founded in 2008, may yet lead to a true South American regional economic institution. Mercosul started out as a joint Argentinean-Brazilian proposal in 1985, with those two countries joining with Paraguay and Uruguay in 1991 as founders. Venezuela joined in 2012, with Bolivia set to join once existing members approve. The three major economies of the Pacific coast, Chile, Peru and Colombia, however, remain outside of full membership in the bloc, and progress toward tariff reduction and other functions have been fairly slow.

Brazil's trade with its immediate neighbors in the Rio de la Plata region is substantial. It has averaged about 30% of Argentina's imports during the 21st century, 19% of Bolivia's, 27% of Paraguay's, and 19% of Uruguay's market. Further afield on the Pacific Coast of South America, however, the numbers are not quite as impressive: 8.8% in Chile, 5.4% in Colombia, 4.7% in Ecuador, and 6.5% of Peru (IMF DOTS 2017).

Brazilian investment in South America is important as well, and though it is welcomed enthusiastically in Uruguay, in Paraguay it is a hypersensitive issue. The migration of *Brasiguayos* (Brazilian-Paraguayans) into the border regions has benefitted Paraguayan agriculture, especially soy beans, but many Paraguayans are suspicious. The terms of the huge Itaipu Dam have been similarly criticized, even though it was a joint venture and Paraguay gets half of the electricity (Lambert 2016: 120–123).

Trade and investment are usually desired by the governments of smaller neighbors of regional hegemons, and the terms of deals can be a measure of regional hegemon activity. They are, along with foreign aid, typically counted as the incentives countries use in their relations with other countries. Tourism is another economic benefit sought by countries, and the rapid rise of American tourists in Europe in the 1960s, of Japanese tourists in the USA in the 1980s and now of Chinese tourists in Asia all have spawned reactions both disdainful and avaricious. Of course, trade, aid, tourism, and investment which are suddenly withheld can be a coercive tool. Russia turned off gas exports to Ukraine in 2009, and indirectly in southeastern Europe as well. The US economic embargo on Cuba in response to the Castro government's policies started a downward spiral in relations that would last into the 21st century. Apartheid-era South Africa was more than willing to "turn the screws" on neighboring black African states. Nepal has felt the bite of Indian trade embargoes several times, and Nigeria cut off trade with Benin and

Ghana in the 1980s. And given the size differential of regional hegemon and other countries, the impact is almost always bigger on the neighbor than the hegemon.

Regional hegemons' policy changes

The preceding exegesis establishes that modern regional hegemons do not exhibit one type of behavior; rather, they exhibit multiple types and phases of behavior. Of the several regional hegemons examined, all exhibited different phases of behavior, roughly categorized as "inactive," "active," and "hyperactive."

The causes of policy and behavioral change are summarized in Table 2.4 below:

Table 2.4 Regional hegemons' reasons for behavioral change

Regional hegemons' reasons for behavioral change			
	Internal	Regional	Extra-Regional
Toward Inactive	• Contraction/ collapse	• Lack of acceptance/ boycott	• Lack of neighbors (colonialism) • Global domination by superpowers/great powers • Focus on global or continental (regional "snobbery")
Toward Active	• Major reform • Leadership Change	• Resistance • Acceptance	• Lack of superpower/great power
Toward Hyper-active	• Increase in resources • Domestic pressures to assert role	• Major regional challenger	• (re) Introduction of extra-regional power • Ideological/global conflict

This table breaks down the reasons for policy changes into three broad areas: internal factors, regional factors, and extra-regional factors. Regional hegemons tend to start with relatively inactive regional policies for historical reasons; they either have few independent neighbors (USA 1776–1820s; South Africa 1910–1960s; China 1644–1948), or their initial foreign relations are dominated by post-colonial ties (Brazil 1822–1850s; Nigeria, 1960–66). In those instances in which they subsequently adopt an inactive behavior, the causes are often related to economic contraction or collapse: Russia 1992–2000, Brazil 1982–85, and Nigeria 1983–85. Regional reactions can also result in a relatively inactive phase of regional behavior: South Africa under apartheid was generally boycotted by its African neighbors, though some functional cooperation did occur. Similarly, the Soviet Union's diplomacy toward its eastern European neighbors prior to 1935 was very constrained. Finally, some regional hegemons gradually begin to ignore their regional neighbors as they become much more powerful and aspire to great power or superpower status; as Lemke characterizes them, regional snobs. This is certainly the case with the United States after WWII, the Soviet Union after the 1950s, and Brazil today.

A much more intriguing question is why regional hegemons shift their policies toward their neighbors toward a more active yet accommodating approach. Of the regional hegemons examined here, all engaged in at least one phase of behavior that resembles what the United States and China both called the "Good Neighbor Policy": the USA 1936–54, the USSR 1987–91, India 1996–98, South Africa 1969–75, Nigeria 1970–75, and Brazil 1900–1950s, 2003–present. Many of these policy changes were associated with domestic policy reforms: the New Deal in the United States, Glasnost' and Perestroika in the USSR, and, as we will see with the policy of Opening Up in China, and Lula's social reforms in Brazil. The end of apartheid in South Africa in 1994 changed Pretoria's regional relations swiftly for the better. Just as domestic policy reforms perforce are an admission that previous policies were not successful, the adoption of an active policy phase toward one's neighbors is an admission that previous relations had been sour.[8] The coincidence of domestic and foreign policy changes is also associated with leadership changes; both democratically achieved and non-democratically. New leaders will often seek to pose their predecessors' foreign policies as needlessly antagonistic toward their neighbors, and it is much easier to improve relations with neighboring leaders when the background of personal distrust and animosity is gone. In several instances, a regional hegemon's recognition that a previous regional action such as the invasion of Czechoslovakia in 1968 led to a moderation of policy, such as the Soviet efforts to subsidize the standards of living in eastern European satellite states. The attempted US invasion of Cuba at the Bay of Pigs in 1961 resulted in foreign aid during the US Alliance for Progress in Latin America. This was also a time that the United States resolved the Chamizal Dispute with Mexico in 1963, putting to rest an issue between the two countries that had lasted since the 19th century, and did so by accepting the 1910 legal recommendation of the Boundary and Water Commission.

Regional resistance is the main reason why regional hegemons often adopt active policies following hyperactive periods. The United States hyperactive period from the beginning of the 20th century to the 1920s had an adverse effect on its regional relations, and military interventions were long, costly and frustrating, as the USA found in Mexico in 1916 and Nicaragua in the 1920s. Hence, the shift to the "Good Neighbor Policy." India had a similar experience with its neighbors, most notably the costly intervention in Sri Lanka in 1984. The opportunity for regional acceptance can also yield a more cooperative phase in policy, as South Africa found after the end of apartheid in 1994 and Nigeria found after the end of the Abacha regime in 1998.

A shift to a hyperactive phase of regional relations is certainly the policy change that attract the most attention in the study of regional hegemons, and one which has a number of origins. The increase in national capabilities is seen in a number of instances of regional hegemons becoming much more assertive toward their neighbors, as well as dabbling in the Globalist phase. In several instances, hyperactive policies were associated with growing economy: the "Roosevelt Corollary" of the USA, the "Continental Jurisdiction" period under Muhammed and Obasanjo in the mid-1970s in Nigeria, the Soviet interventions in Eastern Europe in 1956 and 1968, Quadros's radical phase in early 1960s Brazil, Russian intervention in the "Near Abroad" in the 21st century, and, of course, US intervention in Latin America during the 1950s and 1960s. There have also been periods of hyperactive regional policies that are not associated with growing economic resources, such as the aggressive policies of the 1980s in South Africa which occurred at a time the South African economy was stagnating and declining. The assertive "Indira Doctrine" period in India was not a period of high growth, either. Increasing resources may allow a regional hegemon more leeway to exercise assertive policies, but the resource differentials noted in Table 2.2 are mostly pre-existing conditions. It should be noted, however, that in at least one instance, the USA and its region, assertiveness requires naval resources which are much more expensive than land forces. All other regional hegemons have (and have used) land access to intervene in their neighborhoods.

Domestic political pressures to be more assertive in relations with smaller neighbors are often cited as a reason for a shift to hyperactive policies, and there is little doubt that the image of "teaching them a lesson" plays well to nationalistic domestic audiences. Whether it *causes* these policies is much more difficult to establish. In several of the regional hegemons examined (the USA in the early 20th century, the Russian Federation in the 21st century, Nigeria in the 1970s, and India during the 1960s and 1970s, hyperactive policies were popular insofar in the immediate aftermath of interventions. But there is almost no evidence that public opinion, either broad-based or elite, played a role in prompting the policy changes. It is probably more likely that popular sentiment followed and did not lead the policy shift.

The conflict between two persistent rivals in a regional setting may also prompt a hyperactive shift in policy; here again, the role of asymmetry is important. The regional hegemon, by definition here, is much more powerful than its main regional competitor, yet reacts swiftly to any efforts by the competitor to arm itself and cannot perceive the relationship from the competitor's perspective. Thus, Brazil began a naval arms race with Argentina at the turn of the 20th century, and India continues to build its army against Pakistan, eventually crossing the nuclear arms threshold in 1998, prompting Pakistan to do the same. Regional hegemons find it difficult to see themselves as anything other than reasonable, benign, and self-righteous. They seldom perceive just how big they loom to their neighbors.

What does seem to prompt a dramatic shift in policy toward the hyperactive is the introduction or re-introduction of great powers beyond the region. This was seen in the case of the USA when it perceived Germany to be seizing opportunities in the Caribbean in the early 20th century and again when, in the 1950s and 1960s, the Soviets were the external power. The Soviets were keenly sensitive to United States influence and inspiration in Eastern Europe (along with "Zionists") and again in the case of Central Asia in 2005 and Ukraine in 2004 and again in 2013 saw American and European influence as the hidden hand behind the Tulip, Orange and Maidan Revolutions. The US naval presence in the Indian Ocean during the 1971 East Pakistan war prompted an intensification of the "Indira Doctrine" and Nepalese engagement with China led to Indian economic blockades. South Africa's aggressive policy in the 1980s was prompted by a perception of Soviet and Cuban activity in southern Africa. Nigeria flexed its muscles against Equatorial Guinea when it caught sight of South African influence in the 1970s. In almost every episode of hyperactive policy behavior we have examined, an external great power was associated with a change in policy.

So is Mearsheimer correct in asserting that regional bullies act this way because of external great powers intruding in their neighborhoods? Partly. There is a strong association, but it is not absolute. In the case of Nigeria and France, the reaction of the regional hegemon has been complicated by proposals of joint action in areas of joint concern (Chad and later Mali); the Nigerians certainly do not like the French influence in West Africa, but it has been there for a long while. Nigeria also lacks the resources to do much about *Françafrique*. The other exception is Brazil. Of the regional hegemons examined, it is certainly the most benign in a comparative sense. Since the beginning of the 20th century, it has faced a strongly assertive United States pursuing policies in the Caribbean, Central America, and extending down into the southern cone that is Brazil's primary region. Yet Brazilian foreign policy (with the exception of the brief Quadros period) has generally been not only accepting of the US presence but has been a major "delegate" for extended periods of time. Here again, the long-term persistence of the external great power may be a factor reducing the reaction. It may also be related to unique aspects of Brazilian history. The point is that not all regional hegemons react to an external great power with a hyperactive policy shift; many do, but not all. And the reaction seems to be most related to the *introduction* of a great power into a region and not with the long-term presence of a great power. There is also the possibility that most regional hegemons no longer behave in such an overtly reactive way, though the Russian Federation would seem to be an exception, perhaps an atavistic one. As one scholar of the subject noted almost fifty years ago,

> ... the necessity for spheres of influence, may reflect the lingering of outdated modes of thinking about security which may make security and defense less dependent upon control of territory, these concepts may in time become obsolete.
>
> (Vloyantes 1970: 7)

We will return to the question in the conclusion.

Summary

The above pages may appear to be a taxing exercise in other countries' foreign policies when the subject of this work is ostensibly about Chinese foreign relations with its neighbors. The exercise is necessary, however, if we are to answer the question whether China is behaving in a manner of a regional hegemon, and if so, in which phase of behavior. The balance of the book will be just such an examination. *The argument of this book is that China's regional relations have gone from inactive to hyperactive, to active, and now show some evidence of moving toward hyperactive again.* Figure 2.5 summarizes this movement:

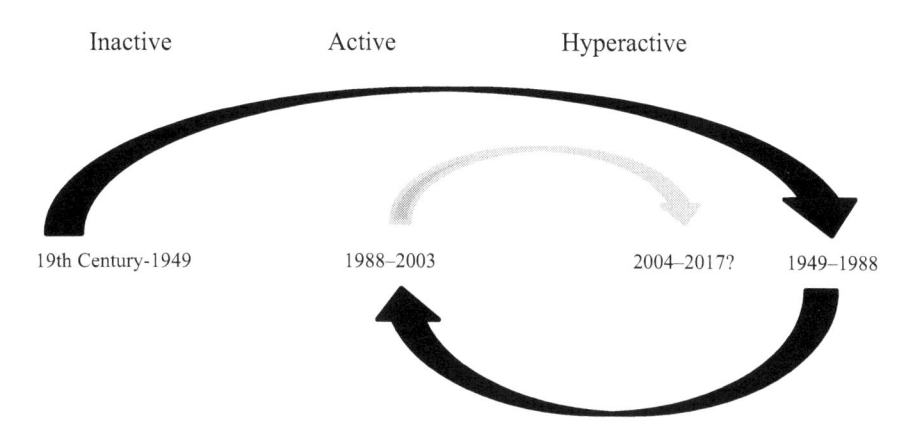

Figure 2.5 Evolution of China's neighboring relations

Six major points are worth remembering:

1. **Hegemons are overwhelming.** Regional hegemons have overwhelming capabilities over their regions. Seven currently exist: USA and Latin America, Russia and the Former Soviet Union, India and South Asia, South Africa and southern Africa, Nigeria and West Africa, Brazil and South America, and China and its four regions in Asia. Overwhelming asymmetric capabilities always lead the smaller states in the region to be much more sensitive to the regional hegemon than the regional hegemon is to its neighbors.
2. **Hegemons are explicitly exclusionary.** Almost all regional hegemons have expressed explicit doctrines of exclusion ("Monroe Doctrines"), and many have also adopted doctrines justifying intervention in the other states in their region.
3. **Hegemons change their policies.** Sometimes they bully their neighbors (hyperactive); sometimes they are neighborly to their neighbors (active); sometimes they have little interaction or attention to their neighbors (inactive). All hegemons examined showed policy changes toward their regions.
4. **External powers can lead to a hegemon's hyperactivity.** The introduction of an external great power into a hegemon's region is the most frequent reason for a regional hegemon to adopt a hyperactive policy, but it is not universal.

5. **Hegemons' hyperactivity leads to resistance; resistance can lead to a policy change.** Regional hegemons hyperactivity results in a variety of responses by regional states: a handful will support the hyperactivity, usually those governments installed by the regional hegemon. Others will actively or passively resist, and, in some cases, the resistance will involve long, difficult wars. The domestic costs of hyperactivity also lead the regional hegemon to reconsider its policies, moving either toward an active or an inactive phase.
6. **Hegemons' activity depends on international institutions they cannot entirely control.** Hegemons that have adopted an active policy need regional institutions that insulate their asymmetry vis-à-vis their neighbors. These are most frequently seen in the economic realm where the provision of public goods is most prominent, but also security public goods. This has led to the creation of overlapping and competing organizations, especially in the 21st century.

Notes

1 Whether China caught up with the rest of Northeast Asia depends largely on which measure of GDP one uses, and in this particular time and with this particular relationship, the distinction of the MER and Purchasing-Power Parity (PPP) measures is critical to the answer (for a longer discussion of the issues involved, see Jackson 2017: 79–83). In MER terms (current US$ and constant 2010 US$), China tripled its share of Northeast Asia's economy, to 46% in the inflation-adjusted figure. In PPP terms, China caught up with Japan and South Korea in 2002/03, helped by the persistent recession in Japan, thereby becoming the regional hegemon according to the definition here.
2 The rapid and unexpected independence of the new Central Asian republics meant that none were entirely prepared for the statistical obligations of being a state. The result is that economic statistics for 1992 are particularly spotty and omitted from consideration here. The population figures are reliable. The power ratios examined here begin in 1993 and show that China began are a roughly equal position in a few categories such as GDP measures, ahead in military personnel by a factor of more than two, but did not pass the SIPRI estimates of Central Asian (read: Russian) military expenditures until 1998. Its population is over six times that of its neighbors combined.
3 The Baltic states, Estonia, Latvia, and Lithuania, which had been part of Tsarist Russian Empire, were annexed in 1940. Königsberg became the Kaliningrad Oblast of the RSFSR as per the Potsdam agreement. Yugoslavia and Albania would both be relatively independent of Soviet influence, and the former would break decisively with Moscow in 1948.
4 The major Nigerian languages differentiate older and younger siblings: in Yoruba, *egbon* is an older sibling, and *aburo* is a younger sibling. In Hausa, an older brother is *yàayáa* and a younger brother is *kânèe*.
5 Franklin Roosevelt was not the first to use the term in relation to US-Latin American diplomacy; his predecessor Herbert Hoover said in 1928, "We have a desire to maintain not only the cordial relations of governments with each other but the relations of good neighbors" (Oxford English Dictionary 1989 s.v., "good neighbour"). FDR got credit for the policy, however.

6 The terms "neighbor" and "neighborhood" are directly related in Hindi: पड़ोसी (Paṛōsī) means "neighbor" and पड़ोस (Paṛōsa) means "neighborhood." "Extended Neighborhood" is विस्तारति पड़ोस (Vistārita paṛōsa).
7 One substantial caveat must be added to the above figures: a large amount of Nigeria's trade with its West African neighbors is informal, and thus not captured by official trade figures. Exactly how much is difficult to determine, but Meagher (2008) estimates that if purely intra-African trade amounts to about 6% of total West African trade, then informal trade is about 4–5% (168).
8 Not all domestic reforms lead to active regional policies; during the mid-1980s in South Africa, a variety of nominal "reforms" of Apartheid were undertaken by the P. W. Botha government at the same time it was attacking ANC facilities in neighboring countries. Needless to say, South African regional relations did not improve much as a result.

Works cited

Abegunrin, Olayiwola. 2003. *Nigerian Foreign Policy under Military Rule, 1966–1999*. New York: Praeger.

Adebajo, Adekeye. 2008. Hegemony on a shoestring: Nigeria's post-Cold War foreign policy, in *Gulliver's Troubles: Nigeria's Foreign Policy after the Cold War*, edited by Adekeye Adebajo and Abdul Raufu Mustapha. Scottsville: University of Kwa-Zulu-Natal Press, 1–40.

Ayoob, Mohammed. 1991. India as a regional hegemon: External opportunities and internal constraints. *International Journal*, 46(Summer), 420–448.

Bandeira, Luiz Alberto Moniz. 2006. Brazil as a regional power and its relations with the United States. *Latin American Perspectives*, 33(3), 12–27.

Barbieri, Katherine, and Keshk, Omar. 2012. Correlates of War project trade data set. <http://correlatesofwar.org>, accessed 14 June 2013.

Basrur, Rajesh. 2014. Paradigm shift: India during and after the Cold War, in *The Engagement of India: Strategies and Responses*, edited by Ian Hall. Washington, DC: Georgetown Press, 169–184.

"Bello: The bets that failed." 2014. *The Economist*, 22 March, 38.

Benjamin, Jules Robert. 1974. *The United States and Cuba: Hegemony and Dependent Development, 1880–1934*. Pittsburgh: University of Pittsburgh Press.

"Boers are moving north." 2011. *Mail & Guardian* [Johannesburg], 3 May. <https://mg.co.za/article/2011-05-03-boers-are-moving-north>, accessed 5 July 2017.

Borgens, Edward G. 2004. *Background of the Monroe Doctrine*. New York: Vantage Press.

Brands, Hal. 2010. *Dilemmas of Brazilian Grand Strategy*. Carlisle, PA: Strategic Studies Institute.

Burges, Sean. 2009. *Brazilian Foreign Policy after the Cold War*. Gainesville: University Press of Florida.

Burges, Sean. 2015. Revisiting consensual hegemony: Brazilian regional leadership in question. *International Politics*, 52(2), 193–207.

Burgess, Stephen F. 2012. South Africa: Benign hegemony and resistance, in *Beyond Great Powers and Hegemons: Why Secondary States Support, Follow, or Challenge*, edited by Kristen P. Williams, Steven E. Lobell, and Neal G. Jesse. Stanford: Stanford Security Studies, 207–221.

Burns, E. Bradford. 1966. *The Unwritten Alliance: Rio-Branco and Brazilian-American Relations*. New York: Columbia University Press.

Burns, E. Bradford. 1980. *A History of Brazil*, 2nd ed. New York: Columbia University Press.
Buzan, Barry, and Wæver, Ole. 2003. *Regions and Powers: The Structure of International Security*. Cambridge: Cambridge University Press.
Chafetz, Glenn R. 1993. *Gorbachev, Reform, and the Brezhnev Doctrine: Soviet Policy toward Eastern Europe, 1985–1990*. Westport, CT: Praeger.
Chaturvedi, S.K., Sharma, S.K., and Kumar, Madhurendra, eds. 2006. *SAARC Yearbook, Vol. 4: Economic Cooperation*. New Delhi: Pragun Publications.
Cooley, Alexander. 2017. Task Force White Paper: Whose rules, whose sphere? Russian governance and influence in post-Soviet states. Carnegie Endowment for International Peace, 30 June. <http://carnegieendowment.org/2017/06/30/whose-rules-whose-sphere-russian-governance-and-influence-in-post-soviet-states-pub-71403>, accessed 2 July 2017.
Crossette, Barbara. 1989. Nepal's economy is gasping as India, a huge neighbor, squeezes it hard. *New York Times*, 11 April. <www.nytimes.com/1989/04/11/world/nepal-s-economy-is-gasping-as-india-a-huge-neighbor-squeezes-it-hard.html>, accessed 27 August 2015.
Destradi, Sandra. 2008. *Empire, Hegemony, and Leadership: Developing a Research Framework for the Study of Regional Powers*. Hamburg: German Institute for Global and Area Studies, GIGA Working Papers, no. 79.
Diamant, Jeff. 2017. Ethnic Russians in some former Soviet republics feel a close connection to Russia. Pew Research Center, 24 July. <www.pewresearch.org/fact-tank/2017/07/24/ethnic-russians-in-some-former-soviet-republics-feel-a-close-connection-to-russia/>, accessed 24 July 2017.
Fenwick, Charles G. 1963. *The Organization of American States: The Inter-American Regional System*. Washington, DC: Kaufman, 52–54.
Gambari, Ibrahim A. 2008. From Balewa to Obasanjo: The theory and practice of Nigeria's foreign policy, in *Gulliver's Troubles: Nigeria's Foreign Policy after the Cold War*, edited by Adekeye Adebajo and Abdul Raufu Mustapha. Scottsville: University of Kwa-Zulu-Natal Press, 58–80.
Gantenbein, James W., ed. 1971. *The Evolution of Our Latin-America Policy: A Documentary Record*. New York: Octogon Books.
Geldenhuys, Deon. 1994. The head of government and South Africa's foreign relations, in *Malan to De Klerk: Leadership in the Apartheid State*, edited by Robert Schirer. New York: St. Martin's Press, 245–290.
Gilderhus, Mark T. 2006. The Monroe doctrine: Meanings and implications. *Presidential Studies Quarterly*, 36(1), 5–16.
Goodman, Joshua. 2009. Brazil: The global power looking for a backyard. *SAIS Review*, 29, 3–10.
Gujral, I.K. 1997. Aspects of India's foreign policy, a speech by I.K. Gujral at the Bandaranaike Center for International Studies, Colombo, Sri Lanka January 20, 1997, Stimson Center website. <http://www.stimson.org/research-pages/the-gujral-doctrine/>, accessed 14 August 2013.
Hagerty, Devin T. 1991. India's regional security doctrine. *Asian Survey*, 31(4), 351–363.
Hast, Susanna. 2012. Beyond the Pejorative: Sphere of Influence in International Theory. Dissertation, University of Lapland.
Henrikson, Alan K. 2004. Good neighbor diplomacy revisited, in *Holding the Line: Borders in a Global World*, edited by Heather N. Nicol. Vancouver: University of British Columbia Press, 18–48.

Hentz, James J. 2005. *South Africa and the Logic of Regional Cooperation*. Bloomington: Indiana University Press.

Herszenhorn, David M. 2014. Away from show of diplomacy in Geneva, Putin puts on a show of his own. *New York Times*, 17 April. <www.nytimes.com/2014/04/18/world/europe/russia-ukraine.html>, accessed 17 April 2014.

Holmes, James R., and Yoshihara, Toshi. 2009. Strongman, constable or free-rider? India's "Monroe doctrine" and Indian naval strategy. *Comparative Strategy*, 28(4), 332–348.

Horowitz, Shale, and Tyburski, Michael D. 2012. Reacting to Russia: Foreign relations of the former Soviet bloc, in *Beyond Great Powers and Hegemons: Why Secondary States Support, Follow, or Challenge*, edited by Kristen P. Williams, Steven E. Lobell, and Neal G. Jesse. Stanford: Stanford Security Studies, 161–176.

Huang, Chiung-Chiu, and Shih, Chih-yu. 2014. *Harmonious Intervention: China's Quest for Relational Security*. Farnham, Surrey: Ashgate.

ICJ [International Court of Justice]. 2002. Communique: Land and Maritime Boundary between Cameroon and Nigeria (Cameroon v. Nigeria: Equatorial Guinea intervening). <www.icj-cij.org/files/case-related/94/094-20021010-PRE-01-00-EN.pdf>

Ihonvbere, Julius O. 1991. Nigeria as Africa's great power: Constraints and prospects for the 1990s. *International Journal*, 46(Summer), 510–535.

IMF DOTS [Direction of Trade Statistics]. 2017. IMF e-library. <data.imf.org/>, accessed 19 January 2017.

Jackson, Steven F. 1995. China's Third World foreign policy: The case of Angola and Mozambique, 1961–1993. *The China Quarterly*, 142, 388–422.

Jackson, Steven F. 2017. Pivots, transitions, and distractions: Power transition theory and the US-Japan-China Relationship 2000–2012, in *The Power Transition in Asia*, edited by David Walton and Emilian Kavalski. Abington: Routledge, 77–103.

Jha, Prashant. 2014. How PM Narendra Modi's "magical address" wooed Nepal's political forces. *Hindustan Times*, 4 August. <www.hindustantimes.com/india-news/how-pm-modi-s-magical-address-wooed-nepal-s-political-forces/article1–1247953.aspx>, accessed 18 August 2015.

Jones, Daniel M., Bremer, Stuart A., and Singer, J. David. 1996. Militarized disputes, 1816–1992: Rationale coding rules and empirical patterns. *Conflict Management and Peace Science*, 163–213.

Jones, Robert A. 1990. *The Soviet Doctrine of "Limited Sovereignty" from Lenin to Gorbachev: The Brezhnev Doctrine*. New York: St. Martin's.

Lambert, Peter W. 2016. Paraguay and the rise of Brazil: Continuity, resistance, and compliance, in *Foreign Policy Responses to the Rise of Brazil: Balancing Power in Emerging States*, edited by Gian Luca Gardini and Maria Herminia Tavares de Almeida. New York: Palgrave Macmillan, 114–128.

Landsberg, Chris. 2000. Promoting democracy: The Mandela-Mbeki Doctrine. *Journal of Democracy*, 11(3), 107–121.

Langley, Lester D. 2002. *The Banana Wars: United States Intervention in the Caribbean, 1898–1934*. Lanham, MD: SR Books.

Lapp, Nancy D. 2012. Resistance is ùtil (useful): Responses to Brazilian hegemony, in *Beyond Great Powers and Hegemons: Why Secondary States Support, Follow, or Challenge*, edited by Kristen P. Williams, Steven E. Lobell, and Neal G. Jesse. Stanford: Stanford Security Studies, 145–160.

Legum, Colin. 2002. South Africa, in *Africa Contemporary Record*, Vol. 26, edited by Colin Legum and Keith Gottschalk. New York: Africana, B735–B736.

Lemke, Douglas. 2002. *Regions of War and Peace*. Cambridge: Cambridge University Press.

66 Regional hegemons

Malamud, Andres. 2011. A leader without followers? The growing divergence between the regional and global performance of Brazilian foreign policy. *Latin American Politics and Society*, 53(3), 1–24.

Malone, David M. 2011. *Does the Elephant Dance? Contemporary Indian Foreign Policy*. Oxford: Oxford University Press.

Mankoff, Jeffrey. 2012. *Russian Foreign Policy: The Return of Great Power Politics*, 2nd ed. Lanham, MD: Rowan & Littlefield.

Mares, David R. 1988. Middle powers under regional hegemony: To challenge or acquiesce in hegemonic enforcement. *International Studies Quarterly*, 32, 453–471.

Meagher, Kate. 2008. New regionalism or loose cannon? Nigeria's role in informal economic networks and integration in West Africa, in *Gulliver's Troubles: Nigeria's Foreign Policy after the Cold War*, edited by Adekeye Adebajo and Abdul Raufu Mustapha. Scottsville: University of KwaZulu-Natal Press, 160–176.

Mearsheimer, John J. 2015. Op-Ed: Don't arm Ukraine. *New York Times*, 8 February. <www.nytimes.com/2015/02/09/opinion/dont-arm-ukraine.html>, accessed 8 February 2015.

Médard, Jean-François. 2008. Crisis, change and continuity: Nigeria-France relations, in *Gulliver's Troubles: Nigeria's Foreign Policy after the Cold War*, edited by Adekeye Adebajo and Abdul Raufu Mustapha. Scottsville: University of Kwa-Zulu-Natal Press, 314–333.

Morris, Edmund. 2002. "A matter of extreme urgency": Theodore Roosevelt, Wilhelm II and the Venezuelan crisis of 1902. *Naval War College Review*, 55(Spring), 73–85.

Myers, David J. 1991. Threat perception and strategic response of the regional hegemons: A conceptual overview, in *Regional Hegemons: Threat Perception and Strategic Response*, edited by David J. Myers. Boulder: Westview, 1–30.

New York Times Editorial Board. 2015. Brazil's dim voice on the world stage. *New York Times*, 21 March. <www.nytimes.com/2015/03/22/opinion/sunday/brazils-dim-voice-on-the-world-stage.html>, accessed 22 March 2015.

"Nigeria set to become Africa's biggest economy (A.P.)." *New York Times*, 6 April. <www.nytimes.com/aponline/2014/04/06/world/africa/ap-af-nigeria-africas-biggest-economy.html>, accessed 6 April 2014.

Nolte, Detlef. 2010. How to compare regional powers: Analytical concepts and research topics. *Review of International Studies*, 36, 881–901.

Obi, Cyril I. 2008. Nigeria's foreign policy and transnational security challenges in West Africa. *Journal of Contemporary African Studies*, 26(2), 183–196.

Osuntokun, Akindjide. 2008. Gulliver and the Lilliputians: Nigeria and its neighbours, in *Gulliver's Troubles: Nigeria's Foreign Policy after the Cold War*, edited by Adekeye Adebajo and Abdul Raufu Mustapha. Scottsville: University of Kwa-Zulu-Natal Press, 141–159.

"The other EU." 2014. *The Economist*, 23 August, 50.

Ouimet, Matthew J. 2003. *The Rise and Fall of the Brezhnev Doctrine in Soviet Foreign Policy*. Chapel Hill: University of North Carolina Press.

PCA [Permanent Court of Arbitration]. 2014. PCA case no 2010–16 in the matter of the Bay of Bengal maritime boundary arbitration between Bangladesh and the Republic of India: Award: Permanent court of arbitration, *The Hague*, 7 July, 1–5.

Pereira, Jorge F. Garzon. 2014. Hierarchical regional orders: An analytical framework. *Journal of Policy Modeling*, 368(2014), S26–S46.

Pike, Frederick B. 1995. *FDR's Good Neighbor Policy: Sixty Years of Generally Gentle Chaos*. Austin: University of Texas Press.

Prys, Miriam. 2010. Hegemony, domination, detachment: Differences in regional powerhood. *International Studies Review*, 12(4), 479–504.

Prys, Miriam. 2012. *Redefining Regional Power in International Relations*. London: Routledge.
Putin, Vladimir. 2014. Vladimir Putin answered journalists' questions on the situation in Ukraine. President of Russia website. <http://eng.kremlin.ru/transcripts/6763>, accessed 15 March 2014.
Raat, W. Dirk. 1992. *Mexico and the United States: Ambivalent Vistas*. Athens, GA: University of Georgia Press.
Roy, Denny. 1994. Hegemon on the horizon? China's threat to East Asian security. *International Security*, 19(Summer), 149–168.
Rutherford, Geddes W. 1926. Spheres of influence: An aspect of semi-suzerainty. *American Journal of International Law*, 20(2), 300–325.
SACU. 2009. *Southern African Customs Union Merchandise Trade 2009*. Windhoek: SACU Secretariat.
Safire, William. 1994. On language: The near abroad. *New York Times*, 22 May.
Schaffer, Howard, and Schaffer, Teresita. 1998. Better neighbors? India and South Asian regional politics. *SAIS Review*, 18(1), 109–121.
Schenoni, Luis Leandro. 2015. The Brazilian rise and the elusive South American balance. Hamburg: German Institute of Global and Area Studies, *GIGA Working Papers*, no. 269 (March).
Schmitt, Eric. 2015. Leading role for France as Africa battles back. *New York Times*, 15 March. <www.nytimes.com/2015/03/16/world/africa/leading-role-for-france-as-africa-battles-back.html>, accessed 16 March 2015.
Scott, David. 2009. India's "extended neighborhood" concept: Power projection for a rising power. *India Review*, 8(2), 107–143.
Seckinger, Ron. 1984. *The Brazilian Monarchy and the South American Republics 1822–1831: Diplomacy and State Building*. Baton Rouge: Louisiana State University Press.
Shambaugh, David. 2013. *China Goes Global: The Partial Power*. Oxford: Oxford University Press.
Shanmugasundaram, Sasikumar. 2012. Regional hegemony and emerging powers: Theorizing India's neighborhood policy. MA Thesis, Central European University, Budapest.
SIPRI Milex. 2017. Stockholm International Peace Research Institute World Military Expenditures Database. <www.sipri.org/research/armaments/milex/milex_database>, accessed 1 May 2017.
Sitaraman, Srini. 2012. South Asia: Conflicts, hegemony, and power balancing, in *Beyond Great Powers and Hegemons: Why Secondary States Support, Follow, or Challenge*, edited by Kristen P. Williams, Steven E. Lobell, and Neal G. Jesse. Stanford: Stanford Security Studies, 177–192.
"Special report Germany: Europe's reluctant hegemon." 2013. *The Economist*, 15 June 2013, 3–16.
Sperling, James. 2001. Neither hegemony nor dominance: Reconsidering German power in post Cold-War Europe. *British Journal of Political Science*, 31, 389–425.
Tan, Alexander C. 2012. China and its neighbors: Too close for comfort?, in *Beyond Great Powers and Hegemons: Why Secondary States Support, Follow, or Challenge*, edited by Kristen P. Williams, Steven E. Lobell, and Neal G. Jesse. Stanford: Stanford Security Studies, 193–206.
Thomas, Ann Van Wynen, and Thomas, Jr., A.J. 1963. *The Organization of American States*. Dallas: Southern Methodist University Press.
Triska, Jan, ed. 1986. *Dominant Powers and Subordinate States: The United States in Latin America and the Soviet Union in Eastern Europe*. Durham: Duke University Press.

Turner, Frederick C. 1991. Regional hegemony and the case of Brazil. *International Journal*, 46(Summer), 476, 481.

Ulam, Adam B. 1974. *Expansion and Coexistence: Soviet Foreign Policy 1917–73*, 2nd ed. New York: Holt, Rinehart and Winston.

UNCTAD WIR [World Investment Report]. 2012. *World Investment Report 2012*. <http://unctad.org/en/Pages/DIAE/World%20Investment%20Report/World_Investment_Report.aspx>, accessed 2013.

Valenta, Jiri. 1991. *Soviet Intervention in Czechoslovakia, 1968: Anatomy of a Decision*, rev. ed. Baltimore: Johns Hopkins University Press.

Vigevani, Tullo, and Cepaluni, Gabriel. 2009. *Brazilian Foreign Policy in Changing Times: The Quest for Autonomy from Sarney to Lula*. Lanham: Lexington Books.

Vloyantes, John P. 1970. *Spheres of Influence: A Framework for Analysis*. Tucson: Institute of Government Research, University of Arizona.

Vorster, B.J. 1975a. Lecture by the honorable the Prime Minister at the first open Autumn School of the University of Stellenbosch in the H. B. Thorn auditorium on 1 April 1975. South Africa History Online. <www.sahistory.org.za/archive/lecture-honourable-prime-minister-first-open-autumn-school-university-stellenbosch-h-b-thorn>, accessed 26 October 2013.

Vorster, B.J. 1975b. New year's message on 31 December 1975. South Africa History Online. <www.sahistory.org.za/archive/>, accessed 26 October 2013.

Waltz, Kenneth N. 1979. *Theory of International Politics*. Reading, MA: Addison-Wesley.

Werner, Jason. 2017. Nigeria and "illusory hegemony" in foreign and security policymaking: *Pax-Nigeriana* and the challenges of Boko Haram. *Foreign Policy Analysis*, 13(3), 638–661.

Whigham, Thomas L. 2002. *The Paraguayan War, Vol. 1: Causes and Early Conduct*. Lincoln: University of Nebraska Press.

Williams, Anthony V. 1991. Nigeria in West Africa, in *Regional Hegemons: Threat Perception and Strategic Response*, edited by David J. Myers. Boulder: Westview, 269–304.

Williams, Kristen P., Lobell, Steven E., and Jesse, Neal G., eds. 2012. *Beyond Great Powers and Hegemons: Why Secondary States Support, Follow, or Challenge*. Stanford: Stanford Security Studies.

Womack, Brantly. 2010. *China among Unequals: Asymmetric Foreign Relationships in Asia*. Singapore, Hackensack, NJ: World Scientific.

Wong, Edward, Perlez, Jane, and Buckley, Chris. 2015. China announces cuts of 300,000 troops at military parade showing its might. *New York Times*, 2 September. <www.nytimes.com/2015/09/03/world/asia/beijing-turns-into-ghost-town-as-it-gears-up-for-military-parade.html>, accessed 8 September 2015.

Wood, Bryce. 1961. *The Making of the Good Neighbor Policy*. New York: Columbia University Press.

World Bank. 2017. World development indicators [Online]. 2017. <http://data.worldbank.org/data-catalog/world-development-indicators>.

Xavier, Constantino. 2017. Paper: India's expatriate evacuation operations: Bringing the diaspora home. *Carnegie India*, 4 January. <http://carnegieindia.org/2017/01/04/india-s-expatriate-evacuation-operations-bringing-diaspora-home-pub-66573>, accessed 5 January 2017.

Ziegler, Dominic. 2017. Special report: Asian geopolitics. *The Economist*, 22 April, 1–12.

3 Legacies of China's regional relations

Inactive: China's neighborly relations from Qing to republic

In the last years of the Qing Empire, China had few neighbors in the sense of the word in English and Chinese: equal, autonomous, distinct, non-related adjacent entities. Across its borders were several European colonies and territories: French Indochina to the southeast, British India to the southwest, and Russian territory to the northwest and northeast. Japanese colonial Korea and Taiwan lay to the east, and further afield were more colonies, Dutch Indonesia and British Malaya, the Spanish then the American Philippines. Only Siam was an independent state. The Qing dynasty's borders were fairly definite, though the relationships were hazy, at least when seen through the eyes of 19th- and 20th-century legal absolutes. Places such as Tibet had a unique style of relationship with the Qing dynasty that is difficult to place into the distinct binary categories of "sovereign" or "not-sovereign" which we use today. The legacy of the Qing empire left tensions for the post-imperial and post-colonial governments of the region, north and south.

The legacy of the emperors

Several of China's modern neighbors were once part of the Qing empire or had a unique relationship to that empire. After the collapse of the Qing state in 1911, some of those parts became independent, and some came under the sovereignty of China, leading to subsequent tensions.

Mongolia is perhaps the best example of this tension. Although the Qing dynasty had tried to prohibit Han Chinese migration into Mongol lands, by the 19th century, these efforts were failing, and the superior weight of population and commerce were slowly exercising a change. An increasing number of Han Chinese were migrating to eastern Inner Mongolia (the area around Hohehot and Baotou), and in some areas, grassland was succumbing to the plow and all that it implied.

Russian penetration of Mongolia did not start in earnest until the Beijing convention of 1860, when the Russians were granted rights to consulates and trade in this previously secluded and neglected area of the Qing empire (Rossabi 1975: 207–211). The threat of Russian influence in such Mongolian cities as Urga (renamed Ulaanbataar in 1924) eventually prompted China to respond by promoting Chinese merchants in Mongolia against their Russian competitors and Han Chinese colonization, which was speeded up by the completion of the Beijing-Zhangjiakou (Peking-Kalgan) railway in 1909. Thus, Qing policy toward Mongolia had become *Chinese* policy toward Mongolia, just as it had toward Manchuria, when Han Chinese immigrants became part of state policy. The last days of the Qing dynasty also saw some of the reforms extended to the administration of Mongolia, which led the Mongol princes of Outer Mongolia to appeal to the Russians once again for help in preserving their autonomy, though not their formal independence. The Russians, however, were cautious and mindful that relations with Beijing were far more important.

The Russians reconsidered their opportunities with the 1911 revolution, and St. Petersburg overcame previous reluctance to help the Mongols and supplied them with arms. China was first forced to recognize the autonomy of Outer Mongolia in 1915, but attempted to reassert control during the hiatus of Russian influence during the Russian revolution when Mongolia was unprotected. But by 1924, Mongolia once again became a Russian – now Bolshevik – satellite. The Yalta agreement in 1945 recognized Mongolian independence much to the chagrin of Chiang Kai-shek, whose efforts in 1946 to recover some control of Mongolia on the basis of ambiguities in the 1924 agreement were unsuccessful.

China had a border with Tsarist Russia as well. The Russian and Chinese empires started to come into contact in the 17th century when Russian settlers started to move into the Amur River basin, an area China considered its own. A small military confrontation ensued which persuaded the Russians to negotiate the Treaty of Nerchinsk in 1689, in which they agreed to stay out of the Amur area. It represented not only the first diplomatic contact of Russia and China, but also the first treaty China negotiated with a Western state on the basis of equality (Westad 2012: 10–11). The Treaty of Kiakhta established the Russo-Qing boundary in northern Mongolia in 1727 and allowed for caravan trade. By the 19th century, during the Second Opium War, the Russians negotiated unequal treaties with China, the 1858 Treaties of Aigun, Beijing, and Tianjin, gaining much of what is now the Russian Far East, down to Vladivostok. The boundary was set by these treaties, but the Russian and Chinese versions differed in key details, and the Russians took advantage and set the boundary as the west bank of the Ussuri River, instead of joint control or division along the *thalweg*, the deepest channel (Stephan 1994: 47–49). The disagreement would last into the 21st century. The other side of the Russo-Qing border, in Xinjiang, was also a source of tension, after a rebellion in the 19th century. The furthest western portion was the Ili Valley (Gulja/Yining); Russian encroachment in 1871 would almost lead to war in 1881. Soviet support for autonomous actors in "East Turkestan" against Chinese control in 1933–34 and 1944–49 would be the source of continued Russo-Chinese tensions and suspicions.

Since the Tokugawa Shogunate isolated itself from the world in 1638, the Qing had only limited commercial contact with Japan through the port of Nagasaki. When Japan was opened forcibly by the United States in 1854, it started down a path that would lead to a long and bloody conflict with China: the first

Sino-Japanese War in 1894–95, which was primarily fought over the control of Korea, but which also separated Taiwan from China, a long period of creeping Japanese imperial predation on Northeast China, then the Second Sino-Japanese War in 1937–45, occupation, massacres, war crimes and national humiliation. All of this is a story that is familiar; its repetition and use as a 21st-century foreign policy tool is dealt with in Chapters 5 and 6. The only matter to add is the creation of a maritime boundary between China and Japan in the Senkaku/Diaoyu islands. Japan's incorporation of the Ryukyu (琉球王国 *Ryūkyū-Ōkoku*; *Liuqiu wangguo* in Chinese) kingdom in 1879 as part of Okinawa Prefecture placed the furthermost island of the Ryukyu chain close to the islands offshore of Taiwan. Japanese authorities claim to have surveyed the islands in the 1880s and found them uninhabited, and thereafter occupied them, for a while operating a fish-processing plant on the largest of those tiny rocks. Chinese claim they were occupied much earlier during the Ming dynasty.

The Qing boundaries with Korea had been largely established even before the dynasty; a palisade had been set up to mark the border, and through which Korean tribute missions passed with suitable formality (see esp. Eggert 1997). The Yalu and Tumen rivers were seen as natural boundaries, but the boundary at Paektusan/Changbaishan was not set until the Kangxi reign in 1712 when the Koreans found themselves at a disadvantage due to poor maps (50–52). But beyond tribute, the Qing did little to rule Korea, its "model tributary state" (Kang 2010: 57). That detached relationship would be shattered by Russo-Japanese rivalry from the 1870s until it was formally independent in 1895 and then formally absorbed by Japan in 1910.

In Southeast Asia, the traditional tributary relationship between imperial China and Vietnam, Cambodia, Laos, Siam, and Burma (mainland Southeast Asia) has been noted by a variety of authors as contributing to a sense of China as the center within Asia. Late imperial and Republican China did establish limited semimodern relations with some of its Southeast Asian neighbors, but most of Southeast Asia was under Western colonial control until after World War II.

China's relations with Vietnam were long and not always favorable. Chinese dynasties had ruled in Vietnam (now primarily northern Vietnam) from 218 BCE to about 939 CE. The result was a profound cultural influence, particularly at the elite level, an economic system based upon intense rice agriculture, the use (later dropped) of Chinese and Chinese-based characters for writing. For the next 500 years, Vietnam was an independent but tributary empire or kingdom, and the linguistic distinction was not a trivial one: the Vietnamese rulers were "kings" (王 *wang/vua*) in their relations to China's emperors, but "emperors" (皇帝 *Huangdi/ Hoàng đế*) in their relations with other countries in Southeast Asia, where they established their own sub-imperium in the Indochina peninsula, accepting tribute from the smaller states and tribes in the region while paying tribute in turn to Beijing (Woodside 1971: chap. 5). During the Ming dynasty, China sought to reimpose direct rule in Vietnam from 1406 to 1427, but the costly war that resulted forced it to withdraw and accept the old tributary relationship (Womack 2006: 128–129). By the Qing dynasty, Chinese officials would "invest" Vietnamese "kings" in a ceremony meant to reinforce the asymmetry of the relationship, the tributary nature of Vietnam, but with no real influence on who ruled or what their policies were (Truong 1968). The Sino-French War of 1883–85 ended China's pretense of a Vietnamese dependent relationship, and ended Vietnam's independence for seventy years. Thus, many of the subsequent territorial and other disagreements between Vietnam and China would be based upon French colonial claims. One such claim was in the islets, reefs and islands in the South China Sea, and in particular the Paracel islands. French colonial claims and Chinese claims to the area date from the 1887 Sino-French Boundary Convention to Qing naval expeditions in 1902 and 1908 (Samuels 1982: 52–54). Periodic efforts by the Chinese Republican government were mostly focused on preventing Japanese development of the islands. These claims were not pressed with much sustained effort, however, and they were secondary to the land boundaries.

Japan then took Vietnam from France in 1945, but when Japan was defeated at the end of World War II, KMT Chinese troops moved into northern Vietnam to accept the Japanese surrender there. Given the traditional antipathy between China and Vietnam, Vietnamese nationalist leader Ho Chi Minh preferred to allow the French to (temporarily) re-establish administrative control. In Ho's pungent words, "It is better to smell the feces of the French for a little while than to eat Chinese excrement all of one's life" (attributed in Chen 1969: 154).

World War II differentiated Southeast Asia in a way that Northeast Asia was not; in Northeast Asia, Japan was seen by Chinese and Koreans as the colonizer and aggressor, a historical legacy that still complicates Japan's diplomacy. But in Southeast Asia, the legacy of the war and Japan was much more differentiated among the countries and peoples of that region, a differentiation that is one important legacy for Chinese in that region and for China's relations with that region, especially in the decades after the war.

Of China's neighbors in Southeast Asia in the late Qing, only one was an independent actor: Siam ("Thailand" after 1939). During the 19th century, Siam had adopted a policy that allowed ethnic Chinese to become Siamese subjects, if they cut off their queues, and adopted other measures to become Siamese (Suryadinata 1997: 7). During WWII, the Republic of China and Thailand were on opposite sides of the war. Thailand, under the military government of Field Marshal Phibul Songgram joined with Japan, attacked French Indochina, declared war on the United Kingdom and the USA in January 1942, and was rewarded by Japan for its assistance. As the war began to go badly for Japan, Phibul fell from power in July 1944, and a "Free Thai Movement" opposed Japan's use of Thai territory, with anti-Japanese guerrillas operating in the northern part of the country (Dear and Foot 1995: 1106–1107).

After the war, despite overtures by Republican Chinese governments, the royal government in Bangkok did not wish to establish diplomatic relations out of the fear of the ethnic Chinese in Thailand. A Treaty of Amity was signed in January 1946, which granted ethnic Chinese in Thailand rights as foreign nationals, but as the KMT government's fortunes sagged in the Chinese civil war, so too did relations between Nanking and Bangkok (Fifield 1958: 260–262).

Malaysia, Indonesia, and Burma were all European colonial territories when they fell to Japanese control, and early on, Japan's "Greater East Asia Co-Prosperity Sphere" (東亜新秩序 *Tōa Shin Chitsujo*) was seen by many Malays, Indonesians, and Burmese as an opportunity to rid themselves of their white colonial masters, only to find that their new Japanese masters were far harsher in their demands, given the desperate conditions of the wartime Japanese economy. In Indonesia, however, the independence-minded leaders such as Sukarno saw the chance as too good to pass up, and in British Malaya, ethnic Malays were favored by the Japanese. Many ethnic Chinese, on the other hand, were staunchly opposed to Japan, and formed the Malayan Peoples Anti-Japanese Army, and retaliated against "collaborators." (Owen 2005: 317–318).

KMT troops did briefly occupy northern Vietnam after Japan's surrender, and Chinese troops had operated in Burma for a while during World War II, but otherwise, China had not intervened militarily in the affairs of its Southeast Asian neighbors in modern times. Thus, diplomatic and strategic relations between China and Southeast Asia were largely inactive until the late 1940s and certainly did not match their commercial exchange.

In South Asia, the borders in the Karakoram and Himalaya mountains are complicated because the legal status of the actors in the period of the Qing and the Raj was (and still are) ambiguous, and their ability to negotiate treaties has been questioned in the 20th century. In particular, the status of Tibet and its right to negotiate a treaty – the 1914 Simla Accord – with the British Raj is the modern legal issue. The Simla Accord established the boundary between Tibet and British India, the McMahon Line along the crest of the eastern Himalayas from Bhutan to Burma. The western and middle boundaries were not defined and remain so. The new government of the Republic of China rejected the Simla Accord after withdrawing from the conference, and all subsequent Chinese governments have insisted that Tibet had no sovereign right to negotiate the border. Thus, the current boundary is still unresolved.

The legacy of the wanderers

Chinese migrants have moved to other countries at least since the Ming dynasty (1368–1644) and particularly in the 19th century. Some moved to places as far and improbable as South Africa and Cuba, but we are concerned with the ethnic Chinese who moved to China's neighboring countries. Chinese migrants are most associated with Southeast Asia, but there were Chinese who moved to India, Russia, Korea, and Japan in the 19th century.

Although this book has used a broad term "ethnic Chinese" in relation to Southeast Asia, it is a community that is hardly unified. Chinese in Southeast Asia are divided primarily by language, length of residence, and degree of integration with local societies. People from Hokkien (Fujian) -speaking Fujian province especially moved to Southeast Asia, although Teochew (Chaozhou) -speaking and Cantonese (Guangdonghua, Taishanhua) -speaking Guangdong province was also prominently represented in Southeast Asia. The Northeast Asian Chinese communities tended to come from Shandong province.

By the end of the Ming dynasty, perhaps 100,000 ethnic Chinese resided in Southeast Asia, and despite Qing dynasty prohibitions, continued to leave China illegally until the formal granting of the right of emigration in 1860, and accelerated in response to the devastating Taiping Rebellion of the mid-19th century. These overseas Chinese often found opportunities and prosperity and in some cases local resentment. As early as the late Ming dynasty, ethnic Chinese could be found in Manila, and by the 1640s in Laos, Cambodia, Vietnam, and places that would later be called Indonesia and Malaysia (Reid 1999: 150–151). But emigrants were not regarded by the Qing government as a major issue of concern. The Chinese imperial court made no protest in response to local attacks on overseas Chinese such as the massacres in the Philippines in 1603 and in Java in 1740, condemning the Chinese as ". . . outcasts who had not hesitated to abandon their homeland for the sake of commerce" (quoted in Fukuda 1995: 21). Thus, the Qing court took relatively little interest in the affairs of Southeast Asian Chinese and perhaps even less in Southeast Asian countries. Only in the last twenty years of the Qing dynasty did the government begin to pay attention to the overseas Chinese, both as a threat to the regime and a resource to be cultivated. Beginning in 1893, the Qing government became more involved in trying to protect overseas Chinese. In 1893, the Qing court did attempt to use overseas Chinese chambers of commerce to promote loyalty to the Manchu dynasty in its last few years, and three missions were sent from Beijing to Southeast Asia in 1907, 1909, and 1911. These missions also sought to persuade overseas Chinese in Southeast Asia to ". . . promote industry and commerce among the overseas Chinese, and to induce them to invest in China" (Yen Ching-hwang 1995: 133–143). The Qing Empire had seen the status and protection of these ethnic Chinese as sufficiently important to establish consulates in Indonesia at the beginning of the 20th century through an agreement with the Dutch government (Netherlands and China 1973). Overseas Chinese played a prominent role in anti-Manchu movements, led by Sun Yat-sen, among others. Some Chinese intellectuals of the late Qing era also saw the ethnic Chinese in the Philippines as a link of oppressed Asian peoples, but after the reactionary coup d'état in Beijing of September 1898, they fled to Japan (Karl 1998: 1105–1106).

Southeast Asian reluctance to acknowledge ethnic Chinese as residents, subjects, citizens, and participants by colonial and national governments has been a political and economic tension within Southeast Asian countries for hundreds of years, and a reason why the Chinese government has itself often expressed its interest in the welfare of ethnic Chinese in the region. Among the colonial administrations, policies toward Chinese varied. The British in Malaya made sure to keep the main ethnic groups, Malays, Chinese, and Indians, separated. The Dutch in their brief attempt at introducing a modicum of parliamentary advice in the 1930s also made sure that each group, Dutch, "Natives," Chinese, and Arabs each had its own slate of electors (Owen 2005: 303). Colonial administrations tended to treat ethnic Chinese as a different category, inferior to the white colonial administrators, but different from "natives," variously defined.

That interest has in turn raised the sensitivities and suspicions of the regional governments, leading to discrimination or differentiation, which led to alienation and Chinese government advocacy for the rights of overseas Chinese, which made Southeast Asian administrations even more suspicious, completing a vicious cycle.

The roles that Chinese migrants took on in many Southeast Asian countries were closely linked to the tensions that were felt in these societies, and even today. In 17th century Dutch Indies, Chinese often took on the role of tax farmers for the Dutch authorities, toll collectors, rice millers, mine operators, as well as craftsmen. Chinese would bid for the right to collect these revenues, both from the Dutch and from native rulers, guaranteeing a fixed income for those rulers, and extracting a profit on top of that (Owen 2005: 27). Chinese also held offices in Siamese kingdom of Ayutthaya and the Vietnamese center of Fai-fo/Quang Nam (Reid 1999: 153). It is the role of merchant and entrepreneur that is most associated with Chinese in Southeast Asia, utilizing their family- and clan-based trust networks of information and private lending, often in association with local wives and concubines who added local knowledge, connections and language skills. In Siam, they would be compelled to adapt to local mores to attain high office, cutting queues and adopting Thai names, and in the Malay and Indonesian archipelagos, many converted to Islam to gain access to Muslim rulers; in Manila, Chinese leaders converted to Catholicism for equivalent reasons. Ethnic Chinese, thanks to their entrepreneurship, became wealthy in many of these societies, and with wealth comes envy and with envy come pogroms; most famously in Manila in 1603, when 23,000 Chinese were slaughtered, and in Batavia (now Jakarta) in 1740 (Owen 2005: 28). The analogy to Jews in Europe was explicitly articulated at the time and frequently mentioned since (Chirot and Reid 1997; Reid 1999: 152). Levantine merchants (Lebanese, Syrians) played a similar role in pre-independence West Africa.

The Chinese were not alone in Southeast Asia; Portuguese, Dutch and for a while English competed with Arabs, Indians, and, until 1638, Japanese for trade. But in terms of long-term influence on the local societies, ethnic Chinese are second to none in Southeast Asia. How many Chinese came to Southeast Asia from the 16th to the 19th centuries is difficult to determine, since local census authorities often disregarded them as "temporary residents." By the early 20th century, however, it was clear that Chinese were in Southeast Asia to stay.

From the foregoing it seems plain that China's regional behavior from the late Qing to the Republican period was fairly inactive. It had few actual independent neighbors with whom they could conduct relations, and much like South Africa after WWII regarded the High Commission Territories as "rightfully theirs," the government in China at the end of WWII had a vague sense of ownership or entitlement to places that had slipped the grasp and Beijing and Nanjing between 1911 and 1945. And like the Russian Federation from 1992 to 1995 in its relations with its former Central Asian parts, the alienation of former territory was not necessarily liked but the former owner, but chaotic politics and economic depression focus attention inward.

Hyperactive: Maoism and anti-hegemonism, 1949–1987

This section is a very brief overview of Chinese foreign policy from the founding of the People's Republic of China to the beginnings of its Good Neighbor Policy. As such, it covers a broad array of events and trends unified by a theme of very poor relations with many of its neighbors, though not universally so. The reasons vary, as discussed below, but generally two major reasons stand out: the Maoist revolutionary foreign policy which gave verbal and sometimes material support for communist revolutionary groups around the world, including China's neighbors, and a Cold War contest with the Soviet Union in particular. The two reasons overlap chronologically, but the revolutionary element declined after 1978, and the Cold War element rose. The effect of both, however, was the same: tense relations with neighboring countries.

Ideational: policies, pronouncements, and doctrines

China's outlook on the world in this period started out with two worlds in conflict – the imperialist world and the socialist world, and added a third with which socialist China could cooperate and eventually to which China would belong. From the founding of the People's Republic of China (PRC) in 1949 through about 1960, China was closely allied with the Soviet Union and saw itself as part of the socialist camp. That was particularly true from 1950 to 1953 when China was fighting a war against the US-led United Nations forces in Korea, and while Soviet leader Josef Stalin was still alive. China signed a military alliance treaty with the USSR in 1950, and almost all of its initial diplomatic interactions were with other socialist countries.

But China had connections with non-communist countries in what would soon be called "the Third World," countries such as India, Burma, Indonesia, Egypt, and others which had been colonies, were not white, and which did not necessarily follow either the USA or the USSR. An element of that feeling was focused on Asia, and when Mao met Indian Prime Minister Jawaharlal Nehru in October 1954, he said, "We Orientals (东方人/*Dongfang ren*) were both bullied by Western imperialism in history. . . . Because of that, we Orientals have the spirit of rallying together . . ." (quoted in Chen Xiangyang 2004: 96). But this occasional reference to commonality was really a recognition of a global phenomenon, not so much as a uniquely Asian phenomenon. Mao's thought was unquestionably globalist in outlook. As the relationship of China and the Soviet Union deteriorated from 1960 to 1963, Mao was increasingly focused on what we now call the Third World, and a sense of belonging to that, given the divisions in the socialist camp. But even in the case of the latter, China did not join the Warsaw Pact, and no multilateral security or economic organization formed among the socialist countries of Asia, even though in the 1950s Mongolia, North Korea, China, and North Vietnam might have done so.

Northeast Asia

China experienced a dramatic loss of position in the 1960s and 1970s within Northeast Asia. As Japan experienced an economic miracle, followed by South

Korea in the 1980s, China's economy was moribund by political chaos and radical economic policies. This relative decline became increasingly obvious to Chinese leaders in the late 1970s when Japan especially, but also Hong Kong and Taiwan (again, the latter two as "family members" not neighbors per se), could be easily seen as growing, modern countries.

China's relations in Northeast Asia effectively started with its intervention in the Korean War in late 1950 when Mao Zedong ordered Chinese troops to save Kim Il-sung's North Korean regime from conquest. For the next several decades, the legacy of the war ensured that South Korea would not establish relations with China and that China would be hostile to the South. China gave a large amount of foreign aid to North Korea over the next decades, and Pyongyang learned to play Moscow and Beijing against each other after the 1963 Sino-Soviet split (Zhang 2014: 176–184). China also did not have diplomatic relations with Japan until 1972, when Tokyo and Beijing normalized their relations following US President Nixon's visit. It was in 1970 that China discovered that it has a territorial dispute with Japan, the Senkaku/Diaoyu Islands. Off the north coast of Taiwan, these uninhabited islands were deemed to have been historically associated with Taiwan, and thus Chinese. Japan in turn noted that it had discovered the islands in the 1880s and which were uninhabited at the time, with no evidence that they had ever been. Chinese fishing boats entered the waters during the negotiations over recognition, but both sides agreed to not raise the issue (Bedeski 1983: 35–36). It would remain, however.

China's relations with Mongolia largely paralleled its relations with the Soviet Union. Mongolia had become independent in 1912 and was the Soviet Union's oldest ally, dating back to 1924, but when Mao and the Chinese communists were in the process of establishing the People's Republic of China, they equivocated about recognizing Mongolia. Chiang Kai-shek had previously agreed to recognize Mongolia's independence (he would go back on this agreement later on Taiwan), but Mao wanted to unify Inner Mongolia and Outer Mongolia as an autonomous region (province) of China. The Soviets backed the Mongolians, and the Chinese backed down. The Mongolians, however, never forgot (Atwood 1999: 156–158). China did establish diplomatic relations with Mongolia and built a connection to the Mongolian railway in 1952 and provided much-needed contracted laborers to Mongolia, the population of which was less than a million at the time. Some limited economic aid was also given beginning in 1956, but China could not compete with the Soviet Union (Zhang 2014: 184–188). China did have something that the Mongolians wanted, namely a border settlement, and in December 1962 signed a settlement that was highly favorable to Mongolia. But when China began to question the legitimacy of the Sino-Soviet border, Mongolia sided with the Soviets, signed an alliance treaty in 1966, and allowed Soviet troops to be stationed along the border (Rossabi 2013: 175–176). The deterioration of relations was manifested along the borders, as described by John Garver:

> As the territorial conflict emerged in 1963–64, both Chinese and Soviet leaders began to fear infiltration and subversion, and the border regime began

to change. . . . Patrols on both sides were strengthened. . . . And, of course, the patrols of the two sides began to encounter each other. Those encounters provided reason for additional patrols and reinforcement. Within a few years, the once-friendly border had been transformed into a militarized standoff.

(Garver 2016: 185)

Southeast Asia

The late 1940s changed China's relations with its Southeast Asian neighbors dramatically, from a rather inactive phase to an almost hyperactive phase, in which Southeast Asian nations perceived a strong policy of interventionism by the new communist government in Beijing. As research by Alastair Iain Johnston (1998: 1–30) has revealed, China became relatively likely to resort to arms to resolve international disputes between 1949 and 1969, and armed clashes occurred between China and India, the Soviet Union, and Vietnam. Relations between revolutionary China and the newly independent nations of Southeast Asia were highly mixed; on the one hand, China did get along well with Indonesia under Sukarno. Its relations with Malaysia, Burma, and Thailand were much more difficult, since China supported communist insurgencies in those countries, and the former had the ethnic Chinese community in Malaya as its main base of support. The Cultural Revolution of China inspired some of the ethnic Chinese youth of several Southeast Asian nations in the 1960s, and this did not do much to alleviate the fears of the governments there, along with race riots in Malaysia and Singapore in 1969, and compounded by the fall of South Vietnam, Laos, and Cambodia to communist governments in the mid-1970s. Chinese criticisms of the government treatment of ethnic Chinese in Southeast Asian nations was another form of intervention that raised suspicion and animosity in capitals such as Jakarta, Bangkok, Rangoon, and Kuala Lumpur.

> They [Southeast Asian nations] were concerned that Chinese could use the development of the communist movement to interfere with their internal governance, some fearing that China could engage in invasion and expansionism. This aside, there were lingering historical questions between China and these countries and they were not disposed of well . . .
>
> (Zhu Tingchan 2001: 17)

After Nixon's opening to China in 1972, several of the Southeast Asian nations followed suit and opened relations with Beijing: Malaysia (1974), the Philippines, and Thailand (1975). Singapore, because of its Chinese majority population and strong informal ties with China pledged that it would be the last of the ASEAN countries to establish diplomatic relations with the People's Republic of China. By the 1980s, that left three major countries in Southeast Asia with which China did not enjoy fully normal relations: Vietnam, Indonesia, and Singapore. Brunei Darussalam became independent in 1984 but did not establish relations with China until the 1990s. In addition, China's relations with Cambodia were with the exiled guerrilla coalition of Democratic Kampuchea, headed by the notorious Khmer Rouge.

Vietnam

More than one author has commented wryly upon the ironic naming of the major pass between China and Vietnam as "Friendship Pass," since in February 1979, it was full of anything but friendship. The name, however, is not entirely inappropriate, since the relationship between China and Vietnam, and similarly between China and the rest of Southeast Asia has been an intense one, tinged with traditional suspicion, rivalry, and enmity to be sure, but also with profound cultural influences, common struggles, and more recently with similar political systems. The nature of the relationships of China and its neighbors to the Southeast have been mixed, but they have never been indifferent or trivial.

Sino-Vietnamese relations improved during the 1949–54 period, when communist China was providing arms, trucks, advisors and a strategic rear area for the Viet Minh, which defeated the French at Dienbienphu in 1954. In the Geneva Peace Conference, however, many Vietnamese felt that the Soviets and particularly the Chinese persuaded them to accept a "half-a-loaf" settlement, since Vietnam was divided at the seventeenth parallel, with only the northern half of the country going to Viet Minh control pending elections. Vietnamese would charge that the Chinese would in effect do the same again nineteen years later in Paris, urging the North Vietnamese and Viet Cong to accept half a victory (Chen 1987: 15–20). The Vietnamese impression – articulated to be sure in the charged atmosphere of 1979 – was that China wanted Vietnam to remain divided, as it has so often been, and thus a weaker neighbor to China's south.

It was the increasing alignment of Vietnam with the Soviet Union and Vietnamese actions in Southeast Asia that turned Chinese suspicion into hostility, however. In a sense, this amounted to inviting an external actor into the region, and was compounded by Vietnam's actions in the rest of Indochina. Not long after the fall of Saigon in April 1975 and the unification of Vietnam, Chinese Vice-Premier Deng Xiaoping indicated to the Secretary-General of the Vietnamese Communist Party Le Duan that China was strongly opposed to the emerging pattern of relations between Vietnam and the Soviet Union (Möller 1984: 327). For the next two years, Vietnam managed to maintain friendly relations with the two hostile communist powers, but increasingly it turned toward the USSR and – axiomatically as far as the leaders in Beijing were concerned – away from China. The deterioration in the Sino-Vietnamese connection began publicly in May 1978, and proceeded rapidly downhill thereafter. Vietnam was admitted to the CMEA (the Soviet trade bloc) in June 1978, and China responded by cutting off all economic aid to Vietnam (Amer 1993: 320).

China then turned off the trade as well. Trade figures for the 1960s and 1970s are fragmentary, and Sino-Vietnamese trade was never a large amount of China's overall trade structure, but it would appear that after a brief period of "normal" trade in 1978, all trade between China and Vietnam effectively stopped in 1979, according to the IMF Direction of Trade Statistics (IMF DOTS 2017). In November 1978, Vietnam signed a Treaty of Friendship and Cooperation with the USSR, moving further in alignment with the USSR.

During this time, relations between the Khmer Rouge regime in Cambodia and Vietnam had deteriorated to a series of border clashes in southern Vietnam. China backed the Khmer Rouge regime as a counterweight to the increasingly pro-Soviet Vietnamese, and possibly also for ideological reasons during the last years of Maoism in China. The Vietnamese army invaded Cambodia on Christmas 1978, and quickly routed the Khmer Rouge, whose remaining forces retreated to the Thai border to continue a guerrilla struggle during the 1980s with Chinese support and assistance. From the Chinese perspective, the Vietnamese installation of a government in Cambodia under Heng Samrin (later eclipsed politically by Hun Sen) allowed Vietnam to dominate the Indochina peninsula, including Cambodia and Laos, to threaten Thailand, and, most importantly, to spread Soviet influence on China's southern flank (Yu Zhengliang 1989: 374). The Khmer Rouge collapse occurred before China could effectively mobilize its forces, and in February 1979, China launched a belated punitive attack on Vietnam, and continued to supply the Khmer Rouge guerrillas during the 1980s. The conflict did have the indirect benefit to China of improving Sino-Thai relations.

Other issues of conflict existed and still exist in the relationship between China and Vietnam, many of which existed separately from the Sino-Soviet Cold War but which that strategic rivalry aggravated. Although ethnic Chinese had been granted the opportunity to become (North) Vietnamese citizens, and after 1975, those *Huaqiao* (华侨 in Chinese, *Hoa* in Vietnamese) in the South suffered discriminatory treatment both as aliens and bourgeoisie, eventually resulting in the expulsion of nearly one million people. This was a serious issue by itself, but coupled with Chinese suspicions of Vietnam and Vietnamese suspicions of China, it became explosive (Ross 1988: 243–246; Wong Kan Seng 1995: 9; Lam 2000: 374–390). Vietnamese war debts to China left over from the 1950s and 1960s added to a Chinese perception of Vietnamese ingratitude.

Lastly, we return to territorial disputes between the two nations. This issue also pre-dates the Sino-Soviet rivalry, but like the ethnic Chinese issue, was made substantially worse by the prevailing strategic atmosphere of the late 1970s and early 1980s. This boundary problem lay in three areas: the land boundary where northern Vietnam meets Guangxi and Guangdong provinces; the Gulf of Tonkin maritime boundary, and the ownership of islands in the South China Sea. The Sino-Vietnamese issues in the South China Sea revolve around two sets of islands, the Paracels and the Spratlys. China seized a portion of the northern Paracel islands in January 1974 from (South) Vietnamese forces, and after 1975 Hanoi began to revive its claims there and in the southern Spratly group, some of which are occupied by mainland Chinese forces, Taiwanese forces, Vietnamese forces, as well as Filipinos and Malaysians. Where the boundary lies depends on which side one asks; the Chinese claim is essentially to all of the islands and waters of the South China Sea. In March 1988, Chinese and Vietnamese naval forces clashed in the Spratlys at Johnson South Reef, killing over sixty Vietnamese (Raine and Le

Mière 2013: 44). Other territorial disputes exist between China and Vietnam, however. The land boundaries between China and Vietnam were the scene of several clashes between Chinese and Vietnamese forces between 1979 and January 1988, boundary markers have been moved, and the Vietnamese accused the Chinese of occupying 8000 hectares of Vietnamese territory at thirty-six points along the border, including Friendship Pass (Gainsborough 1992: 206).

Indonesia

The Chinese-Indonesian connection prior to 1965 was close – too close in fact for many Indonesians. From the establishment of relations in August 1950 to their "freezing" in October 1967, Indonesia was China's most important Third World friend, with increasing political, economic and social ties. Trade with China was between 3 and 4% of Indonesia's overall trade in the early 1960s, and between 3 and 5% of overall Chinese trade during that period, and even more if indirect trade through Hong Kong were counted. After the Indonesian Communist Party (PKI) attempted a coup d'état in September 1965, however, Indonesia became a strongly anti-communist, anti-Chinese force in Southeast Asia, aligned with the West and incredibly suspicious of China and Chinese. Beginning in 1972, however, China made overtures to Jakarta to normalize their relations, but for the next eighteen years, Indonesia was uninterested even after Malaysia, the Philippines, and Thailand had established relations with China.

What, then, were the outstanding issues between China and Indonesia? The primary issue can be summarized in two words: Indonesian suspicion. Out of a population in 1989 of about 175 million, approximately 3.5% were ethnic Chinese, or about 6 million people (Bresnan 1993: 255). A treaty of dual citizenship allowed ethnic Chinese to adopt Indonesian citizenship in 1955, and about 65% of the then 2.45 million Chinese did become citizens by 1962, but there were still more than one million alien Chinese in Indonesia in the late 1960s. More important than numbers was the role the ethnic Chinese played in the Indonesian economy – fully 80% of private sector economic activity was in ethnic Chinese hands (Chin 2000: 13). Somewhat like the *Norteamericanos* who dominated the plantation, mine and export sectors of Central America during the late 19th and early 20th centuries, or Levantine Arabs in West Africa, resentment against wealth and a group which did not wholly assimilate into the native culture(s) led to a dangerous situation.

From many Indonesians' perspective, PRC concern for the ethnic Chinese community in Indonesia was violating that nation's newly-found sovereignty and competing for the loyalty of their citizens and residents. The growing connection between China and the Communist Party of Indonesia (PKI) during the 1960s further aggravated the suspicions of conservative elements of Indonesian society, especially the military and Muslim organizations (Taylor 1976: 108–119). When the PKI came out in support of the coup attempt of 30 September 1965, it sealed its fate; the party and its organizations were smashed, and Indonesia erupted in violence, much of it directed against the Chinese community. Estimates of deaths run into the hundreds of thousands, principally in rural areas of former PKI organization (Bresnan 1993: 23). Chinese resident in Indonesia were thereafter regarded by many as "Fifth Columnists" and subjected to restrictions and discrimination. China sent ships to evacuate ethnic Chinese from Indonesia, and their condition, which was of great concern to China, was complicated further by the fact that hundreds of thousands of ethnic Chinese in Indonesia were still stateless persons: not Indonesian citizens and yet without (mainland) Chinese passports. Throughout the 1970s, the government of Indonesia stated the need to "re-educate" ethnic Chinese in Indonesia as the main reason for delaying normalization of relations (Nastic 1985: 24). Although the costly and difficult Indonesian process of naturalization was eased somewhat in 1980, many ethnic Chinese remained suspicious of a government which was suspicious of them. Opposition to normalizing relations with China was greatest in the Indonesian military and the state intelligence body, Bakin (McDonald 1989: 10). Perhaps most important was the reluctance of President Suharto, who stubbornly insisted on a Chinese apology for its alleged role in the 1965 coup attempt and for ceasing support for subversive movements in Southeast Asia.

History and Indonesian suspicions aside, there were two additional issues separating Beijing and Jakarta. The first was the settlement of Indonesian debts to China left over from the heyday of the 1960s. This totaled over US$100 million (Vatikiotis and Delfs 1990: 10). This, however, was overshadowed by the growing bilateral trade between China and Indonesia, a trade that was substantially in Indonesia's favor. China and Indonesia signed a memorandum of understanding (MOU) for bilateral trade in July 1985, which grew rapidly to over $800 million in 1987, and over $1 billion in 1989 (Tasker 1988: 66; IMF DOTS 2017). Indonesian exporters saw China as an excellent market for timber-related exports, and the Indonesian government recognized the chance to diversify its exports away from petroleum and Western markets. The exporters, however, found the lack of formal relations to be an impediment and the Indonesian Chamber of Commerce and Industry (Kadin) was a force pushing for the normalization of relations, as was the Indonesian Foreign Ministry by the 1980s (Tasker 1988: 66–67; Vatikiotis 1989: 36).

The end of the 1980s saw the Chinese and Indonesian perspectives on crucial third county issues far apart as well. Indonesian attitudes toward the Vietnamese invasion of Cambodia were not nearly as strident as China's, and in general Indonesia was not as strongly anti-Soviet as the Chinese. Instead, Indonesia's suspicions remained fixed on China and Chinese.

Burma

If the relations of Vietnam and Indonesia with China went from decidedly good to decidedly bad in the 1960–70s, Chinese policy toward Burma (after 1989 Myanmar) were simply undecided from the 1950s to the 1980s. Although initially hostile to the "bourgeois" government of U Nu in 1949, Beijing's leadership reached an accommodation with Burma by 1950. Despite moves by the government in Rangoon (since 1989 Yangon) to restrict ethnic schools and newspapers among

Burma's 3% Chinese minority in 1964, the relationship remained correct. China maintained its options toward Burma by continuing support for the main faction of the Burmese Communist Party (BCP), but such support was discreet and conducted on a low level (Taylor 1976: 199–203). The Cultural Revolution in China managed to change fairly good Sino-Burmese relations in a matter of weeks. A series of incidents which in other times might have been resolved at the consular level escalated into a major rift between the two countries, with China becoming particularly vicious in its press attacks on the government in Rangoon. Much of the conflict stemmed from the assertion of Beijing of a special relationship with ethnic Chinese in Burma and the rights of the latter to wear Mao buttons, study the works of Mao, praise Mao, etc. Attacks on Chinese businesses and groups in Rangoon concerned Beijing, and it demanded compensation and apology for the incidents. Chinese aid to the BCP insurgency increased, including involvement of Chinese advisors and personnel, and a base along the Sino-Burmese border allowed the BCP to conduct an insurgency and anti-Rangoon radio broadcasts (Taylor 1976: 221–239). Although the relationship improved somewhat during the early 1970s, due to both the calm Burmese reaction to provocative Chinese behavior and regularized Chinese diplomacy, Burmese suspicions remained. China maintained a link with the BCP through the 1970s at the same time that it regularized its official relations with the government in Rangoon, a curious and singular instance of Chinese foreign policy indecision.

Malaysia

The Malaysian government was highly suspicious of China, largely because of the ethnic Chinese element in its population. From 1948 to 1960, the British and then the Malaysian government fought a counter-insurgency with Commonwealth assistance against the Malayan Communist Party, the membership of which was overwhelmingly ethnic Chinese. That rebellion was put down in 1960, but sprang up again in 1968 as ethnic Chinese youth, inspired by Chairman Mao's Cultural Revolution, the war in Vietnam, and everything else that made 1968 an exciting year, launched their own effort. Operating from the Thai border, the fighting peaked in 1969 but as splits had occurred within the Red Guards in China, so, too the MCP, though it would remain in existence until 1989. The Malaysian government enacted a variety of restrictions on its ethnic Chinese citizens, such as prohibitions against young Chinese-Malaysians traveling to China, political restrictions on anyone formerly associated with the MCP, and a variety of other mechanisms that implicitly questioned the loyalty of ethnic Chinese.

Central Asia

China's relations with the Soviet Union went from outstanding to standing conflict between 1949 and 1963. The borders between the two countries were disputed by China, which claimed that the treaties between Qing Dynasty China and Tsarist Russia were unequal. Serious armed clashes occurred along the border in March

1969, resulting in several hundred casualties. Thereafter the relationship was antagonistic, and transcended the neighborhood to the global level. The tension was eased marginally in the early 1980s when the Soviets sought better relations to pry China loose from its alignment with the United States, but the Soviet invasion of Afghanistan in 1979, the Soviet-backed Vietnamese invasion of Cambodia in 1978 and the Soviet arms buildup created a substantial gap in relations.

South Asia

"New China's" relations with South Asia started off well. There was the period of "*Hindi-Chini bhai-bhai*" (हिंदी-चीनी भाई-भाई "Indians and Chinese are brothers") friendship, and India recognized the PRC in 1950. In April 1954, China and India signed an agreement in which India recognized China's rights in Tibet, which had been at issue (Garver 2001: 51). Relations between 1954 and 1958 were particularly good, as India – though a democracy – recused itself from taking sides in the Cold War, as the United States had wanted. The agreement also mentioned the Five Principles of Peaceful Co-existence, which would become a centerpiece of Chinese foreign policy rhetoric ever after.

The brief period of amiable Sino-Indian relations of the mid-1950s quickly deteriorated when the Tibetan rebellion in 1959 forced the Tenzin Gyatso, the 14th Dalai Lama to flee to India, and China fully occupied Tibet. The western border was not well defined, however, and neither side entirely accepted the MacMahon Line, which separated China from India in the eastern sector, a dispute going back to the 19th century. Chinese suspicion of US and Indian sponsorship of Tibetan guerrillas, and Nehru's ill-advised "forward policy" led to a brief but important border war between China and India in October-November 1962, in which China's army decisively defeated Indian forces before withdrawing. That left an enduring legacy of bitterness and suspicion in New Delhi. Chinese soldiers had also secretly entered Nepal in 1960 (with Nepalese government assent) to clear out a Tibetan refugee camp the Chinese government claimed was also a guerrilla base (Garver 2001: 148). Clashes on the border between Tibet and Sikkim between Chinese and Indian forces in September 1967 left hundred dead after China started pushing up against a no-man's-land area (Garver 2001: 171). China also started aid to the Maoist Naxalites in India around this time, though like much of China's "support" of Maoist organizations during the Cultural Revolution, it involved more rhetoric than reality (Lintner 2015: 266–267).

Chinese aid to India's arch-rival in South Asia, Pakistan, was much more substantial and further aggravated relations. When India and Pakistan fought a brief border war in the Punjab in 1965, Chinese military movements along the Himalayan border helped pressure India to end the clash. In 1971, however, the devastation of the Cultural Revolution in China was such that it could do little to help its Pakistani ally from being dismembered by India, establishing Bangladesh (China would not recognize that state until after a coup in Dhaka led it to break diplomatically with India in 1975). Thereafter, Indian diplomacy moved toward the Soviet Union during the 1970s. The Cold War had crept around the world, combined with local disputes and formed a very dangerous mixture: the Chinese joined with Pakistan and the United States in supporting the Mujahideen in Afghanistan from 1980 to 1989.

Works cited

Amer, Ramses. 1993. Sino-Vietnamese relations and Southeast Asian security. *Contemporary Southeast Asia*, 14(March), 320.

Atwood, Christopher P. 1999. Sino-Soviet diplomacy and the second partition of Mongolia, 1945–46, in *Mongolia in the Twentieth Century: Landlocked Cosmopolitan*, edited by Stephen Kotkin and Bruce A. Elleman. Armonk, NY: M.E. Sharpe, 135–159.

Bedeski, Robert E. 1983. *The Fragile Entente: The 1978 Japan-China Peace Treaty in a Global Context*. Boulder, CO: Westview.

Bresnan, John. 1993. *Managing Indonesia: The Modern Political Economy*. New York: Columbia University Press.

Chen, King C. 1969. *Vietnam and China, 1938–1954*. Princeton: Princeton University Press.

Chen, King C. 1987. *China's War with Vietnam, 1979: Issues, Decisions, and Implications*. Stanford, CA: Hoover Institution Press.

Chen Xiangyang. 2004. *Zhongguo mulin waijiao: sixiang, shijian, qianzhang* [China's good-neighbour diplomacy: Though, practice, prospect]. Beijing: Shishi chubanshe.

Chin, Ung Ho. 2000. *The Chinese of South-East Asia*. London: Minority Rights Group International Report.

Chirot, Daniel, and Reid, Anthony, eds. 1997. *Essential Outsiders: Chinese and Jews in the Modern Transformation of Southeast Asia and Central Europe*. Seattle: University of Washington Press.

Dear, I.C.B, and Foot, M.R.D., eds. 1995. *The Oxford Companion to World War II*. Oxford: Oxford University Press.

Eggert, Marion. 1997. A borderline case: Korean travelers' views of the Chinese border (eighteenth to nineteenth century), in *China and Her Neighbours: Borders, Visions of the Other, Foreign Policy 10th to 19th Century*, edited by Sabine Dabringhaus and Roderich Ptak. Wiesbaden: Harrassowitz Verlag, 49–78.

Fifield, Russell H. 1958. *The Diplomacy of Southeast Asia: 1945–1958*. New York: Harper & Brothers.

Fukuda, Shozo. 1995. *With Sweat & Abacus: Economic Roles of Southeast Asian Chinese on the Eve of World War II*, ed. George Hicks. Singapore: Select Books, [orig. pub: 1937].

Gainsborough, Martin. 1992. Vietnam II: A turbulent normalisation with China. *The World Today*, 1 November, 205–207.

Garver, John W. 2001. *Protracted Contest: Sino-Indian Rivalry in the Twentieth Century*. Seattle: University of Washington Press.

Garver, John W. 2016. *China's Quest: The History of the Foreign Relations of the People's Republic of China*. New York: Oxford University Press.

IMF DOTS [Direction of Trade Statistics]. 2017. IMF e-library. <data.imf.org/>, accessed 19 January 2017.

Johnston, Alastair Iain. 1998. China's militarized interstate dispute behaviour 1949–1992: A first cut at the data. *The China Quarterly*, 153, 1–30.

Kang, David C. 2010. *East Asia before the West: Five Centuries of Trade and Tribute*. New York: Columbia University Press.

Karl, Rebecca E. 1998. Creating Asia: China in the world at the beginning of the twentieth century. *American Historical Review*, 103(October), 1096–1118.

Lam, Tom. 2000. The exodus of Hoa refugees from Vietnam and their settlement in Guangxi: China's refugee settlement strategies. *Journal of Refugee Studies*, 13, 374–390.

Lintner, Bertil. 2015. *Great Game East: India, China and the Struggle for Asia's Most Volatile Frontier*. New Haven: Yale University Press.

McDonald, Hamish. 1989. Breaking the ice. *Far Eastern Economic Review*, 9 March, 10–11.

Möller, Kay. 1984. *China und das wiedervereinte Vietnam: Pax Sinica contra Regionalhegemonie* [China and reunified Vietnam: Pax Sinica versus regional hegemony]. Bochum: Studienverlag Brockmeyer.

Nastic, Dragan. 1985. Sino-Indonesian relations. *Review of International Affairs: Politics, Economics, Law, Science, Culture*, 36(5 September), 23–25.

Netherlands and China. 1973. *Treaties and Agreements with and Concerning China, 1894–1919*, vol. 1, ed. John V.A. MacMurray. New York: Howard Fertig.

Owen, Norman G. 2005. *The Emergence of Modern Southeast Asia: A New History*. Honolulu: University of Hawai'i Press.

Raine, Sarah, and Le Mière, Christian. 2013. *Regional Disorder: The South China Sea Disputes*. London: International Institute for Strategic Studies.

Reid, Anthony. 1999. Economic and social change, c. 1400–1800, in *The Cambridge History of Southeast Asia, Vol. 1, Part Two: From c. 1500 to c. 1800*, edited by Nicholas Tarling. Cambridge: Cambridge University Press, 116–163.

Ross, Robert S. 1988. *The Indochina Tangle: China's Vietnam Policy, 1975–1979*. New York: Columbia University Press.

Rossabi, Morris. 1975. *China and Inner Asia: From 1368 to the Present Day*. New York: PICA Press.

Rossabi, Morris. 2013. Sino-Mongol border: From conflict to precarious resolution, in *Beijing's Power and China's Borders: Twenty Neighbors in Asia*, edited by Bruce A. Elleman, Stephen Kotkin, and Clived Schofield. Armonk, NY: M.E. Sharpe, 168–189.

Samuels, Marwyn S. 1982. *Contest for the South China Sea*. New York: Methuen.

Stephan, John J. 1994. *The Russian Far East: A History*. Stanford: Stanford University Press.

Suryadinata, Leo. 1997. Ethnic Chinese in Southeast Asia, in *Ethnic Chinese as Southeast Asians*, edited by Leo Suryadinata. New York: St. Martin's, 1–25.

Tasker, Rodney. 1988. Business leads the way. *Far Eastern Economic Review*, 28 April, 66–67.

Taylor, Jay. 1976. *China and Southeast Asia: Peking's Relations with Revolutionary Movements*, 2nd ed. New York: Praeger.

Truong, Buu Lam. 1968. Intervention versus tribute in Sino-Vietnamese relations, 1788–1790, in *The Chinese World Order*, edited by John King Fairbank. Cambridge, MA: Harvard University Press, 165–179.

Vatikiotis, Michael. 1989. Another step closer. *Far Eastern Economic Review*, 30 November, 36.

Vatikiotis, Michael, and Delfs, Robert. 1990. Burying the past. *Far Eastern Economic Review*, 12 July, 10–11.

Westad, Odd Arne. 2012. *Restless Empire: China and the World Since 1750*. New York: Basic Books.

Womack, Brantly. 2006. *China and Vietnam: The Politics of Asymmetry*. Cambridge: Cambridge University Press.

Wong Kan Seng. 1995. Ethnic Chinese in Southeast Asia, in *Southeast Asian Chinese and China: The Politico-Economic Dimension*, edited by Leo Suryadinata. Singapore: Times Academic Press, 1–20.

Woodside, Alexander Barton. 1971. *Vietnam and the Chinese Model: A Comparative Study of Vietnamese and Chinese Government in the First Half of the Nineteenth Century*. Cambridge, MA: Harvard University Council on East Asian Studies.

Yen Ching-hwang. 1995. Ch'ing China and the Singapore Chinese Chamber of Commerce, 1906–1911, in *Southeast Asian Chinese and China: The Politico-Economic Dimension*, edited by Leo Suryadinata. Singapore: Times Academic Press, 133–143.

Yu Zhengliang et al. 1989. *Zhanhou guoji guanxi shigang* [Outline history of post-war international relations]. Beijing: Shijie zhishi chubanshe.

Zhang, Shu Guang. 2014. *Beijing's Economic Statecraft during the Cold War, 1949–1991*. Washington, DC: Woodrow Wilson Center Press.

Zhu Tingchan. 2001. Lun Zhongguo mulin zhengce de lilun yu shijian [Discussing the theory and practice of China's Good Neighbor Policy]. *Guoji guancha* [International Observations], 2(2001), 12–18, republished in *Zhongguo waijiao*, 8(2001), 16–21.

4 Restructuring of relations
The "Good Neighbor" 1988–2004

Period overview

In the middle of the Sichuan capital of Chengdu stands an immense statue of the late Mao Zedong, waving to the masses who no longer pay it any attention, a monstrous relic of another era in Chinese politics, and one of the few left in China anymore. Near that statue in October 1990, Vietnamese and Chinese officials secretly met to discuss the normalization of their bilateral relations (Zhang Qing 2000: 44–46). Only sixteen months before in the same city, demonstrations against the Chinese Communist Party had been suppressed with the same fury that had been unleashed in Tiananmen Square, a provincial echo of a national tragedy. The sequence was not coincidental; for although the underlying reasons for the Good Neighbor Policy was in part a response by an aspiring regional hegemon to a rapidly changing global and regional international environment and domestic changes, the immediate causes of China's Good Neighbor Policy were largely – but not wholly – an outgrowth of two events of May-June 1989: the Sino-Soviet normalization of relations and the Tiananmen Square massacre.

The international outrage at the Tiananmen Square massacre of 4 June 1989 resulted in a flurry of Chinese diplomatic visits. The year 1990 was particularly notable for Chinese diplomacy, because of the normalization of diplomatic relations with Singapore and Indonesia. Premier Li Peng visited Indonesia and Singapore, as well as Thailand, Malaysia, the Philippines, Laos, and Sri Lanka. Other top leaders visited India, Thailand, North Korea, Pakistan, and Japan. Precisely at a time when Western Europe and the United States imposed sanctions against China and limited high-level contacts between Chinese and Western leaders, China's diplomacy turned toward its neighbors, including Vietnam. In late 1990, Foreign Minister Qian Qichen characterized this thrust as China's "Good Neighbor Policy," and the 1991 *Zhongguo waijiao gailan* [hereafter *ZGWJGL*, see note in Works Cited] summarized, "In the past year, China's good-neighbor relations with Asian countries have had comprehensive development, relations with bordering countries have emerged as their best period since the founding of the country" (Scalapino 1991: 63; *Zhongguo waijiao gailan* 1991: 23, hereafter *ZGWJGL*). Chinese Premier Li Peng said in 1991 that "[d]eveloping good neighborly relations with bordering countries comprises an important part of our foreign policy" (Li Peng 1991). In July and August 1991, the warming between China and Vietnam continued when General Le Duc Anh (second in rank in the Vietnamese Politburo) and Vice-Foreign Minister Nguyen Dy Nhien visited Beijing, arranging for the November visit of Premier Vo Van Kiet and Party Leader Do Muoi to the Chinese capital (Hiebert and Cheung 1991a, 1991b).

As seen in Chapter 2, the USA's own Good Neighbor Policy initiative in the 1930s had two unspoken targets for its Good Neighbor Policy: fascism and communism – it was attempting to support the ideology of democratic free market capitalism against challenges at a time when totalitarian ideologies were serious competitors. Just as the Great Depression humbled the United States as the paragon of capitalism and forced it to reconsider its appeal to countries around the world, so too, China was a model of economic growth and economic reform before the crisis of June 1989 caused an enormous crisis of confidence and prestige.

Ideational: policies, pronouncements, and doctrines

Ideology

The period in question is book-ended by two disasters from the Chinese leadership perspective: the collapse of the Soviet Union and communism in that country and eastern Europe, and the American invasion of Iraq which seemed an ominous warning not only the "Axis of Evil" in the world but to any country that stood in the way of the United States. China's own brush with democratization in May/June 1989 led the leadership of the Communist Party of China to begin worrying that regime change remained a core strategic goal for the USA and the West. The question was how China would deal with a broader world that was threatening and yet its own region that showed greater promise than ever before with the problems of Soviet influence disappearing. Furthermore, the decline of communism as a rigid ideology and its use as a bogeyman by Asian governments to oppose opening relations with China also went away in the late 1980s, giving China opportunities that had been previously closed. The answer to these threats and opportunities would lie in two important phrases: Deng Xiaoping's dicta related to "laying low" and Jiang Zemin's implementation of "Good Neighbor Relations."

Seeking a stable international environment within which to promote economic growth became a long-term goal of the Chinese communist leadership. Paramount leader Deng Xiaoping's famous dictum, *taoguang yanghui* (韬光养晦 and sometimes abbreviated TGYH) is associated with the 1989–1995 period. Translations vary, but often include elements of "lay low," "hide your capabilities, develop some strength," or more fully, "keep a low profile and bide your time, while also getting something accomplished") The full phrase is 冷静观察、沉着应付、稳住阵脚、韬光养晦、有所作为 *Lengjing guancha, chenzhuo yingfu, wen zhu zhenjiao, taoguangyanghui, you suo zuowei* [calmly observe, calmly cope, stabilize the position, keep a low profile, make a difference]. Deng had a number of closely related phrases in the same vein. Chinese and foreign scholars have written extensively on the issue, especially in the 2008–11 period when some Chinese

90 The "Good Neighbor"

began to question the utility of it as a strategy (see Chen and Wang 2011). At the time the emphasis was on the *taoguang yanghui* element of the phrase, which many regarded as meaning that China should avoid conflicts with other countries. By the mid-1990s, some began to give equal emphasis to the *you suo zuowei* ("make a difference"/"do something"), but it would be fair to say that the phrase and other dicta that Deng uttered at this period constituted a strategy of caution.

Chinese foreign relations at the beginning of this period also avoided multilateralism beyond its participation in the United Nations. By the early 21st century, however, it was participating in a variety of regional organizations for the Asia-Pacific and sub-regions. This shift from the "hub-and-spokes" (辐辏结构 *fucou jiegou*) approach of bilateralism represented both a cautious approach – fearing to be left out and isolated – and a step toward dealing with other countries as an equal neighbor.

"Good Neighbor Relations"

If China was laying low in its global relations, there was no doubt that it had opportunities in its regional situation. The two were virtually simultaneous in their origin: May-June 1989. The normalization of Sino-Soviet relations and Soviet leader Mikhail Gorbachev's visit to Beijing met all of the previous Chinese demands for normalization: Soviet withdrawal from Afghanistan, Vietnamese withdrawal from Cambodia, and a military pull back from the Sino-Soviet border. Furthermore, it was already obvious by the late 1980s that Gorbachev was not going to dictate the affairs of Soviet friends and allies and that the Soviet economy could not much longer afford to subsidize them. That meant that formerly hostile relations with countries such as Vietnam, Laos, India, and Mongolia which had stood with (or leaned toward) the Soviets during the Cold War might be improved. When the Soviet Union collapsed in 1991, China also acquired three new contiguous neighbors, Kazakhstan, Kyrgyzstan, and Tajikistan, and moved quickly to establish good relations, as will be discussed below.

The idea of good neighbor relations meshed well with existing foreign policy doctrines, most notably the Five Principles of Peaceful Co-existence. Chinese scholars naturally began to rummage for examples from Mao's era of neighborliness (see Zhu Tingchan 2001: 16–17; Chen Xiangyang's 2004: book, *Zhongguo mulin waijiao/China's Good-Neighbour Diplomacy* traces the ideas back to ancient China. See also Zhang Shengjian and Hu Weining 2010). The phrase is first used officially in the *ZGWJGL* 1989, where it appears in one of the major headings, "Diligently develop good-neighborly relations, actively strengthen friendly cooperation with various countries" (14). One of the first uses of the phrase in the post-Tiananmen period appears to have been by then Premier Li Peng, in the Government Work Report of 1993, who urged the "energetic development of good-neighborly relations with surrounding countries . . ." (quoted in Zhu Tingchan 2001: 16). But the phrase and policies are strongly associated with Jiang Zemin (1989–2005) who as leader of the Communist Party, President, and Chair of the Central Military Commission was the official leader of China, particularly after the death of Deng Xiaoping in 1997 (Fang Chunsheng 2005: 47). Jiang made it a particular point in the 15th CCP Party Congress in 1997, saying, "[We] must support good neighborliness. This is what our country has consistently stood for, and it absolutely will not change" [要坚特睦邻友好。这是我国的一贯主张，决不改变] (quoted in Zhu Tingchan 2001: 16). Jiang also used the phrase in his April 1997 visit to Russia and, at the 1997 ASEAN summit, pledged that China would always be a "good neighbor, good partner, and good friend" (Chen Xiangyang 2004: 126–127). In 1999 in the visit of Vietnamese Communist leaders, Party ideologues went so far as to try to float it as a "16 Character Directive" ("长期稳定, 面向未来, 睦邻友好, 全面合作" roughly meaning "Long-term stability, looking toward the future, friendly neighborliness, comprehensive cooperation") as an addition to Deng's *taoguang yanghui* dicta (Li Chengren 2010: 25; Zhu Tingchan 2001: 19). The Good Neighbor Policy was also seen as integral to the domestic economic reform policies (Zhu Tingchan 2001: 17). At least as early as 2001, Chinese analysts were seeing the Good Neighbor Policy as an important way to reassure worrying countries nearby that China's rise was not threatening (Ya Xin 2001: 19; see also Chung 2010: chap. 2 for a review of the Good Neighbor Policy and Southeast Asian relations).

At its broadest level, however, China's Good Neighbor Policy has an unspoken target, as well as its primary weakness: United States foreign policy. It is no coincidence that Chinese spokespersons regularly invoke the Five Principles of Peaceful Co-existence and terms of "good neighborliness" in speaking to their neighboring countries in Asia. The third principle of the Five Principles is non-interference in each other's internal affairs (不干涉原则, *bu ganshe yuanze*). Whereas the West in general and the United States in particular has placed substantial emphasis on human rights conditions in its foreign policy, Chinese leaders in their relations with Southeast Asian countries especially have stressed the common ground of opposition to human rights conditions and considerations in foreign relations (Nathan 1994: 632–633; Ya Xin 2001: 52–53). Foreign policy issues between the United States and Southeast Asian states have revolved around American allegations of violations of human rights, press freedom, criminal procedure and the like. Press freedom in Singapore, American criticism of Indonesia for its actions in East Timor, conflicts with Malaysia over rain forest depletion, and even with democratic India over the violation of human rights in Kashmir formed a nexus of disagreement between the United States and Asia.

China countered with an appeal to a common cultural heritage. An editorial in *People's Daily* during the 1994 APEC meeting outlines this sense of common ground:

> … the common characteristics of east Asian culture, such as attaching importance to education, and harmonious human relations, are positive factors in economic development. The Western countries enjoy talking about pluralization. While encouraging the developing countries to achieve pluralization in political affairs, they should also respect the pluralization existing in the world and the national culture of other countries. In fact, only

by respecting the inherent cultural heritages and value concepts of various countries can the common achievements of human civilization be more effectively used. . . . Just as Jiang Zemin pointed out in Singapore: "Asian civilization, once a force pushing history forward, will show new splendor in mankind development in the new era."

(FBIS 1994a: 6)

Chinese leaders were seeking to use these conflicts, coupled with their own Good Neighbor Policy to convince Asian countries of their common ground.

Northeast Asia

Security

It is often said that the Cold War never ended on the Korean peninsula: a constant confrontation between two hostile regimes, one communist, the other not, with a militarized border and angry rhetoric punctuated by occasional militarized incidents. It certainly looks and feels like the old Cold War, but in some important ways it is not. The collapse of the Soviet Union and the dramatic economic changes in China led the regime in Pyongyang to question its security guarantees and in 1992 when China established diplomatic relations with the Republic of Korea (ROK), North Korea's security context deteriorated further, and it would begin to seek the protection of the ultimate weapon. At the time, however, the Korean peninsula and the broader security context of Northeast Asia was improving from China's perspective, with good relations with Japan, new relations with South Korea, the disappearance of the Soviet threat, and the beginning of amiable relations with the Russian Federation.

Territorial disputes

The resolution of territorial disputes through legal means, including long-standing ones, is a mark of an active phase regional hegemon, such as the India-Bangladesh maritime settlement in the World Court in 2014 (during the brief period in which the new Modi government was trying to improve its regional relations). China resolved its long-standing northeastern border issue with Russia during this time, and we will see also with its new Central Asian neighbors. Although for purposes of analysis the Russian Federation is treated as Central Asia in this study, the boundary resolution in the Amur and Ussuri regions will be dealt with here. A total of 4,300km length of the boundary was in dispute. The areas in question were in the Manzhouli-Zabaikalsk area near the tripoint with Mongolia, the area at the confluence of the Amur and Ussuri rivers, opposite the city of Khabarovsk, and a salient across the river from Blagoveshchensk. The negotiations were reopened by the Gorbachev government in 1987, and outlasted the Soviet Union; the treaty was negotiated and signed by the USSR in 1991, but ratified by its successor state, the Russian Federation in 1992. The process of establishing the *thalweg* (deepest part of the channel) was made more difficult because of the local geography of tiny river islands, and an additional agreement was negotiated in 2004 to finalize the border. In general, the two sides split the difference fairly evenly between them, and what had been a long and vexing boundary dispute ceased to be a problem (Galeotti 2013: 257–259).

China and South Korea have two maritime disputes, one of which was negotiated during this period, and the other which was ignored. Although the land border between China and the DPRK were resolved in 1963, neither of the Koreas have resolved the issue of overlapping Exclusive Economic Zone (EEZ) claims in the Yellow Sea. This is an important fishing ground for all three states, but the maritime border has never been resolved. China and South Korea negotiated an agreement in 2001 which established a Provisional Measures Zone (PMZ), and two Transitional Zones, which by agreement became part of China and South Korea's EEZs four years later, but the patrolling and monitoring of the middle PMZ was left such that each country monitored its own country's fishers. The ownership issue was over Socotra Rock (Ieodo/Suyan), a submerged feature 150km southwest of Cheju island. South Korea built a research station there between 1995 and 2001, despite Chinese claims (Armstrong 2013: 121).

Border management with North Korea became a significant regional issue for China during this time. In the case of North Korea, the border has been clearly set and agreed to since 1963. In addition to a minor issue concerning islands in the Tumen and Yalu rivers, a much bigger problem exists between the two countries: refugees. Given the grim economic conditions in North Korea, and draconian policies of that government, it should not be surprising that many North Koreans have slipped across the Yalu river into adjacent Chinese province of Jilin, where a sizeable ethnic Korean community exists in the Yanbian Korean Autonomous Prefecture (Choi 2011: 507–527; Lankov 2004). The issue had existed for several years beginning with economic reform and prosperity in China, and though the central government in China never acknowledged turning a blind eye to the North Korean refugee issue, it was also clear that returning these people was not a high priority so long as the issue was quiet. That ended in 2002 when a group of North Koreans left the Northeast and came to Beijing and managed to scale the US and German embassy walls (Rosenthal 2002). This set off a diplomatic stand-off that the Chinese government could no longer pretend did not exist, and which the North Korean government would have to make an issue out of. The stand-off ended when the North Koreans were sent indirectly to South Korea, but ever after the border between North Korea and China remains more tightly controlled, with walls and fences at potential crossing areas (Choi 2011: 517) and North Koreans living in China without authorization lead a much more surreptitious existence, often accused of causing crime (Choi 2011: 522).

Issues concerning the China-Mongolia border had been frequent during the Cold War, the 1963 Treaty establishing the boundary notwithstanding. There were disputes along the 4,645km border, but following the Soviet lead in 1987, negotiations between Chinese and Mongolian sides yielded a new treaty. It was also an agreement that favored the Mongolian side, and though the two countries have had political and economic issues since then, the border is not one of them (Rossabi 2013: 178–179).

Finally, the Senkaku/Diaoyu Island dispute still existed, but in 1978 during the Sino-Japanese Treaty negotiations, Deng Xiaoping explicitly placed it on the back burner of territorial disputes, saying that it was a problem that should be left to later generations (quoted in Zhu Tingchan 2001: 19). Provocative actions by Hong Kong and other Chinese in response to private Japanese provocations in the 1990s generally did not produce lasting incidents (Fravel 2008: 270).

Military intervention

China did not invade, attack or intervene in Northeast Asia during this time period. There have been rumors that China supported the Mongolian Democratic Union party against the supposedly pro-Russian MPRP, and the Mongolian press often reprints rumors of Chinese intentions to annex Mongolia, but there is no evidence of this (Rossabi 2005: 240).

External major powers

The United States, enjoying its "peace dividend" after the Cold War, reduced forces deployed around the world from a peak of 2.15 million during the Reagan administration to 1.4 million in the Clinton administration, much of the reduction occurring in Europe. Military personnel in East Asia and the Pacific did not see as much of a reduction, going from a Cold War peak of 130,000 down to 97,000. But from China's perspective, the relative US power in East Asia was even more overwhelming given the collapse of the Soviet Union. The US response to the 1995–96 Taiwan Straits crisis certainly demonstrated that American power was still active and involved in East Asia during this time, a substantial setback for China's cross-straits relations. The forced landing of a US Airforce EP-3 surveillance aircraft created a minor crisis in US-China relations in April 2001, and in far-off Belgrade, Yugoslavia, in 1999, the bombing of the Chinese embassy there was seen by the Chinese public and government as not the accident the US government claimed it had been and instead as a signal meant to intimidate China. And hanging over US-China relations has been issues of the Tiananmen Square massacre, human rights, the rights of Tibetans, and the suspicion of the Chinese Communist Party leadership that the USA would like to see China go the same way as the communist countries of Eastern Europe and the Soviet Union, toward liberal democracy.

In contrast to the USA, the USSR in speech and deed was very different. Mikhail Gorbachev's July 1986 Vladivostok speech and his 1988 Krasnayorsk speech both signaled the Soviets' willingness to come to an understanding with China in Asia. Soviet troops withdrew from Afghanistan, drew down along the Chinese border in both the Soviet Union and Mongolia, and pressured the Vietnamese to withdraw from Cambodia. Gorbachev's visit to China in May 1989 might have been a high point in Sino-Soviet relations and Chinese diplomacy if it were not for the student demonstrators in Tiananmen Square, many inspired by Gorbachev's *glasnost'* and *Demokratizatsiya* policies. The shock and horror of what followed in June would lead directly to the collapse of communism in eastern Europe as countries there began a whole-scale rejection of communist parties and their rule, and to the collapse of the Soviet Union itself.

The Yeltsin era (1991–99) saw the drastic contraction of the Russian economy, with the accompanying reduction of Russian strategic assets in general and in East Asia especially. The once-fearsome Soviet Pacific Fleet was either returned to European waters or deteriorated due to lack of maintenance. The Russian population in the Far East declined, and Russian influence in Northeast Asia dropped substantially. Sino-Russian relations in this period will be treated under "Central Asia."

Diplomatic relations with regional states

China expanded its diplomatic presence in Northeast Asia during the 1990s, establishing formal ties with South Korea, while maintaining relations with North Korea, improving its relations with Japan, and harmonizing its ties with Mongolia.

Japan

China began the period afraid that Japan would be pressured into economic sanctions by the West in response to Tiananmen, and it did suspend the yen loans, the latest batch of which had been made just in August of 1988. Prime Minister Kaifu Toshiki announced the resumption of the loans in July 1990, and broke the isolation of China among the advanced industrial democracies in August 1991 by his visit; both sides avoided deep discussions of unfortunate history. Chinese President Jiang Zemin made a visit to Japan in April 1992, and during Emperor Akihito's return state visit to China – the first by any Japanese emperor – in October 1992, historical subjects were merely alluded to by both sides. When Prime Minister Hosokawa Morihiro visited in March 1994, the issue was again avoided. A fourth yen loan was extended in December 1994.

The wartime history was still there, but in some ways growing, not shrinking in importance of the Sino-Japanese relationship; a "patriotic education campaign" began in earnest in 1994 which emphasized China's historical humiliation by Western powers and its victimization by Japan in the Second Sino-Japanese War in particular (Wang 2012: 99). Prime Minister Murayama Tomiichi in August 1995 made the most direct apology for the past, stating, "Japan . . . caused tremendous damage and suffering to the people of many countries, particularly to those of Asian nations . . . I . . . express here once again my feelings of deep remorse and state my heartfelt apology." (MOFAJ 1995). From the Japanese perspective, that ended the issue.

During Jiang Zemin's second visit to Japan in November 1998, however, the Chinese decided it was time to make the Japanese fully apologize. It didn't go well. The Chinese side wanted a written apology similar to what the South Korean

President had recently received. The Japanese would only go so far as an oral statement of "deep remorse." They repeated the 1972 declaration, and though the foreign ministries of both countries hailed the visit as a success, most analysts saw it as a major Chinese failure (Wan 2006: 129–130). The Prime Ministership of Koizumi Junichiro (April 2001-September 2006) was a particularly difficult period in Sino-Japanese political relations, given his visits to the Yasukuni Shrine (seen by Chinese as a symbol of unrepentant Japanese militarism) and close relationship with the USA and the George W. Bush Administration. Although further high-level visits occurred, the political relationship cooled after this even as the economic relationship was booming, the period often called "cold politics and hot economics" (Yahuda 2014: 73).

South Korea

China established diplomatic relations with the Republic of Korea on August 24, 1992, formalizing what was already an economic relationship that was growing as quickly as North Korea's was stagnating. That China could establish simultaneous relations with both Koreas was no small feat, given the two regimes were competing governments of the same nation, not unlike China and Taiwan. Unlike China and Taiwan, however, the Koreans followed the German *Ostpolitik* solution, and allowed dual recognitions after the 1970s. The Soviet Union had done so in September 1990, enduring the indignant scorn of the North Korean press. But this was during a period when North and South Korea had entered into a period of reconciliation in 1990–91, signed a joint agreement and both entered the United Nations simultaneously in September 1991. Qian Qichen, then China's Foreign Minister, was in Seoul in November 1991 when China joined APEC, and when he met with President Roh Tae-woo, the latter raised the prospect of establishing relations. The problem, of course, was North Korea. Jiang Zemin had told Kim Il-sung told during his 1989 and 1990 visits to Beijing and Shenyang that China was going to establish trade relations and unofficial trade offices, and Kim agreed (Qian 2005: 117–118). The issue of establishing diplomatic ties had been hinted at by Yang Shangkun in his visit to Pyongyang in April 1992, but in July the Chinese had made their decision, and Qian Qichen was dispatched to Pyongyang to inform Kim Il-sung. The meeting was brief, but Kim curtly said, "We understand China's independent foreign policy." China and the ROK established formal relations the next month (Qian 2005: 123–125). Roh Tae-woo made a state visit to China a month later.

North Korea

The collapse of the Soviet Union left North Korea with fewer options than it had previously exploited. Kim Il-sung died in July 1994, bequeathing to his son and successor Kim Jong-il a massive famine and a nuclear crisis. Nuclear weapons and regime stability became the two main concerns for China in its relations with the DPRK, and for a while it appeared that China had helped negotiate a solution to the first issue. In 1993, when the IAEA was unsatisfied that North Korea was in compliance with it Non-Proliferation Treaty (NPT) declaration, Pyongyang threatened to pull out of the NPT altogether, leading to the first North Korean nuclear crisis. The United States and North Korea reached the Agreed Framework in 1994, in which the USA and a consortium which included South Korean and Japanese funding would build a light-water reactor and supply fuel oil to North Korea in exchange for denuclearization. China was not a major participant in this deal. By 2003, the North Koreans again threatened to pull out of the NPT, and the government in Beijing organized and hosted the Six Party Talks (China, Russia, USA, South Korea, North Korea, Japan) in a grand gesture of "responsible great power" status. The results will be discussed in Chapter 6.

China did supply North Korea with about $800 million worth of arms between 1988 and 1995, according to SIPRI, but no arms transfers are recorded thereafter (SIPRI TIV 2017). There were also the usual high-level mutual visits, such as Chinese President Yang Shangkun's 1992 official visit to North Korea, and Kim Jong-il's 2001 tour of China, meant to convince him of the need for economic reforms.

Mongolia

Mongolia, as the oldest Soviet ally, followed trends in Moscow closely, and when reforms began there in the mid-1980s, the previous hard-line leader, Tsendenbal, was eased out of power and replaced by Jambyn Batmünkh, who was cut from the same cloth as Gorbachev. Relations with China improved quickly after Gorbachev's 1986 Vladivostok speech, despite decades of intense Mongolian suspicion and hostility, a product of the most asymmetrical relationship China has with its contiguous neighbors: at the time, 2.1 million Mongolians facing 1.1 billion Chinese in China. Consulates were opened, leaders visited, and trade flourished. Chinese President Yang Shangkun in meeting with the Mongolian Foreign Minister in July 1989 ended the interview with a profoundly neighborly statement: "China and Mongolia are equal" (Rossabi 2005: 228–230).

The asymmetry of the relationship has not gone away, nor have Mongolian fears of Chinese moving into to sparsely-populated Mongolia. During the 1990s, Mongolia went the way of Eastern Europe, democratizing, privatizing, and adopting liberal free-market policies, in many cases much too quickly. The democratically elected President of Mongolia, Punsalmaagin Ochirbat, visited China twice in 1991, and President Yang Shangkun returned the favor that summer and signed a variety of agreements, including loans, aid, trade, and exchanges. The Mongolians pledged to protect Chinese investments in Mongolia. Both sides pledged not to interfere in each other's internal affairs. Li Peng followed in 1994 and signed a treaty, once again pledging not to interfere in each other's internal affairs, and Mongolia restating its observance of the one-China policy (Rossabi 2005: 232–233). There were, to be sure, irritants in the relationship. China's two nuclear tests in 1994 and another in 1996 in Xinjiang drew protests from Mongolia (Madhok

2005: 213–214) (Nigeria similarly protested French nuclear tests in the Sahara in the 1960s).

Regional international organizations

Northeast Asia per se does not have a regional international organization the way Southeast Asia, South Asia, and Central Asia do. There are, however, two bodies that encompass Northeast Asia. APEC – Asia-Pacific Economic Cooperation – began as an Australian proposal in early 1989, and it received a cool response from Southeast Asia, especially Malaysia, which had its own idea for an East Asian Economic Group that would not include Australia, Canada, New Zealand, and the USA. APEC, however, won out and has expanded ever since. When in 1991 China had the opportunity to join, it did so quickly so as to further escape its post-Tiananmen isolation. The trick was Taiwan: since APEC was technically a meeting of "economies" and not states, there might be room for both the PRC and ROC-Taiwan in the same organization. Joining as "Chinese Taipei," "Hong Kong, China," and "the People's Republic of China," the three economies attended the third summit at Seoul in November 1991 (Qian 2005: 107–110). China hosted the 13th meeting in Shanghai in 2001 and has been active in the organization since. The organization, however, has spread to include Mexico, Chile, Peru, Papua New Guinea, and Russia. It has been focused on trade, investment, and related economic issues, but political and security issues have come onto the agenda, such as terrorism. The organization has evolved over time, and much of the debate has been over the nature of the body and its decision-making (or lack thereof). A legalistic approach supported by the Western members dominated 1989–93 and focused on trade liberalization in the region. The Southeast Asian states were concerned as APEC grew that it would outweigh ASEAN, and China has been a staunch supporter of the "Asian Approach" to decision-making in APEC, which began to emerge in the mid-1990s (Chung 2010: 29–32). It is part of China's increasing commitment to multilateralism during this period, so long as the organization did not intrude upon sovereignty matters and showed its commitment to cooperation with its neighbors (Heilmann and Schmidt 2014: 24–25; Wu 2009).

ASEAN Plus Three and the ASEAN Regional Forum (ARF) are two outgrowths of the Association of Southeast Asian Nations. These will be discussed at greater length below, but one aspect of these dialogue relationships (as ASEAN describes them) does represent the only entity that could be described as a purely Northeast Asian regional organization. The dialogue relationship began during the 1997 Asian financial crisis, focusing on stabilizing the affected countries. This led to Chiang Mai initiative, and the formalization of the dialogue: the "+3" countries, China, Japan and South Korea, join the ten countries of ASEAN after the main meeting, but beginning in 1999, China, Japan, and South Korean minister-level representatives have met on their own before attending the ASEAN+3 meeting. At the 2002 summit, China also pushed for ASEAN +3 to consider non-traditional security issues, such as piracy, terrorism, and crime (Chung 2010: 74–77).

Hegemon's expatriates, co-ethnics

Unlike Southeast Asia, there were far fewer ethnic Chinese communities in Northeast Asia. In Japan, the *kakyō* (華僑/かきょう) have a long history there, but less political impact. Tens of thousands of Chinese students came to Japan during this period, occasionally raising questions of whether they were studying or illicitly working. Issues such as Taiwanese versus mainland ownership of a dormitory in 1987 did periodically rise to the national level of the relationship (Whiting 1989: 152–155), but generally, matters remained at the consular level.

Korea also had an "old" ethnic Chinese community (화교/*hwagyo*) of over 60,000 people going back in history, though by the end of World War II most had gone, either back to their native Shandong or elsewhere. Of those who remained, most went south in the division of Korea, and discriminatory policies of the Syngman Rhee government and intermarriage also reduced the numbers who identified as Chinese, and then in the 1970s and 1980s emigrated to the United States or Taiwan. The 1997 Asian financial crisis hit the remaining number, many restauranteurs and small shopkeepers hard as well, and about 22,000 are left, mostly with ROC citizenship (Rhee 2009: 114–117). But just as that group was declining in the 1990s, a group of "new" overseas Chinese, many of them ethnic Koreans with Chinese citizenship, arrived in Korea.

Of these overseas Chinese communities – real or perceived – the one with a substantial political impact was in Mongolia where memories of "usurious Chinese merchants" and fears die hard. In the late 1980s, the sensitivity was still there, as aptly summarized by Rossabi, "The two sides had complementary needs. Mongolia required skilled labor, while China could profit from Mongolia's animal and mineral resources. Yet Mongolia still feared that these Chinese workers would be the first wave in an onslaught of Chinese who would migrate and overwhelm Mongolia, as they had done in Inner Mongolia" (Rossabi 2005: 229). China has sought to use its Inner Mongolians as a bridge to the new government in Ulaanbaatar in the new relationship, with scholarships, exchanges and the like.

Provision of public goods

Unlike Southeast Asia or Central Asia in this period, there was little explicit Chinese provision of security public goods. Although still allied with North Korea, the leadership in Pyongyang clearly had reasons to question the credibility of Chinese guarantees, especially after the 1992 recognition of South Korea and the subsequent blossoming of that relationship. And with the Soviet Union gone and Russian Federation in disarray, Kim Il-sung and his successor Kim Jong-il no longer had a second friendly power to play off the Chinese as they had done for decades. When North Korea announced its intention to leave the NPT in 1994, the Chinese response to possible UN Security Council sanctions was tepid. Years later, the Chinese became much more involved in Korean nuclear diplomacy in the Six Party Talks, discussed in Chapter 6.

Economic

Northeast Asia became the center of China's economic gravity in the 1990s, the source of much of its capital, trade, technology, and economic growth. Aided by World Trade Organization membership in 2001, China's economic growth was impressive by most standards in the 1990s. Japan, on the other hand, saw its much-vaunted high levels of economic growth of the 1980s slow to a crawl and then went into a long-term recession beginning in 1993 and would stay there for most of the decade. South Korea would suffer from a short but sharp recession resulting from the 1997 Asian Financial Crisis.

Trade

China's trade with Northeast Asia increased impressively during 1988–2003 period, as shown in Table 4.1.

Chinese trade with the four states in the region increased by a factor of ten between 1988 and 2003. Most impressive of the group was South Korea, which had no (official) trade with China in 1988–99, to almost half of Japan's trade in 2003.[1] As a region, Northeast Asia was China's most important trade partner: fully 19% of China's world trade was with Northeast Asia in 1988 and it grew to about a quarter of the total during the 1990s and early 2000s. In contrast, trade with the

Table 4.1 China: total trade with Northeast Asia, 1988–2003

China: total trade with Northeast Asia, 1988–2003 (current US$, million)

	Japan	South Korea	North Korea	Mongolia
1988	$19,109	$0	$579	$25
1989	$18,929	$0	$562	$29
1990	$16,866	$669	$491	$40
1991	$20,284	$3,245	$610	$46
1992	$25,385	$5,061	$694	$183
1993	$39,085	$8,220	$898	$151
1994	$47,809	$11,694	$624	$119
1995	$57,474	$16,976	$550	$164
1996	$60,078	$20,012	$566	$199
1997	$60,809	$24,021	$656	$252
1998	$58,025	$21,286	$408	$243
1999	$66,167	$25,036	$370	$263
2000	$83,174	$34,500	$488	$323
2001	$87,888	$35,940	$737	$362
2002	$101,972	$44,089	$738	$363
2003	$133,573	$63,231	$1,023	$440

Source: IMF DOTS (2017).

USA during the same period was around 10% of China's total in the late 1980s and early 1990s, growing to 15–16% in the early 2000s.

What is particularly interesting about these data is that they show the shifting economic relationship between Japan and China from the early 1990s to the early 2000s. At the beginning of the period, the trade was an asymmetrical dependency: Japan was much more important to China's foreign trade than China was for Japan's trade. China bought over 22% of its goods from Japan in 1994 and sold over 20% of its goods to Japan in 1996. Japan, on the other hand, began in 1988–92 selling only 2–3% of its goods to the China market and importing 5–7% of its total from China. As the years went by, however, China became more and more of a vital market and source of goods for Japan. By 2003, the two were fairly close. But the trends would continue into the next period, with China becoming less dependent on Japan, and Japan becoming more dependent on China.

South Korea's trade with China grew by a factor of almost one hundred from its beginnings in 1990, and also showed signs of increasing mutual dependency. It is notable that South Korea exported less in 1998–99 to China as a result of the 1997 Asian financial crisis, though by 2000 it was growing again. A broader and more important trend is that whereas China stabilized at about 10% of imports and 4% of exports from South Korea in the mid-1990s, South Korean dependence on China continued to grow, reaching 12% imports from China and 18% exports to China. Like Japan, this asymmetrical relationship would continue into the 21st century. At the time it was seen as sign both of a healthy and mutually beneficial economic relationship, as well as a solid political relationship, helped by common antipathy toward what they perceive to be Japanese wartime amnesia.

Mongolia, on the other hand, saw its trade with China flourish, the export side especially. Unlike North Korea, Russian goods did not completely disappear from Mongolian markets but did drop from half to about one-third from 1992 to 2003. But Russian's economic decline of the 1990s strongly affected the purchase of Mongolian commodities, and it would be China that would take up the slack.

Southeast Asia

China is and has been substantially larger than its Southeast Asian neighbors combined and overtook the collective region in the early 1990s in all measures of capability considered here. The most telling of the ratios encountered here is the GDP, and this disparity rose even faster in the 21st century.

Security

Territorial disputes

China largely resolved its land-based territorial disputes in Southeast Asia in this period, and ignored its maritime disputes. Security issues in Southeast Asia were still tense in 1988, less than a decade since the Sino-Vietnamese war. There were minor clashes along the land border of China and Vietnam into 1987. China's

March 1988 seizure of Johnson Reef in the Spratlys, resulting in over 80 Vietnamese casualties also set the region on edge in 1988. But in 1989–90, China launched into a determined effort to improve its relations with its neighbors with some notable successes.

The Declaration on the Conduct of Parties in the South China Sea (DOC) between China and ASEAN in November 2002 was one of a flurry of China-ASEAN agreements that year, though it had the potential for being one of the most important for security in Southeast Asia, since it addressed the problem of maritime incidents and interaction in the South China Sea (*China's Foreign Affairs* [hereafter *CFA*] 2003: 65).

Vietnam

There were three areas of territorial dispute between China and Vietnam in 1988; by the end of the period, two of them were resolved diplomatically. After the normalization of relations between Beijing and Hanoi in 1991 (see below), experts and ministers from the two countries began the long work of dealing with the border issues, starting with the land boundaries, and then turning to the Gulf of Tonkin/Beibu Gulf. A total of 227km^2 was in dispute, and at the end of 1999, the two countries agreed to split the difference almost exactly, meeting a mutually imposed deadline and a year later reached agreement on the division in the gulf, in which Vietnam received over 53% of the area in dispute. The two sides also concluded an agreement on fishing in 2004 (Amer 2013: 295–303). The South China Sea, however, eluded a negotiated solution, and the Chinese and Vietnamese have not yet agreed as to where the Gulf of Tonkin/Beibu Gulf ends and the South China Sea begins.

Laos

The border between China and Laos had been established in 1895 by the Sino-French agreement, but as is often the case in the 19th-century colonial history, the actual boundary was not demarcated. China and Laos signed a treaty in 1991 establishing a boundary commission, and a supplementary agreement was signed in 1994, and the Sino-Laotian-Vietnamese trijunction was established in 2006 (Townsend-Gault 2013: 149).

South China Sea

In contrast to the relatively harmonious resolution of China's other border disputes during this period, the South China Sea continued to be an area of disagreement, although at a somewhat lower level than the period that would follow. Deng Xiaoping had discussed the issue vaguely in 1984, saying, "In the Nansha [Spratlys], historical maps delimit as part of China, belonging to China, now except for Taiwan occupying one island, the Philippines occupies several islands, Vietnam occupies several islands, Malaysia occupies several islands. What to do about this in the future? One method is to use military force to take them back; one is method is to shelve the sovereignty question, and jointly develop, this could eliminate many cumulative problems in the future" (Zhu Tingchan 2001: 19). This was then crafted in a "Sixteen Character Policy" in 1990. In the case of China and Vietnam, most of the effort and attention from 1992–2000 had been on the land and gulf boundaries, and when the matter of the South China Sea was raised, the two sides could not get beyond the agenda-setting stage and the expert level. In August 1991, Li Peng agreed to participate in exploratory workshop talks in Bandung sponsored by Indonesia so long as territorial sovereignty was not on the agenda (Vatikiotis 1991: 19).

Periodic voyages of exploration ships resulted in diplomatic protests in 1998, but in general these two sides seemed to be working toward and managing the disputes and reducing outright conflict (Amer 2013: 303–305). China did little about the Malaysian or Brunei claims during this time, but the Philippines was another matter. In 1995, Chinese started setting buoys, markers, and shelters on Mischief Reef, claimed but not occupied by the Philippines. Manila protested but did not use naval force, and the two sides later agreed to a bilateral dispute mechanism (Raine and Le Mière 2013: 46). During Jiang Zemin's 1996 visit to Manila, he proposed "shelving" the dispute over sovereignty. As we will see below, it was also addressed multilaterally in ASEAN.

Military intervention

One of the key touchstones of Chinese foreign policy since the 1950s had been the Five Principles of Peaceful Co-existence, the third of which is non-interference in internal affairs. Beginning in the late 1980s, China began to take this much more seriously than previously, especially in its relations with Southeast Asia. This period begins with the end of China's most significant intervention in Southeast Asia, the Communist Party of Burma's (CPB) twenty-year insurgency.[2] China's support had begun to wane in 1977, when reports of the CPB disappeared from the Chinese press after the Burmese government of Ne Win recognized China's client Democratic Kampuchea (Khmer Rouge Cambodia). China had continued some support until the 1980s, trying to lure the aging leadership of the CPB to quiet retirement in China. Some did, but the last hold-outs, clinging to their hard-line Stalinist/Maoist ideology refused and renounced the leaders in Beijing as "revisionists." Whether urged by China's leaders or of their own volition, the CPB army struck in a coup against the leaders on April 17, 1989, who fled, thus ending the last tiny remnant of China's sponsoring of world-wide revolution (Lintner 2015: 193–194). China continued working with the Wa State in Myanmar across the border from Yunnan province, though it had neither created nor recognized it as a government.

China did not militarily intervene in any other of its neighbors during this period of time, the disputed area of the South China Sea notwithstanding. China did express itself forcefully in an "internal" matter in 1995–96 in the Taiwan Straits after Taiwan's president, Lee Teng-hui visited the United States; China lobbed missiles near Taiwan to demonstrate its outrage, the United States sailed two aircraft carrier groups through the Straits as a signal, and in the 1996 Taiwan presidential election, Lee won by an even greater margin. The mainland assumption of sovereignty over Hong Kong (1997) and Macao (1999), however, showed an impressive degree of restraint during the period and China's leaders hoped the "One Country, Two Systems" concept might sell in Taipei.

External major powers

The last echo of the Cold War in Southeast Asia was in Cambodia, where the Soviet Union and Vietnam had been backing Hun Sen's government against a coalition of forces which included Royalists, remnants of the Khmer Rouge, and the US-backed Lon Nol forces. China supplied weapons, Thailand supplied safe havens across the border, and the USA gave diplomatic support. By 1988, with Soviet support declining, Vietnam was looking for a diplomatic solution. The last of the Vietnamese troops withdrew in September 1989, while the negotiations about the nature and duration of the transition of government in Cambodia were beginning, and in April 1991, a ceasefire began. The final accord was signed in Paris in October 1991.

> Here, the five permanent members of the UN Security Council (P5) and Australia took centre stage, to some extent at ASEAN's expense . . . the second sitting in 1991 resulted in a diplomatic settlement that led to the signing of the Final Act of the Paris Conference on 23 October 1991.
>
> (Acharya 2012: 198)

It marked the end of the Cold War in Southeast Asia, and the Soviet Union had only two months left to live.

The USA withdrew from its bases in the Philippines in 1992 after the government in Manila terminated the leases on US Naval Base Subic Bay and Clark Airbase. Yet with the end of the Cold War and the collapse of the Soviet Union, US relative power was at its apex. American triumphalism of the 1990s also coincided with the Clinton Administration's emphasis on human rights as a major foreign policy issue. This ran directly into China's policies of trying to separate economic reform from political reform, and Chinese leaders continued to talk of the importance of sovereignty in international relations. The emphasis on sovereign control of internal affairs was reiterated by Jiang Zemin during his 1994 Southeast Asian tour, saying that "China firmly advocates that the internal affairs of Southeast Asian countries should only be solved by the people of those countries . . ." (FBIS 23 Nov. 1994b: 12). In discussing relations with both India and Vietnam, the common opposition toward American human rights policies, arms transfers policies, and other conflicts have been stressed (FBIS 1994a: 6).

This is not to say that China is seeking to form a bloc or formal coalition against the United States; conflict gets in the way of prosperity, and Chinese leaders were not seeking to become the major opponent to the sole remaining superpower. Indeed, with the American 2001 "War on Terrorism," they saw an opportunity to improve relations with the United States as a cooperative partner, such as the designation of an obscure Xinjiang organization as a "terrorist group" and the placement of China on a backburner of American foreign policy. Furthermore, so long as Malaysian Prime Minister Mohamed Mahathir and Singaporean leader Lee Kwan Yew stood as articulate spokesmen for an "Asian position" on human rights which supported the Chinese stance, there is no reason for the Chinese to take a strong lead in organizing Asian opposition to the United States. However, the US War on Terrorism also had an enormous price for China's regional policy: it could not exclude the USA from Southeast Asia after terrorist bombings and acts in the Philippines and Bali. Furthermore, the United States had and is likely to continue to have the capacity for intervention either diplomatically, militarily, or financially in any part of South or Southeast Asia. Thus, China could not effectively exclude this major actor from interacting with its region.

Diplomatic relations with regional states

China's establishment of diplomatic relations with all of its neighbors in Southeast Asia was one of the great achievement of this period of good neighborly relations. In 1988, China's relations with Indonesia, Vietnam, Laos, Singapore were either non-existent, "frozen," or frosty. Within four years, China had flourishing relations with all of its Southeast Asian neighbors, with frequent leadership visits and a variety of exchanges.

Vietnam

The normalization of relations between China and Vietnam saw the resolution of many – but not all – of the remaining issues which had separated the two countries. Most of the issues had been resolved or mitigated by the decline and subsequent collapse of the Soviet Union first as a superpower and then as an international entity. The Vietnamese army pulled out of Cambodia in September 1989 and pulled troops it had in Laos out in spring of 1988. Still, China did not begin to improve its relations with Vietnam until October 1990 and did not formalize the new relationship until November 1991, shortly after the Cambodian peace agreement was signed in Paris, when Communist Party leader Doi Muoi and Premier Vo Van Kiet visited Beijing. Their meetings resolved the debt issue (Vietnam repaid China $200 million) and the ethnic issue, Vietnam agreed to resettle 200,000 ethnic Chinese refugees who had fled or were expelled from Vietnam in 1978 (Sutter 1993: 34). Several agreements were signed between China and Vietnam covering a variety of issues (*ZGWJGL* 1992: 49–51). The visit of Jiang Zemin to Hanoi in 2002 saw all but the fisheries issue put to rest. According to one source familiar with the negotiations, the Vietnamese were quite frank that the economic deterioration of Vietnam after the collapse of the Soviet economy was a primary factor in the negotiations (Zhang Qing 2000: 44–46).

The desperate need for foreign goods and trade was a major factor in Vietnamese foreign policy calculations from 1989 to 1993. During this time, the Soviet and

CMEA economies collapsed, taking with them a vast majority of Vietnam's foreign trade. The United States continued to enforce an economic embargo against Vietnam at the time, leaving the government in Hanoi with only three options only: first, to normalize its relations with its neighbors, particularly China and the ASEAN states (Zhang Qing 2000: 44–46); second, to rapidly improve its relations with Japan, South Korea, Australia, and New Zealand, the advanced industrial nations of the western Pacific, and third, to continue to pursue the possibility of lifting the American economic embargo and normalizing Vietnamese relations with the West (Ni Xiayun 1994b: 11). Vietnam's leaders pursued all three courses, with much greater success among its neighbors than the more distant states.[3]

The Chinese and Vietnamese also share an ideological affinity of market socialism (or authoritarian capitalism, depending upon one's perspective). Both have discarded most aspects of a command economy, first in agriculture and later and only partially in industry, with impressive results (Williams 1992: 39–58). Foreign investment and trade play a major role in both economies, but political freedoms do not. The leaders in both Beijing and Hanoi are acutely aware that they represent two of the most significant remaining communist regimes, and the only two which seem to be economically viable. The Vietnamese reforms were inspired to no small extent by those in China, and the Chinese press has begun to recognize in turn that the Vietnamese have progressed further and faster in their reforms than China has in many important aspects (Ni Xiayun 1994a: 39–42). The two Communist Parties maintain separate party-to-party relations, giving them a second and secret channel of communication which has been used during tensions and crises.

Indonesia

If Sino-Vietnamese relations were normalized in the wake of mass slaughter, it was the death of one man which provided the opportunity for Sino-Indonesian normalization. The death of the Showa Emperor of Japan (Hirohito) in early 1989 would bring both Chinese Foreign Minister Qian Qichen and Indonesian President Suharto to Tokyo for the funeral. The Chinese approached the Indonesians on February 6, proposing a meeting between Qian and Suharto, and, to everyone's surprise, Suharto accepted (McDonald 1989: 10). The major issues appear to have been settled at the February 23 Tokyo meeting, but the devil remained in the details. Talks at the United Nations were held over the process of normalization in November 1989, but Suharto continued to imply that the process might take longer. It was not until July 3, 1990 that the announcement of the resumption of relations was finally made, scheduled for August 8 during Li Peng's visit to Jakarta. Significantly, the Chinese leader was to visit Indonesia before any major Indonesian officials were to visit Beijing, an alteration of the normal pattern of state visits in which the foreigner initiates and the Chinese reciprocate the first visit. An embassy was opened (albeit initially merely a room in a hotel), and relations generally developed smoothly.

Three incidents after 1994 demonstrated that Sino-Indonesian relations were still somewhat delicate. First, Taiwanese President Lee Teng-hui made a "private" visit to Indonesia in February 1994, prompting the Chinese embassy in Jakarta to issue a note protesting the visit. The second incident was a somewhat oblique effort by Indonesia to invite an external actor – Australia – into the security of the region by signing the Agreement on Maintaining Security in December 1995. Although China was not an explicit target of the security exchange, it was confirmed informally to be the primary reason, especially given potential Chinese maritime claims near Indonesia's Natuna islands (Storey 2000: 145). Indonesia's actions in East Timor in 1999 destroyed the basis of its security cooperation with the Australian military, but the effort demonstrated the intentions of Jakarta to invite external actors into Southeast Asia. The third incident was riots that appeared to target ethnic Chinese in 1994 and again in 1998. More on this will be discussed below.

Myanmar

China's relations with its other neighbors were also upgraded during the 1990s, and China's relations with Myanmar (Burma) in particular improved, despite (or because of) the international opprobrium of the State Law and Order Restoration Council (SLORC), the military junta running the country. After the military shot protesters on August 8, 1988 (the "8/8/88 Incident"), the military brushed aside its own civilian puppet government and sought to stage an election its endorsed candidates could win. Instead, the May 1990 election went to Aung San Suu Kyi's National League for Democracy (NLD), and the military tightened its grip. China, following its policy of non-interference, continued to work with the existing Myanmar government, regardless of how it got into power. Chinese government officials visited – 66 delegations in 1990 alone, five of them at vice-ministerial level or higher – and Myanmar became more dependent on trade with China, as discussed below (*ZGWJGL* 1991: 57). In the immediate aftermath of Tiananmen Square massacre, Myanmar was one of the few places in the world where Chinese officials were heartily welcomed with the Pawk Phaw sentiment (胞波 – *baobo*, brotherly).

China also sold Myanmar weapons, with sales in the early 1990s of over US$1 billion in Chinese military equipment to the SLORC regime in Yangon (Rangoon) (Lintner 1993: 26). The terms of the arms deals are obviously secret, but it appears that the total cost for the arms was US$1.3–1.4 billion at "Friendship Prices," of which US$400 million was paid up front, with the remainder to be paid back largely in barter trade. SIPRI's Trend Indicator Values estimate the 1988–2003 amount to be US$1.745 billion (SIPRI TIV 2017).

Thailand

Next door to Myanmar is Thailand, which, like China, was never formally colonized by the West, and which was much wealthier and rapidly-developing in the 1980s. It was not, however, immune from military coups d'état. Another one occurred in 1991, and then came mass demonstrations after elections in May 1992, called "Bloody May." The intervention of the King brought a period of democratic governance, first under Chuan Leekpai and the rise of Thaksin Shinawatra, the popular Prime Minister from 2001–06. In each case, China shifted to recognize each government in turn and to try to maintain its traditionally good relations with Thailand. China also sold Thailand about US$1.2 billion worth of arms in this period (SIPRI TIV 2017). The more important action would come in 1997 when Thailand's currency collapsed and China would step in, discussed below.

Philippines

The fall of the Marcos government in February 1986 during the "People Power" uprising did not have a strong effect on Sino-Philippines relations; the government in Beijing quickly sent its customary congratulations to the new President Corazon Aquino (*ZGWJGL* 1987: 72–73). The idea that such movements would, within three years, topple communist governments around the world and occupy Tiananmen Square was probably inconceivable to China's leadership at the time.

Li Peng visited the Philippines in 1990, and Qiao Shi, Chair of the National People's Congress (NPC) in August 1993. President Jiang Zemin in November 1996, Premier Zhu Rongji in November 1999 and Li Peng (again, this time as Chair of the NPC) in September 2002. Corazon Aquino visited China in April 1988, met all of the relevant leadership, and in emphasizing the strong ties with China, pointed to her paternal great-grandfather who emigrated from Fujian (*ZGWJGL* 1989: 67). Jiang's visit in 1996 was a key event because it both upgraded the relationship, and both sides agreed to "shelve" any disagreements about territorial sovereignty in the South China Sea.

Laos

Laos was a dependent of a dependent of the Soviet Union during the Cold War, supported by Vietnam which was supported by the Soviets, in some ways akin to Nicaragua during that period (dependent on a Soviet dependent, Cuba). The result of Soviet decline was to bring pressure on Vietnam and in turn Laos, which started its own economic reforms in 1986. China and Laos gradually normalized their relations between 1986 and 1989 (Zhang Ruikun 2010: 12). A number of economic agreements were signed in 1989, and when Laos was hit by the economic backwash of the 1997 Thai financial crisis, the Chinese gave an interest-free loan in 1999 (Crispin and Lintner 2000). By 2001, China was the fifth-largest foreign aid donor to Laos (Zhang Ruikun 2010: 13–14). President Khamtai Siphandon visited China in July 2000, and Jiang Zemin returned the favor in November, the first Chinese leader to ever visit Laos. The two sides pledged themselves as, "Committed to the development of the 21st century long-term stability, good neighborliness, mutual trust, comprehensive cooperation" as part of the policy of "good neighborly relations" (Zhang Ruikun 2010: 12). Not all was well in Laos at the time. In 2000, the Lao People's Revolutionary Party appeared to break into pro-Vietnamese and pro-Chinese factions, the latter led by the Foreign Minister

Somsavat Lengsavad, who was ethnic Chinese and who had negotiated the 1999 loan (Crispin and Lintner 2000).

Cambodia

It is one of the more remarkable changes in Chinese diplomacy during this period that China established relations with the government in Phnom Penh after spending a decade supporting the fight against it. The Paris Conference in October 1991 had placed Cambodia under UN administration and thousands of peacekeepers, including over 400 Chinese, sought to rebuild an impoverished and shattered country. Elections in May 1993 allowed the UN to withdraw and left Norodom Ranariddh, Prince Sihanouk's son, as first prime minister and Hun Sen as second prime minister. The old and ailing Sihanouk became king.

Hun Sen seized power in a coup d'état on July 5, 1997 at a time when China was enjoying the smooth takeover of Hong Kong less than a week before, and Thailand's currency crisis was about to turn into a regional disaster. ASEAN foreign ministers were reluctant to interfere with Cambodia's internal affairs, though the body did delay Cambodia's entry into ASEAN. Two scholars characterize the Chinese response: "China adopted an indulgent attitude toward Hun Sen's coup. Hun Sen curried Chinese favor on July 23 by expelling Taiwan's Economic and Cultural Representative Office. On July 25, the Chinese ambassador in Cambodia joined Hun Sen in hosting a discussion with the Chinese community in Phnom Penh aimed at restoring confidence. Hun Sen urged China to provide assistance for infrastructure projects" (Brown and Zasloff 1998: 268).

Malaysia

China's relations with Malaysia in beginning of this period were official, formal and cool. The clash between China and Vietnam in 1988 on Second Johnson Reef did not reassure Malaysia, given its claims in the South China Sea, that China would be peaceful, and one Malaysian strategic analyst prominently stated, "Malaysia has, and will in the foreseeable future, regard China as its greatest threat in one form or another" (quoted in Ngeow 2015: 271). China sought to improve relations. Premier Li Peng made a highly-publicized official visit in December 1990 as part of his diplomatic tour of Southeast Asia, and much like the opening with Indonesia, the Chinese visit was first, and the Malaysian visit came the next year (*ZGWJGL* 1991: 62, 1992: 62–63). Over the next years, Prime Minister Mahathir would make seven visits to China. One factor that improved the relations between Kuala Lumpur and Beijing came in December 1989: the final end of the Malayan Communist Party insurgency, which the Malaysian government suspected of being or having been supported by China. A second improvement was the development of military exchanges between the two countries, starting with visits by the defense ministers in 1992, posting of military attachés in their respective embassies in 1995, and, more broadly, a 1999 Framework for Future Bilateral Cooperation (Ngeow 2015: 272). The third was the further improvement in economic relations, discussed below.

Singapore

Deliberately last in establishing full diplomatic relations with China among the Southeast Asian nations was Singapore, on October 3, 1990. Lee Kuan Yew had stated that in deference to Indonesian sensitivities, Singapore – over 75% ethnic Chinese – would be last among the ASEAN nations to formalize ties with Beijing. The two countries had extensive trade and investment relations and had commercial offices prior to 1990. Lee had visited China in September 1988 and met all of the top leaders (*ZGWJGL* 1989: 64), and Li Peng visited in August 1990, shortly before the establishment of diplomatic relations, and Lee came back to Beijing in October (*ZGWJGL* 1991: 63–65). The relationship continued to improve in the 1990s.

Regional international organizations

China began participating in regional international organizations in the 1990s, and in Southeast Asia this meant working with ASEAN. The Cambodian war divided Southeast Asia at the beginning of this period into two camps: the six ASEAN members (Brunei, Indonesia, Malaysia, Philippines, Singapore, and Thailand), and Vietnam, Cambodia, Laos, and Myanmar. By the end of 1999 all had joined ASEAN: Vietnam in 1995, Laos and Myanmar in 1997, and finally Cambodia in 1999. Beginning in 1994, the ASEAN Regional Forum (ARF) was created to discuss security issues. Economic issues and occasionally other matters are handled in the Asia-Pacific Economic Cooperation (APEC), founded in 1989. A variety of ancillary dialogues had begun such as ASEAN +3, and thus Southeast Asia became arguably the most institutionalized region in Asia, and the center of other regional organizations for East Asia.

One organization that did not come to fruition in this time was the East Asia Grouping, a Malaysian proposal identified with Mahathir bin Mohamad in 1991. The idea was to create an international organization for the region of the (then) six ASEAN states plus China, South Korea and Japan. It would not include the white countries: Australia, New Zealand, and the United States. Japan opposed the idea, and the proposal became the East Asia Economic Caucus within APEC and briefly was revived as the East Asian Summit (EAS) in 2005 but then the USA, Russia, and India joined in 2011 making the organization a substantial overlap with APEC. The initial Malaysian proposal, however, was China's best opportunity to join an exclusionary organization that it had not created but which would keep the USA and others out. It did not pursue the option.

"The ASEAN Way" is a shorthand description of the decision-making processes in ASEAN and its related bodies such as the ARF and ASEAN +3 and ASEAN +1 [China]. It emphasizes consultation and consensus in decision-making and unanimity. Most decisions are expressed by a joint communique. In practice, this can mean that decisions are slow and individual states can effectively veto. But it was an arrangement that all members undertook from the beginning in 1967 and to which the dialogue partners agree as well.

The ARF formed in 1994 in response to desires by Australia and others to have a place where all East Asian countries could at least discuss security matters.[4]

It meets after the regular ASEAN Summit, so the Southeast Asian nations have an advantage of prior discussions among themselves. It does not have a formal secretariat, a charter, or the ability to move beyond the "comfort level" of the least comfortable member, and in practice this limits discussion of important but touchy subjects. China joined with some reluctance. As Chien-peng Chung summarizes,

> Initially reluctant, the PRC agreed to join the ARF because, in the aftermath of the Tiananmen incident, it felt the need to establish its credentials as a responsible international actor, a force for peace, and a good neighbor.... The PRC was also wary of being left out of a regional security organization that included major Asia-Pacific rivals like the USA and Japan.
> (Chung 2010: 49)

China joined, but was reluctant to see the ARF move too far, too quickly. But in 1995, after the Mischief Reef incident, China did agree to follow a peaceful solution in the South China Sea disputes (Chung 2010: 50).

ASEAN Plus Three grew out of the 1997 Asian financial crisis, when China and Japan (along with South Korea) met with Southeast Asian countries to help deal with their currency crises. Over the next two years later, the idea was given further depth and in May 2000 a currency-swap deal known as the Chiang Mai Initiative came into being. The economics of the arrangements are discussed below, but for the purposes of this discussion it is important to note that the ASEAN +3 and ASEAN +1 bodies represents the only fora in which China deals with Southeast Asia without the United States, Australia, New Zealand or Canada present. Not surprisingly, this suits China, and beginning in 2002, China has suggested that the ASEAN +3 group also deal with political and security issues in addition to currency ones. In 2003, China linked it to its Good Neighbor Policy: "At the ASEAN +3 Summit in October 2003, PRC Premier Wen Jiabao formally enunciated the 'Good Neighbor Policy' to realize a 'friendly neighborhood, secure neighborhood, and prosperous neighborhood' for China and its Asian neighbors, which it had already been practicing since the 1980s, albeit then on a largely bilateral basis" (Chung 2010: 74).

China did negotiate with ASEAN as a body the Declaration of Conduct of the parties (DOC) in November 2002, probably the height of its cooperation with Southeast Asia's regional international organization. The significance of the agreement is outlined by Amitav Acharya:

> The most significant words of the DOC concerned an undertaking by the parties to "exercise self-restraint in the conduct of activities that would complicate or escalate disputes and affect peace and stability including, among others, refraining from action of inhabiting on the presently uninhabited islands, reefs, shoals, cays, and other features and to handle their differences in a constructive manner." The DOC did not include a specific commitment to freeze erection of new structures in the disputed area, a commitment sought by the Philippines, but refused by China.
> (Acharya 2015: 68)

The non-binding 2002 DOC was supposed to be followed by a Code of Conduct (COC), a detailed agreement on how to interact and behave in the South China Sea, but specifically did not propose to resolve the issue of territorial sovereignty. In October 2003, China acceded to the Treaty of Amity and Cooperation (TAC) in Southeast Asia with ASEAN as a body (*CFA* 2004: 381–382). It was to be the pinnacle of China's institutionally linked cooperative approach to its Southeast Asian neighbors. By 2005, China would begin to back away from multilateralism with ASEAN, especially over territorial issues.

Hegemon's expatriates, co-ethnics

The deep suspicion of some Southeast Asian governments toward ethnic Chinese residing in their countries has been discussed in previous chapters. Beginning in the 1990s, this issue began to be gradually resolved, with the Chinese government moving away from advocating for ethnic Chinese, and Southeast Asian governments moving away from seeing ethnic Chinese as communist agitators and rootless millionaires.

Diplomatic relations notwithstanding, anti-Chinese incidents continued to occur in Indonesia. In a 1994 riot in the Sumatran city of Medan, crowds attacked ethnic Chinese persons and property. The Chinese Ministry of Foreign Affairs issued a statement expressing "concern" about the incident, to which the Indonesians responded sharply, the Justice Minister saying, "China had better mind its own internal affairs. Events such as took place in Medan happen in many other countries" (quoted in Sukma 1994: 36). The issue arose again in 1998 when riots broke out in Jakarta, and roving gangs were systematically raping ethnic Chinese women. Once again, the Chinese Ministry of Foreign Affairs was left between the horns of the dilemma: whether to treat this as an entirely internal Indonesian affair, thus preserving the "Good Neighbor Policy" or to issue a statement protesting the inability of the Indonesian government to prevent these incidents from happening, even if it meant "intervening" in Jakarta's business. The issue was undecided for several weeks, and it was other Chinese groups – including the government in Taipei – that broke the silence by criticizing the Indonesian government's inaction in the face of outrages against ethnic Chinese. Once a competitive regime began to make representations about the situation in Indonesia, the Chinese communist government issued its own statement protesting the situation, and China's Xinhua News Agency stated that "[i]t is an unshirkable responsibility of the Chinese government to do its utmost to show concern for and give assistance to Indonesian Chinese" (Zha 2000: 557–575; Bolt 2000: 123). Sensitivity to issues of sovereignty remains acute for both countries.

In Malaysia, ethnic relations between Chinese and other citizens of Malaysia improved during this time, though with some notable tensions. As mentioned, the Malayan Communist Party's second insurgency ended in December 1989. The group's guerillas had been a major threat to the government in the 1950s during the First Malayan Emergency, and then started a new insurgency in 1968, with far less success. China's support for the insurgency during this second time was minimal but the overwhelming number of the MCP insurgents were ethnic Chinese, either from Malaysia or Thailand, and that led to Malay suspicions of ethnic Chinese. The restrictions that had been placed on young Chinese-Malaysian visiting mainland were eased (ZGWJGL 1990: 61, 1991: 62).

Provision of security public goods

In one respect, China did provide modest public security goods in Southeast Asia, beginning with the UNTAC in Cambodia in 1992, in which China provided over 400 troops. In East Timor in 1999, China voted in favor of UN Security Council Resolution 1272, which authorized a PKO even though it was clear that Indonesia was very reluctant to allow such an intervention in the escalating crisis.

Economic

If China's contribution to public goods in the security realm of Southeast Asia during this period was minimal, its contributions to the economic realm were maximal. At a critical time in 1997–99, when the Asian financial crisis was wrecking the economies of the region, China stepped forward and lent billions of dollars that Japan seemed unable to – and the IMF unwilling to – lend to desperate countries in Southeast Asia. That China's trade with the world grew enormously during this period is well known; its trade with Southeast Asia also grew, and this region became more important to the Chinese economy from 1988–2003, just as China became much more important for Southeast Asian economies, many increasingly bound into Japanese-managed production chains and networks.

For all of the dramatic rise in capabilities seen during this period and as outlined in Chapter 2, there was also a rise in vulnerability for China: the economy of China began to consume imported raw materials at an accelerating rate. The autarkic policies of the Maoist period were discarded, and China became a net importer of a number of strategic materials, particularly petroleum and iron ore. Given world prices during this period, it made sense: OPEC had effectively collapsed in 1986, and petroleum prices made foreign purchases easier at exactly the time China's economy was starting to boom. Crude oil dropped by half from 1984 to 1986, to around $14/bbl, and during the 1990s remained fairly low. China became a net crude oil importer in 1996, as domestic production – though growing steadily – failed to match skyrocketing demand. Beginning in 2000, however, the price went up again and Chinese imports by volume almost doubled in a short space of time, from 36 million tons per year (mty) to 72 mty (Zha 2005: 40–41); Beijing's leadership began to recognize that energy security was a pressing long-term problem involving diversification of sources and import routes.

Trade

The growth in trade between China and Southeast Asian nations is shown in Table 4.2:

Table 4.2 China: total trade with Southeast Asia, 1988–2003

China: total trade with Southeast Asia, 1988–2003 (current US$, million)

	Brunei	Cambodia	Indonesia	Laos	Malaysia	Myanmar	Philippines	Singapore	Thailand	Vietnam
1988	$9	$1	$918	$21	$878	$271	$404	$2,512	$1,144	$0
1989	$12	$3	$805	$16	$1,045	$314	$322	$3,191	$1,256	$8
1990	$12	$3	$1,250	$21	$1,222	$373	$295	$2,865	$1,240	$3
1991	$13	$3	$1,884	$13	$1,332	$392	$384	$3,077	$1,269	$32
1992	$15	$13	$2,026	$32	$1,475	$390	$365	$3,268	$1,319	$179
1993	$11	$22	$2,139	$41	$1,788	$489	$495	$4,892	$1,351	$399
1994	$16	$36	$2,641	$40	$2,741	$512	$748	$5,044	$2,024	$533
1995	$35	$57	$3,491	$54	$3,346	$767	$1,306	$6,898	$3,363	$1,054
1996	$39	$70	$3,717	$31	$3,620	$659	$1,387	$7,366	$3,150	$1,151
1997	$33	$121	$4,518	$29	$4,406	$643	$1,662	$8,707	$3,507	$1,436
1998	$9	$162	$3,633	$26	$4,269	$595	$2,016	$8,126	$3,593	$1,241
1999	$8	$160	$4,830	$32	$5,279	$508	$2,287	$8,563	$4,216	$1,318
2000	$74	$224	$7,464	$41	$8,045	$621	$3,142	$10,821	$6,624	$2,466
2001	$165	$240	$6,735	$62	$9,429	$632	$3,567	$10,938	$7,216	$2,815
2002	$263	$276	$7,928	$64	$14,271	$862	$5,259	$14,023	$8,558	$3,264
2003	$346	$321	$10,229	$109	$20,128	$1,077	$9,400	$19,352	$12,655	$4,634

Source: IMF DOTS (2017).

Compared to Northeast Asia and the United States, of course, Southeast Asia was less important in China's total trade. The former averaged 23% of China's trade in 1988–2003 and the latter about 14%. But Southeast Asia rose steadily from 6% to 9.2% of China's trade during this time, much greater than Central Asia or South Asia's proportions. One of the trade partners began with no trade with China: Vietnam. By the end of the period its total trade was over $4.6 billion annually. The dependency of Southeast Asian countries during this time on China was both as a source of goods and as a sales destination. All grew during the period, though most remained under ten percent except Myanmar, which was particularly dependent on Chinese imports from 1990 to 2003. These trends seen here would continue to grow into the next period. China also proposed the China-ASEAN Free Trade agreement in 2000, which was agreed to in 2003, though implemented only in 2010, discussed in Chapter 7.

Provision of public goods

Regional leadership also involves a certain amount of sacrifice on behalf of the regional cause, and in this respect, China contributed significantly during the 1997–99 financial crisis in the region, pumping over $2 billion to Thailand to support the baht, supporting additional financial aid from international organizations, and by avoiding the temptation to devalue their own currency at a time when the baht, ringgit, rupiah, and won were all in apparent free-fall:

> When Southeast Asia was dragged down in the crisis with Thailand as the main actor, there was a very great risk that China too would be pulled in. The logical action from China, bearing in mind China's earlier inaction, would have been an isolationist move to protect itself from the crisis. . . . China had a relatively strong economy with a very strong currency reserve that potentially could keep China out of the crisis and most of its loans were long-term loans with sound bases. The Chinese action was somewhat surprising. China was one of the main supporters of the grant of Special Drawing Rights (SDR) 2.9 billion (US $3.9 b) to Thailand in August and moreover pledged US$2 billion (China and HK) to support Thailand . . . China also refused to devalue its currency during the crisis to avoid spreading the problem . . . and to create a platform for regional leadership. . . . In addition to the financial question marks, China could create a platform for regional leadership by acting as the regional stabilizer. China reacted rapidly to the situation and was one of the first to give credits to Thailand on the eve of the crisis. Japan was slower and, despite its very high stakes in the region, reluctant to give credits to individual states. China was consequently perceived by the states in the crisis as being more generous than Japan, despite the fact that Japan gave substantially larger credits.
>
> (Swanstrom 2001: 136–137)

This provision of public goods was and still is one of most important acts of China during this active phase of its relations to Southeast Asia. The Malaysians in 2015 still refer to this and blamed Western monetary speculators such as George Soros and "Washington Consensus" policies. Other regional hegemons have provided monetary assistance, though the United States usually works through the IMF and thus is linked to the highly unpopular conditionality of those terms. The Soviets had forgiven Polish government debt in 1956 when it ran out of money, but earned little thanks (Chafetz 1993: 24).

China also began financing a joint ASEAN-China fund for projects. During the 2003 ASEAN summit, Chinese Premier Wen Jiabao hit upon a phrase that was meant to deal with the undeniable size of China within the region: "A Friendly Elephant" (Lee 2001: 66). How friendly it actually would be is the subject of the later chapters.

Central Asia

China lost a neighbor on Christmas Day 1991, and it gained six, the newly independent states of Central Asia: Turkmenistan, Uzbekistan, the Russian Federation (the Soviet successor state), Kazakhstan, Kyrgyzstan, and Tajikistan. It also gained three new international borders in the process, with the latter three. In the two other instances of regional hegemons suddenly acquiring newly independent neighbors, South Africa in the 1960s and the Russian Federation in the 1990s, the results have not been particularly harmonious. China's response was a marked contrast of cooperation and the construction of a multilateral security and economic institution, the Shanghai Cooperation Organization (SCO).

Security

China's relations with Central Asia during this period underwent a complete transformation, from non-existent to active, and from a conventional military vulnerability to potential Soviet invasion to an unconventional vulnerability linked to ethnic relations in the far western provincial area of Xinjiang. And unlike China's relations with Southeast Asia in which Beijing sought to limit the multilateral nature of interactions initially, only to embrace them at the turn of the century, China advocated a multilateral institution in the form of the Shanghai Five and later SCO fairly early on.

Resistance to Chinese governance in Xinjiang was not new, but incidents continued, despite economic and social reforms occurring in China in general. The first incident that might have been described as Uighur resistance was an April 1990 uprising in Baren, near Kashgar, possibly with heavy casualties. These incidents were not reported in the Chinese media. That changed in 1996 when the government in Beijing acknowledged what was happening, and posed it as part of a larger international problem (Gill and Murphy 2005: 24). After riots in Yining (Gulja) in 1997, the government in Beijing applied more force. China has used overwhelming numbers of paramilitary People's Armed Police (PAP, 中国人民武装警察部队 *Zhongguo renmin wuzhuang jingdui*) to monitor potential trouble spots and an impressive array of technological tools to monitor the situation in

Xinjiang. A series of bombs in 1992–98 killed several people in Ürümqi, Kashgar (Kashi), Hotan (Hetian), and targeted assassinations of government, party and government-sanctioned religious leaders, both Han Chinese and Uighurs, arson, and riots all pointed to what Chinese leaders saw as a serious threat to domestic stability ("Major terrorist cases" 2001). Most serious was the rioting in Ghulja (Yining) in 1997, during which Chinese security forces killed over 150 (Wayne 2009: 250). This marked a peak in activity in Xinjiang, which receded for a while, only to pick up again in the 21st century, which will be discussed in Chapter 8. But it is in this context that China's relations with its new neighbors must be considered, since they were smaller, weaker, and less capable than the Soviet state from which they descended.

Territorial disputes

The first step toward controlling a border is finding where exactly the border is. The Soviet Union and China had negotiated a border treaty between 1987 and 1991. The issues surrounding the northeastern Russian boundary are addressed above in the chapter section on Northeast Asia. The northwest Sino-Russian boundary is a 46-km section that separates Kazakhstan and Mongolia, which was not in dispute. The difficulty in 1992 lay in the fact that none of China's new contiguous neighbors, Kazakhstan, Kyrgyzstan, and Tajikistan, had any access to the maps and treaty documents that the Soviets had negotiated: those were all in Moscow's keeping. Thus, joint discussions made sense (Yahuda 2008: 77). In 1998, a multilateral summit was held which produced the first border agreements between China and the new Central Asia republics, which were then to be approved by their respective bilateral partners.

China and Kazakhstan share the longest border in Central Asia, 1,765 km. There was a dispute over 187km² and in the 1998 Sino-Kazakhstani agreement, China got 43% and Kazakhstan 57% of the disputed area (Blank 2013: 97). Kyrgyzstan's border with China is shorter than Kazakhstan's at 1,063km, but more controversial. The Kyrgyzstan-China border is near to Aksu (Akesu) and Kashgar in China, and China had a large historical claim along the border. In the 1999 agreement, Bishkek ceded 1,240km² to China. This led to rumors that the Kyrgyz president, Askar Akayev, had personally profited from the deal, and in early 2002, protests about the alleged corruption in Kyrgyzstan were violently repressed (Marat 2013: 127), but the controversy would eventually lead to the 2005 "Tulip Revolution," a seminal event for China's relations with Central Asia which will be dealt with in Chapter 8.

China's border with Tajikistan is 477km long and in some of the world's most remote locations in the Pamir mountains. As one analyst characterized it, ". . . the land in question in the Tajik-China case was not hotly contested. It concerns a remote and sparsely populated region, not a vital portion of Tajik territory. Nor is it inherently an important area for strategic or commercial purposes for China" (Gleason 2013: 283). Border negotiations were concluded in 1999 with China receiving 200km² of disputed territory and then modified in a 2002 agreement to

1122km². But it would take until 2011 for the Tajikistani parliament to ratify the agreement, given its concession of any land to China.

Military intervention

China did not intervene in the newly independent countries of Central Asia. It did cooperate with the governments through the informal "Shanghai Five" and the formal Shanghai Cooperation Organization in joint military exercises, training, and anti-terrorism work, discussed below.

External major powers

The Russian Federation may have lost Central Asia, but Russian influence there remained high after the collapse of the USSR in a variety of aspects. Russian attention from the collapse until the mid-1990s was generally internal, focusing on the economic crisis and looking to the West for inspiration or at least help. Central Asia returned to the Kremlin's agenda when President Boris Yeltsin promoted Yevgeny Primakov first as Foreign Minister (1996–98) and then as Prime Minister (1998–99). His successor, Vladimir Putin first as Prime Minister and then as President continued to see the former Soviet republics as areas of importance where Russian influence could and should be paramount (Mankoff 2012: 244–247). All of the leaders of the newly independent states of Kazakhstan, Kyrgyzstan, Tajikistan, Turkmenistan, and Uzbekistan were former Soviet communist leaders, spoke Russian, and governed states that were organized along Soviet lines. All but Tajikistan had significant ethnic Russian minorities, though these would gradually decline as many would emigrate to the Russian Federation. The Russians continued to occupy a military base in Tajikistan, where the 201st Motor Rifle Division was stationed after the war in Afghanistan, and then during the civil war in Tajikistan between 1992 and 1997 as part of the CIS Peacekeeping Force. Russian economic ties were also strong in Central Asia, helped by existing transportation and commercial networks. The Russians also monopolized the Central Asian countries' arms purchases, and China sold no weapons to these countries during this period (SIPRI TIV 2017).

After September 11, 2001, the USA became a Central Asian power: it invaded Afghanistan, overthrew the Taliban government, fought the remnants of Al-Qaeda, and stayed. Transport into land-locked Afghanistan was essential, since the United States does not fight wars without an enormous logistical effort. Pakistan was naturally the first and most important approach, but access to the northern areas of Afghanistan and air transit rights were needed as well. The USA and Kyrgyzstan reached an agreement for the use of what would be later called Manas Air Base in December 2001, for transport and air-combat purposes. The USA reached a similar agreement with Uzbekistan for the use of Karshi-Khanabad Air Base. Other NATO partners in International Security Assistance Force had Central Asian air bases as well.

China's initial reaction to the developments was mixed. On the one hand, it perceived itself as having a common cause with the United States: fighting Islamic terrorism. Michael Yahuda summarizes this attitude:

> Notwithstanding the views expressed in some Chinese strategic journals that China faced a renewed danger of encirclement by the United States, the Chinese government made no objections to the physical presence of American power for the first time near its vulnerable Western region of Xinjiang and, in fact, it lent its support to the American defeat of the Taliban in Afghanistan and the American attempt to establish a democratic government there. Beijing sent a lone police officer to serve with UN peace-keepers in Afghanistan . . . his presence spoke volumes about China's official approval of the American-led venture.
> (Yahuda 2008: 82)

The United States in 2002 did China a favor in return and declared the East Turkestan Islamic Movement to be a terrorist organization, one of a handful of organizations seeking to end Chinese presence in Xinjiang ("East Turkestan"). The US State Department summarized its dual position, however:

> Previous Chinese crackdowns on ethnic Uighurs and others in Xinjiang raised concerns about possible human rights abuses . . . while the United States designated the East Turkestan Islamic Movement as a terrorist organization . . . [but] the war on terrorism must not be used as a substitute for addressing legitimate social and economic aspirations.
> (US State Department, Office of the Coordinator for Counterterrorism 2003)

China was also concerned, however, that with the USA making bilateral agreements with Kyrgyzstan and Uzbekistan without reference to the SCO, that body was becoming a marginal player in the rapidly changing strategic situation in Central Asia. China held joint military exercises with Kyrgyzstan in 2002, and in 2003, multilateral military exercises were held in Kazakhstan (Wang 2008: 108–109). Ultimately, the American presence there would become a major issue for China, but not until 2005, which will be dealt with in Chapter 8.

Diplomatic relations with regional states

When the Soviet Union broke up in the wake of the abortive August 1991 coup, China was quick to extend recognition and invitations to the leaders of the newly-independent central Asian states, many of whom visited in 1992. Premier Li Peng returned the favor in April 1994 with a visit through Uzbekistan, Turkmenistan, Kazakhstan, and Kyrgyzstan (FBIS 1994c: 15). Jiang Zemin visited in July 1996, and his speech at Almaty in Kazakhstan was a major statement on the importance of China's neighborly relations.

Russian Federation

No longer burdened by Cold War enmity, the Chinese and the Russians got along well after the collapse of the Soviet Union, though the economic distress, social disarray and political chaos of post-Soviet Russia was an object lesson for China's post-Tiananmen leaders in why opposing democracy movements was absolutely necessary. Russia was also the first of China's neighbors to become a "partner," first part of the "Constructive Partnership" in 1994 and then the "Strategic Partnership of Coordination" in 1996. Trade fluctuated between the two, but by 2001 exceeded $10 billion total and continued to rise. In July 2001, the two sides signed the Treaty of Good-Neighborliness and Friendly Cooperation Between the People's Republic of China and the Russian Federation, which was a twenty-year treaty. China also purchased $15.5 billion of dollars' worth of military technology from the Russians (SIPRI TIV 2017).

Regional international organizations

The origins of the SCO lie in the collapse of the USSR. Following Mikhail S. Gorbachev's visit to Beijing in 1989, the Soviet Union and China had undertaken a variety of Confidence-Building Measures (CBMs) along their borders, pulling back troops, and reducing the aggressive patrolling that had previously been taking place. The CBMs continued under the new governments, and in 1996 Russia, China, Kyrgyzstan, Kazakhstan and Tajikistan signed the "Agreement on Confidence-Building in the Military Field Along the Border Areas," and the grouping was nicknamed the "Shanghai Five" after the summit meeting in that city. This was followed by the 1997 "Agreement on Reducing Each Other's Military Forces Along the Border Regions" (Yahuda 2008: 77). To the extent that the "Shanghai Five" could be considered an organization, it was a summit-only one; it featured meetings among the heads of state only in its Moscow (1997), Almaty (1998), Bishkek (1999), and Dushanbe (2000) summits.

The shift to the SCO occurred in Shanghai in June 2001 (before 9/11 and the US invasion of Afghanistan), when Uzbekistan joined the group and the SCO was formally created. Turkmenistan is the lone hold-out, though it is often invited to SCO meetings as a guest. The difference of this approach is well-summarized by Wang Jianwei:

> Northeast Asia and Central Asia have had little tradition of multilateralism, due to the polarizing effect of the Cold War . . . China could deal bilaterally with the Soviet Union as well as other former Soviet republics bordering China. But China chose a different approach. Here the issue of border disputes common to all parties involved facilitated this choice. . . . To a great extent, multilateralism in this area is more an unintended result of practice rather than of design.
> (Wang 2008: 105)

China was a major force behind the increasing institutionalization of the SCO. The organizational momentum of the SCO is largely due to Chinese enthusiasm.

As Song Weiqing observes, "... this organization is largely a Chinese initiative and ... China plays a 'leading role' in the SCO process. China is clearly more motivated to promote the SCO than the other members" (Song 2014: 87). The Secretariat formally opened in January 2004, headquartered in Beijing, and with formal meeting mechanisms for the heads of state, heads of government, foreign ministers, heads of agencies.

A center point of the SCO from early on was the fighting of the "Three Evils" of terrorism, separatism, and extremism. Chinese leaders were particularly interested in setting up a joint anti-terrorism mechanism. This would be accomplished with the Regional Counter-Terrorism Structure (RCTS but also called the Regional Anti-Terrorist Structure, or RATS), which was agreed to in 1999 but not implemented until 2004 and is discussed in Chapter 8. China did engage in a bilateral joint counter-terror military exercises with Kyrgyzstan in October 2002, the first joint military exercise China had participated in, and a broader exercise in 2003 in both Kazakhstan and Xinjiang involving hostage rescue, terrorist base destruction, air drops, and aircraft interception (Yang Tao 2012: 97).

Why, then, did China move from its previous "hub-and-spokes" style of bilateralism to an institutionalized multilateral approach in the SCO? Part of the answer lies in the increasing asymmetry of China and its neighbors. As noted, the material capabilities of China vis-à-vis its neighbors went from a substantial advantage in the early 1990s when the Soviet Union broke up to overwhelming by the beginning of the 21st century. As China's relative power grew, the potential for fear, resentment, and counter-balancing was also present. Thus, creating and further institutionalizing an international organization in which each member, even tiny Tajikistan, sits as an equal helps relieve that potential reaction. But the process of building the SCO also helped change Chinese attitudes toward multilateralism. As Yahuda (2008) points out:

> It was the experience of cultivating better relations with neighbouring states that led China towards the embracing of multilateral associations of states as vehicles within which to work with others on cooperative endeavours and within which it could also enhance its own interests. In the process, China has not only changed fundamentally the character of its relations with neighbouring countries, but it has also begun to challenge, and perhaps change, the character of international order within its region.
>
> (75)

Hegemon's expatriates, co-ethnics

In the late 1980s, cross-border migration from China to the Kirghiz SSR (now Kyrgyzstan) developed on a small scale, primarily involving Chinese vegetable farmers coming to state farms on a seasonal contract basis. Chinese "shuttle traders" also came to trade in Naryn, but generally did not stay long. After the collapse of the Soviet Union, Chinese shuttle traders competed with Kyrgyz shuttle traders for a while, but as time went on, Chinese traders won out (Zhaparov 2008: 81–83).

122 *The "Good Neighbor"*

Shuttle trade in general started to die out by the late 1990s as regular large-scale corporate trade took over.

Many of the "Chinese" who acted as cross-border traders at this point were ethnic Uighurs from Xinjiang, who often worked in family-related groups and partnered with Dunggan (Hui – ethnic Chinese Muslim citizens of the USSR, especially Kirghiz SSR) (Zhaparov 2008: 83–84) or Kyrgyz. These traders included Rebiya Kadeer, a Uighur business woman who became quite wealthy in the process and was a member of China's National People's Congress until her arrest in 1999 and expulsion in 2005.

Provision of security public goods

The first and most important part of providing security public goods is reducing the threat of war, deliberate or accidental. In Central Asia, this was started with the CBMs that first the Soviets then the Russians and Chinese undertook beginning in 1989 of pulling troops back from their borders, meetings of military leaders, exchange of information, and, eventually, the 1996 Agreement on Confidence-Building in the Military Field Along the Border Areas, and then the 1997 Agreement on Reducing Each Other's Military Forces Along the Border Regions.

The second provision of public security goods is the Chinese participation in SCO-sponsored military exercises, which began modestly in 2003 but have grown gradually in the 21st century. But the real provider of security public goods in the region remains Russia, primarily unilaterally or through the CSTO.

Economic

Trade

It is no mere coincidence that the first major Chinese official to visit the newly independent Central Asian republics in January 1992 was Li Lanqing, the Minister of Foreign Trade; China recognized the potential of Central Asia to supply or transit energy to western China and to buy Chinese goods in return. Transportation was (and is) a major problem, and China was seeking to improve communications with Central Asia long before Xi Jinping's One Belt One Road proposal in 2013.

Table 4.3 shows the total trade China did with Russia and the Central Asian republics from 1992–2003. Trade figures for 1992–93 must be taken with some caution, but by 1994 they are consistent (if not reliable).

The importance of Russia in China's regional trade is clear, and only Kazakhstan has more than $1 billion in trade among the Central Asian republics. But compared to Northeast Asia and Southeast Asia, this was not as important to China's overall world trade: it averaged 2.5% of total China trade during this period.

The data from 1992 are the Russian Federation only. For Russia, Chinese imports begin around 2.5% of its total imports in 1994, and within nine years more than double to 5.8%, a trend we will see increase even more dramatically in

Table 4.3 China: total trade with Central Asia, 1992–2003

China: total trade with Central Asia, 1992–2003 (current US$, million)

	Kazakhstan	Kyrgyzstan	Russia	Tajikistan	Turkmenistan	Uzbekistan
1992	$363	$16	$5,849	$3	$4	$52
1993	$435	$102	$7,677	$12	$5	$54
1994	$336	$98	$5,044	$3	$11	$134
1995	$391	$231	$5,473	$24	$18	$118
1996	$460	$106	$6,849	$12	$11	$187
1997	$527	$107	$6,119	$20	$14	$201
1998	$636	$198	$5,459	$19	$13	$90
1999	$1,139	$135	$5,720	$8	$9	$40
2000	$1,557	$178	$8,003	$17	$16	$51
2001	$1,289	$119	$10,674	$11	$33	$58
2002	$1,956	$202	$11,927	$12	$88	$132
2003	$3,286	$314	$15,761	$39	$83	$347

Source: IMF DOTS (2017).

the next period. In the meanwhile, Russia is becoming more dependent on exports, primarily commodities but also weapons, to China, from 4.5% to 6.2%. China, on the other hand, saw its proportion of both exports to and imports from Russia go down. The amounts of trade with all of the other countries, except Kazakhstan, were fairly small. Russia maintained a substantial market share in most of these countries during this period. Kazakhstan imported 43% of its goods from Russia on average during the period, but began to sell more and more of its commodities to China, eventually over 13%. Kyrgyzstan saw its imports from China go up, whereas Tajikistan became more dependent on Russia during this period. Turkmenistan did remarkably little trade with China during this time, though that would change once a natural gas pipeline was constructed. Uzbekistan saw its trade with Russia decline as a percentage of its overall imports and exports, though it was still the dominant partner. China's trade with Uzbekistan was beginning to grow, however.

South Asia

China's relations across the Himalayas in the late 1980s stood where they had been for a long while. They got on famously with the Pakistanis, poorly with the Indians, and episodic openings to other smaller countries in India's neighborhood were often discouraged by New Delhi's sense of regional exclusion. By the beginning of the 21st century, relations with all actors had improved, but the fundamentals of Sino-Indian rivalry remained, somewhat reduced by diplomacy and trade. Of all of the regions in which China sought to use its Good Neighbor Policy, this one had the greatest challenges.

Security

This period opens with the same strategic triangle that existed in 1962: Pakistan and India often on the brink of war, China staunchly backing Pakistan, now much weaker due to the loss of Bangladesh in 1971. But the decline of the Soviet Union and after 1989 its withdrawal from Afghanistan and the easing of the Cold War also meant that China had an opportunity to try to lessen its tensions with India, while simultaneously maintaining its friendship with Pakistan. To a substantial degree, China achieved this during the period in question.

The "delinking" of China's relations with Pakistan from its relations with India was a key goal for Beijing, which had tried to approach the Indians as far back as 1981 on the proposal but had been rebuffed. Then in 1987 the Indians began to warm to the idea, and after Li Peng's (1991) trip to India, the joint communique made it clear that Sino-Indian relations were not dependent on or directed at other countries (Garver 2001: 220–222). The Soviets were out of Afghanistan; China had established relations with India and still had its ties with Pakistan intact.

Territorial disputes

The territorial disputes between China and India that led to a war in 1962 had not been resolved since. China's relations with India have improved considerably from 1986–1987, when the government in New Delhi granted state status to Union Territory of Arunachal Pradesh (prior to 1972 the North-East Frontier Agency) in the disputed region between China and India, causing China to send troops to the region in protest (Chanda 1987: 42–43). The Sino-Indian joint border commission met periodically to resolve the claims, and the two sides signed an agreement during Rao's visit undertaking to peacefully resolve their disputed border, and setting up regular meetings in border areas between the two countries' armed forces (Ma Jiali 1994: 28).

Military intervention

After the Soviet withdrawal from Afghanistan, China's support for the Mujahideen ended, and China did not intervene in any other areas in South Asia. Bertil Lintner's careful 2015 study of external support for various rebels such as the Naxilites in India shows that China had no further interest in subversion (267–268). China was simply interested in relations with established governments.

External major powers

With the Soviet withdrawal from Afghanistan, and its collapse two years later, South Asia's strategic environment changed substantially. The Cold War was over, and it was not yet clear what would replace it. The role of the United States in Central Asia has been discussed above; the same can be said of South Asia, where after 9/11, it was forced to be expedient in working with Pakistan despite sanctions imposed on it and India in 1998 after their nuclear weapons tests.

Diplomatic relations with regional states

India

Prime Minister Rajiv Gandhi paid an official visit to Beijing in December 1988 and the two sides established a joint working group to deal with the border issue (Malik 1995: 318). Li Peng visited India in 1991 after the elections there, and both India's President R. Venkataraman and Prime Minister P. V. Narasimha Rao visited China in May 1992 and September 1993, respectively. Extensive border trade resumed for the first time since the 1962 war. Issues remained, to be sure, in the Sino-Indian relationship, particularly China's growing military links with Myanmar, but the two countries began to enjoy their best relations since Zhou Enlai's trip to New Delhi in 1954, when the Chinese first articulated their "Five Principles of Peaceful Co-existence." In November 1996, Jiang Zemin made a state visit and established "All-around constructive partnership relations" (*Zhongguo waijiao* [hereafter *ZGWJ*] 1997: 115).

Relations cooled during the BJP government (1998–2004) when in May 1998, India conducted its first nuclear weapons tests, prompting Pakistan to respond with its own.[5] Since the Indian test was first, China condemned it roundly, as well as the BJP government, pointing to the "China threat" as its justification (*ZGWJ* 1999: 100).

Pakistan

China condemned the Indian nuclear test in May 1998 but not the Pakistani response. China's comparative silence about Pakistan's nuclear tests was due to its covert program to transfer critical nuclear weapons and missile technologies to Pakistan during this time. Doing so not only showed the Pakistanis that China still was their staunch defender, it was giving Islamabad the ultimate protection (Garver 2001: 220–225). China also sold or transferred $3.8 billion in conventional weapons to Pakistan during this time, out of total Pakistani imports of $9.7 billion (SIPRI TIV 2017). Indicative of Pakistan's unwavering support of China's leaders, top Pakistani leaders including Foreign Secretary Humayun Khan visited Beijing right after the Tiananmen massacre and Li Peng's first foreign visit after that was to Pakistan, something the Chinese official media pointed to as evidence of the firmness of Pakistani support (*ZGWJ* 1990: 68). The summer of 1989 was also a time when India-Pakistan relations were improving, and Rajiv Gandhi visited Pakistan and met with Benazir Bhutto, the first such visit in almost thirty years, and the only time the son and daughter of previous prime ministers have met as prime ministers themselves.

Jiang Zemin made a state visit to Pakistan in December 1996 after visiting India, touting the Good Neighbor Policy along the way, saying "A century of good neighborliness creates a bright future" (世代睦邻友好、共创美好未来/*shidai mulin youhao, gong chuang meihao weilai*) (*ZGWJ* 1997: 95). But the Chinese backing of Pakistan would only go so far. In 1999, the Pakistani government began a limited war in Kargil, on the Indian side of the Line of Control in Kashmir, apparently hoping to create a crisis that would raise the Kashmir issue to the UN Security Council. This gambit vastly underestimated Indian military resolve and overestimated Chinese backing. In three months of tough fighting, the Indian army cleared the Pakistanis from the heights they had occupied, and though China continued to express its friendship with Pakistan, its position in public statements was carefully neutral (Garver 2001: 239). But when General Pervez Musharraf staged a coup d'état in October 1999, China had little reaction other than to recognize him and continue the relationship (*ZGWJ* 2000: 105).

Bangladesh

The foreign relations of Bangladesh are highly politicized between the two major parties, the Awami League and the Bangladesh Nationalist Party (BNP), the leaders of which have alternated as Prime Ministers since 1991. The BNP has a reputation as being more hostile to India than the Awami League, and was in power 1991–96 and again from 2001 to 2006. The Awami League government, however, was also careful not to damage good relations with China, and Sheikh Hasina Wajid, the new Prime Minister, made her first official foreign visit in office to China (*ZGWJ* 1997: 111). China had begun to supply Bangladesh with military equipment, US$862 million during this period, most of it from 1988–95 (SIPRI TIV 2017). Military exchanges between Chinese and Bangladeshi military services continued after 1996, and Bangladesh would continue to try to use its Chinese connection to avoid being completely dominated by India. And China would continue to develop this relationship to keep its doors open in South Asia.

Nepal

Nestled in the foothills of the Himalayas between China and India, Nepal is of critical strategic importance to India, which sees it as a shield against China. More than any other country in South Asia, India seeks to limit Sino-Nepalese relations, especially military relations. The period began with the Nepalese government finding out just how seriously the Indians took Chinese arms sales to Kathmandu. When trucks with $20 million worth of small arms and anti-aircraft guns arrived from China in June 1988, India reacted: in March 1989 it shut down almost all trade with Nepal, and Nepal's economic situation became dire. If Nepal had expected China to come to its rescue, it was disappointed, despite having been warned that Chinese transportation into Nepal could not make up for an Indian blockade. Nor was Chinese rhetorical support particularly strong, though Li Peng did visit Kathmandu in November 1989 and offered sympathy for the "difficulties" that Nepal was experiencing. Chinese officials were also visiting India during this episode, and there was little that China could do for Nepal's economy, given the limited transportation links between Tibet and Nepal (Garver 2001: 154–160).

The "Good Neighbor" 127

Bhutan

The tiny, isolated kingdom of Bhutan had (and has) limited relations with any countries other than India. The 1949 treaty governing the two countries' relations gave India a primary role in determining Thimpu's contacts with the outside world, though in 1984, it allowed direct talks between Beijing and Thimpu, but the two did not establish diplomatic relations nor a border agreement (Garver 2001: 182–185).

Sri Lanka

India and Sri Lanka had in 1987–90 experienced a traumatic episode during the Sri Lankan civil war; India had intervened in the Sri Lankan rebellion of the Tamils and in 1987 signed a peace accord with the Sri Lankan government in which the latter recognized Indian security concerns and made concessions to the Tamil minority. An Indian peacekeeping force arrived to disarm the rebel groups, but one group, the LTTE, refused, and the Indian army found itself in a long counter-insurgency it had not planned on. Indian forces pulled out in 1990. Although Chinese analysts were critical of Indian coercion of Sri Lanka in the 1987 peace accord in private, Chinese reporting on the conflict was generally neutral (Garver 2001: 307–309).

Afghanistan

After the Soviet withdrawal from Afghanistan in 1989, China's relations with Kabul were minimal, largely because the Najibullah government was seen (accurately) as a Soviet installation. It fell in 1992, and the Taliban took over Kabul in 1996, but the civil war would last until the American invasion in 2001. Typical of the period was *Zhongguo waijiao*'s assessment of 1999: "In 1999, the People's Republic of China continued to keep friendly good relations with the Islamic State of Afghanistan, but the situation in Afghanistan is volatile, limiting the cooperation and exchanges between the two sides" (*ZGWJ* 2000: 107–108).

Maldives

China had established diplomatic relations with the Maldives in 1972, and Huang Hua had visited in 1981. Total trade was seldom more than $1 million a year, and China did not designate the islands as a "neighbor" until 2004.

Regional international organizations

SAARC had been founded in 1985, largely at the urging of the smaller South Asian nations. Initial membership was limited to Bangladesh, Bhutan, India, Maldives, Nepal, Pakistan, and Sri Lanka. It is not a particularly effective organization at resolving security issues in the sub-continent. Afghanistan applied for members after founding, leading to a debate among the members as to its South Asian versus

128 The "Good Neighbor"

Central Asian identity. Its occupation by Soviet troops was also an issue. China was not a member, and the organization did not have external observers until 2005.

Economic

China's economic relations with South Asia were secondary to the security equation in this period, and the region represented less trade than the other three regions examined. That is not to say that China and the South Asian countries were uninterested in trade, and a substantial exchange began in the 1990s.

Trade

Table 4.4 shows the development of trade between China and South Asia from 1988 to 2003.

China started out the period with Pakistan as its leading trade partner, not surprising given the close political relations of the two. Trade with India came next, and then Bangladesh and Sri Lanka; Nepal and Afghanistan were about equal, and Bhutan and Maldives were negligible. As India's economy became more open and grew during the 1990s, it gradually overtook Pakistan's position as China's leading trade partner in South Asia, displacing it in 1995. By the end of the period, India's trade with China was three times Pakistan. Bangladesh's trade also increased by a

Table 4.4 China: total trade with South Asia, 1988–2003

China: total trade with South Asia, 1988–2003 (current US$, million)

	Afghanistan	Bangladesh	Bhutan	India	Maldives	Nepal	Pakistan	Sri Lanka
1988	$25	$129	$0	$246	$0	$25	$386	$92
1989	$11	$227	$0	$271	$0	$33	$592	$73
1990	$24	$173	$0	$270	$1	$47	$575	$97
1991	$27	$213	$0	$265	$1	$34	$687	$123
1992	$26	$221	$0	$339	$1	$36	$643	$110
1993	$35	$195	$0	$671	$4	$35	$849	$143
1994	$39	$387	$0	$893	$2	$42	$768	$152
1995	$48	$678	$0	$1,163	$1	$54	$1,012	$241
1996	$35	$690	$0	$1,417	$1	$40	$966	$195
1997	$33	$747	$0	$1,835	$0	$68	$1,072	$255
1998	$25	$687	$0	$1,924	$1	$72	$915	$298
1999	$20	$715	$1	$1,988	$1	$215	$971	$268
2000	$25	$918	$2	$2,911	$1	$204	$1,162	$458
2001	$17	$975	$2	$3,603	$2	$153	$1,300	$401
2002	$20	$1,101	$1	$4,947	$3	$110	$1,800	$349
2003	$27	$1,368	$2	$7,595	$3	$127	$2,430	$524

Source: IMF DOTS (2017). Data for Bhutan prior to 2000 are incomplete.

factor of ten, whereas Afghanistan, Nepal, and Sri Lanka had much more modest increases.

The two Asian giants did not start out trading much with each other; neither one's trade with the other was more than 0.6% of their total imports or exports. As the 1990s went on, the trade importance of each rose gradually. By the 21st century, however, the asymmetry was beginning: both exports to and imports from China became more important to India than India was to China.

Provision of public goods

China gave modest amounts of foreign aid to the countries of South Asia in this time period, though given the opaque nature of China's foreign aid statistics, it is difficult to make broad statements about them. There is little question but that Pakistan was the largest recipient, and Nepal was given some token aid during the Indian embargo, but China was not the major provider that it was in Southeast Asia in 1997–98.

Conclusion

What kind of regional hegemon was China during this period? The balance of evidence would point toward an *active* phase of regional hegemon behavior. In ideology, the emphasis on "neighborliness" and on regional focus is unmistakable. China's global-level connections were suddenly curtailed by Western condemnation and sanctions after June 4, 1989. But within China's own region, there were multiple governments which were willing to overlook Tiananmen, and not only because of their authoritarian nature; some, such as Pakistan, were then democratic. Others, such as Myanmar, were themselves under sanctions. In a world context in which the "Third Wave of Democracy" seemed to be washing across the world, China's leaders went back to the Five Principles of Peaceful Co-existence and its non-interference principle. China sought relations with all of its neighbors, and showed little outward preferences in their type of governance, except perhaps for stability. As seen in Chapter 2, other regional hegemons had been in similar situations. Apartheid South Africa briefly tried to use "Détente" to open relations with its neighbors after continued condemnation by Western countries in the late 1960s and early 1970s, though with limited success.

In the security realm, the resolution of territorial disputes was impressively legal and negotiated, not unlike Brazil's border negotiations at the turn of the 20th century with its neighbors. This was the case in Kazakhstan, Kyrgyzstan, Tajikistan, Russia, the land and Tonkin/Beibu Gulf with Vietnam, Laos, and Mongolia, all of which were negotiated and most of which were settled equitably. There were three exceptions: the South China Sea, the Senkaku/Diaoyu islands and the Sino-Indian border. In these cases, the dispute was not so much resolved as "shelved": China did not enter into negotiations over the sovereignty of these disputed areas, but did in some cases engage in joint development of resources. In the Sino-Indian border, China did elevate the level of discussion. In the South China Sea, the Chinese agreement with ASEAN with the DOC was a hopeful sign of adopting a diplomatic approach in a regional organization. In Central Asia, the Shanghai Five and SCO showed a Chinese acceptance of multilateralism as well.

Intervention was the most important change in China's policy toward its neighbors during this period. Support for two remnant insurgencies in Myanmar and Malaysia ended, and thereafter China's military did not intervene in any of its neighbors' land territories. And there is very limited evidence that China engaged in the sort of sponsorships, partisan subsidies, or work to influence the internal politics of its neighbors that all other regional hegemons have. Non-interference is a serious Chinese policy principle. The best analog to this was Gorbachev's renunciation of the Brezhnev doctrine, when the Soviets refused to intervene in the eastern European countries when they began to leave the bloc in 1989. In the latter case, though, it was much more of an explicit change of policy as well as behavior, and for China, it was a gradual change of behavior.

The role of and reaction to external major powers is complex in this period. On the one hand, the Soviet Union and Russia were much less active outside of Central Asia. The United States, however, was highly active in South Asia after 9/11, where it had been previously peripatetic and Central Asia, where it had never been before. In Southeast Asia, however, the closure of US bases in the Philippines did show a limited withdrawal. China did not register substantial objection to this introduction of an external power.

Diplomatically, China established its formal relations with all but one of its neighbors, a major accomplishment: South Korea, Indonesia, Singapore, as well as the post-Soviet states. It also started formal relations with ASEAN, joined ARF and APEC, and founded the SCO, and worked intensively with all of these organizations. Only in Northeast Asia where there was no body, and South Asia, where the regional organization was weak and did not accept observers yet was China not yet a member of a regional organization. But in no cases was China a member of an organization that provided explicit security public goods.

In arms sales, China did sell a good deal of weaponry to its neighbors, but in only one case was it the overwhelming seller: Myanmar. Even Pakistan continued to purchase its arms from a variety of different sources, Chinese and Western. In sharp contrast, India and Russia have both been highly sensitive to their neighbors' purchasing of other major powers' weapons, as Nepal found to it considerable discomfort.

The expatriate population of China was an issue during this period, and in particular the Indonesian case shows that sensitivity on this issue was still high. At the same time, China did not intervene in this case, and its protests were mild at most. In Malaysia, the dropping of travel restrictions showed that the Malay-dominated government in Kuala Lumpur was moving away from previous suspicion. China and Vietnam resolved their mutual expatriate population problem, and elsewhere in Southeast Asia the overseas Chinese were a well-integrated – if recognized – part of the citizenry. In Northeast Asia the Chinese population was not an issue, despite Mongolian suspicions, nor were they in Central Asia or South Asia. Unlike ethnic Russians in the "near abroad" in the former Soviet states or *Norteamericanos* in Central America in the early 20th century, the ethnic Chinese generally continued to integrate into their countries of residence and citizenship.

In the economics of the relationships, levels of trade in all regions of China increased during this period, though China's trade with Northeast Asia was far greater than the other three regions combined. Southeast Asia become more important as the period went on, but for Central Asia the trend was unclear, and for South Asia, the trade was generally the same. China did not seek to use its trade as a foreign policy weapon during this time against any of its neighbors. Investment was not a significant part of the economic relationship yet, either, except as a net recipient. But in one major region, Southeast Asia, China was a major provider of economic public goods. The 1997–98 Asian financial crisis represented a major step forward for China in taking on an active regional hegemon role. We will examine how this developed in further chapters.

Causes of shift

This chapter has pointed to the Tiananmen Square massacre and the international reaction to that as a major part of the shift in China's relations with its neighbors. That is not the only cause of the change, though easily the most dramatic. The shift in China's relations from a confrontational, almost hyperactive phrase to an active phase, was more complex than that.

Internal

Just as with most other regional hegemons, internal reforms were associated with an active behavioral phase. China's economic reforms began in 1979, stalled in 1989, revived in 1992 and then continued. The progress of reform in China was incremental and sometimes haphazard, changing one sector and then shifting to another. Certain fundamental changes were deferred until later, just as in regional relations key territorial issues such as the Sino-Indian border and the South China Sea were also shelved for later. That would yield a series of impressive successes, but it also meant deferring the hard issues until later.

Regional

Within the different regions that China is a part of, the opportunities provided by the Soviet weakening, withdrawal and collapse were substantial: it opened up relations with the Central Asian republics, forced Mongolia, Vietnam, and Laos to be much more flexible and ended the Cold War's manifestations in Indochina and South Asia especially, and eliminated the ideological rift of Asia. Regional relations eased in many of the regions of Asia, with the ending of the Cambodia conflict and the periodic easing of the India-Pakistan conflict. For China, the standard rhetoric that it wanted a peaceful regional environment was a core policy, and, as its trade with neighbors increased, it become more important.

Extra-regional

Strategically, the collapse of the Soviet Union's economy, and then its political system, led to a situation almost akin to a "reverse domino" effect, in which the curtailment of Soviet economic and military aid, diplomatic and political support for friends and allies led to strategic readjustments in regions around the world. In Asia, for instance, the loss of aid, trade, and arms flowing from the Soviet Union to Vietnam caused a concomitant loss of Vietnamese aid for the Phnom Penh regime in Cambodia and the government in Laos, in effect, the imperium and sub-imperia of the USSR. In the Western hemisphere, the reduction of Soviet aid to Cuba contributed to a settlement of the civil war in Nicaragua, and an attempt to solve the civil war in Angola. In South Asia, the Soviets withdrew from Afghanistan. With the decline in Soviet influence, each of the Soviet Union's friends and allies has been placed in a difficult position of either trying to maintain its sub-imperium, or conceding the presence of regional competitors. Most prominent among these regional competitors is China, both in Northeast and Southeast Asia.

Notes

1 The trade with North Korea increased much more modestly, and the figures from the IMF Direction of Trade Statistics must naturally be taken with a dose of skepticism in general and with the more specific objection that barter trade between China and North Korea would not be included in the statistics.
2 These were also known as the "White Flag" communists because of their distinctive banner.
3 The large level of Taiwanese investment in Vietnam has been seen by Chinese analysts as part of Taipei's "southern entry" strategy, which normalization and investment between the mainland and Vietnam might impede (Ni Xiayun 1994a: 14). Continued visits and exchanges between Vietnam and Taiwan are a definite source of concern for China, and for good reason; if Ho Chi Minh was willing in the 1940s to play French off of Chinese, Doi Muoi in the 1990s could play Chinese off of each other (Gainsborough 1992: 206). Thus, although the Chinese consistently deny that they made any concessions to Vietnam in the process of normalization, the Vietnamese were not wholly without leverage (Guo Ming 1992: 215–216).
4 Members include Australia, Bangladesh, Brunei Darussalam, Cambodia, Canada, China, Democratic People's Republic of Korea, European Union, India, Indonesia, Japan, Lao PDR, Malaysia, Mongolia, Myanmar, New Zealand, Pakistan, Papua New Guinea, Philippines, Republic of Korea, Russia, Singapore, Sri Lanka, Thailand, Timor-Leste, United States, and Vietnam.
5 India's nuclear test in 1974 code named "Smiling Buddha" or Pokhran-I was officially designated as a "Peaceful nuclear explosion." In the 1950s and 1960s there had been some consideration of the use of nuclear explosions for construction purposes, such as digging a canal. The US and Soviet Union banned such uses in 1976.

Works cited

Acharya, Amitav. 2012. *The Making of Southeast Asia: International Relations of a Region*. Singapore: Institute of Southeast Asian Studies.
Acharya, Amitav. 2015. *Indonesia Matters: Emerging Democratic Power*. Singapore: World Scientific.

Agence France Presse. 2002. Vietnam insists progress made in China border talks, 15 March.
Amer, Ramses. 2013. Sino-Vietnamese border disputes, in *Beijing's Power and China's Borders: Twenty Neighbors in Asia*, edited by Bruce A. Elleman, Stephen Kotkin, and Clive Schofield. Armonk, NY: M.E. Sharpe, 295–310.
Armstrong, Charles K. 2013. Sino-Korean border relations, in *Beijing's Power and China's Borders: Twenty Neighbors in Asia*, edited by Bruce A. Elleman, Stephen Kotkin, and Clive Schofield. Armonk, NY: M.E. Sharpe, 110–125.
Blank, Stephen. 2013. Kazakhstan's border relations with China, in *Beijing's Power and China's Borders: Twenty Neighbors in Asia*, edited by Bruce A. Elleman, Stephen Kotkin, and Clived Schofield. Armonk, NY: M.E. Sharpe, 96–109.
Bolt, Paul J. 2000. *China and Southeast Asia's Ethnic Chinese: State and Diaspora in Contemporary Asia*. New York: Praeger.
"Brief introduction to the Shanghai Cooperation Organisation." n.d. SCO website. <www.sectsco.org/EN123/brief.asp>, accessed 28 March 2013.
Brown, MacAlister, and Zasloff, Joseph J. 1998. *Cambodia Confounds the Peacemakers, 1979–1998*. Ithaca: Cornell University Press.
CFA [China's Foreign Affairs]. Annual. Beijing: Ministry of Foreign Affairs of the People's Republic of China. This is the official yearbook of the Ministry of Foreign Affairs of the People's Republic of China. Beginning its publication in 1987 as 中国外交概览 China's Foreign Affairs review, it is hereafter referred to as ZGWJGL, and after 1995 中国外交 it is renamed Zhongguo waijiao (ZGWJ) for the Chinese language version, and China's Foreign Affairs or CFA for the English-language version, which began publication in 2003. See also ZGWJ.
Chafetz, Glenn R. 1993. *Gorbachev, Reform, and the Brezhnev Doctrine: Soviet Policy toward Eastern Europe, 1985–1990*. Westport, CT: Praeger.
Chanda, Nayan. 1987. Heading for a conflict. *Far Eastern Economic Review*, 4 June, 42–43.
Chen, Dingding, and Wang, Jianwei. 2011. Lying low no more? China's new thinking on the *tao guang yang hui*. *China: An International Journal*, 9(2), 195–216.
Chen Xiangyang. 2004. *Zhongguo mulin waijiao: sixiang, shijian, qianzhang* [China's good-neighbour diplomacy: Though, practice, prospect]. Beijing: Shishi chubanshe.
Choi, Eunyoung Christina. 2011. Everyday practices of *bordering* and the threatened bodies of undocumented North Korean border-crossers, in *Ashgate Research Companion to Border Studies*, edited by Doris Wastl-Walter. Farnhame, Surrey: Ashgate, 507–527.
Chung, Chien-peng. 2010. *China's Multilateral Cooperation in Asia and the Pacific: Institutionalizing Beijing's "Good Neighbour Policy"*. Abingdon: Routledge.
Crispin, Shawn W., and Lintner, Bertil. 2000. Laos: Behind the bombings. *Far Eastern Economic Review*, 27 July. <www.feer.com/articles/2000/0007_27/p26regional.html>, accessed 2001.
Fang Chunsheng. 2005. Lun Jiang Zemin zhu zheng qijian dui woguo mulin youhao zhengce de fazhan [On Jiang Zemin's development in our good-neighborliness and friendliness policy]. *Huangshan xueyuan xuebao* [Journal of Huangshan University], 7(1), 47–52.
FBIS [Foreign Broadcast Information Service]. 1994a. *Daily Report: China*, 16 November, 6.
FBIS [Foreign Broadcast Information Service]. 1994b. *Daily Report: China*, 23 November, 12.
FBIS [Foreign Broadcast Information Service]. 1994c. *Daily Report: China*, 9 November, 15.
Fravel, M. Taylor. 2008. *Strong Borders Secure Nation: Cooperation and Conflict in China's Territorial Disputes*. Princeton: Princeton University Press.

Gainsborough, Martin. 1992. Vietnam II: A turbulent normalisation with China. *The World Today*, 1 November, 205–207.

Galeotti, Mark. 2013. Sino-Russian border resolution, in *Beijing's Power and China's Borders: Twenty Neighbors in Asia*, edited by Bruce A. Elleman, Stephen Kotkin, and Clive Schofield. Armonk, NY: M.E. Sharpe, 250–265.

Garver, John W. 2001. *Protracted Contest: Sino-Indian Rivalry in the Twentieth Century*. Seattle: University of Washington Press.

Gill, Bates, and Murphy, Melissa. 2005. China's evolving approach to counterterrorism. *Harvard Asia Quarterly*, (Winter/Spring), 21–32.

Gleason, Gregory. 2013. Tajikistan-China border normalization, in *Beijing's Power and China's Borders: Twenty Neighbors in Asia*, edited by Bruce A. Elleman, Stephen Kotkin, and Clive Schofield. Armonk, NY: M.E. Sharpe, 282–291.

Guo Ming. 1992. *ZhongYue guanxi yanbian sishi nian* [Forty years of the evolution of Sino-Vietnamese relations]. Nanning: Guangxi renmin chubanshe.

Heilmann, Sebastian, and Schmidt, Dirk H. 2014. *China's Foreign Political and Economic Relations: An Unconventional Global Power*. Lanham: Rowan & Littlefield.

Hiebert, Murray, and Cheung, Tai Ming. 1991a. Comrades again. *Far Eastern Economic Review*, 22 August, 8–9.

Hiebert, Murray, and Cheung, Tai Ming. 1991b. A lesson in ideology. *Far Eastern Economic Review*, 21 November, 10–11.

IMF DOTS [Direction of Trade Statistics]. 2017. IMF e-library. <data.imf.org/>, accessed 19 January 2017.

Lankov, Andrei. 2004. North Korean refugees in Northeast China. *Asian Survey*, 44(6), 856–873.

Lee, Lai To. 2001. China's relations with ASEAN: Partners in the 21st century? *Pacifica Review*, 13(February), 61–71.

Li Chengren. 2010. Shenhua mulin youhao cujin quanmian hezuo [Deepen good-neighborly relations, promote comprehensive cooperation]. *Dangdai shijie*, (10), 25–29.

Lintner, Bertil. 1993. Arms for eyes. *Far Eastern Economic Review*, 16 December, 26.

Lintner, Bertil. 2015. *Great Game East: India, China and the Struggle for Asia's Most Volatile Frontier*. New Haven: Yale University Press.

Li Peng. 1991. *Guangming ribao*, 13 December 1991, quoted in Zhang Zhongguo, Dui jiushi niandai Zhongguo waijiao de sikao [Reflections on Chinese diplomacy in the '90s]. *Anhui sheng weidang jiaoxuebao*, 1(1991), 71–74.

Madhok, Shakti. 2005. *Sino-Mongolian Relations, 1949–2004*. New Delhi: Reliance Publishing House.

Ma Jiali. 1994. Hou lengzhan shidai Indu de dui Hua guanxi [India: Post-Cold War relations with China]. *Xiandai guoji guanxi* [Contemporary International Relations], 3(1994), 26–29.

"Major terrorist cases committed by 'Three Forces' first time exposed in Xinjiang." 2001. *People's Daily* (English), 11 December 2001 in China.org.cn. <www.china.org.cn/english/government/23429.htm>, accessed 11 January 2017.

Malik, J. Mohan. 1995. China-India relations in the post-Soviet era: the continuing rivalry. *The China Quarterly*, (142, June), 317–355.

Mankoff, Jeffrey. 2012. *Russian Foreign Policy: The Return of Great Power Politics*, 2nd ed. Lanham, MD: Rowan & Littlefield.

Marat, Erica. 2013. Kyrgyzstan: China's regional playground?, in *Beijing's Power and China's Borders: Twenty Neighbors in Asia*, edited by Bruce A. Elleman, Stephen Kotkin, and Clive Schofield. Armonk, NY: M.E. Sharpe, 126–141.

McDonald, Hamish. 1989. Breaking the ice. *Far Eastern Economic Review*, 9 March, 10–11.
MOFAJ [Ministry of Foreign Affairs of Japan]. 1995. Ministry of Foreign Affairs of Japan: Statement by Prime Minister Tomiichi Murayama "On the occasion of the 50th anniversary of the war's end", 15 August 1995. <www.mofa.go.jp/announce/press/pm/murayama/9508.html>, accessed 5 May 2017.
Nathan, Andrew J. 1994. Human rights in Chinese Foreign Policy. *China Quarterly*, 139(September), 632–633.
Ngeow, Chow Bing. 2015. Comprehensive strategic partners but prosaic military ties: The development of Malaysia-China defence relations, 1991–2015. *Contemporary Southeast Asia*, 37(2), 269–304.
Ni Xiayun. 1994a. Yuenan jingji zai gaige zhong qude jiaokuai fazhan [Vietnam's economy: A relatively repaid progress in reform]. *Xiandai guoji guanxi* [Contemporary International Relations], 4, 39–42.
Ni Xiayun. 1994b. Yuenan waijiao qianxi" [An initial analysis of Vietnam's foreign policy]. *Xiandai guoji guanxi* [Contemporary International Relations], 6, 11–14.
Qian Qichen. 2005. *Ten Episodes in China's Diplomacy*. New York: HarperCollins.
Raine, Sarah, and Le Mière, Christian. 2013. *Regional Disorder: The South China Sea Disputes*. London: International Institute for Strategic Studies.
Rhee, Young Ju. 2009. Diversity within Chinese diaspora: Old and new Huaqiao in South Korea, in *Diasporas: Critical and Interdisciplinary Perspectives*, edited by Jane Fernandez. Freeland: Interdisciplinary Press, 111–126.
Rosenthal, Elizabeth. 2002. North Koreans seek asylum at consulates in China. *New York Times*, 9 May. <http://www.nytimes.com/2002/05/09/world/north-koreans-seek-asylum-at-consulates-in-china.html>, accessed 1 August 2014.
Rossabi, Morris. 2005. *Modern Mongolia: From Khans to Commissars to Capitalists*. Berkeley and Los Angeles: University of California Press.
Rossabi, Morris. 2013. Sino-Mongol border: From conflict to precarious resolution, in *Beijing's Power and China's Borders: Twenty Neighbors in Asia*, edited by Bruce A. Elleman, Stephen Kotkin, and Clive Schofield. Armonk, NY: M.E. Sharpe, 168–189.
Scalapino, Robert A. 1991. China's relations with its neighbors. *Academy of Political Science, Proceedings*, 38(2), 63–74.
SIPRI TIV [Stockholm International Peace Research Institute]. 2017. *Importer/Exporter Arms Transfers TIV Tables*. Stockholm: Stockholm International Peace Research Institute. <http://armstrade.sipri.org/armstrade/page/values.php>, accessed 13 April 2017.
Song, Weiqing. 2014. Interests, power and China's difficult game in the Shanghai Cooperation Organization (SCO). *Journal of Contemporary China*, 23(85), 85–101.
Storey, Ian James. 2000. Indonesia's China policy in the new order and beyond: Problems and prospects. *Contemporary Southeast Asia*, 22(April), 145.
Sukma, Rizal. 1994. Recent developments in Sino-Indonesian relations: An Indonesia view. *Contemporary Southeast Asia*, 16(1), 40–43.
Sutter, Karen M. 1993. China's Vietnam policy: The road to normalization and prospects for the Sino-Vietnamese relationship. *Journal of Northeast Asian Studies*, 12(2), 21–46.
Swanstrom, Niklas. 2001. *Foreign Devils, Dictatorship, or Institutional Control: China's Foreign Policy towards Southeast Asia*. Uppsala: Uppsala University Department of Peace and Conflict Research.
Townsend-Gault, Ian. 2013. The China-Laos boundary: Lan Xang meets Middle Kingdom, in *Beijing's Power and China's Borders: Twenty Neighbors in Asia*, edited by Bruce Elleman, Stephen Kotkin, and Clive Schofield. Armonk, NY: M.E. Sharpe, 142–153.

US State Department, Office of the Coordinator for Counterterrorism. 2003. Patterns of global terrorism. 30 April 2003. <www.state.gov/j/ct/rls/crt/2002/html/19983.htm>, accessed 30 March 2013.

Vatikiotis, Michael. 1991. Eye on the Islands. *Far Eastern Economic Review*, 4 July, 19.

Wan, Ming. 2006. *Sino-Japanese Relations: Interaction, Logic, and Transformation*. Washington, DC: Wilson Center.

Wang Jianwei. 2008. China and SCO: Towards a new type of interstate relations, in *China Turns to Multilateralism: Foreign Policy and Regional Security*, edited by Guoguang Wu and Helen Lansdowne. London: Routledge, 104–126.

Wang, Zheng. 2012. *Never Forget National Humiliation: Historical Memory in Chinese Politics and Foreign Relations*. New York: Columbia University Press.

Wayne, Martin I. 2009. Inside China's war on terrorism. *Journal of Contemporary China*, 18(59), 249–261.

Whiting, Allen S. 1989. *China Eyes Japan*. Berkeley and Los Angeles: University of California Press.

Williams, Michael C. 1992. *Vietnam at the Crossroads*. London: Royal Institute of International Affairs.

Wu, Xinbo. 2009. Chinese perspectives on building an East Asian community in the twenty-first century, in *Asia's New Multilateralism: Cooperation, Competition, and the Search for Community*, edited by Michael J. Green and Bates Gill. New York: Columbia University Press, 55–77.

Yahuda, Michael. 2008. China's multilateralism and regional order, in *China Turns to Multilateralism: Foreign Policy and Regional Security*, edited by Guoguang Wu and Helen Landsdowne. London: Routledge, 75–89.

Yahuda, Michael. 2014. *Sino-Japanese Relations after the Cold War: Two Tigers Sharing a Mountain*. Abingdon, Oxon: Routledge.

Yang Tao. 2012. Jiaqiang Shanghai Hezuo Zuzhi fankong hezuo mianlin de tiaozhan yu yingdui cuoshi [Strengthening the Shanghai Cooperation Organization's anti-terrorism cooperation and response measures]. *Hubei jingguan xueyuan xuebao*, (3), 96–98.

Ya Xin. 2001. Mulin youhao gonggu zhoubian [Good neighborly, strong all around]. *Liaowang* [Outlook], 27, 52–53, republished in *Zhongguo waijiao*, 11(2001), 19–20.

ZGWJ [Zhongguo waijiao]. Annual. Beijing: Ministry of Foreign Affairs of the People's Republic of China. This is the official yearbook of the Ministry of Foreign Affairs of the People's Republic of China. Beginning its publication in 1987 as 中国外交概览 China's Foreign Affairs review, it is hereafter referred to as ZGWJGL, and after 1995 中国外交 it is renamed Zhongguo waijiao (ZGWJ) for the Chinese language version, and China's Foreign Affairs or CFA for the English-language version, which began publication in 2003.

ZGWJGL [Zhongguo waijiao gailan]. See ZGWJ.

Zha, Daojiong. 2000. China and the May 1998 Riots of Indonesia: Exploring the issues. *The Pacific Review*, 13, 557–575.

Zha, Daojiong. 2005. China's energy security and its international relations. *China and Eurasia Forum Quarterly*, 3(3), 39–54.

Zhang Qing. 2000. Dujin quebo xiongdi zai: yi shixian Zhong-Yue guanxi zhengchanghua de "Chengdu huiwu" [Recollection of the "Chengdu meeting" in the normalization of Sino-Vietnamese relations]. *Zhongguo waijiao*, 5, 44–46.

Zhang Ruikun. 2010. Zhengchanghua yilai de Zhong Lao guanxi [China-Laos relations since regularization]. *Dongnanya Nanya yanjiu*, (4), 12–15.

Zhang Shengjiang, and Hu Weining. 2010. Zhongguo mulin waijiao chuantong de wenhua diyun [The heritage of China's traditional good-neighbor diplomacy]. *Nanjing zhengzhi xueyuan xuebao* [Journal of PLA Nanjing Institute of Politics], 26(5), 69–71.

Zhaparov, Amantur. 2008. The issue of Chinese migrants in Kyrgyzstan. *China and Eurasia Forum Quarterly*, 7(1), 79–91.

Zhu Tingchan. 2001. Lun Zhongguo mulin zhengce de lilun yu shijian [Discussing the theory and practice of China's Good Neighbor Policy]. *Guoji guancha* [International Observations], 2(2001), 12–18, republished in *Zhongguo waijiao*, 8(2001), 16–21.

5 "Friendly Elephant" or assertive Dragon? 2004–present

Period overview

Has China become "more assertive," as many in the media assert, and if so, when it this trend begin? Periodization is a tricky academic exercise at the best of times; sometimes your subject obligingly has a clear and pronounced break with the past, such as 1949 or 1989; in other cases, the transition is so subtle that it is difficult to put an exact date on it. That is the nature of this latest period in China's relations with its neighbors. The period begins less with a sharp policy break seen in previous periods of China's regional relations than a gradual policy transition, culminating in some evidence for an increasingly hyperactive phase in China's Northeast and Southeast neighboring relations, though less in its South or Central Asian relations. David Shambaugh, one of the most astute observers of China's foreign relations, summarizes China's relations with its neighbors at the beginning of 2005 this way:

> Bilaterally and multilaterally, Beijing's diplomacy has been remarkably adept and nuanced, earning praise around the region. As a result, most nations in the region now see China as a good neighbor, a constructive partner, a careful listener, and a nonthreatening regional power.
>
> (Shambaugh 2005: 64)

Premier Wen Jiabao adopted a vivid analogy when he related an anecdote: "[This] reminds me of an ASEAN meeting I attended last year. I remember on that occasion Mr. Mahathir and Mr. Goh Chok Tong drew a vivid analogy between China and a 'friendly elephant.' They told me the rise of China would not pose a threat to their countries" (Wen Jiabao 2004).

Yet Shambaugh notes that this quickly became antagonistic in 2009/10: "What was painstakingly built by Beijing over the decade 1998–2008, however, quickly unraveled in the short span of eighteen months from mid-2009 through 2010. During this brief period, China got into diplomatic scrapes with virtually *every* one its neighbors, with the net result that the previously positive perception of China in the region plummeted. This has become known as the period of China's 'assertiveness'" (Shambaugh 2013: 99). The contrast was bluntly made by Yang Jiechi in 2012: "China's foreign minister, Yang Jiechi, facing a barrage of complaints about his country's behaviour in the region, blurted out the sort of thing polite leaders usually prefer to leave unsaid. 'China is a big country,' he points out, 'and other countries are small countries, that is just a fact'" ("The Dragon's New Teeth" 2012). This chapter and the following ones will argue that the situation was not as comprehensively bad as Shambaugh states, but much more complex in its origins.

Furthermore, the transition in Chinese outlook and ideational aspects of its foreign policy preceded its behavioral transition by over four years; China began to *think* increasingly as a hyperactive regional hegemon in the 2004–07 period and began to *act* that way in 2009. The reasons are many, and Chinese analysts pose the change as a result of cumulative issues, primarily in US-China relations, such as aerial and maritime surveillance and the bombing of the Chinese embassy in Belgrade (Zhu 2013: 54). Yet these incidents occurred long before 2009, and one is left wondering why Chinese behavior seems to have taken a turn in that year. The broad world economic recession of 2009 left China both relatively unaffected and increasingly skeptical of American world leadership after the "Washington Consensus" managed to lead the world off of a financial cliff. One possibility that has been overlooked is the continued American presence in Central Asia. Whereas Chinese leaders had been understanding of the United States invasion of Afghanistan in 2001 and the accompanying basing agreements in Central Asian states, the invasion of Iraq in 2003 was a very different matter. The 2005 "Tulip Revolution" in Kyrgyzstan and protests in Uzbekistan reinforced the impression that the American presence in Central Asia was not temporary and purely focused on fighting Al Qaeda and the Taliban in Afghanistan, but a broader and permanent presence that was attempting to democratize China's neighbors. American efforts at democratization of the world were among the ideas that China's scholar/advocates have condemned. Jin Canrong and Dai Weilai point to Condoleezza Rice's 2006 speech at Georgetown University as a turning point in this effort to spread democratic values (2009: 5–6), Qin Yaqing traces it back to 9/11 and the war on terror, and other analysts have different dating, but the idea is common: United States policy is to push democracy and universal human rights (2011: 8). In 2005, China began to harden parts of its foreign policy by adopting the concept of "Core National Interests," and publicly using the term in 2007. Further south, the US-India civil nuclear agreement in 2006 harmed both Sino-American and Sino-Indian relations. By 2009, confrontations with Japan, and then Vietnam and Philippines put a chill on China's image with its neighbors. But for every over-publicized incident such as the South China Sea, it is useful to remember that there are also boringly harmonious ties that do not grab headlines.

If the beginning of this period is ambiguous, there is also a question of whether the period changes around 2009/2010, when many western analysts began to assert that a "New Assertive China" was beginning to throw its weight around the region (see, inter alia, Shambaugh 2013: 99; Roy 2013: 2; Beeson and Li 2014; Rozman 2010). There is certainly no question but that this is an assertion in the media, but as Johnston demonstrated in 2013, the evidence for this idea is mixed. By 2016 at least some Chinese scholars were attributing foreign policy changes to the rise of Xi at the 18th CCP Congress in late 2012 and the Neighboring Diplomacy Work

Conference in October 2013 as a rapid change that "... emphasized that sovereign interests should be prioritized before security and development interests. This idea now guides Chinese regional diplomacy" (Luo Yongkun 2016: 87–89). This chapter will examine evidence for a change of thinking in China's regional relations, and Chapters 6, 7, 8, and 9 will look at the evidence of behavioral changes in China's four regions.

China's capabilities are not solely economic, either. China's military has been the focus of exceptional attention in the past decade, as analysts frequently talk about China's "assertiveness." Yet China's total number of military personnel went down in this period. China's President Xi Jinping announced the demobilization of 300,000 soldiers in September 2015, bringing China well below three million (Wong et al. 2015). China's military expenditures, though difficult to estimate, have clearly gone up during this period of time, even by China's own accounting. The estimates of SIPRI as a regional ratio are shown in Chapter 2. China's spending represents a significant shift away from land forces toward air and naval forces, which are more expensive. There is evidence that this rate of increase that roughly tripled China's military expenditures from $72 billion a year to over $214 billion a year is slowing down: budgetary announcements have pointed to a 7% increase for 2017, the slowest in several years (Page and Wong 2017).

The energy supply vulnerability noted in the previous chapter grew as China's economy did, and China became the world's largest importer of petroleum in 2014 and had total consumption of 10.7 million bbl/d, less than half of it domestically produced (EIA 2014). Future growth in Chinese petroleum consumption is therefore likely to come from abroad. This in turn means that diversification of energy sources and suppliers became a major foreign policy goal of China. This became known as the "Malacca Dilemma" (马六甲困境 *maliujia kunjing*), both in recognition that most of China's petroleum supplies from the Middle East passed through the Straits of Malacca, and of the growing Chinese interest in the chokepoint theory of turn-of-the-century US naval theoretician Alfred Thayer Mahan. The prospect of a hostile foreign power – read "The United States" – choking off China's oil supply in the narrow passage became part of a broader Chinese initiative. Discussions of the problem had begun earlier by Hu Jintao after the 16th CCP Congress in 2002 (Sun Xingjie 2013: 25). In addition, some Chinese analysts have pointed out the other problems of the Straits, including its high and growing traffic density, and piracy problems (Huang Pengzhi 2014: 11–12). Myanmar and the pipeline built there between 2005 and 2014 would be able to supply oil to Kunming without going through the straits, and the oil and gas pipelines from Central Asia would also help supply western China. The prospect of a pipeline running up Pakistan is part of this idea as well. These will be discussed in the following chapters.

China's resources in foreign direct investment, official development assistance, and a variety of prominent projects such as the Beijing Olympics in 2008, a manned space program and the like were similarly cited by Chinese and foreign analysts alike as evidence of China's leaders attempting to translate these impressive increases in capabilities into "Soft Power" as well as hard power. By virtually

"Friendly Elephant" or assertive Dragon? 141

all measures, China's capabilities placed it as the most prominent of the great powers during the 2004–2016 period.

Ideational: policies, pronouncements, and doctrines

China's Good Neighbor Policy continued to be used and cited during the 2004–2014 period as the basis for its regional relations, but reflecting a greater role for Chinese foreign policy in other regions, additional policies were added to the official external ideology of China's leaders, each new leader adding new catch-phrases to the previous ones. During a visit to Tajikistan, incoming President Hu Jintao reaffirmed that China would continue to pursue his predecessor Jiang Zemin's "neighbor" policy, an indication that it was most strongly associated with Jiang. Hu Jintao himself announced a policy of "Harmonious World" (和谐世界 *hexie shijie*) in 2005, which was meant to be the foreign policy analog to the domestic policy of building a Harmonious Society (Guo and Blanchard, eds. 2008: 1–4). After his departure from office, however, the phrase dropped out of current use. The foreign policy establishment of Beijing cast this policy as a new development, but most of its content was similar to previous policy statements: China emphasizes peaceful relations as a means to development, adheres to the concepts first articulated in Zhou Enlai's Five Principles of Peaceful Coexistence and seeks good relations with all states. As Emilian Kavalski notes, the Chinese policies regardless of their exact phrasing encompasses a narrative of a "peaceful rise" (和平崛起 *heping jueqi*) or "peaceful development" and non-interference in other countries' affairs, creating normative power within a variety of places such as Central Asia where the appeal of Western-style democracy may not be as firm as US government officials would like (Kavalski 2012: 110–111).

The incoming leader Xi Jinping continued the trend started by Hu Jintao of developing a brand-new catch-phrase linking domestic and foreign policy: The "Chinese Dream" (中国梦 *Zhongguo meng*), which has a variety of interpretations of national revival, prosperity, ambition. Beginning in 2012, Xi Jinping began to articulate a new policy, or at least a new phrase, characterizing China's foreign relations: "New Type of Great Power Relations" (新型大国关系 *xinxing daguo guanxi*), which was highlighted during his June 2012 trip to California in which he spent time with US President Barack Obama. Perhaps the most important element of this policy is the explicit equality of China and the United States in relations.

The scope of China's reach did change during the 21st century, and China reached out to Latin America, Africa, the Middle East in commercial, diplomatic and in some cases strategic cooperation. China's interactions with Africa in particular garnered a great deal of attention in western academia and media, and yielded the image of China as a global power now expanding beyond its Asian neighborhood. The Chinese navy is engaged in anti-piracy efforts in the Gulf of Aden, and in July 2017 established a supporting military base in Djibouti. It has sent a large number of troops overseas to act as peacekeepers and observers under UN auspices, with 1,900 currently operating in Lebanon, Western Sahara, Congo, Liberia, Cote d'Ivoire, Sudan, Darfur, South Sudan, and Cyprus (*China's Foreign*

Affairs [hereafter *CFA*] 2013: 322). China is also actively engaged in the Middle East, using its navy to escort vessels involved in the destruction of chemical weapons in Syria, but at the same time vetoing efforts to sanction the government of Syria in the United Nations Security Council (along with the Russian Federation). China reached north and became a Permanent Observer on the Artic Council in 2013 (Myers 2013). China's diplomacy also was focused on reform of the UN Security Council, the World Bank and IMF, among other global institutions, and the upshot of this is that China would appear to be focused on the "Globalist" phase as outlined in Table 2.3, and as Shambaugh characterizes it, *China Goes Global* (2013).

Does this mean that China has become a "regional snob," out-growing its previous focus on East Asia? Do the foreign policies of China under Hu and Xi constitute a return to a globalist ideology? There are relatively few Chinese foreign policy statements that point to the broad-brush images of a "primary contradiction" that the Maoist and immediate post-Maoist eras had; most statements during this period repeat the basic formula that Chinese foreign policy is meant to serve domestic development and that regional and world stability are the best ways to achieve this goal.

Beginning in 2009, Chinese academic and policy-oriented authors began to publish a variety of pieces with "Great Power" in the title and China in their contents (see inter alia, Qin Yaqing 2011; Jin Canrong, ed. 2011; Tang Jin, ed. 2009). Most have painted with a broad brush the relative decline of American power (though not denying its continued superpower status), due to several factors that few American analysts could disagree with: the long "war on terror" and the military commitments in Afghanistan and Iraq, with consequential damage to American "soft power"; the financial crisis beginning in 2008, and the rise of new actors such as the BRICS (Brazil, Russia, India, China, and, after 2010, South Africa). "Snobbish" priority to major countries notwithstanding, China's foreign relations continue to place great emphasis on relations with their neighbors in the 21st century.

Occasionally, Chinese analysts have recognized the asymmetry in the relationship between China and other countries. Jin Canrong wrote in 2009 that Chinese tend to see the singular or particular with a victim mentality (受害主义思想 *shouhai zhuyi sixiang*), and fail to recognize that foreigners see China's enormous GDP growth and see China as extremely powerful (Jin Canrong and Dai Weilai 2009: 16). Many Chinese academics recognized in 2013 that China's size and growth were a factor in its neighbors' perceptions of it. Feng Zhongping saw this, saying, "A key and long-term challenge for China's periphery diplomacy is to ease its neighbors' concerns over China's rise, especially from those smaller nations" (Feng Zhongping 2013: 50). Wu Zhicheng, writing in 2015, said that "[f]orestalling impressions that China is trying to dominate its neighbors, clarifying Chinese intentions, and fostering mutual trust rather than suspicion is the right way to go" (Wu Zhicheng 2015: 64). But there has been a continued and more vocal sense of victimization in Chinese statements, coupled with proclamation of great power status, such as Foreign Minister Yang Jiechi's "China is a big country, and other countries are small countries, that is just a fact" reply to ASEAN noted above. Despite Chinese academics' urging, Chinese government speeches – not to mention its behavior – have not reassured the neighbors.

China lost most of its "neighbors" in the 21st century; it gained "partners" instead, a shift in language that reflected a shift in policy, one that had previously accepted nearby countries as they were and sought merely peaceful and stable relations, and replaced it with a more transactional relationship. In a sense, the shift is within the general active phase of regional hegemons, moving from the less active toward the more active, but not yet into the hyperactive. The rhetoric of "neighbor" continued to be used in the 21st century, though its uses have begun to vary from the "Good Neighbor Relations" period of the 1990s, which one Chinese scholar characterized as the "old policy" in 2015 but nevertheless held that elements contained in it continued to be applicable to Chinese regional relation (Du Yanjun 2015: 110). The same scholar also stated that ". . . China will treat its neighbors like relatives and frequent meetings will draw them closer." The shift from "neighbor" to "partner" began in 2003, at the 16th CCP Congress, when China introduced a new phrase, "与邻为善、以邻为伴" *yu lin wei shan, yu lin wei ban*, a rhyme that does not translate well into English, but might be rendered, "With neighbors act friendly, take neighbors as partners" and is officially translated as "developing good-neighborly relationships and partnerships" (*China's Foreign Affairs* [hereafter *CFA*] 2004: 39; 中国外交/*Zhongguo waijiao* [hereafter *ZGWJ*] 2004: 30). The phrase was supplemented by the phrase 睦邻、安邻、富邻的政策 (*mulin, anlin, fulin de zhengce*, literally "Harmonious neighbor, peaceful neighbor, prosperous neighbor policy," and officially translated as "Policy of bringing harmony, peace and prosperity to neighbors"). By the second decade of the 21st century, however, fewer and fewer or China's neighbors were being formally designated as "neighbors" (邻国 *lin guo*) as China's diplomats sought to promote the status of contiguous and proximate states to "partner" (伙伴 *huoban*) status. The official State Council White Paper on China's Policies on Asia-Pacific Security Cooperation officially defined the nature of the "partner" status in January 2017:

> Countries may become partners when they have the same values and ideals, but they can also be partners if they seek common ground while reserving differences. The key is to remain committed to treating each other as equals and carrying out mutually beneficial cooperation.
> (State Council Information Office 2017)

Of course, there are partners and then there are *partners*; China's partnership designations have a variety of nuances which forms a hierarchy of partnership statuses, as seen in Table 5.1:

Thus, fully twenty-one of China's neighbors had some sort of "partnership" designation, two more have "strategic cooperative relations" and four have no designation: Bhutan, with which China has no diplomatic relations, Timor Leste, which China only recognized as a "neighbor" in 2014, North Korea, described as a "traditional friendship" and Japan, which is a "close and important neighbor."

144 *"Friendly Elephant" or assertive Dragon?*

Table 5.1 Hierarchy of Chinese partnership designations

Hierarchy of partnership designations

Level	English	Chinese	Examples
1	Comprehensive strategic partnership of coordination	全面战略协作伙伴关系	Russian Federation
	All-Weather strategic cooperative partnership	全天候战略合作伙伴关系	Pakistan
2	Comprehensive strategic partnership of cooperation	全面战略合作伙伴关系	Cambodia, Laos, Myanmar, Thailand, Vietnam
3	Strategic and cooperative partnership	战略合作伙伴关系	Afghanistan, S. Korea, India
4	Comprehensive strategic partnership	全面战略伙伴关系	Kazakhstan, Malaysia, Mongolia, Indonesia
5	Strategic partnership	战略伙伴关系	Kyrgyzstan, Tajikistan, Turkmenistan, Uzbekistan
6	Comprehensive cooperative partnership	全方位合作伙伴关系	Singapore
	Comprehensive partnership of cooperation	全面合作伙伴关系	Bangladesh, Nepal
7	Strategic cooperative relations	战略合作关系	Brunei, Philippines

Source: Liu Bowen and Fang Changping (2016: 74). The level hierarchy is from Liu and Fang. English translations from *China's Foreign Affairs*, except for Pakistan. The Maldives is not listed in Liu and Fang's analysis but was designated as "Comprehensive Friendly and Cooperative Partnership" in 2014.

The individual promotions in status will be dealt with below in each bilateral relationship, from "neighbor" to "partner," but the overall chronology shows two peaks: there were nine partnership designations in 2003–05 and twelve in 2012–15.

Perhaps recognizing that its aspirations to great power status were leading to the neglect of relations with its neighbors, the Chinese leadership attended an October 2013 conference on diplomacy with its neighbors (周边外交工作座谈会 *zhoubian waijiao gongzuo zuotan hui*, which is sometimes translated as the "peripheral diplomacy" and sometimes as "neighboring diplomacy") in Beijing, attended by the entire Politburo Standing Committee, ambassadors, CCP Central Committee members responsible for foreign relations. It was, in the words of veteran China-watchers Bonnie Glaser and Deep Pal, the first major foreign policy gathering in China since 2006 (Glaser and Pal 2013) and in the words of China's Foreign Ministry, the first of its kind ever. It was described as having ". . . set out the strategic objectives, basic principles and overall plan for its neighborhood diplomacy in the next five to ten years" (*CFA* 2014: 38). One of the conference organizers, Jin Canrong of the School of International Studies at Renmin University announced that "[i]t does not mean we do not attach importance to big nations or developing countries, but neighbors will be the focus of the moment" (Li Xiaokun 2014). Xi's speech to the conference emphasized China's relations with neighbors and characterized them as "... mostly stable, friendly and cooperative" (Xi Jinping 2013). Xi repeated the phrase of "与邻为善、以邻为伴" (*yu lin wei shan, yi lin wei ban*) as a central principle. Xi also emphasized the "New Silk Road" and "Maritime Silk Road" proposals, later simplified as One Belt One Road (一带一路 *yilu yidai*), as well as free trade agreements. It would appear that the conference also made the decision that diplomatic relations with China's neighbors should be upgraded to the various "partner" arrangements that had already been assigned to some neighbors, yet it would appear that the conference also made the decision that not all neighbors would be favored: "Efforts were discernable during the CPC Central Committee symposium to consider further overall arrangements and to raise the profile of diplomacy in peripheral areas as well as to strengthen relations with *most* neighboring countries" (Wu Zhicheng 2015: 62, emphasis added).

An academic roundtable followed the leadership conference, published in 现代国际关系/*Contemporary International Relations*, one of China's most influential foreign policy publications, and the authors were among the most prominent scholars of China's foreign relations. The articles represent a debate within the influential academic community over priorities and approaches to neighboring countries, and the role of outside powers – most notably the United States – in the region.

Within weeks of the neighboring diplomacy work conference, however, there is evidence that the Chinese leadership decided to test one of its neighbors, Vietnam, by setting up a drilling rig near the disputed Paracel Islands, as discussed below. A Japanese reporter for *Asahi Shimbun*, citing an unnamed Chinese researcher, claimed that the decision to move the rig was made at the start of 2014, roughly two months after the conference, despite concerns of the Chinese Ministry of Foreign Affairs which (rightfully) feared the move might damage regional relations (Hayashi 2014).

Finally, a key question is whether China has shown any proclivity toward regional exclusion doctrines that we saw characterized other regional hegemons' behavior in Chapter 2. China's recent behavior toward its neighbors in Northeast and Southeast Asia have led some analysts to discuss "China's Monroe Doctrine." This phrase has been cropping up with increasing frequency in the popular and academic media (see especially Li Zhonglin 2013, for a very good Chinese review of the term and Jackson 2016 for an English-language discussion).

The direct answer is no, though the evidence is mixed and there are some trends that may point in that direction. First, Chinese officials themselves specifically and emphatically deny that it has a Monroe Doctrine (门罗主义 – *Menluo zhuyi*, literally "Monroe-ism"). State Councilor Dai Bingguo was the top-level leader with responsibility for foreign affairs under President Hu Jintao. His speech in December 2010 "Adhere to the Path of Peaceful Development" was considered by Chinese and outsiders as a major statement on China's outlook and is particularly worth examining precisely because it engages issues of neighboring relations and doctrines of exclusion directly.

Dai's statement is quite pacific, which is not terribly surprising: "... China's strategic intention can be defined in two words: peaceful development, i.e., harmony and development at home and peace and cooperation abroad" (Dai Bingguo 2010). It also stands as a response to the advocates of the *wu suo wei* portion of Deng Xiaoping's 24 character *taoguang yanghui* foreign policy dictum (Chen and Wang 2011). What is particularly important from a comparative historical perspective: "We do not seek hegemony and will never compete with other countries for leadership in our region, seek so-called 'joint hegemony' or follow so-called 'Monroe Doctrine.' ... the bilateral and multilateral agreements we have signed with Asian countries no not have a single article that is exclusive" (Dai Bingguo 2010).

Chinese scholars have also delved into the Monroe Doctrine with extensive analyses as to why China's policies do not compare to the Monroe Doctrine (Li Zhonglin 2013; Yang Cheng 2014; Wang 2015). Official Chinese sources have stressed that the policies of China do not seek to exclude external actors from the region: "China consistently stressed that Asia is open and welcomes a positive and constructive role from non-regional members, a stance that is essentially different from the Monroe Doctrine. China ... has never pursued a sphere of influence ..." (Zheng Xiwen 2014). This statement has been repeated by Foreign Ministry spokesmen and women as well. The most logical target of such a policy, the United States, has been specifically mentioned as a state that China does not seek to exclude: Wang Yiwei, director of the Institute of International Affairs at Renmin University, writing in the usually provocative *Global Times* also made this point clear: "Beijing has stated on many occasions it welcomes Washington to play a positive and constructive role in Asia and it is therefore unnecessary and impossible to exclude the world's greatest power" (Wang Yiwei 2014). Jin Canrong and Duan Haowen of the School of International Studies at Renmin University, the former a frequent commentator on China's East Asian relations, called for "Open Regionalism" as China's policy: "... we must adhere to the principle of open regionalism. As the Asia-Pacific has become the biggest engine of the world economy, external powers are all eager to participate in Asia-Pacific economic activities in order to obtain reasonable rights and interests. China, whether out of consideration for its own relationships with other major powers or Asia-Pacific economic growth, should adhere to the principle of open regional cooperation ..." (Jin Canrong and Duan Haowen 2013: 30). The point is reinforced by Han Caizhen and Shi Yinhong, writing in the same forum, "China's rapid rise is misunderstood as a bid by China to expand its regional power and to exclude the U.S. This is in spite of the fact that China has repeatedly said it welcomes a constructive role of the U.S. in East Asia" (Han Caizhen and Shi Yinhong 2014: 30–31). Thus, at least at the level of officially articulated policy, China has not engaged in the construction of a regional exclusion doctrine seen in other regional hegemons' behavior. Unlike the USA, USSR/Russia, India, and Nigeria in Chapter 2, there is no explicit Chinese "keep out" sign.

There have been hints, however.

The October 2013 Peripheral Strategy Conference and its academic follow-on conference may have made some modifications to this approach. One of the more provocative articles from the conference was by Li Yonghui, Dean at Beijing Foreign Studies University, who explicitly called for China to establish a "strategic peripheral belt" (周边战略依托带 *zhoubian zhanlüe yituo dai*) in the region (Li Yonghui 2013: 66). Li explicitly pointed to the unsuccessful efforts of Germany and Japan to establish such belts in their regions, and the more successful effort of the USA in its "Good Neighbor Policy" (68). Li concludes that ". . . China can set up its strategic belt with its twenty-odd neighbors, of course, but it also can construct a larger strategic belt with the countries of the Middle East, the Pacific Rim, and the Indian Ocean" (69). Other scholars, most notably CICIR President Ji Zhiye have disagreed with this proposal, saying,

> History shows how some big powers turned their neighborhood (周边 *zhoubian*) into colonies by imposing their systems, laws and even languages on them; others set up spheres of influence around themselves . . . still others sought to establish their hegemony by using alliances or institutions. All of these efforts have met with failure.
> (Ji Zhiye 2013: 4)

Ji continues and allows the United States a role in the region, saying,

> Since China is blazing a trail in the field of neighboring diplomacy, it will naturally not reject the legitimate interests of the other major powers on her periphery. In this regard, China needs to learn how to co-exist peacefully with other major powers, notably the United States.

The role of the United States in the region will be examined below.

Perhaps the most noted hint that China was moving toward a Regional Exclusion Doctrine was President Xi Jinping's statement about "New Asian Diplomacy" and a "New Asian Security Concept" to the Fourth Conference on Interaction and Confidence Building Measures in Asia (CICA)[1] in May 2014 in Shanghai, when he stated in a prepared speech, that, "In the final analysis, it is for the people of Asia to run the affairs of Asia, solve the problems of Asia and uphold the security of Asia. The people of Asia have the capability and wisdom to achieve peace and stability in the region through enhanced cooperation" (Xi Jinping 2014). Many analysts, both foreign and Chinese, jumped on the (officially translated) phrase "it is for the people of Asia to run the affairs of Asia" (亚洲国家主导亚洲事务 *Yazhou guojia zhudao Yazhou shiwu*. The verb could be translated as "leading," "guiding," or "dominating") as an exclusion of non-Asian powers. Chinese scholars and policy analysts quickly sought to deny such an interpretation. The official China Internet Information Center engaged the issue directly, noting the use of ". . . the phrase 'having Asian countries manage Asian affairs' more frequently. They [Western and neighboring media] interpreted it as 'China's Monroe Doctrine,' because it shows China's urge for a greater role in Asian affairs. . . . But [that] term filled with hegemony, cannot truthfully summarize China's activities in its peripheral regions" (Cui Heng

2014). It is well worth noting that the next paragraph in Xi's speech denies any effort at exclusion:

> Asia is open to the world . . . countries in Asia must firmly commit themselves to cooperation with countries in other parts of the world. . . . We welcome all parties to play a positive and constructive role in promoting Asia's security and cooperation and work together to achieve win-win outcomes for all.
> (Xi Jinping 2014)

Xu Qingchao of the Shanghai Academy of Social Sciences while noting the rise of China and the importance of Xi's "New Asian Diplomacy" also specifically denied it to be a "Chinese Monroe Doctrine" (Xu Qingchao 2014: 1). Interestingly, several Chinese commentators also pointed out that ". . . Asian states even including Japan have misgivings about whether the US can provide permanent security for them, Xi's remarks indicate that it is never reliable to bind your own security to another's wagon" (Wang Yiwei 2014). Interestingly, this questioning of the US security commitment to Asia has been posed not as an actor to exclude, but rather as a public security good which the USA may fail to provide (Yang Cheng 2014: 2). Other Chinese authors equivocated on the issue of China's potential domination of its neighbors similar to other historical great powers. Yan Xuetong, writing in *China Daily*, said,

> Historically, all global powers rose as regional powers before becoming global powers. In the early stages of its rise, the US implemented the Monroe Doctrine and focused on Latin America; after World War II, the Soviet Union, which was growing in strength, took Europe as the focus. China will be no exception, so it too needs a successful neighborhood policy first. That move can help win friends among its neighbors, because after World War II it is already an established rule that sovereignty and territory should not be violated; both the US and the Soviet Union influenced neighbors' politics but without incorporating territory as they had done in the past.
> (Yan Xuetong 2015)

In addition to these statements, there has been some Chinese behavior that some analysts have specifically cited as showing at least some evidence of exclusion: Chinese activity in the South China Sea claimed by the "Nine-Dashed Line," a self-declared "Air Defense Identification Zone (ADIZ) in the East China Sea near the Senkaku/Diaoyu Islands in 2013.

As noted above, the "Nine Dashed Line" (revised in 2013 to a "Ten-Dashed Line" on official Chinese maps to more explicitly include Taiwan) represents a claim that pre-dates the People's Republic of China. What is ambiguous is whether the dashes on Chinese maps are a simple map-making convention, grouping the islands, islets, reefs, and rocks of the South China Sea together for purposes of clarity but not claim, or a full maritime sovereignty claim to the *entire* South China Sea: water, islands, rocks, and reefs (US State Department, Bureau of Oceans and

International Environmental and Scientific Affairs 2014; Odgaard 2015). Although a territorial claim, the Chinese statements concerning the South China Sea are not exactly a regional exclusion doctrine as we have defined it here. First, the area is unpopulated and not exactly a region; all other regional exclusion doctrines have spanned broader identifiable regions, encompassing multiple sovereign populated countries. Second, the claim is not particularly new, though the construction of artificial islands on top of reefs is, as is the use of Coast Guard and naval resources to patrol and enforce Chinese claims. Third, although Chinese documents and announcements regularly reiterate their claims to the South China Sea, there has been no effort to categorically deny entrance or transit to other countries' ships or aircraft in the area, and given its importance to international shipping, such a move would be impossible to enforce. The Chinese foreign ministry stated, "The Chinese side respects and safeguards the freedom of navigation and over-flight in the South China Sea to which all countries are entitled under international law" (MOFA 2015).

Chinese statements specifically on the US presence in the area have been contradictory. On the one hand, when the USA announced that Japan might join the USA in aerial patrols of the South China Sea, Chinese spokesman said in 2015 that the USA and Japan were "not involved in the South China Sea issue" and should not do anything to "complicate the situation," which would imply staying out (Kubo et al. 2015). Furthermore, Chinese naval units have protested US "Freedom of Navigation Exercise" within 12 nautical miles (nm) of Chinese-occupied reefs (Torbati 2015; MOFA 2015). On the other hand, Chinese statements have alluded to future US use of weather stations and search and rescue facilities in the South China Sea reefs being reclaimed by China (Blanchard 2015a). Thus, there seems to be a fine difference between a sign that says "Keep Out" and one that says, "I Own This."

The announcement of an East China Sea Air Defense Identification Zone (ADIZ)[2] in the East China Sea near the disputed Senkaku/Diaoyu Islands in November 2013 was seen by some analysts as another assertion of Chinese primacy in the region, and at the least the advancement of a territorial claim against Japan ("Banyan: Crossing a line in the sky" 2013: 44; "Regional turbulence" 2013: 39). The rhetoric associated with the announcement of the zone was clearly anti-Japanese, but did not seemed aimed at the USA (Perlez and Fackler 2013). Somewhat akin to the position on the South China Sea, China's announcements sought to differentiate civil and non-civil intrusions into "their" sovereign territory:

> China's establishment of the zone is aimed at safeguarding national sovereignty and security of territory and territorial airspace. . . . The Chinese government . . . explicitly point out that normal flight activities by foreign international airlines within the East China Sea ADIZ will not be affected at all.
>
> (MOFA 2013)

But at least one Chinese scholar was explicit in linking the zone to a broader idea: ". . . [the] main reasons for the establishment of the ADIZ: it is an important measure towards improving geopolitical security structures in the East China Sea and building the 'strategic buffer zone'[战略缓冲区 – *zhanlüe huanchong qu*]" (Lin Hongyu 2014: 17). Other Chinese authors pointed out that the USA has its own ADIZ, and the rules involving them are substantially similar (Cao Qun 2014). US policy makers did not see it that way, and the strong US reaction to the announcement of the zone – sending two B-52 bombers flying through it unannounced – and the negative reaction by other countries such as South Korea, whose EEZ claim is overlapped by the Chinese ADIZ – resulted in China stepping back from enforcing its zone (Perlez 2013).

All of this makes it difficult to say that China has a Monroe Doctrine; it may be moving toward one, but one would expect, based upon the behavior of most similar regional hegemons in the 19th and 20th centuries, that just such a doctrine would be explicitly declared. Why not?

Explaining non-behavior is, of course, much more difficult than explaining behavior, so what follows in somewhat speculative. The first possible reason why China does not have a Monroe Doctrine is precedent: it has explicitly decried any such Regional Exclusion Doctrine in the past, and has stated in official terms that it would never adopt such a doctrine. To adopt such a doctrine now or in the near future requires an explicit statement, and would naturally beg the question of why the previous policy had changed. It has occurred in the past, of course, that states have openly repudiated previous policies. Government or regime change is one such instance, but it seems unlikely in the foreseeable future for China.

A second possible reason for the lack of a Chinese Monroe Doctrine is a historical Chinese aversion to Regional Exclusion Doctrines. The first reference to other countries having their own "Monroe Doctrine" was the relationship of Imperial Japan to East Asia, during World War I (Reid 1915). By the 1930s, Japan's "Greater East Asian Co-Prosperity Sphere" (東亜新秩序 *Tōa Shin Chitsujo*) was not only a Regional Exclusion Doctrine based upon the slogan of "Asia for the Asians" it was also a thinly veiled justification for rapacious Japanese imperialism. This history is well known in China, and scholars have written on the subject of "Japan's Monroe Doctrine" (Chen Xiuwu 2014). Qing dynasty China also had to endure European spheres of influence in its territory during the late 19th and early 20th centuries, as well as formal colonies and leaseholdings. China's recent historical experiences with regional exclusion are not positive.

A third potential reason for China eschewing a formal Regional Exclusion Doctrine would be the precedent it would set for its relations with South Asia and Central Asia. In both regions, China's economic reach is already intruding into areas which the Indians and the Russians explicitly believe they have primacy and have said so on several occasions. Yet President Xi Jinping's (2013) initiative, the "Silk Road Economic Belt" and the "Maritime Silk Road" concept expanding infrastructure, transportation and trade links between China, Southeast Asia, South Asia, Central Asia, the Middle East and all the way to Europe would intrude. For China to seek to exclude other powers from East Asia while pushing ahead into Russia and India's regions would doubtlessly provoke charges of hypocrisy and resistance. China is seeking to expand its influence globally, not to limit it.

Fourth, the original Monroe Doctrine is now defunct. In a move that attracted more attention in Latin America and China than the United States, the Obama Administration's Secretary of State John Kerry in a major speech at the Organization of American States officially renounced the Monroe Doctrine in November 2013: "The era of the Monroe Doctrine is over. . . . Many years ago, the United States dictated a policy that defined the hemisphere for many years after. We've moved past that era" (Kerry 2013). Officially, of course, this means nothing to China. In reality, it deprives China from using the same excuse for having a Regional Exclusion Doctrine that so many other regional hegemons have invoked: the USA has one, too. Chinese scholars wrote several articles on the issue, some such as Sun Hongbo (2014) and Zhao Lingmin (2013) saw it primarily as a response to declining US power and an effort to improve Latin American relations. Other scholars looked at it from a broad view of historical development (Xing Yue 2014; Sun Xihui 2014), but it seems likely that Chinese policy makers would have been made aware of the announcement.

The final possibility is, of course, that China's leaders do not think that the time is ripe yet for such an announcement, but will in the future. Paramount leader Deng Xiaoping's famous dictum, *taoguang yanghui* (韬光养晦) still has a powerful influence on Chinese strategic thinking. Trying to exclude foreign powers from Southeast and Northeast Asia means trying to exclude the United States. And few Chinese authors, scholars, or even bloggers argue that China currently has that capability, and no Chinese leaders or official sources openly advocate that path. At least, not yet. Indeed, on more than one occasion, Chinese scholars and spokespeople have accepted that the United States has a role within the Asian political system, Chen Xiangyang going so far as to label it a "special sort of neighbor" (特殊的邻国 *teshu de linguo*) (2004: 305, 311).

Other aspects of China's ideational foreign relations remained strongly rooted in the active phase of regional hegemonic behavior as outlined in Table 2.3. China's main concern about the domestic political systems of its neighbors remained largely stability. After the Kyrgyz "Tulip Revolution" in 2005, despite a democratic upheaval in that country, China still maintained diplomatic relations with Bishkek. The opening of the Myanmar government in 2011–12 to greater democratic participation was met with formal congratulations upon the new leaders' elections, and Chinese analysts noted that Myanmar's new government continued its good relations with China (Liu Xinsheng 2013). Any reservations China's leaders may have had about the changes in that country and Aung San Suu-kyi's National League for Democracy were kept private, though Chinese academics have been critical.

China's leaders also undertook a major effort to promote China's "Soft Power" and public diplomacy during this period. The use of 'soft power' by China has been the subject of considerable scholarly attention, both in the West and in China (*inter alia*: Shambaugh 2013; Ding 2008; Kurlantzick 2007; Liu Yumei 2007; Yu Xintian 2008; Wang Xiaozhi et al. 2012). Chinese scholars have written extensively on issues of 'soft power' (软实力 *ruan shili* or 软权力 *ruan quanli*) and 'public diplomacy,' (公共外交 *gonggong waijiao*). Chinese scholars point to their history, culture, cuisine, and social reputation as parts of their 'soft power' that could be used around the world, including in Asia. These include the number of Confucius institutes, foreign aid, medical teams, and most recently the immense eye-catching infrastructure projects that China has undertaken domestically in the last decade or more, and which it is now proposing in the One Belt One Road idea to bring to its neighbors. Or perhaps Chinese foreign policy thinkers are suffering from Maslow's Law of Instrument: when all you have is a hammer, every problem looks like a nail. For Xi Jinping, every diplomatic challenge among China's neighbors looks like an infrastructure problem.

Finally, the role of nationalism must be briefly addressed. Of all of the ideologies that affect foreign policy, this is one of the most basic: it privileges the nation over self, family, locality or region, and sets nation against other nations, "us" versus "them." There is little question but that nationalism is a large and potent force in Chinese foreign policy today; a quick reading of editorials in *Global Times* will show resentment, grievance, provocations, conspiracies, deep wounds, an insult to the dignity of the Chinese people, undeniable facts, irrefutable proof. This is the dark side of China's foreign policy (Wang 2012). Nationalism needs an *other* to hate. Since 1989, that has been increasingly the United States. Within China's neighbors, Japan is the obvious example and has been for over one hundred years. Other neighbors have been less frequently mentioned, except as allies, enablers, and co-conspirators. Of the other regional hegemons examined, the Russian Federation comes the closest to having a long-standing, historically based sense of injury form the basis of a nationalistic foreign policy.

Notes

1 CICA was founded in 1999 and encompasses a large number of countries from Egypt and the Middle East, South Asia, Central Asia, and East Asia. The USA and Japan are observers, and South Korea is a member. <www.s-cica.org>, accessed 27 December 2015.
2 Japan has an ADIZ around it since 1969. These have been self-proclaimed zones since the Cold War, and many other countries have announced them.

Works cited

"Banyan: Crossing a line in the sky." 2013. *The Economist*, 30 November, 44.
Beeson, Mark, and Li, Fujian. 2014. *China's Regional Relations: Evolving Foreign Policy Dynamics*. Boulder, CO: Lynne Rienner.
Blanchard, Ben. 2015a. China says U.S. welcome to use civilian China sea. *Reuters*, 30 April. <www.reuters.com/article/us-china-usa-southchinasea-idUSKBN0NM31620150501>, accessed 2 May 2015.
Cao Qun. 2014. ZhongMei fangkong shibiequ guize shi fou cunzai fenqi? [Are there differences between Chinese and American rules governing Air Defense Identification Zones (ADIZ)]. *Dangdai YaTai* [Journal of Contemporary Asia-Pacific], 2, 27–53.
CFA [China's Foreign Affairs]. Annual. Beijing: Ministry of Foreign Affairs of the People's Republic of China. This is the official yearbook of the Ministry of Foreign Affairs of the People's Republic of China. Beginning its publication in 1987 as 中国外交概览 China's

Foreign Affairs review, it is hereafter referred to as ZGWJGL, and after 1995 中国外交 it is renamed Zhongguo waijiao (ZGWJ) for the Chinese language version, and China's Foreign Affairs or *CFA* for the English-language version, which began publication in 2003. See also ZGWJGL.

Chen Dingding, and Jianwei, Wang. 2011. Lying low no more? China's new thinking on the *tao guang yang hui*. *China: An International Journal* 9(2), 195–216.

Chen Xiangyang. 2004. *Zhongguo mulin waijiao: sixiang, shijian, qianzhang* [China's good-neighbour diplomacy: Though, practice, prospect]. Beijing: Shishi chubanshe.

Chen Xiuwu. 2014. Riben de "Yazhou Menluo zhuyi" [Japan's "Asia Monroe Doctrine"]. *Waiguo wenti yanjiu*, 214(4), 3–8.

Cui Heng. 2014. The strategic coupling of Sino-Russian relations. China.org.cn [State Council Information Office]. <www.china.org.cn/opinion/2014-05/25/content_32473565.htm>, accessed 6 April 2015.

Dai Bingguo. 2010. Zhongguo guowu weiyuan Dai Bingguo: zhichi zou heping fazhan daolu [State Councilor Dai Bingguo: Adhere to the path of peaceful development]. Zhonghua Renmin Gongheguo zhongyang renmin zhengfu [Central People's Government of the People's Republic of China] website, 6 December 2010. <www.gov.cn/ldhd/2010-12/06/content_1760381.htm>, accessed 25 April 2013. Translation at http://china.usc.edu/ShowArticle.aspx?articleID=2325

Ding, Sheng. 2008. *The Dragon's Hidden Wings: How China Rises with Its Soft Power*. Lanham, MD: Lexington Books.

"The Dragon's new teeth: China's military rise." 2012. *The Economist*, 7 April. <www.economist.com/node/21552193>, accessed 9 January 2016.

Du Yanjun. 2015. What's new in Chinese diplomacy? – An interpretation of Xi Jinping: The governance of China. *Contemporary International Relations*, 25(3), 108–115.

EIA [US Energy Information Agency]. 2014. China in now world's largest importer of petroleum and other liquid fuels. US EIA website, 24 March. <www.eia.gov/todayinenergy/detail.php?id=15531>, accessed 6 June 2017.

Feng Zhongping. 2013. Periphery strategy should focus on innovative security cooperation. *Contemporary International Relations*, 23(6), 50–53.

Glaser, Bonnie, and Pal, Deep. 2013. China periphery diplomacy initiative: Implications for China's neighbors and the United States. China-US Focus, 7 November. <www.chinausfocus.com/foreign-policy/chinas-periphery-diplomacy-initiative-implications-for-china-neighbors-and-the-united-states/>, accessed 8 March 2014.

Guo, Sujian, and Blanchard, Jean-Marc F., eds. 2008. *"Harmonious World" and China's New Foreign Policy*. Lanham: Lexington Books.

Han Caizhen, and Shi Yinhong. 2014. Bottlenecks in East Asia's regional cooperation. *Contemporary International Relations* (English), 24(3), 29–37.

Hayashi, Nozumu. 2014. China approved South China Sea oil drilling in early 2014. Asahi Shimbun Asia-Japan Watch, 29 May. <http://ajw.asahi.com/article/asia/china/AJ201405290049>, accessed 30 May 2014.

Huang Pengzhi. 2014. Guanyu "Maliujia kunjing" de san zhong chengyin fenxi [Analysis of the three causes of the "Malacca dilemma"]. *Xue lilun* (33), 11–12.

Jackson, Steven F. 2016. Does China have a Monroe Doctrine? Evidence for regional exclusion. *Strategic Studies Quarterly*, 10(4), 64–89.

Ji Zhiye. 2013. China's neighboring diplomacy demands top-level design. *Contemporary International Relations*, 23(6), 1–4.

Jin Canrong, ed. 2011. *Da guo de zeren* [Big power's responsibility]. Beijing: Zhongguo renmin daxue chubanshe.

Jin Canrong, and Dai Weilai. 2009. Daguo guanxi bianhua de xin qushi ji yinxiang [New tendencies and influences in the changes in great power relations], in *Daguo waijiao*, edited by Tang Jin. Beijing: Hua wen chubanshe, 1–26.

Jin Canrong, and Duan Haowen. 2013. New features of the surrounding international environment and China's response. *Contemporary International Relations*, 23(6), 24–30.

Kavalski, Emilian. 2012. *Central Asia and the Rise of Normative Powers: Contextualizing the Security Governance of the European Union, China, and India*. New York: Bloomsbury.

Kerry, John. 2013. Remarks on U.S. policy in the Western hemisphere. US Department of State, 18 November. <www.state.gov/secretary/remarks/2013/11/217680.htm>, accessed 8 June 2015.

Kubo, Nobuhiro, Kelly, Tim, and Brunnstrom, David. 2015. Exclusive: Japan considering joint U.S. air patrols in South China Sea – sources. *Reuters*, 29 April. <www.reuters.com/article/us-usa-japan-southchinasea-idUSKBN0NK15M20150429>, accessed 29 April 2015.

Kurlantzick, Joshua. 2007. *Charm Offensive: How China's Soft Power Is Transforming the World*. New Haven: Yale University Press.

Li Xiaokun. 2014. Diplomacy to focus on neighborhood. Xinhuanet, 2 January. <http://news.xinhuanet.com/english/2014-01/02/c_133012471.htm>, accessed 8 March 2014.

Li Yonghui. 2013. Constructing a strategic peripheral belt to support the wings of China's rise. *Contemporary International Relations*, 23(6), 66–70.

Li Zhonglin. 2013. Ping suowei Zhongguo ban "Menluo zhuyi" [Comment on the so-called "Chinese Monroe Doctrine"]. *Heping yu fazhan*, (4), 103–115.

Lin Hongyu. 2014. Sino-Japanese relations and the ADIZ. *Contemporary International Relations* (English), 24(2; March/April), 16–21.

Liu Bowen, and Fang Changping. 2016. Zhoubian huoban guanxiwang gei yu Zhongguo zhoubian anquan huanjing [Partnership networks and the security environment in China's periphery]. *Dangdai YaTai*, (3), 68–100.

Liu Xinsheng. 2013. Miandian da biange ji qi dui Zhong-Mian guanxi de yingxiang [Large change in Myanmar and its influence on China-Myanmar relations]. *Dongnanya zongheng* [Around Southeast Asia], (1), 36–40.

Liu Yumei. 2007. 'Ruan shili yu Zong Fei guanxi de fazhan [Soft power and the development of Sino-African relations]. *Guoji wenti yanjiu*, 3(2007), 16–21.

Luo Yongkun. 2016. Changes in China's Southeast-Asia policy. *Contemporary International Relations*, 26(1), 87–100.

MOFA. 2013. Foreign ministry spokesperson Qin Gang's regular press conference on November 25, 2013. <http://az.china-embassy.org/eng/fyrth/t1102346.htm>, accessed 19 August 2014.

MOFA. 2015. Foreign Ministry spokesperson Lu Kang's regular press conference on October 27, 2015. Ministry of Foreign Affairs, People's Republic of China. <www.fmprc.gov.cn/mfa_eng/xwfw_665399/s2510_665401/2535_665405/t1309625.shtml>, accessed 28 October 2015.

Myers, Steven Lee. 2013. Arctic council adds 6 nations as observer states, including China. *New York Times*, 15 May. <www.nytimes.com/2013/05/16/world/europe/arctic-council-adds-six-members-including-china.html>, accessed 17 August 2014.

Odgaard, Liselotte. 2015. China's dangerous ambiguity in the South China Sea: Op-Ed. *New York Times*, 10 December. <www.nytimes.com/2015/12/11/opinion/chinas-dangerous-ambiguity.html>, accessed 10 December.

Page, Jeremy, and Wong, Chun Han. 2017. China eases foot off gas on military spending. *Wall Street Journal*, 4 March. <www.wsj.com/articles/china-raising-military-budget-by-about-7-1488601110>, accessed 26 April 2017.

Perlez, Jane. 2013. After challenges, China appears to backpedal on air zone. *New York Times*, 27 November 2013. <www.nytimes.com/2013/11/28/world/asia/china-explains-handling-of-b-52-flight-as-tensions-escalate.html>, accessed 8 April 2014.

Perlez, Jane, and Fackler, Martin. 2013. China patrols air zone over disputed islands. *New York Times*, 28 November. <www.nytimes.com/2013/11/29/world/asia/japan-south-korea-fly-military-planes-in-zone-set-by-china.html>, accessed 4 December 2013.

Qin Yaqing. 2011. *Da guo guanxi yu Zhongguo waijiao* [Great power relations and China's diplomacy]. Beijing: Shijie zhishi chubanshe.

"Regional turbulence: The East China Sea." 2013. *The Economist*, 30 November, 39.

Reid, Gilbert. 1915. An imitation Monroe Doctrine. *Journal of Race Development*, 6(July), 12–22.

Roy, Denny. 2013. *Return of the Dragon: Rising China and Regional Security*. New York: Columbia University Press.

Rozman, Gilbert. 2010. *Chinese Strategic thought toward Asia*. New York: Palgrave Macmillan.

Shambaugh, David. 2005. China engages Asia: Reshaping the regional order. *International Security*, 29(3), 64–99.

Shambaugh, David. 2013. *China Goes Global: The Partial Power*. Oxford: Oxford University Press.

State Council Information Office. 2017. China's policies on Asia-Pacific security cooperation. Xinhua, 11 January. <http://news.xinhuanet.com/english/china/2017-01/11/c_135973695.htm>, accessed 14 January 2017.

Sun Hongbo. 2014. Meiguo gaobie "Menluo zhuyi" de yingxiang ji weilai de MeiLa guanxi [America bids farewell to the "Monroe Doctrine's" influence and the future of US-Latin American relations]. *Dangdai shijie* [Contemporary World], (3), 37–40.

Sun Xihui. 2014. "Menluo zhuyi" zhi hui zhongjie ma? [Can the "Monroe Doctrine" really be ending?]. *Xin Shijie* [New Horizons], 39(1), 80–81.

Sun Xingjie. 2013. Miandian, guoji diyuan xin wutai [Myanmar, new international geographic stage]. *Qingnian cankao*, 7 February 2012 in *Ganbu wenzhai*, 2013(4), 25.

Tang Jin, ed. 2009. *Daguo waijiao* [Great power diplomacy]. Beijing: Hua wen chubanshe.

Torbati, Yeganeh. 2015. "Hope to see you again": China warship to U.S. destroyer after South China Sea patrol. *Reuters*, 5 November. <www.reuters.com/article/us-southchinasea-usa-warship-idUSKCN0SV05420151106>, accessed 5 November 2015.

US State Department, Bureau of Oceans and International Environmental and Scientific Affairs. 2014. *Limits in the Seas: China: Maritime Claims in the South China Sea*. no. 143, December. Washington, DC: US State Department.

Wang, Dong. 2015. Is China trying to push the US out of East Asia? *China Quarterly of International Strategic Studies*, 1(1), 59–84.

Wang Xiaozhi, Huang Lizhi, and Liu Haifang. 2012. Fansi Zhongguo dui Fei gonggong waijiao [Reflections on China's public diplomacy], *Dangdai shijie*, 3(2012), 34–37.

Wang Yiwei. 2014. Outsiders unreliable as security providers. *Global Times* (China), 7 July. <www.globaltimes.cn/content/869253.shtml>, accessed 29 August 2015.

Wang, Zheng. 2012. *Never Forget National Humiliation: Historical Memory in Chinese Politics and Foreign Relations*. New York: Columbia University Press.

Wen Jiabao. 2004. Premier Web Jiabao meets the press (2004). 14 March. Chinese Government's Official Web Portal. <http://english.gov.cn/official/2005-07/26/content_17183.htm>, accessed 9 April 2014.

Wong, Edward. 2015. Security law suggests a broadening of China's "core interests". *New York Times*, 2 July. <www.nytimes.com/2015/07/03/world/asia/security-law-suggests-a-broadening-of-chinas-core-interests.html>, accessed 3 July 2015.

Wong, Edward, Perlez, Jane, and Buckley, Chris. 2015. China announces cuts of 300,000 troops at military parade showing its might. *New York Times*, 2 September <www.nytimes.com/2015/09/03/world/asia/beijing-turns-into-ghost-town-as-it-gears-up-for-military-parade.html>, accessed 8 September 2015.

Wu Zhicheng. 2015. Strategic planning for its neighboring diplomacy. *Contemporary International Relations*, 25(2), 62–65.

Xi Jinping. 2013. Xi Jinping zài zhōubiān wàijiāo gōngzuò zuòtán huì shàng fābiǎo zhòngyào jiǎnghuà [Xi Jinping delivered an important speech at the neighboring diplomacy work conference]. 25 October. Ministry of Foreign Affairs. <www.fmprc.gov.cn/mfa_chn/zyxw_602251/t1093113.shtml>, accessed 8 March 2014.

Xi Jinping. 2014. New Asian security concept for new progress in security cooperation. 5 May. Remarks at Fourth Summit of the Conference on Interaction and Confidence Building Measures in Asia. Ministry of Foreign Affairs, People's Republic of China. <www.fmprc.gov.cn/mfa_eng/zxxx_662805/t1159951.shtml>, accessed 27 December 2015.

Xing Yue. 2014. San wen "Men Luo zhu yi" [Three questions about the Monroe Doctrine]. *Zhongguo shehui kexue bao* [China Social Sciences], international edition, B04(12 February), 1–2.

Xu Qingchao. 2014. Zhongguo xin Yazhou waijiao bushi Zhongguo ban "Luomen zhuyi". *Zhongguo shehui kexue bao*, 18 July, A07.

Yan Xuetong. 2015. Diplomacy should focus on neighbors. *China Daily*, 27 January. <http://usa.chinadaily.com.cn/epaper/2015-01/27/content_19419558.htm>, accessed 29 August 2015.

Yang Cheng. 2014. "Zhōngguó bǎn mén luó zhǔyì" de cuòwù zhījué [The misperception of "China's Monroe Doctrine"]. *Dongfang zaobao*, 19 May, A09.

Yu Xintian. 2008. Ruan shili jianshe yu Zhongguo dui wait zhanlue [Soft power construction and China's external strategy]. *Zhongguo yu shijie tanlun*, (2), 15–20.

ZGWJ. See ZGWJGL.

ZGWJGL [Zhongguo waijiao gailan] [Survey of China's diplomacy]. Annual. Beijing: Ministry of Foreign Affairs of the People's Republic of China. This is the official yearbook of the Ministry of Foreign Affairs of the People's Republic of China. Beginning its publication in 1987 as 中国外交概览 China's Foreign Affairs review, it is hereafter referred to as ZGWJGL, and after 1995 中国外交 it is renamed Zhongguo waijiao (ZGWJ) for the Chinese language version, and China's Foreign Affairs or CFA for the English-language version, which began publication in 2003.

Zhao Lingmin. 2013. Meiguo gaobie "Menluo zhuyi?" [America says farewell to the "Monroe Doctrine?"]. *Huaxingbao*, 23(28 November), 1–2.

Zheng Xiwen. 2014. No Asian Monroe Doctrine. *China Daily*, 29 September. <www.chinadaily.com.cn/opinion/2014-09/29/content_18679191.htm>, accessed 29 August 2015.

Zhu Feng. 2013. Chinese perspectives on the U.S. role in Southeast Asia, in *Southeast Asian Affairs 2013*, edited by Daljit Singh. Singapore: ISEAS–Yusof Ishak Institute, 51–60.

6 China and Northeast Asia in the 21st century

Northeast Asia is the region of some of China's worst foreign relations during this period and in recent years has become even worse. Of the six states within the region (not counting Taiwan), China, Japan, South Korea, North Korea, and Mongolia, none of the bilateral relations are particularly warm, and several are openly hostile. The region is only marginally and peripherally institutionalized in its international organization through Southeast Asian fora, ASEAN + 3, ASEAN +1, the ASEAN Regional Forum (ARF), the newly developed East Asian Summit, and APEC. Yet, the region does have enormous economic links even between the hostile parties.

China's only real regional challenger, Japan, is in Northeast Asia, as is one of its most dangerous territorial disputes; if there is evidence that China is behaving more like other regional hegemons in their hyperactive phases, this is one of the two the sub-regions, Southeast Asia being the other. China's position in Northeast Asia was, for the first time in 110 years, becoming dominant. As we will see when discussing trade below, that condition would also apply to economics.

Security

Territorial disputes

Japan

China has one explicit territorial dispute in Northeast Asia, the maritime border, including the Senkaku/Diaoyu island group, and two additional latent issues, which are somewhat minor. A full discussion of the Senkaku/Diaoyu dispute is beyond the scope of this volume; whether it is resolved legally or forcefully is (for the Chinese side of the dispute, see Guo Jiping 2012 and for the Japanese, see MOFAJ 2013). As we have seen, hyperactive regional hegemons tend to use force in the resolution of territorial issues, whereas active hegemons tend to use legal or negotiated means. As seen in Chapters 3 and 4, the Senkaku/Diaoyu issue had been lurking in Sino-Japanese relations for a long time, coming up periodically when minor incidents occurred but generally remained a minor unresolved irritant in the broader Sino-Japanese relationship. That began to change in the 21st century, when a variety of factors forced the issue back to the top of the relationship. The actual dry land territory involved in the Senkaku/Diaoyu dispute is absurdly small, around 5.17km², or about eight times the size of the Washington Mall; China's perspective is that its Exclusive Economic Zones (EEZs) would be furthered by ownership of the Senkaku/Diaoyu islands, which is much more expansive. The Chinese legal position is that the United Nations Conference on Law of the Sea's idea of an EEZ grants a country added legal protections above the right to control economic activity in the area (Bush 2010: 67–68); the Chinese claim that the area and beyond become "jurisdictional waters" (Dutton 2014: 14) and in November 2013 explicitly added an Air Defense Identification Zone over its claimed EEZ ("Regional turbulence" 2013; Perlez and Fackler 2013). To be sure, Japan also has a very expansive Air Identification Zone and declared it well before the Chinese did, in 1969 (Bush 2010: 68). The Chinese side, after seeing a substantial US military reaction to the ADIZ subsequently down-played its significance (Perlez 2013a). China's claims and its interpretation of its rights within an EEZ and ADIZ represent a significant increase in what constitute "its" waters, and since these claims overlap considerably with what Japan considers to be "its" waters, the dispute is not about 8 square kilometers of land; it is over hundreds of thousands of kilometers of ocean.

Finally, in terms of territorial disputes, unofficial Chinese sources have also been making vague assertions about historical association between Okinawa/the Ryukyus and Qing dynasty China (Wu Di 2011; Perlez 2013b; Bradsher 2013). Given the unpopularity of US bases in Okinawa with local residents and with the central government in Tokyo, the area and potential claim might be another way in which the government in Beijing can provoke Japan (Fackler 2013b). Japan's 2014 Defense White Paper noted this current in Chinese press, but also indicated that such assertions were not official Chinese government policy (Japan Ministry of Defense 2014: "China" fn. 1). It is not clear that this is a serious claim, let alone a territorial dispute, but it could indicate that the existing dispute is likely to continue.

Korea

As noted, China and South Korea have a minor dispute over a submerged rock in the Yellow Sea as well (Ieodo in Korean, Suyan in Chinese, aka Socotra Rock) which influences EEZ claims, but unlike the Senkaku/Diaoyu stand-off, it has remained largely low-key (Zhang Huizhi and Wang Xiaoke 2013: 103). The maritime intersection of Chinese and South Korea EEZs has been the focus of sporadic talks since 1996, but little progress has been made because of the continued disagreement over this rock ("S. Korea, China hold closed talks on maritime border" 2014).

Old historical issues have alluded to a potential territorial issue between China and Korea in a dispute that started in 2004 when Chinese scholars characterized the ancient kingdom of Koguryo (37 BCE–668 CE) as a regional part of China, and which South Korean scholars consider to be a Korean kingdom that lay in what is now northeastern China (Jae Ho Chung 2009: 472–479). The Chinese side apparently had concerns that the historical debate might represent an effort by the South Koreans to raise a territorial claim for the far distant future of a reunified Korea, and the Koreans saw the Chinese claim to deny an independent historical identity for Korea. Deft diplomacy in the late summer of 2004 agreed that the issue was a purely academic one, but the asymmetry of the two actors beginning in the first decade of the 21st century produced increased sensitivity of the Korean side over a minor academic point.

The border between China and North Korea remains tightly controlled. The two sides have been slowly developing protocols and procedures for joint border inspections, though as of 2012 these negotiations had not yet been completed, let alone the actual inspection. Border trade is down, hurting Chinese traders (Liu 2017) and individual North Koreans (including soldiers) in late 2014 and early 2015 snuck across the border looking for food and murdered a handful of Chinese residents in at least three incidents (Perlez 2015; Ramzy 2015). China has since stepped up its patrols.

External major powers

The Chinese perspective on its relations with Japan are strongly linked to the enduring US-Japan Security Treaty. The US position concerning the Senkakus is that they are currently administered by Japan, and as such come under the umbrella of US protection. China's reaction to the issue of the islands has increasingly focused on the United States role in backing Japan's stance. Especially after the September 2012 crisis, Chinese diplomats strongly linked Japan's behavior with American backing, such as Chen Jian's statement to the Hong Kong Press Club at the end of October 2012 (Perlez and Bradsher 2012) and former Defense Ministry spokesman Qian Lihua's statement that ". . . the US has fostered Japan to keep challenging the limits of China's tolerance," (Wang Wei 2013). A *People's Daily* editorial linked the issue to the US "Pivot to Asia" explicitly: "In recent years, the eastward shift of the US strategy has given Japan an opportunity to seize the Diaoyu Islands" ("Hegemony of Japan-US alliance" 2013). When US Secretary of State Clinton reiterated the US position of neutrality on the issue of the islands' sovereignty but that the USA would be obligated to defend them under the US-Japan Security Treaty in January 2013, the Chinese Foreign Ministry criticized the US position, and again when President Barrack Obama did the same in April 2014 (Xinhua 2014). Chinese analysts, however, have been linking China's difficulties in its relations with its neighbors to the actions of the United States since at least 2004 when Chen Xiangyang wrote extensively on the subject (287–291).

Diplomatic relations with regional states

China has formal diplomatic relations with all four independent Northeast Asian states during this time period. South Korea was elevated to an "All-Round Cooperative Partnership" in 2003 and to a "Strategic Cooperative Partnership" in 2008.

China established a "Strategic Partnership" with Mongolia in 2011, and in 2014 a Comprehensive Strategic Partnership with Ulaanbaatar. But neither Japan nor North Korea have become "partners" with China, an indication of the diplomatic tensions in Northeast Asia. Japan is a "close and important neighbor," by the end of this period one of the few nearby states to still be regularly described as a "neighbor" in the Chinese diplomatic lexicon, and North Korea was described as having "traditional and cooperative" relations with China.

Japan

The alternative explanation for the territorial conflict between China and Japan is that the Senkaku/Diaoyu islands stand as a proxy for other issues in the Sino-Japanese relationship, political and resource-based. For China, the islands stand in for over 110 years of Japanese aggression against China beginning with the first Sino-Japanese war in 1894–95 when Japan seized Taiwan and the Diaoyu islands. If China and Japan shared another border, then that would be the "issue." *Incidents* happen regularly, but China makes them an *issue* when Japan's leaders visit the Yasukuni Shrine or engage in other behavior or promote policies that China's leaders interpret as historically insensitive. In this interpretation, China's ambitions for the islands are secondary to the need for historical reassessment and an appropriate resolution of the historical grievance with Japan.

The long prime ministerial term of Koizumi Junichiro (2001–2006) saw several incidents involving the Senkaku/Diaoyu islands for the first time since China and Japan had concluded a confidence-building measures agreement in February 2001. China protested the report in January 2003 that the Japanese government had secretly leased three of the five islands from private owners, a prelude to the September 2012 incident. In March 2004 and again in June 2004 Chinese maritime activity in both the overlapping EEZ and (unofficial) Chinese protesters on the islands themselves resulted in Japanese diplomatic protests and arrests by Japanese authorities, and a Chinese submarine was discovered near Okinawa in November (Wan 2006: 26–29). In each case, the incidents followed Prime Minister Koizumi's visit to the Yasukuni Shrine. The Japanese response in early 2009 was to publicly assert that the islands were covered by the US-Japan Security Treaty and thus protected by both Japanese and US militaries.

The arrest of a Chinese fishing boat captain who rammed his boat into Japanese coast guard vessels in September 2010 led to Chinese economic retaliation in the form of a temporary rare earth metals embargo (see below). The most serious recent episode over the Senkaku/Diaoyu islands began in September 2012 when the Japanese central government purchased some of the privately owned islands, ostensibly to forestall their purchase by former Tokyo governor and nationalist firebrand Ishihara Shintaro. The Chinese reacted much more harshly than in 2003 when the Japanese government had leased the islands, seeing this as a violation of the "Gentlemen's Agreement" to shelf the status of the islands. Chinese maritime patrol boats entered the area in protest in numbers far above previous levels (MOFAJ 2014), and popular protests erupted in Chinese cities, some of which turned violent (Johnson and Shanker 2012; Perlez 2012a). Chinese aircraft violated the airspace over the islands in December 2012, as opposed to flying nearby, and the Japanese Coast Guard continues to record intrusions into the 12 nautical mile territorial limits of Japan around the islands, averaging over ten a month since September 2012 (Tabuchi 2012; Fackler 2014; Japan Coast Guard 2017).

To be sure, for every incident and period of tension, Japan and China have managed the crisis as well as might be expected, given the emotions and nationalism on both sides. Less than a month after the September 2012 crisis, China had secretly opened discussions with Japan (Fackler 2012; MOFA 2012). Neither side has sent actual naval (Maritime Self-Defense Force in the case of Japan) units into the area, instead using vessels of the Japan Coast Guard (海上保安庁/*Kaijō Hoan-chō*) and China Coast Guard vessels (中国海警/*Zhongguo haicha*, a 2013 consolidation of the State Oceanographic Administration's Marine Surveillance, Maritime Safety Administration and other marine-related bureaus. Gong Jianhua 2012; Erickson and Collins 2013). The Chinese Coast Guard now has a numeric advantage over the Japanese Coast Guards in large patrol craft (see Table 7.1 in the next chapter), but Japanese Coast Guard vessels retain a number of technological and logistical advantages, being based closer to the disputed area than the Chinese. Both sides' Coast Guard vessels have been upgraded in what appears to be a (un)-arms race, albeit one with naval backing (Bush 2010: 72–75). There have been instances in which Chinese naval vessels have passed near the islands (Perlez 2012b). In most incidents, Chinese intrusions have been fairly brief, so that Japanese patrol craft or aircraft arrive after the Chinese departure, though one incident in January 2013 a Chinese ship lingered thirteen hours (Fackler 2013a). By the end of January 2013, the new Chinese president, Xi Jinping, was being somewhat conciliatory (Perlez 2013c). The potential for war which captured headlines in late 2012 receded, though neither side's rhetoric has changed. Xi Jinping and Abe Shinzo met in April 2015 at the neutral site of Jakarta, and though the handshake was clearly strained, the relationship is no longer on edge.

But just as it seems that China will not necessarily use force to resolve its territorial dispute with Japan, it also seems unlikely that legal mechanisms are being used. China and Japan established a "mechanism of high-level consultation on maritime issues" in December 2011 during Japanese Prime Minister Noda Yoshihiko's visit to Beijing (*CFA* 2012: 437), though by September 2012 it was effectively just a forum for exchanging diplomatic protest notes. To their credit, the Chinese have registered their claim before the United Nations Commission on Limits of the Continental Shelf (CLCS) set up by UNCLOS. China deposited a Maritime Zone Notification on September 21, 2012 and Japan responded with its objection three days later. This would give the Chinese a geological edge in its argument for possession of the islands, since they do appear to be on the continental shelf as opposed to the Ryukyu Island chain which are on the other side of the Okinawa Trench. Needless to say, Japan objects. And as we will see in the next section, the legal approach is only valid for the Senkaku/Diaoyu dispute and not the South China Sea, as far as China is concerned.

Whether China uses force to enforce its territorial claim against Japan depends partly on the perceived stakes. Natural gas fields lie substantially to the north of the Senkaku/Diaoyu chain, and the islands' status plays a role in establishing a maritime division of the Chinese and Japanese EEZs that do affect the gas fields. If the Diaoyus are Chinese, then China's EEZ could be moved further out to include most of the natural gas fields; if the Senkakus are established as Japanese, the EEZs overlap and the most likely resolution, a median line division, would split the gas fields in two. Estimates of how much gas is at stake vary enormously. The US government estimate from the Energy Information Agency (EIA) is that the East China Sea contains 1–2 trillion cubic feet of proven and probable reserves; Chinese estimates go up to 250 trillion, mostly in undiscovered formations (EIA 2012: 3).[1] As we will see below, Chinese estimates for energy reserves in the South China Sea are also much higher than those of the EIA, raising the disturbing prospect that Chinese leaders may be making critical decisions based upon significantly different calculations of interests.

Disputes over energy have been seen in a number of other regional hegemons' behavior, from the US economic embargo on Cuba in 1960 prompted by the latter's importation of Soviet oil, to the Russian Federation's 2009 economic coercion of Ukraine and other neighbors using a natural gas shut-off. Nigeria also cut off Ghana's oil in 1980 in a dispute over illegal migrants (Abegunrin 2003: 103–105). The attempt to seize territory and risk war for its *potential* energy resources, however, does not appear as common behavior, simply because the expense and damage of a modern war far outweighs most conceivable benefits derived. Even if China were to seize the Senkakus in a lightning operation, it would not make Japan more willing to accept China's advanced maritime EEZ claim, nor would it entice international oil corporations to explore in the disputed area. The more logical approach would be joint production, such as between Brazil and Paraguay in the Itaipu Dam project. To be sure, the even division of the dam's electricity seems somewhat unfair to many Brazilians, given that Paraguay immediately resells it (at a negotiated markup) to Brazil. Joint development is, nevertheless, a logical and cheaper alternative to conquest. China and Japan have held discussions on joint development of gas fields in the East China Sea, and Japanese government financing built an oil and gas pipeline from the Pinghu field to the ports of Shanghai and Ningbo in 1983 (EIA 2012: 2). In the 21st century, both China and Japan have made proposals for joint production that the other side has rejected.

Fish are another issue that makes the dispute in the East China Sea potentially worth fighting about; indeed, the name of the main island in the Senkaku/Diaoyu group is "fishing island" in both Chinese and Japanese: 钓鱼岛 (*Diaoyudao*) and 魚釣り島 (*Uotsurijima*). Though it may seem like a trivial dispute to 21st-century readers, Chinese and Japanese take their fish seriously, and thus the extent of the EEZs, which allow countries to regulate fishing, are of vital importance. China surpassed Japan as the largest fishing nation in East Asia in 1992, and its marine capture totals began to increase massively in the late 1990s, and though the growth slowed in the early 21st century, by 2012, China became the world leader in marine capture fish by an enormous margin, with a total catch of almost 14 million tons, about 17% of world total, and leading Indonesia and the USA, which produce a bit more than 5 million tons each (FAO 2012). Of the major fishing grounds worldwide, the North-Western Pacific, broadly defined (area 61 in the FAO designation), is the most important, but the precise amount fished from the East China Sea is difficult to determine, because the fishing there is not under the statistical aegis of the FAO's Asia-Pacific Fishery Commission. It is probably sufficient to say that Japan and China's overlapping EEZs in the East China Sea represent for each an immensely important resource that is currently productive, unlike most of the putative hydrocarbons in the area. Other regional hegemons have had fishing disputes as well; India regularly deals with fishing disputes around Sri Lanka and Bangladesh, and the United States in the 1960s and 1970s had a serious dispute with Ecuador over its unilateral 200-nm EEZ, in what was called the "Tuna War" which in 1963 led to the suspension of US military sales to Ecuador (Cascon 2008).

Korea

China's relations with the two Koreas have an element of a love triangle to it: China is firmly committed to North Korea by history, treaty, and communist party ties, yet its economic and increasingly political ties with South Korea clearly pull China's leaders toward Seoul. Managing the relationship is one of China's Northeast Asian headaches, just as managing the relationship between South Korea and Japan is one of America's major worries. And there is little doubt but that China's relationship with Pyongyang has deteriorated seriously in the 21st century. Both in nuclear policy and domestic economic policy, China has sought to change North Korean behavior, one of the few instances of China explicitly acting to constrain a neighbor, albeit with little success.

Chinese leaders have been restrained in their advocacy for economic reforms in North Korea, to be sure. But Kim Jong-il's tour of Shanghai's Pudong district in 2001 clearly impressed the North Korean leader to at least rhetorically reform the Stalinist economy in the "July 1 Measures" (Park 2009: 535–536). The foreign economic zones set up in North Korea were inspired by Chinese experience, and strongly supported by Jang Song-thaek. Unfortunately, his demise in late 2013 has left the zones and economic reforms in North Korea without an advocate, and it is unclear what the zones' future is.

North Korea in turn has shown little inclination to restraint, and has generally become more belligerent as it has become more isolated. China's ability to influence North Korean behavior is the subject of intense debate among western scholars and policy makers; it is clear that China's influence in the 21st century is limited, and that one of its main contacts in the North Korean inner circle of power, Jang Song-thaek, is now dead, executed by orders of Kim Jong-un, the third generation of the Kim family to govern (Pollack 2014). As of August 2017, the youngest Kim has not been invited to visit Beijing, although Chinese President Xi Jinping enjoyed a warm visit in Seoul in 2014, a move probably calculated as much as a signal to the North as an effort to woo South Korea away from the US orbit (Perlez 2014).

North Korea's has two tools for manipulating its international environment: nuclear weapons on missiles and potential instability, and it uses both. China has been hosting the Six Party Talks (USA, Russia, China, South Korea, Japan and North Korea) since they began in 2003. The talks in turn were China's best opportunity to demonstrate its "responsible great power" status, serving as the only party capable to bringing North Korea to the hexagonal table. This represented China's primary contribution to security public goods in the region. Despite an apparent breakthrough in 2007, North Korea's violation of UN sanctions with a (failed) satellite (ICBM) launch in 2009 led to Pyongyang's withdrawal from talks, and UN Security Council sanctions against North Korea, for which China voted, another act of "responsible great power" status. Subsequent North Korean behavior, including the sinking of a South Korean warship, shelling of inhabited off-shore islands, and announcements of intention to launch satellites and especially its 2013 third nuclear weapons test have not endeared the North Koreans to the major powers in East Asia. And though Chinese statements are reluctant to admit it, the North Korean threat is one very clear reason why Japan has sought defense modernization. As one Chinese scholar of the North notes, "A nuclear-armed D.P.R.K. will provide South Korea and Japan excuses to beef up their armed forces – especially Japan which is hankering after a reason to justify a revival of its military" (Huang Fengzhi and Sun Guoqiang 2013: 66). North Korea's potential for nuclear missiles also is an American justification for missile defenses in Northeast Asia, which China opposes. And of course, China charges that the North Korean nuclear program helps justify the American "pivot" back to Asia (67).

Particularly after the 2013 North Korean nuclear test, the relationship between Beijing and Pyongyang has been strained. Chinese sources no longer refer to the "Resist American Aggression, Aid Korea" war and instead now use the more neutral (and compact) "Korean War" (Huang Fengzhi and Sun Guoqiang 2013: 68), noting that "[t]hese moves have shifted China away from its historical and ideological path . . . North Korea's brinksmanship, such as the third underground nuclear test, its abandonment of the Korean Armistice Agreement and its announcement that it was restarting the Yangbyon nuclear reactor, China's security interests have been under serious threat" (69). Indeed, there has been a recent debate in China: "China held some heavy discussions on the issue: is North Korea a strategic asset or a heavy burden for China?" (74–75). And just to be truly annoying, the North Koreans tested missiles during Xi Jinping's vaunted May 2017 Belt and Road Forum, just to spoil the party.

And yet China tolerates North Korea, like a dysfunctional family member one does not like but cannot possibly avoid because they live next door. The official Chinese designation of the relationship is "traditional friendship and cooperation" (传统友好合作关系 *chuantong youhao hezuo guanxi*), and even in 2013 Chinese scholars writing at the limits of policy noted, "China will not forsake Kim Jong-un's regime and side with Washington . . ." (Huang Fengzhi and Sun Guoqiang 2013: 71). Whether the common communist party system, or the contemporary historical legacy of fighting side-by-side in the Korean war has any remaining appeal to China is a question; Xi Jinping had just been born when the Korean war ended, and it is doubtful that there are any Korean war veterans left on active duty in the PLA. In large part, the fear of instability in North Korea is a strong motivator for China; if mass unrest were to break out in North Korea, the prospect of millions of refugees crossing the very narrow Tumen river into China is quite conceivable. The 1971 India-Pakistan war started because of Bengali refugees fleeing into India. A war on the peninsula has happened before and a desperate and unstable regime in Pyongyang has shown that it is very willing to engage in brinksmanship. Even a peaceful unification of the peninsula à la East and West Germany poses an uncomfortable prospect for China: a unified Korea, allied with the United States, could put American troops back on the Yalu river across from China. North Korea is a classic buffer state, and China seems willing to tolerate its behavior so long as it remains stable.

This problem of a regional hegemon which is unable to discipline a smaller ally has occurred elsewhere, such as South Africa's relations with Rhodesia, and though not a regional relationship, one might see the US-Israeli relationship as having elements: a larger power unable to discipline its smaller ally because the smaller ally is well aware that the larger power cannot possibly cut the small one loose, thus, its behavior is unconstrained.

China's relations with the other side of the triangle, however, have been generally very good. The major element of this, of course, is a solid economic relationship, but some of the strength of the relationship also lies in a common historical grievance against Japan. Every visit by a Japanese political leader to the Yasukuni Shrine is an opportunity for China to join with South Korea in condemning Japanese militarism and Tokyo's historical insensitivity. Otherwise, the South Korean security relationship with the USA remains very strong, and strengthened with each North Korean provocation that China does not strongly condemn or actually punish.

Xi Jinping's state visit to South Korea in July 2014 marked the pinnacle of Chinese efforts to court South Korea. In 2016–17, the relationship between China and South Korea soured. Much of the effort that Xi Jinping had put into developing a personal relationship with President Park Geun-hye came to naught in December 2016 when she was impeached for corruption. Then, after North Korean missile tests and demonstrations, South Korea went ahead with the installation of the THAAD anti-missile system. Chinese reaction was quick and harsh. Contending that the American AN/TPY-2 radar associated with the system could spy on Chinese defense electronics (and privately worried that an effective anti-missile system could nullify China's own ICBMs), the Foreign Ministry lodged protests and Chinese citizens in turn turned against South Korean products and firms. Whether the newly-elected President of South Korea, Moon Jae-in, will repair the Sino-Korean relationship remains to be seen.

Mongolia

Mongolia's position in the world is defined by two giant rival neighbors, barely more than 2.9 million people, and too much space. As noted, its border with

China has been delimited and demarcated in 1988; the asymmetry of the relationship remains and has grown. Direct threats are absent, no military intervention or clashes have occurred and leadership meetings are frequent. The two sides declared theirs to be a "good neighborly partnership of mutual trust" in 2003 (*CFA* 2005: 244). Mongolia's President Bagabardi Natsagiin paid a state visit to China in January 2004, and his successor Enkhbayar visited in November 2005. Chinese leaders frequently use the sidelines of the Shanghai Cooperation Organization (Mongolia is an observer in that body) Summit and Prime Ministerial meetings to meet with their Mongolian counterparts, and in 2011 the relationship was upgraded to a "strategic partnership" (*CFA* 2012: 214. Note this was two years after the Russian Federation had similarly upgraded their relations to "strategic partner"; see Bulag 2009: 101). Xi Jinping's state visit to Mongolia in August 2014 to celebrate the 60th anniversary of Sino-Mongolian diplomatic relations being the most recent.

Mongolian leaders are well aware that their position between two giants is an inherently limited one, and the first guiding principle of Mongolian foreign policy is "Maintaining friendly relations with the Russian Federation, People's Republic of China" (MOFAMG 2011). Mongolian relations with Russia, however, have been somewhat limited, and their economic relationship has declined relative to that of China (Campi 2014). Russia does have a strong position in Mongolian transportation, since the rail links have traditionally been toward the north and railway gauges are Russian.

Mongolia's democratic government has sought to create a "third neighbor" from a number of other countries, most notably the United States, Japan and India. Mongolia's "Third Neighbor" policy has been part of a broader effort to diversify its international contacts and raise its global profile. It participates in a very small annual military exercise called Khaan Quest with the United States and is a "Partnership for Peace" partner with NATO and sent troops to Afghanistan (NATO 2012). US President George W. Bush visited Ulanbaatar in 2005, and Vice President Joseph Biden in 2013, Secretary of State Clinton in 2012 and Kerry in 2016, as well as state visits from Mongolian leaders to Washington. Mongolia became an observer in the Shanghai Cooperation Organization in 2004, but according to one analyst turned down the offer of full membership (Jargalsaikhan 2014). It has also joined ASEAN Regional Forum in 1998, the Bo'ao Forum for Asia in 2001, among others.

The US policy toward Mongolia has been to hold it up as an example of stable democracy and economic transformation in East Asia, a contrast with China's authoritarian industrialization (Campi 2012a). And Mongolia has been a champion of democracy in the 21st century, chairing the Community of Democracies (COD) from 2011–13. The American contrast of democratic Mongolia and China has been a minor irritant in the relations between Beijing and Ulaanbaatar but more so between China and the United States, another in China's perceived efforts of the USA to push a democracy agenda on East Asia (Campi 2012a). Chinese analysts have characterized Mongolia's "Third Neighbor" policy as a successful effort of a land-locked country to develop its diplomatic contacts and economic ties despite overwhelming dependency on China and Russia, and note the role of Mongolia as a Western, and especially American "model democracy" (Chen Xiang 2014: 11). In this instance, despite strong ties to an extra-regional power, the United States, China has not apparently regarded this as a threatening intrusion into its "neighborhood." Despite Mongolia's status as a multiparty democracy the relationship with China is stable, and despite the personal antipathy that many Mongolians feel for China and Chinese, the Mongolian leadership is well aware of its limited options and maintains friendly relations with the giant to the south. Like Nepal, it is a "sandwich state," though China is not as hypersensitive as India.

In only one regard has China sought to squeeze Mongolia, namely its relations with the Dalai Lama; since most Mongolians are Tibetan Buddhists, the Dalai Lama is very popular there and has visited a number of times, but China's objections have led to the curtailment of his visits such as in 2011, and outright cancellation in 2014 prior to Xi Jinping's visit (Meng 2014). In 2002, during one of the Dalai Lama's visits, China shut down its rail link to Mongolia in retaliation (Bayartsogt 2011).

Military intervention

Despite the poor relations and cat-and-mouse games of Chinese Coast Guard ships and aircraft around the Diaoyu/Senkakus, it is important to remember that there has been no armed intervention by China in Northeast Asia during the 2004–2016 period. Indeed, if one examines the Militarized Interstate Dispute database, very little shows up during this period and region beyond the North Korean nuclear crisis.[2]

Regional international organizations

As noted in Chapter 4, Northeast Asia itself does not have a regional organization, and the primary mechanism for East Asia regionalism is an adjunct of Southeast Asian regionalism, namely the "ASEAN + 3" concept, adding China, South Korea and Japan to the ten ASEAN states, which began in 1997. China holds that this body represents, ". . . the main vehicle for East Asia cooperation" (State Council Information Office 2017). The "+3" states themselves began to meet prior to ASEAN meetings in 1999, though these were initially low-key summits and meetings of foreign, finance, and trade ministers. These have gradually expanded into other ministerial meetings, and the forum of China-Japan-ROK Cooperation (first recognized as a separate mechanism in the *ZGWJ* 2008: 239) meetings began to take place outside of the ASEAN meeting in 2008, and in 2011 a small secretariat was established in Seoul (*CFA* 2014: 391). Of these trilateral discussions, foreign policy was the most common topic, but the potential Free Trade Agreement and cultural and functional cooperation were also held, as discussed below. Most of the focus on regional international organizations in East Asia and the Asia Pacific is linked to Southeast Asia and will be discussed below.

Hegemon's expatriates

Chinese students continue to study in Japan, political tensions aside, and Chinese tourists travel to Japan and South Korea. Few incidents of Chinese in Japan or Korea have been politicized, and though Chinese tourism to Japan did drop significantly from 2010 to 2011, this can also be explained by the Tohoku earthquake/tsunami/nuclear disaster as well as rising Sino-Japanese tensions in late 2010. In the case of South Korea, the "old" Chinese community has largely disappeared, but replaced by a "new" community, generally Mandarin-speaking, and much of it ethnic Koreans with PRC citizenship, who have taken on an important role as intermediaries in the Sino-South Korean relationship (Rhee 2009: 117–118).

There is an alternative interpretation about a hegemon's expatriates that should, however, be considered, namely fishers as expatriates. Of the recent incidents in the East and South China Seas involving Chinese use of Coast Guard and other maritime units to enforce Chinese claims to islets and reefs, all initially involved law enforcement of claimant states against Chinese fishers. The 2010 incident in the Senkakus involved a Chinese fishing captain detained by Japanese authorities. In 2012 and 2013, Chinese boats were seized by North Korean authorities, which drew indignant protests from Chinese netizens (Buckley 2013). There have been repeated incidents with South Korea, and fatalities on both sides (Choe 2011; Choe 2014). The standard interpretation of these incidents are that they are China using the fishermen as an excuse to enforce territorial claims, what Dupont and Baker (2014) call the "fish, protect, contest, and occupy" strategy (87). That certainly may be the case, but we must consider that the Chinese behavior in these cases are not primarily territorial aggression but citizen protection, not unlike Americans in coastal Nicaragua in the early 20th century or Russians in eastern Ukraine in the early 21st. Hyperactive regional hegemons protect their citizens, whether abroad or in ambiguous areas. It's what they do.

Provision of security public goods

If China is to be a regional hegemon, one of the expectations found in other regional hegemons is the provision of public security goods; protection is the obvious one, but there are other ways in which a regional hegemon helps to secure its region, even if it means taking on more burdens proportionately than the countries it is helping to protect. In Northeast Asia, there is little that China provides. In one area it has been important, namely in the Korean nuclear issue. China is the primary diplomatic conduit to North Korea, and China was a major advocate for the Six Party Talks (China, USA, Russia, South Korea, North Korea, and Japan), which have been seeking a way to curtail North Korea's nuclear weapons ambitions. Unfortunately, these efforts have since broken down, and North Korea has continued to test both nuclear weapons and longer-range missiles, in violation of UN Security Council resolutions and Chinese urgings. North Korea's defiance of the Six Party Talks has also nullified one of China's few arguments that it is helping preserve peace and security in the region.

Economic

Trade

China's economic relations with Northeast Asia in the 21st century have sometimes been described as the "hot" or "warm" side of the relationship, especially with Japan. In recent years, China's trade with South Korea has also boomed, and now almost equals its trade with Japan. Yet China's global trade patterns – boosted by WTO membership in 2001 – have begun to diversify, with less percentage of trade with the advanced industrial economies of North America, Europe and Japan, even as the total trade with all economies has gone up enormously. China's market presence in neighboring economies is another theme that will be developed in this chapter and subsequent ones: China's neighbors are buying more and more of their products from China. Finally, trade and investment and other economic interactions serve as a dual vehicle of relations: an incentive, a reward, but it can also be used as a coercive tool. As Table 6.1 below shows, China now does over half a trillion dollars' worth of trade in the region:

Table 6.1 China: total trade with Northeast Asia, 2004–2015

China: total trade with Northeast Asia, 2004–2015 (current US$, million)

	Japan	South Korea	North Korea	Mongolia
2004	$167,728	$89,975	$1,377	$693
2005	$184,565	$111,991	$1,581	$859
2006	$207,583	$134,377	$1,700	$1,578
2007	$236,020	$160,173	$1,974	$2,008
2008	$266,984	$186,080	$2,787	$2,443
2009	$228,973	$156,140	$2,680	$2,355
2010	$296,566	$206,834	$3,466	$3,966
2011	$341,700	$244,598	$5,629	$6,399
2012	$329,236	$254,237	$5,931	$6,591
2013	$312,132	$274,056	$6,547	$5,946
2014	$312,137	$290,688	$6,364	$7,287
2015	$278,613	$275,717	$5,430	$5,325

Source: IMF DOTS (2017).

Obviously, trade with Mongolia is much smaller both because of the small population there, and because commodity prices have declined in recent years. Trade with North Korea is constrained by political issues and UN sanctions. For all of the security and political difficulties between China and Japan, the two are strongly linked economically.

From China's perspective, trade with Japan has been growing in absolute terms, though it has run a consistent bilateral trade deficit. However, as shown in Table 6.2, China's dependence on Japan for trade has declined during this period:

Table 6.2 China and Japan: mutual trade dependency, 2004–2015

China and Japan: mutual trade dependency, 2004–2015 (% total imports/exports)

	Japan		China	
	Imports from China	Exports to China	Imports from Japan	Exports to Japan
2004	20.7%	13.1%	16.8%	12.4%
2005	21.0%	13.4%	15.2%	11.0%
2006	20.5%	14.3%	14.6%	9.5%
2007	20.5%	15.3%	14.0%	8.4%
2008	18.8%	16.0%	13.3%	8.1%
2009	22.2%	18.9%	13.0%	8.2%
2010	22.1%	19.4%	12.6%	7.6%
2011	21.5%	19.7%	11.2%	7.8%
2012	21.3%	18.1%	9.8%	7.4%
2013	21.7%	18.1%	8.3%	6.8%
2014	22.3%	18.3%	8.3%	6.4%
2015	24.8%	17.5%	8.9%	6.0%

Source: IMF DOTS (2017).

The trends showed a reversal of the asymmetry of trade relations from earlier periods when Japan was more important to China than China was to Japan. Now the China market is crucial to Japan, making up over 18% of its exports, and even more important as a source of goods, making up about a quarter of Japanese imports. Yet for China, which once received over a quarter of its goods from Japan, it now is around 9%, not small, to be sure, but far less than in earlier decades. Even more important, the Japan market just isn't as large as it once was for Chinese exporters, about 6% of the total.

In short, trade with China matters more to Japan than trade with Japan matters to China. This asymmetry is particularly noted in the last ten years, and Chinese economists have pointed out the link between China's territorial dispute and the greater sensitivity and vulnerability (to use Keohane and Nye's terms) of the Japanese economy: "Considering the effects of the Diaoyu Islands incident on Japan's economy, politics, social life and strategic adjustments, interdependence between China and Japan has obvious asymmetry, and Japan's 'sensitivity' and 'vulnerability' in interdependent relations are greater than those of China" (Duan Xia and Shen Yan 2013: 118–119). But Duan and Shen also wisely note that the Chinese trade relationship with other countries in East Asia is much more complex than the simple figures of bilateral exchange would imply. China is deeply integrated into production chains, usually involving Japanese corporations and shipping intermediate products back and forth in the assembly process, especially of high-value electronics (Yeung 2016: chap. 4). For China to try to use its trade asymmetry with countries such as Japan and South Korea, it would have to be prepared to suffer as well.

China's trade with South Korea has over doubled in the last twelve years. Here, too, an asymmetry has formed: South Korea, with its much smaller economy, depends on China more than China depends on South Korea. Table 6.3 shows the figures:

Table 6.3 China and South Korea: mutual trade dependency, 2004–2015

China and South Korea: mutual trade dependency, 2004–2015 (% total imports/exports)

	South Korea		China	
	Imports from China	Exports to China	Imports from South Korea	Exports to South Korea
2004	13.2%	19.6%	11.1%	4.7%
2005	14.8%	21.8%	11.6%	4.6%
2006	15.7%	21.3%	11.3%	4.6%
2007	17.7%	22.1%	10.9%	4.6%
2008	17.7%	21.7%	9.9%	5.2%
2009	16.8%	23.9%	10.2%	4.5%
2010	16.8%	25.1%	9.9%	4.4%
2011	16.5%	24.2%	9.3%	4.4%
2012	15.5%	24.5%	9.2%	4.3%
2013	16.1%	26.1%	9.4%	4.1%
2014	17.1%	25.4%	9.7%	4.3%
2015	20.7%	26.0%	10.9%	4.4%

Source: IMF DOTS (2017).

The trade situation with North Korea is increasingly political, given repeated North Korean violations of UN sanctions in its nuclear and missile programs. Even more so now than in earlier periods, Pyongyang is almost completely dependent on China, though economic relations with North Korea are small and difficult to assess. The official IMF Direction of Trade Statistics trade between China and North Korea does not capture barter trade, which may be significant but is not reported. Regardless, the dependency of North Korea on trade with China is nearly complete, with three quarters of imports and exports to and from China, according to the IMF.

Recent satellite evidence reported by CSIS would seem to indicate that the UN Security Council economic sanctions against North Korea are making themselves felt in trade between China and North Korea ("Imagery suggests . . ." 2016).

Table 6.4 Mongolia: trade dependency on China and Russia, 2004–2015

Mongolia: trade dependency on Russia and China, 2004–2015 (% total imports/exports)

	Russia		China	
	Imports from Russia	Exports to Russia	Imports from China	Exports to China
2004	33.5%	2.4%	25.1%	47.6%
2005	35.6%	2.6%	25.8%	48.2%
2006	38.3%	2.9%	25.5%	68.1%
2007	36.2%	3.0%	27.7%	72.5%
2008	38.4%	3.4%	27.8%	64.5%
2009	35.9%	3.6%	24.7%	73.9%
2010	26.8%	2.6%	41.4%	81.5%
2011	23.0%	2.1%	42.8%	85.8%
2012	25.9%	1.4%	37.1%	88.2%
2013	25.0%	1.0%	38.9%	83.7%
2014	27.2%	0.7%	41.3%	88.5%
2015	28.4%	1.0%	39.9%	83.9%

Source: IMF DOTS (2017).

China very publicly turned North Korean coal ships away in an indication of increased sanctions enforcement in April 2017 (Ruwitch and Meng 2017), but other reporting is much more suspicious of China's enforcement (Forsythe 2016; Page and Solomon 2017).

Lastly, there is trade with Mongolia. The former Soviet satellite still does a good deal of trade with the Russian Federation, especially its imports, but its exports now go almost completely to China, as seen in Table 6.4: Russia is barely a destination for Mongolian exports, and though Russian exports are about a quarter of Mongolia's total, that percentage has been declining while China's is now over 40%. Mongolia's foreign trade and investment are dominated by China, and much of the investment in energy and mineral extraction that Mongolia depends on for foreign exchange is Chinese. Neither the United States nor Japan's trade positions in Mongolia have been above single digits in the 21st century.

Investment

China is still a net recipient of foreign direct investment, but its outward investments have grown substantially in the 21st century, including its northeast Asian neighbors. Table 6.5 shows the flows and overall net stock from 2004 to 2014, using the Chinese Ministry of Commerce annual statistics.[3]

From this, it is clear that although China is a substantial investor in Northeast Asia, only in the case of Mongolia does it provide much more than 1% of FDI,

Table 6.5 China: foreign direct investment in Northeast Asia, 2004–2014

China: foreign direct investment in Northeast Asia, 2004–2014 (current US$, million)

Year	Japan	South Korea	North Korea	Mongolia
2004	$15.3	$40.2	$14.1	$40.2
2005	$17.2	$588.8	$6.5	$52.3
2006	$39.5	$27.3	$11.1	$82.4
2007	$39.0	$56.7	$18.4	$196.3
2008	$58.6	$96.9	$41.2	$238.6
2009	$84.1	$265.1	$5.9	$276.5
2010	$338.0	–$721.7	$12.1	$193.9
2011	$149.4	$341.7	$56.0	$451.0
2012	$210.7	$942.4	$109.5	$904.0
2013	$434.1	$268.8	$86.2	$388.8
2014	$394.5	$548.9	$51.9	$502.6
outward net stocks, 2014	$2,547.0	$2,771.6	$611.6	$3,762.5

Source: Ministry of Commerce, PRC (2014).

according to IMF CDIS data. South Korea is its largest investment destination, but it does not rank in that country's top 10 of foreign investors.

The political tensions between China and Japan do not seem immediately apparent in the flow of FDI during this period; in the 2010 period when Sino-Japanese relations were experiencing some of their worst downturns, Chinese investment in Japan went up. Chinese investments in North Korea appear to be a nominal stake in a poor and risky market, whereas South Korea received four times the investment. The Chinese investment in Mongolia is perhaps the most sensitive of the Northeast Asian economic interactions; China invested nearly $2.4 billion in an economy with a total GDP of only $11 billion at Market Exchange Rate between 2005 and 2012, prompting the Mongolian government to pass limits on foreign mining ownership, mostly Chinese but also Russian (Campi 2012b: 2; Levin 2012). It should also be noted that Chinese FDI gives Beijing both a large incentive and a potential coercive mechanism in its relations with its much smaller neighbors, the central government is growing increasingly concerned that capital outflows from China could create an economically destabilizing force for China's domestic economy and has tried to reel in some of it (Wu and Chatterjee 2017).

The politicization of commercial disputes is one possible indicator of hyperactive hegemonic behavior, and there have been a handful of incidents between China and Japan in the 2009–14 period that would appear to be just that. The first was a dispute over rare earth metals in 2009–2014. China is the world's leading exporter of these minerals which have substantial uses in electronics, automotive and energy industries. Beginning around 2006, China began to restrict its export quotas for these minerals (Bradsher 2009). In September 2010, however, it apparently cut off all exports of rare earth metals to Japan only, following the arrest of a Chinese fishing boat captain near the Senkaku/Diaoyu islets (Bradsher 2010). Chinese officials claimed that export restrictions on rare earth metals were prompted solely by environmental concerns as well as a concern over maintaining stable prices, and in 2014, the WTO ruled against China's restrictions as economically-motivated (WTO 2014). The restrictions on exports to Japan had been lifted, and by the time of the WTO ruling on the economic aspects of the case, China had begun to import rare earth metals (Reuters 2012). The export quota restrictions would seem to have been a simple case of China seeking to profit from its export dominance; the specific (if temporary) ban on exports directed at Japan, however, seems to have been quite clearly the politicization of a commercial transaction.

South Korea has also felt the economic sting of China's displeasure: in 2016–2017 with South Korea fearing North Korean missiles, it began negotiations with the United States to install the THADD system. China, in addition to diplomatic protests, Chinese citizens were encouraged to boycott the South Korean store chain Lotte, South Korean cosmetics, tourist visits, and even K-Pop (*Nationalism unleashed* 2017: 41–42; Rich 2017; Qin and Choe 2016; Yiu 2017).

Mongolia also learned the economic costs of offending China. In 2006, after the Dalai Lama visited the country (invited by private Buddhist groups in Mongolia where lamaistic Buddhism is prevalent), China responded by cancelling air travel between Beijing and Ulaanbaatar. In November 2016 after another visit, China began charging commodity import fees and additional transit costs (Shepherd 2017a, 2017b). The Mongolian Foreign Ministry has since announced that His Holiness has not been invited back (Edwards 2016).

Provision of economic public goods

In addition to the bilateral trade and investment positions noted above, China has been negotiating a trilateral free-trade deal with South Korea and Japan, despite diplomatic tensions with the latter. Negotiations were announced in November 2012 during the Trilateral meeting before the ASEAN 10+3 Summit in Phnom Penh, and ten rounds of talks, most recently in March 2016, have occurred. Actual progress is difficult to judge, and Chinese scholars have been pessimistic: "China-Japan-South Korea free trade negotiations were not halted by the chilly Sino-Japanese and Japan-South Korea relations of late, but until things can be improved, substantive progress is a chimera" (Li Xiangyang 2015: 28). But the fact that the talks are still ongoing does speak to a certain degree of separation of politics and economics in northeast Asia.

China has also provided foreign aid and investment to North Korea, though bilateral aid figures are not available. RAND estimates that in 2011 $7.1 billion went to the Dandong port facility, and another $2 billion for infrastructure in the Rason Special Economic Zone (Wolf et al. 2013: 45).

Currency swaps are another example of public goods provision in economics which China has used both to improve trade relations and diplomatic relations in the region. China has two currency swap agreements, with South Korea and with Mongolia. Given inflation and fluctuations in the tögrög, China is accepting a less stable currency in its countertrade, but the August 2014 swap deal is only for RMB15 million (about US$2.2 m). A much bigger deal is the RMB360 million (about US$53m) deal with South Korea, China's biggest bilateral currency swap with an independent state, which has a much greater total amount of trade with China than Mongolia, but which also has a more stable currency, the Won. This in a sense represents Seoul's willingness to hold RMB as a reserve, and given its high levels of trade with China makes sense as a currency hedge. We will see that currency swaps are even more important as a mechanism of monetary diplomacy in Southeast Asia.

Infrastructure and transportation in Northeast Asia primarily focus on Mongolia, since Japan and South Korea are effectively cut off from land transportation to China. Mongolia's economic connection to China is stymied to an extent by the railway gauge issue: Mongolia uses the 1520mm Russian gauge, and China uses the 1435mm Standard gauge, causing trans-shipment costs at the border. Proposals to build Standard gauge lines from copper and coal mines in Mongolia to link up with Chinese lines in Inner Mongolian Autonomous Region make economic sense but Mongolian politicians are hypersensitive to the issue, and only recently has Mongolia agreed to build one such line to the Tavan Tolgoi coal mine, but no construction has yet begun and the coal is currently trucked out (Kohn 2014). The construction of a paved highway between China and the Oyu Tolgoi copper mine has also been agreed to. Mongolia's place in Xi Jinping's much-vaunted "One Belt One Road" proposal is vague. Although Chinese officials have indicated that Mongolia may play a role in the idea, firm proposals are lacking (Campi 2015). China does provide Mongolia with its primary outlet to the sea in Tianjin, as per the 1991 agreement, and that was expanded to other northern Chinese ports during Xi Jinping's visit to Mongolia in 2014.

Notes

1 As a means of comparison, the state of Pennsylvania in 2012 was estimated to have 36 trillion cubic feet in reserves and the United States as a whole 308 trillion (EIA 2014).
2 The latest version of the MID database (version 10, July 2010), however, only goes up to 2007 at the time of this writing (August 2014), so the 2010 and 2012 Diaoyu/Senkaku crises would be chronologically excluded. ICB data collections. www.cidcm.umd.edu/icb/data/, accessed 31 August 2014.
3 Determining Chinese FDI is another statistical challenge for foreign observers; the Chinese Ministry of Commerce's yearbook *Statistical Bulletin of China's Outward Foreign Direct Investment* shows both FDI flows and stocks by country from 2004 to the present. Its figures, however, are derived differently from the IMF's Coordinated Direct Investment Survey. UNCTAD also produces an annual *World Investment Report*. In addition, the American Enterprise Institute issues the China Global Investment Tracker, based primarily on press reports. None entirely agree, and the patterns of discrepancy are inconsistent.

Works cited

Abegunrin, Olayiwola. 2003. *Nigerian Foreign Policy under Military Rule, 1966–1999*. Westport, CT: Praeger.

Bayartsogt, Khaliun. 2011. Mongolia cuts short Dalai Lama lecture tour under China pressure. *Reuters*, 8 November. <http://uk.reuters.com/article/uk-mongolia-dalai-idUK-TRE7A71U420111108>, accessed 21 July 2016.

Bradsher, Keith. 2009. China tightens grip on rare minerals. *New York Times*, 1 September. <www.nytimes.com/2009/09/01/business/global/01minerals/htm>, accessed 17 May 2014.

Bradsher, Keith. 2010. Amid tension, China blocks vital exports to Japan. *New York Times*, 22 September 2010. <www.nytimes.com/2010/09/23/business/global/23rare.html>, accessed 17 May 2014.

Bradsher, Keith. 2013. Okinawa piques Chinese papers. *New York Times*, 8 May. <www.nytimes.com/2013/05/09/world/asia/okinawa-piques-chinese-papers.html>, accessed 9 May 2013.

Buckley, Chris. 2013. North Korea seizes Chinese boat. *New York Times*, 19 May. <www.nytimes.com/2013/05/20/world/asia/north-korea-seized-chinese-fishing-boat.html>, accessed 17 May 2017.

Bulag, Uradyn E. 2009. Mongolia in 2009. *Asian Survey*, 50(1), 97–103.

Bush, Richard J. 2010. *The Perils of Proximity: China-Japan Security Relations*. Washington, DC: Brookings.

Campi, Alicia. 2012a. The message behind Secretary Clinton's trip to Mongolia. *Asia Pacific Bulletin* (no. 172), 26 July.

Campi, Alicia. 2012b. Mongolia's turn at the "great game". *Asia Pacific Bulletin* (no. 184), 1 November.

Campi, Alicia. 2014. Mongolian foreign relations surge indicates new activist agenda for 2014. *Asia Pacific Bulletin* (no. 254), 25 March.

Campi, Alicia. 2015. Mongolia's place in China's "One Belt, One Road". *China Brief*, 15(16). <https://jamestown.org/program/mongolias-place-in-chinas-one-belt-one-road/>, accessed 31 October 2017.

Cascon. 2008. Cascon case EUS: Ecuador-USA 1963–1975. MIT Cascon system for analyzing international conflict. <http://web.mit.edu/cascon/cases/case_eus.html>, accessed 17 May 2017.

CFA [China's Foreign Affairs]. Annual. Beijing: Ministry of Foreign Affairs of the People's Republic of China. This is the official yearbook of the Ministry of Foreign Affairs of the People's Republic of China. Beginning its publication in 1987 as 中国外交概览 China's Foreign Affairs review, it is hereafter referred to as ZGWJGL, and after 1995 中国外交 it is renamed Zhongguo waijiao (ZGWJ) for the Chinese language version, and China's Foreign Affairs or CFA for the English-language version, which began publication in 2003. See also ZGWJ.

Chen Xiang. 2014. Menggu tuixing "Di San Linguo" waijiao de yuanyin tanxi [Exploratory analysis of the causes of Mongolia's "Third Neighbor" foreign policy]. *Guoji yanjiu cankao*, (10), 8–11.

Chen Xiangyang. 2004. *Zhongguo mulin waijiao: sixiang, shijian, qianzhang* [China's good-neighbour diplomacy: Though, practice, prospect]. Beijing: Shishi chubanshe.

Choe, Sang-hun. 2011. Chinese fisherman kills South Korean coast guardsman. *New York Times*, 12 December. <www.nytimes.com/2011/12/13/world/asia/chinese-fisherman-kills-south-korean-coast-guardsman.html>, accessed 30 September 2016.

Choe, Sang-hun. 2014. Fisherman from China dies in clash off S. Korea. *New York Times*, 10 October. <www.nytimes.com/2014/10/11/world/asia/chinese-fishing-captain-killed-in-clash-with-south-korean-coast-guard.html>, accessed 30 September 2016.

Chung, Jae Ho. 2009. China's "soft" clash with South Korea: The history war and beyond. *Asian Survey*, 49, 468–483.

Duan Xia, and Shen Yan. 2013. Some considerations on the asymmetry of the Sino-Japanese economic interdependency. *Contemporary International Relations*, 23(1), 110–122.

Dupont, Alan, and Baker, Christopher. 2014. East Asia's maritime disputes: Fishing in troubled waters. *Washington Quarterly*, 37(1), 79–98.

Dutton, Peter A. 2014. China's maritime disputes in the East and South China Seas. *Naval War College Review*, 67(3), 7–18.

Edwards, Terrence. 2016. Mongolia says Dalai Lama won't be invited again. *Reuters*, 22 December. <www.reuters.com/article/us-mongolia-china-idUSKBN14B0N5>, accessed 7 June 2017.

EIA [US Energy Information Agency]. 2012. East China Sea. US EIA website. <www.eia.gov/countries/analysisbriefs/east_china_sea/east_china_sea.pdf>, accessed 25 September 2012.

EIA [US Energy Information Agency]. 2014. Expected future production of dry natural gas. US EIA website. <www.eia.gov/dnav/ng/ng_enr_dry_dcu_NUS_a.htm>, accessed 10 April 2014.

Erickson, Andrew, and Collins, Gabe. 2013. New fleet on the block: China's coast guard comes together. *Wall Street Journal*, 11 March. <http://blogs.wsj.com/chinarealtime/2013/03/11/new-fleet-on-the-block-chinas-coast-guard-comes-together/>, accessed 22 May 2014.

Fackler, Martin. 2012. China and Japan say they held talks over islands dispute. *New York Times*, 12 October. <www.nytimes.com/2012/10/13/world/asia/china-and-japan-say-they-held-talks-over-islands-dispute.html>, accessed 12 October 2012.

Fackler, Martin. 2013a. Japan summons China's envoy after ships near disputed islands. *New York Times*, 8 January. <www.nytimes.com/2013/01/09/world/asia/japan-summons-chinas-envoy-after-ships-near-islands.html>, accessed 8 January 2013.

Fackler, Martin. 2013b. In Okinawa, talk of break from Japan turns serious. *New York Times*, 5 July. <www.nytimes.com/2013/07/06/world/asia/in-okinawa-talk-of-break-from-japan-turns-serious.html>, accessed 6 July 2013.

Fackler, Martin. 2014. Japan raises alarm on Chinese flybys in overlapping air zones. *New York Times*, 25 May. <www.nytimes.com/2014/05/26/world/asia/japan-east-china-sea.html>, accessed 25 May 2014.

FAO. 2012. Fisheries and aquaculture department: FAO global capture production database updated 2012: Summary information. <www.fao.org/fishery/statistics/en>, accessed 27 May 2014.

Forsythe, Michael. 2016. U.S. says Chinese executives helped North Korea dodge sanctions. *New York Times*, 27 September. <www.nytimes.com/2016/09/28/world/asia/china-north-korea-sanctions-ma-xiaohong.html>, accessed 27 September 2016.

Gong Jianhua. 2012. Need for unified coast guard. *China Daily*, 19 October. <http://usa.chinadaily.com.cn/opinion/2012-10/19/content_15829823.htm>, accessed 22 May 2014.

Guo Jiping. 2012. Ironclad evidence shows that Diaoyu Dao is China's territory. Ministry of Foreign Affairs, China. <www.fmprc.gov.cn/mfa_eng/topics_665678/diaodao_665718/>, accessed 9 May 2014.

"Hegemony of Japan-US alliance". 2013. *People's Daily Online* [English], 23 January. <http://english.people.com.cn/90777/8103153.html>, accessed 26 January 2013.

Huang Fengzhi, and Sun Guoqiang. 2013. China-U.S. joint cooperation over D.P.R.K. *Contemporary International Relations*, 24(1), 59–75.

"Imagery suggests downtick in Chinese-North Korean economic interaction since January 2016 nuclear test". 2016. Beyond Parallel, Center for Strategic and International Studies, 22 April. <http://beyondparallel.csis.org/decrease-in-trade-after-nuclear-test/>, accessed 22 August 2016.

IMF DOTS [Direction of Trade Statistics]. 2017. IMF e-library. <data.imf.org/>, accessed 19 January 2017.

Japan Coast Guard. 2017. Vessels entering contiguous zone or territorial sea around the Senkaku_Diaoyu Islands [spreadsheet]. JCG LINK. <www.kaiho.mlit.go.jp/mission/senkaku/senkaku.html>, accessed 27 June 2017.

Japan Ministry of Defense. 2014. *Defense of Japan 2014*. Tokyo: Ministry of Defense. <www.mod.go.jp/e/publ/w_paper/2014.html>, accessed 16 August 2014.

Jargalsaikhan, Mendee. 2014. Khaan Quest 2014: A small exercise with big implications: Pacific forum center for strategic and international studies. *PacNet* (no. 45), 19 June. <http://csis.org/publication/pacnet-45-khaan-quest-2014-small-exercise-big-implications>, accessed 4 August 2014.

Johnson, Ian, and Shanker, Thom. 2012. China warns of "further actions" as anti-Japan protests resume. *New York Times*, 18 September. <www.nytimes.com/2012/09/19/world/asia/china-warns-japan-over-island-dispute.html>, accessed 18 September 2012.

Kohn, Michael. 2014. Mongolia embraces China with compatible rail to cut costs. Bloomberg News, 24 October. <www.bloomberg.com/news/articles/2014-10-24/mongolia-embraces-china-with-railway-to-lower-transport-costs>, accessed 26 July 2016.

Levin, Dan. 2012. In Mongolia, a new, penned-in wealth. *New York Times*, 26 June. <www.nytimes.com/2012/06/27/world/asia/mongolias-coal-deposits-draw-neighbors-attention.html>, accessed 27 June 2012.

Li Xiangyang. 2015. The development trend in China's surrounding areas. *Contemporary International Relations*, 25(2), 25–28.

Liu, Coco. 2017. Sanctions are fine, but what about the Chinese who depend on trade with North Korea? *South China Morning Post*, 9 July. <www.scmp.com/week-asia/business/article/2101743/sanctions-are-fine-what-about-chinese-who-depend-trade-north>, accessed 9 July 2017.

Meng, Angela. 2014. Xi Jinping looks to deepen ties in visit to "wary" Mongolia. *South China Morning Post*, 21 August. <www.scmp.com/news/china/article/1577929/xi-jinping-looks-deepen-ties-visit-wary-mongolia>, accessed 21 July 2016.

Ministry of Commerce of the PRC. 2011–2014. Statistical bulletin of China's outward foreign direct investment. Beijing: China Statistics Press. Annual.

MOFA. 2012. Vice Foreign Minister Zhang Zhijun gave briefing to Chinese and foreign journalists on the Diaoyu Dao issue (transcript). Ministry of Foreign Affairs of China, 27 October. <www.fmprc.gov.cn/mfa_eng/topics_665678/diaodao_665718/t983015.shtml>, accessed 9 May 2014.

MOFAJ. 2013. Japanese territory: Senkaku Islands Q&A, 5 June. <www.mofa.go.jp/region/asia-paci/senkaku/qa_1010.html>, accessed 12 May 2014.

MOFAJ. 2014. Ministry of Foreign Affairs of Japan: Japanese territory: Trends in Chinese government and other vessels in the waters surrounding the Senkaku Islands, and Japan's response, 2 May. <www.mofa.go.jp/region/page23e_000021.html>, accessed 12 May 2014.

MOFAMG [Mongolia Ministry of Foreign Affairs]. 2011. Mongolia's foreign policy in the political field. <www.mfa.gov.mn/en/index.php?option=com_content&view=article&id=

80%3Aii-&catid=36%3A2009-12-20-21-52-14&Itemid=55&lang=en>, accessed 4 August 2014.

"Nationalism unleashed: China and South Korea." 2017. *The Economist*, 28 March, 42–42.

NATO. 2012. NATO's cooperation with Mongolia: North Atlantic Treaty Organization, 23 March. <www.nato.int/cps/en/natolive/topics_85297.htm>, accessed 5 August 2014.

Page, Jeremy, and Solomon, Jay. 2017. Chinese-North Korean venture shows how much sanctions can miss. *Wall Street Journal*, 7 May. <www.wsj.com/articles/chinese-north-korean-venture-shows-how-much-sanctions-can-miss-1494191212>, accessed 8 May 2017.

Park, Yong-soo. 2009. The political economy of economic reform in North Korea. *Australian Journal of International Affairs*, 63(4), 529–549.

Perlez, Jane. 2012a. China alters its strategy in diplomatic crisis with Japan. *New York Times*, 28 September. <www.nytimes.com/2012/09/29/world/asia/china-alters-its-strategy-in-dispute-with-japan.html>, accessed 28 September 2012.

Perlez, Jane. 2012b. China steps up pressure on Japan in island dispute. *New York Times*, 15 December. <www.nytimes.com/2012/12/16/world/asia/china-steps-up-pressure-on-japan-in-island-dispute.html>, accessed 16 December 2012.

Perlez, Jane. 2013a. After challenges, China appears to backpedal on air zone. *New York Times*, 27 November 2013. <www.nytimes.com/2013/11/28/world/asia/china-explains-handling-of-b-52-flight-as-tensions-escalate.html>, accessed 8 April 2014.

Perlez, Jane. 2013b. China looks West as it bolsters regional ties. *New York Times*, 7 September. <www.nytimes.com/2013/09/08/world/asia/china-looks-west-as-it-strengthens-regional-ties.html>, accessed 8 September 2013.

Perlez, Jane. 2013c. Chinese leader eases tone in meeting with Japan envoy. *New York Times*, 25 January. <www.nytimes.com/2013/01/26/world/asia/chinese-leader-eases-tone-in-meeting-with-japan-envoy.html>, accessed 25 January 2013.

Perlez, Jane. 2014. Chinese president's visit to South Korea is seen as way to weaken US alliances. *New York Times*, 2 July. <www.nytimes.com/2014/07/03/world/asia/chinas-president-to-visit-south-korea.html>, accessed 2 August 2014.

Perlez, Jane. 2015. China wary as violence spills from North Korea. *New York Times*, 29 January. <www.nytimes.com/2015/01/30/world/asia/for-north-koreans-on-chinese-border-welcome-turns-into-wariness.html>, accessed 6 February 2015.

Perlez, Jane, and Bradsher, Keith. 2012. Ex-envoy says US stirs China-Japan tensions. *New York Times*, 30 October. <www.nytimes.com/2012/10/31/world/asia/in-speech-organized-by-beijing-ex-diplomat-calls-islands-dispute-with-japan-a-time-bomb.html>, accessed 31 October 2012.

Perlez, Jane, and Fackler, Martin. 2013. China patrols air zone over disputed islands. *New York Times*, 28 November. <www.nytimes.com/2013/11/29/world/asia/japan-south-korea-fly-military-planes-in-zone-set-by-china.html>, accessed 4 December 2013.

Pollack, Jonathan D. 2014. Why does China coddle North Korea? *New York Times*, 12 January. <www.nytimes.com/2014/01/13/opinion/why-does-china-coddle-north-korea.html>, accessed 13 January 2014.

Qin, Amy, and Choe Sang-hun. 2016. South Korean missile defense deal appears to sour China's taste for K-Pop. *New York Times*, 7 August. <www.nytimes.com/2016/08/08/world/asia/china-korea-thaad.html>, accessed 30 September 2016.

Ramzy, Austin. 2015. China confirms killings on border with North Korea. *New York Times: Sinosphere Blog*, 29 April. <https://sinosphere.blogs.nytimes.com/2015/04/29/china-confirms-killings-on-border-with-north-korea/>, accessed 29 April 2015.

"Regional turbulence: the East China Sea." 2013. *The Economist*, 30 November, 39.

Reuters. 2012. China, a rare earths giant, set to start importing the elements. *New York Times*, 11 July 2012. <www.nytimes.com/2012/07/12/business/global/china-a-rare-earaths-giant-set-to-start-importing-the-elements.html>, accessed 17 May 2014.

Rhee, Young Ju. 2009. Diversity within Chinese diaspora: Old and new Huaqiao in South Korea, in *Diasporas: Critical and Interdisciplinary Perspectives*, edited by Jane Fernandez. Freeland: Interdisciplinary Press, 111–126.

Rich, Motoko. 2017. As leaders argue, South Korea finds China is no longer an easy sell. *New York Times*, 8 March. <www.nytimes.com/2017/03/08/world/asia/china-south-korea-economy.html>, accessed 8 March 2017.

Ruwitch, John, and Meng Meng. 2017. Exclusive: North Korean ships head home after China orders coal returned. *Reuters*, 11 April. <www.reuters.com/article/us-china-northkorea-coal-exclusive-idUSKBN17D0D8>, accessed 11 April 2017.

Shepherd, Christian. 2017a. China says Dalai Lama "provokes" with visit to disputed border with India. *Reuters*, 12 April. <www.reuters.com/article/us-china-india-dalailama/china-says-dalai-lama-provokes-with-visit-to-disputed-border-with-india-idUSKBN17E1EZ>, accessed 12 April 2017.

Shepherd, Christian. 2017b. China says hopes Mongolia learned lesson after Dalai Lama visit. *Reuters*, 24 January. <www.reuters.com/article/us-china-mongolia-dalailama-idUSKBN158197>, accessed 24 January 2017.

"S. Korea, China hold closed talks on maritime border". 2014. Yonhap News Agency, 17 June. <http://english.yonhapnews.co.kr/full/2014/06/17/34/1200000000AEN20140617001800315F.html>, accessed 19 August 2014.

State Council Information Office. 2017. China's policies on Asia-Pacific security cooperation. Xinhua, 11 January. <http://news.xinhuanet.com/english/china/2017-01/11/c_135973695.htm>, accessed 14 January 2017.

Tabuchi, Hiroko. 2012. Japan scrambles jets in island dispute with China. *New York Times*, 13 December 2012. <www.nytimes.com/2012/12/14/world/asia/japan-scrambles-jets-in-island-dispute-with-china.html>, accessed 13 December 2012.

Wan, Ming. 2006. *Sino-Japanese Relations: Interaction, Logic, and Transformation*. Washington, DC: Wilson Center.

Wang Wei. 2013. US plays disgraceful role in China-Japan ties: Qian Lihua. Xinhua News Agency website. <http://news.xinhuanet.com/english/china/2013-03/08/c_132218496.htm>, accessed 23 March 2013.

Wolf, Charles, Wang Xiao, and Warner, Eric. 2013. *China's Foreign Aid and Government-Sponsored Investment Activities: Scale, Content, Destinations, and Implications*. Santa Monica: RAND Corporation.

WTO. 2014. China – Measures related to the exportation of rare earths, tungsten, and molybdenum: Reports of the panel. WT/DS431/R/Add.1, WT/DS432/Add.1, WT/433/Add.1. 26 March. <www.wto.org/english/tratop_e/dispu_e/431_432_433r_a_e.pdf>, accessed 17 May 2014.

Wu Di. 2011. Qing dai Zhong Liu guanxi gaishu [Overview of China-Ryukyu relations during the Qing dynasty]. *Hotan shifan zhuanke xuexiao xuebao*, 30(1), 10–11.

Wu, Kane, and Chatterjee, Sumeet. 2017. Exclusive: China regulators plan to crack down further on overseas deals. *Reuters*, 4 August. <www.reuters.com/article/us-china-conglomerates-idUSKBN1AK195>, accessed 5 August 2017.

Xinhua. 2014. Chinese analysts criticize US president's remarks on Diaoyu islands. Xinhua News Agency, 30 April. <http://news.xinhuanet.com/english/china/2014-04/30/c_133302253.htm>, accessed 22 May 2014. Available at <www.globaltimes.cn/content/857778.shtml>, accessed 2 November 2017.

Yeung, Henry Wai-chung. 2016. *Strategic Coupling: East Asian Industrial Transformation in the New Global Economy*. Ithaca: Cornell University Press.

Yiu, Enoch. 2017. Vietnam is in, France is no not, as 200 million Chinese tourists prepare to hit the road by 2020. *South China Morning Post*, 20 July. <www.scmp.com/business/companies/article/2103479/vietnam-france-so-not-200-million-chinese-tourists-prepare-hit>, accessed 20 July 2017.

ZGWJ [Zhongguo waijiao] [China's diplomacy]. Annual. Beijing: Ministry of Foreign Affairs of the People's Republic of China. This is the official yearbook of the Ministry of Foreign Affairs of the People's Republic of China. Beginning its publication in 1987 as 中国外交概览 China's Foreign Affairs review, it is hereafter referred to as ZGWJGL, and after 1995 中国外交 it is renamed Zhongguo waijiao (ZGWJ) for the Chinese language version, and China's Foreign Affairs or CFA for the English-language version, which began publication in 2003.

Zhang Huizhi, and Wang Xiaoke. 2013. China-South Korea Relations. *Contemporary International Relations*, 23(2), 101–116.

7 China and Southeast Asia in the 21st century

The relationship between China and its Southeast Asian neighbors has shown the most change since the Qing dynasty: it has shifted, often dramatically, from an inactive, indifferent relationship, to a hyperactive relationship based upon revolutionary appeal and Cold War rivalry, to an earnest Good Neighbor Policy that opened China's ties with the ten nations of ASEAN by the beginning of the 21st century. The focus on much of the scholarship and media of the world is now on whether China is once again shifting toward a hyperactive phase. This chapter will seek to answer that question, arguing that China's behavior toward Southeast Asia has shown some evidence of hyperactivity toward a limited number of its neighbors, such as Vietnam and the Philippines, but less so with most of its neighbors.

Security

China's rise during the period beginning 2002 increased its already considerable dominance over Southeast Asia, as seen in Chapter 2.

Territorial disputes

China's land borders with its Southeast Asian neighbors were finalized and resolved during this period; its maritime boundaries, on the other hand, continued to be source of tension, especially in the South China Sea. Of the land borders, the Sino-Vietnamese was the most sensitive, but as seen in Chapter 4, resolved diplomatically and equitably, the land boundary at the end of 1999 and the Gulf of Tonkin/Beibu Gulf at the end of 2000. China's borders with Laos and Myanmar have been similarly resolved and demarcated (Amer 2013: 300). The key land boundary dispute was resolved in 2000, with the two sides splitting the difference almost exactly. The last point was the China-Laos-Vietnam tripoint border, fixed by treaty in 2006 (Townsend-Gault 2013: 149).

But that leaves the South China Sea unresolved, and the issue in many ways is getting more dangerous. Map 7.1 shows the competing claims of the actors: China/Taiwan, Vietnam, Philippines, Malaysia, Brunei, and possibly Indonesia.

If the Diaoyu/Senkaku dispute is largely just a rocky symbol of broader issues in Sino-Japanese relations, the South China Sea is a much different dispute. The area in dispute is infinitely greater – about the size of India – the stakes are substantially

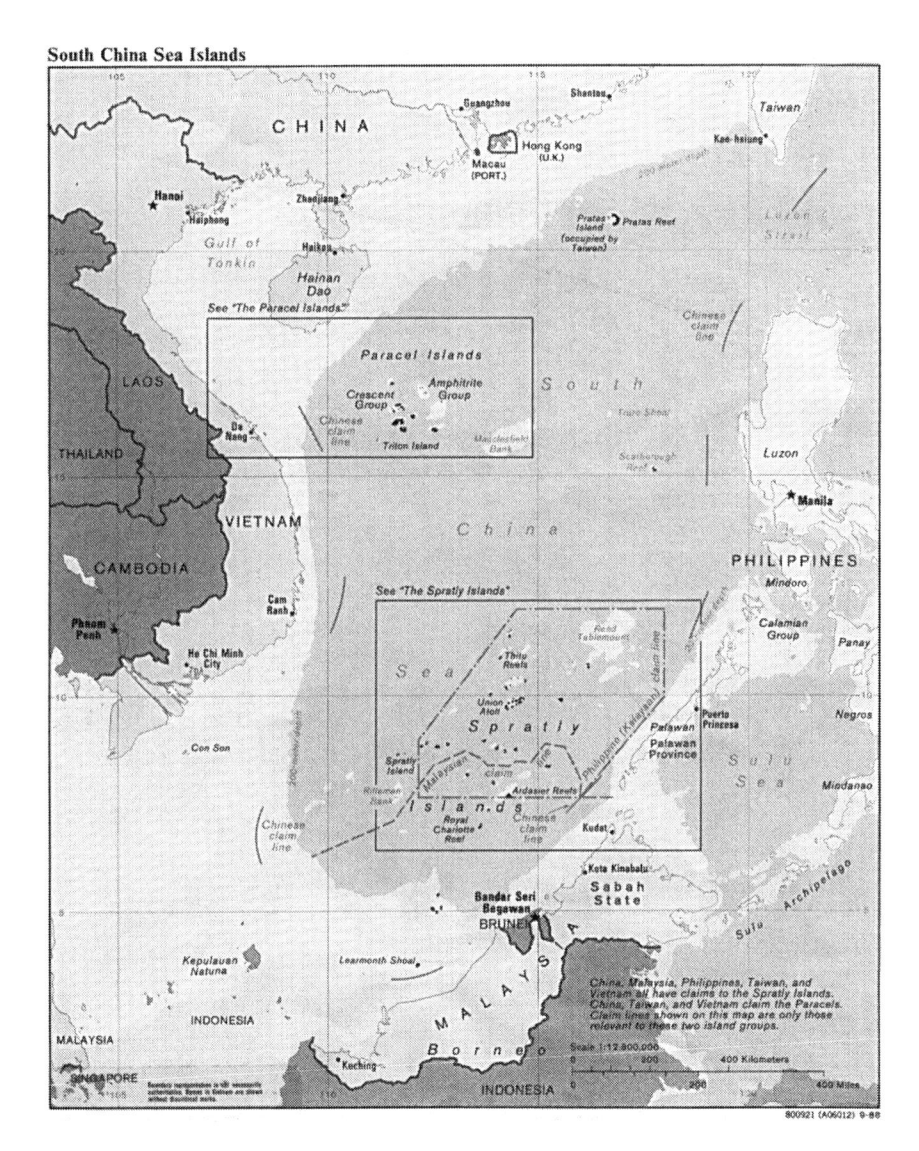

Map 7.1 Map of South China Sea claims

Source: Central Intelligence Agency. University of Texas Library, Perry-Castañeda Library Map Collection <www.lib.utexas.edu/maps/middle_east_and_asia/schina_sea_88.jpg>, accessed 2 September 2014.

higher, and the number of participants is greater. Unlike the Diaoyu/Senkaku dispute, which is a tiny set of islands that might influence an EEZ claim, China's claim to the South China Sea may be a territorial claim to the entire maritime area, what was previously known as the "Nine-Dashed Line"(九段线 *jiu duan xian*) and then in June 2014 the "Ten-Dashed Line" or sometimes the "U-Dashed Line"

(U形线). As noted in Chapter 4, China has been vague about whether the dashes indicate a convenient map grouping, a territorial claim based upon a continental shelf, or the sea where its island claims are and thus limited to the 12 nautical mile areas around those few specks of dry land in the Spratlys and the Paracels. (US State Department, Bureau of Oceans and International Environmental and Scientific Affairs 2014; Odgaard 2015). Nor are precise locations indicated, unlike most other maritime claims, which are precisely delimited in longitude, latitude, degrees, minutes, and seconds.

The legal arguments of China concerning the South China Sea were substantially (but not completely) scuttled on 12 July 2016 when the Permanent Court of Arbitration (PCA) in The Hague ruled that China could not establish an Exclusive Economic Zone based upon the Nine-Dashed Line concept since none of the islets and reefs in the South China Sea were, legally speaking, *islands* as far as the UNCLOS Treaty was concerned. The PCA ruling did not, however, rule on the sovereignty of the sea, only on the question of whether the Chinese-occupied and Chinese-claimed reefs could legally be used as the basis for such a claim (PCA 2016). China, of course, refused to cooperate with the arbitration which had been brought by the Philippines, and has refused to recognize the results, claiming that the provisions of UNCLOS allow it to do so. The ruling was a diplomatic defeat for China, though it has changed nothing in the South China Sea itself.

The South China Sea dispute has been around for a while, as noted in previous chapters, yet the Declaration on the Conduct of Parties in the South China Sea of a (usually shortened as the "Declaration of Conduct" or DOC) in late 2002 seemed to point to a diplomatic approach to the issue, if not an actual resolution. China and ASEAN declared a "Strategic Partnership" in 2003. The non-binding 2002 DOC was supposed to be followed by a Code of Conduct (COC), a detailed agreement on how to interact and behave in the South China Sea, but specifically did not propose to resolve the issue of territorial sovereignty. But during the period in question, the issue of the South China Sea has remained unresolved, and initial hopes based upon the Code of Conduct have given in to frustration and, in the last few years, increasing acrimony and conflict.

Putting details into the Code has proven next to impossible because of the principle of consensus ("the ASEAN Way"): reaching an agreement with ten members plus China has been unworkable. An ASEAN-China Joint Working Group was created in 2004, and an agreement to draft specific guidelines were adopted in 2011. But an initial plan to fully operationalize the DOC within ten years eventually ran into its deadline at the July 2012 ASEAN meeting in Cambodia, and the host nation scuttled even a vague resolution urging the completion of the task (Chheang 2012). Many analysts believe that China is in no hurry to ever conclude a COC (Tiezzi 2014). At the August 2005 joint working group meeting in Manila, China raised its objection to all of the ASEAN states caucusing before the meeting, and sought to only involve the "relevant parties" (i.e., claimants). It has explicitly indicated that a gradual approach, satisfying all concerns of all relevant parties would be the best way to proceed. Although Beijing did agree in July 2013 to talks about the COC, China would appear to be more interested in negotiating in a series of bilateral agreements with other claimant states. Chinese diplomats did sign protocols on communications at sea, the Code for Unplanned Encounters at Sea (CUES) at the Vientiane summit in September 2016, which was a step forward . . . after fourteen years.

Much has been made of the potential for energy in the South China Sea, too much in this author's opinion. The Energy Information Agency (EIA) in 2013 estimated that the hydrocarbons lie primarily in off-shore waters, not in the Spratlys or the center of the sea (EIA 2013). Just as in the East China Sea, estimates of energy potential vary significantly: "EIA estimates the South China Sea contains approximately 11 billion barrels of oil and 190 trillion cubic feet of natural gas in proved and probable reserves," but Chinese estimates of gas are much higher, around 500 tcf (2). The issue of fish and fisheries there has not been sufficiently seen, both as a resource issue and as an expatriate citizen issue. Fishing boats there are in desperate need of better management.

There is little question that the fisheries of the South China Sea are in ecological danger, not helped in the least by the political wrangling of the disputant states. Part of the reason for the rise in tensions in the Spratlys is that the northern parts of the South China Sea have been significantly fished out. Maximum Sustainable Yields (MSY) for Northern South China Sea areas for China is 1.9 million tons and for Vietnam is 1.5 million tons, yet each exceeds that number significantly, China by 1.3 million tons and Vietnam by over 800,000 tons. The Asia Pacific Fishery Commission puts the matter plainly: "The picture that emerges is one of a subregional fishery that has been under heavy fishing pressure for more than 30 years and which has been fished down considerably. . . . there remains a clear trend of a declining catch of large demersal and pelagic species . . ." (APFIC 2012: 10–12). The big fish are gone, and fishers venture further south in pursuit of them, and run into fishers from other nations.

China's fisheries' total fish catch grew in the 1990s, but then peaked in 1998 at 15.4 million tons of fish, a time associated with its "Good Neighbor Policy," and then declined to 14.4 mt in 2001–02. Yet by 2010, catches were going up again, and exceeding previous levels, 17.1 mt in 2014, the latest year of figures. Some of this trend reflects an effort by China to actually reduce catches in stressed fisheries. A summer time ban on fishing in the Paracels, and parts of the Spratlys, initially imposed in 1999, can be seen to have had an effect. Of course the summer time ban is also useful in excluding other nations from fishing in the South China Sea, and China asserts the right to maintain the fishing ban, and to force all other fishers to obtain permits in Hainan to fish in the South China Sea (Dupont and Baker 2014: 85, 90–91). The ban also helped reduce the total number of Chinese fishers from 9.2 million people in 2000 down to 8.3 million in 2005. But the number of Chinese fishers fishing and the fish caught both gradually crept up, and in 2014 there were around 9.1 million Chinese fishers, up from 8.3 in 2005 (FAO 2016: 17). Given the distances involved, however, China has fewer but larger boats in the South China Sea compared to other claimants. The Asia Pacific Fishery Commission estimates a total Chinese fishing fleet in the South China Sea per se to be around 92,312 vessels, compared to 129,519 Vietnamese, and over 1.3 million Filipino vessels, overwhelmingly small, unpowered boats (APFIC 2012: 26).

Perhaps most disturbing is the expansion of Chinese fishing activities and conflicts into areas not previously seen. Conflicts and incidents in 2009, 2010, 2013, and 2016 conflicts between Indonesian law enforcement and Chinese fishers near the Natuna Islands, an area within Indonesia's claimed EEZ and not clearly even within the Chinese "Ten-Dashed Line" claims push the issue even further. When asked about the incident, the Chinese Foreign Ministry claimed that the fishers were within their "traditional fishing grounds," even though it is over 1,000 miles to the nearest (undisputed) Chinese port (Cochrane 2016).

Vietnam

The Vietnamese claim is fairly clear: it claims the entirety of the Paracel (*Hoàng Sa*) and the Spratlys (*Trường Sa*) and an EEZ associated with them. The Vietnamese Foreign Ministry made its position quite clear: "Viet Nam resolutely protests those actions and asks China to respect Viet Nam's sovereignty [over the Paracel and Spratlys], end the aforesaid wrongful actions and to strictly observe the Declaration of the conducts of parties in the South China Sea and the Viet Nam-China Agreement on basic principles guiding the settlement of maritime issues" (MOFAV 2016).

Vietnam and China have had violent clashes as far back as 1974 and as recently as May 2014, both near the Paracels. Although Chinese and Vietnamese Communist Party officials have sought to calm matters down after the 2014 clash over a Chinese drilling rig near the Paracels, it is fairly clear that Vietnam intends to follow a strategy that is largely what might be called an external balancing one: bringing together parties in an informal arrangement to seek to balance China's maritime might, India, Japan, Australia, Philippines (see below). Vietnam is also distinctive in its military spending and foreign weapons purchases. It is the only country that can be said to continue a "hard balance" strategy by developing its own military further as seen in spending figures. Diplomatic lines are open, and after the oil rig incident in 2014 Nguyen Phu Trong, General Secretary of the Vietnamese Communist Party, visited Beijing in April 2015 as both states tried to put their relations back on a more stable, if not friendly path (Blanchard 2015b).

Philippines

The Philippines as an archipelago has a "baseline" claim to an EEZ, and occupies several small features in the Spratlys. The most recent and contentious dispute with China, however, is over Scarborough Shoal and the Macclesfield Bank, two rich fishing grounds near the large, long island of Palawan. A Defense and Security Consultation mechanism was initiated in 2005, the Chinese and Philippine navies conducted visits and small joint exercises in 2006.

Maritime incidents with China began in 2011 and in 2012, China blocked entrance to the lagoon harbor at Scarborough with large Coast Guard vessels and has not withdrawn since. Chinese Coast Guard and naval ships have closely monitored Philippines outposts in the Spratlys such as Second Thomas Shoal. Manila sought help both from the United States, its treaty ally, and upgraded its security relations with the United States under the 2014 Enhanced Defense Cooperation Agreement, including joint maritime patrols, rotation of US military personnel in the Philippines, and use of Philippines' military bases (Ferdinando 2016). Manila also worked with other actors in the Asia-Pacific (see below); however, its domestic military spending has not risen dramatically, nor has it spent much on foreign military equipment.

The Philippines also brought a case against China in an international court, the PCA in The Hague. This, more than anything on the water, aggravated Sino-Philippines relations, since it effectively set China into a no-win situation: either it participated in the hearings, in which case if it lost it would be even more bound to their results in the court of international public opinion, or if it refused, it would be revealed to be both unconfident in the legal basis of its claims and petulant. As Jesse et al. observe, hegemons don't like to be "bound" in security issues (2012: 14). The PCA case also made this an issue for ASEAN members, since the case would have legal implications for the other three claimants, and policy implications for all other members: they would have to discuss the matter. Several, such as Singapore, indicated that the Philippines' decision was a unilateral one, and did not represent ASEAN opinion. Prior to the ruling, most ASEAN members (even Cambodia) were cagey about their stances, and afterwards either acknowledging the ruling without calling for compliance or making neutral statements. The Philippines and Vietnam called for the ruling to be respected, as did the United States, Japan, and most Western countries (Arbitration Support Tracker 2016).

And then came Duterte.

Just two weeks before the PCA ruling, the new president of the Philippines, Rodrigo Duterte assumed office, having been elected in May on an anti-crime, anti-drugs platform. His administration almost immediately made it clear that it would not press the PCA ruling. China in turn has indicated it is willing to "play nice" with the Philippines: Filipino fishers have been allowed access to the exterior of Scarborough Shoal and nearby areas, though there is a question whether the Chinese Coast Guard continues to block the entrance (Paddock 2016).

Malaysia

Malaysia's claim to the South China Sea overlaps Brunei's (see below) and China's and Indonesia's, but not Vietnam's. Indeed, Vietnam and Malaysia issued a joint submission to the Commission on the Limits of the Continental Shelf (Permanent Mission of the Socialist Republic of Viet Nam to the UN 2009). That was the last bold move Malaysia has made in the South China Sea; thereafter, Malaysia has been a relatively quiet claimant (Forbes 2013). Unlike the Philippines and Vietnam, which have had significant clashes with China, Malaysia's claims have not been sharply contested by China, and Malaysia in turn has done relatively little since the 1990s to assert them. Malaysia's position in the South China Sea may be described as "hedging": it remains a claimant, but there is little doubt but that it has moved noticeably toward a more accommodationist position vis-à-vis China in the last year, and bilateral relations have improved, as discussed below.

Brunei Darussalam

The tiny sultanate of Brunei Darussalam has a claim in the South China Sea that is highly ambiguous, and which has in no clear way affected the relationship of that country with China. On maps, the Bruneian claim is certainly distinct: a rectangle thrusting out straight from the coast toward Louisa Reef. This conflicts most notably with Malaysia's claim, though it also overlaps the Chinese Nine-Dashed Line. Those two apparently settled their differences in 2009 with an exchange of letters, though both seem to be fairly quiet about the details (Sands 2016). Brunei avoids discussing the South China Sea issue, but as ASEAN Chair in 2013 it could not avoid it, and the ASEAN-China meeting issued a communique in which China agreed to start formal negotiations for the COC. Brunei also barely mentioned the issue in the August 2016 "Joint Statement Between Brunei Darussalam and the Socialist Republic of Viet Nam" (MOFAT 2016).

If anything, China has been trying to use its relationship with Brunei as a demonstration of how it sees a possible *modus vivendi* in the South China Sea region: bilaterally negotiated, economically based, and leaving the tough issue of territorial sovereignty aside.

Indonesia

Do Indonesia and China have conflicting territorial claims in the South China Sea? The answer is unclear. In the 1990s, the ambiguity was reassuring; now it is disturbing. The issue surrounds an archipelago called the Natuna Islands, which lie northwest of Borneo, and the EEZ it generates. Unlike the Spratlys, these are clearly large, legal islands and well-inhabited with over 80,000 people. In the 1980s, before the restoration of diplomatic relations, China vaguely assured Indonesia that there was no territorial dispute between the two of them (Acharya 2015: 66). The issue resurfaced in the 1990s, however, when China produced its newer "Nine-Dashed Line" map which seemed to overlap Chinese dashes with Indonesia's EEZ around the Natuna Islands (Johnson 1997: 153). China has sought to raise the potential negotiation of a maritime boundary with Indonesia, but the Indonesian government does not even acknowledge a territorial dispute. China would appear to be increasingly willing to push the issue; Chinese fishing boats' activities in Indonesia's EEZ occurred in 2009 and 2010 and Chinese patrol vessels responded aggressively, claiming the area as "traditional Chinese fishing grounds"; the Indonesians apparently let the issue drop (Arsana and Schofield 2013: 66–70). Recent clashes between Chinese fishing vessels in the area, Indonesian naval vessels – not fisheries enforcement – and Chinese Coast Guard ships in March 2016 have raised an issue of whether a generally low-level functional issue – conflict over fishing rights – may in fact be elevated to a higher-level territorial conflict (Wood 2016: 2; Cochrane 2016).

Indonesia has sought to pose itself as a neutral party to the larger South China Sea issue, and had emphasized its diplomatic initiatives to resolve the matter peacefully:

> Indonesia is not a claimant State to the sovereignty disputes in the South China Sea, and as such Indonesia has played an impartial yet active role in establishing confidence building measures among the claimant states and creating an atmosphere of peace through a series of workshops on the South China Sea since 1990.
> (Permanent Mission of the Republic of Indonesia to the UN 2010: 1–2)

Indonesia also stated in polite but clear terms that it does not regard the "Nine Dashed Line Map" to have legal basis, nor do any of the small features of the South China Sea generate an EEZ: "Indonesia also follows closely the debate over the above mentioned map which has also been referred to as the so-called 'nine-dotted-lines map'. Thus far, there is no clear explanation as to the legal basis, the method of drawing, and the status of those separated dotted-lines . . ." (Permanent Mission of the Republic of Indonesia to the UN 2010: 1–2). It would seem that China is seeking to force the Indonesians to the negotiations table and to recognize its dashes where they overlap with Indonesia's EEZ, possibly making Indonesia the first ASEAN state to recognize them in what would be a low-cost concession from Jakarta.

In this respect, Chinese diplomacy seems to be working with the non-claimants against the primary claimants (Vietnam and, until recently, the Philippines) and at the same time trying to minimize conflict with the three southern-most South China Sea claimant states, Brunei, Malaysia and potentially Indonesia. The ASEAN joint communique coming out of the Myanmar summit in August 2014 did make reference to "increased tensions" in the sea, possibly an indication that at least some of the ASEAN members are beginning to work together. Earlier meetings of the Senior Officials group in Suzhou in September 2013 yielded a vague statement in favor of "gradual progress and consensus through consultations," but it is unclear whether any progress or consensus has been reached.

China's characterization of the issues in the South China Sea has been first and foremost to allude to "some countries outside of the region" (clearly meaning the United States) "hyping up of the so-called tension" (Wang Yi 2014). And the United States did indeed propose a freeze in construction and provocative acts on islands, reefs, rocks, and shoals, a proposal China categorically rejected, announcing it could build whatever it liked on its sovereign territory.

Most of the Chinese patrols in the South China Sea are China Coast Guard vessels, and unlike the roughly even match they face with the Japanese Coast Guard in the Senkaku/Diaoyu dispute, the Chinese Coast Guard is much larger than any of the Southeast Asian nations' equivalent forces. Table 7.1 shows the comparison: China has an overwhelming capacity even in this less aggressive form of maritime coercion: bigger ships, and more of them, a substantial advantage in those situations in which "push comes to shove" but not shooting. One analyst of the subject

Table 7.1 East Asian Coast Guard and maritime enforcement units

East Asian Coast Guard and maritime enforcement units: ocean-going vessels (>1,000t)

	2012	2013	2014	2015	2016
China	51	78	80	105	119
Indonesia	4	4	6	6	6
Japan	71	85	68	70	70
Malaysia	2	2	2	2	2
Philippines	5	5	5	5	5
Vietnam		1	2	5	5

Source: IISS, *Military Balance 2012–2016.*

was quite clear on its function: ". . . China now possesses the world's largest bluewater coast guard fleet . . . it uses the law-enforcement cutter as an instrument of foreign policy" (Martinson 2015: 25). It has used them to block out Filipino vessels from disputed atolls' lagoon entrances, drag Chinese fishing boats away from Indonesian patrols that had seized them and literally ran over a Vietnamese vessel in 2014. The dominance in Coast Guard vessels would also give China a huge advantage should any future regional or bilateral agreements limit the presence of *naval* vessels in the South China Sea. The United States has responded by transferring a used Coast Guard Cutter (USCGC *Morgenthau*) to Vietnam in May 2017 and smaller vessels as well (LaGrone 2017).

Many of China's actions in the South China Sea have been designed to avoid the appearance of outright military aggression, and indeed in some cases appear to be banal to parties which either do not want to become involved or which do not share the Southeast Asian nations' hypersensitivity due to the vast asymmetry of relations: the publication of Chinese passports with the "Nine-Dashed Line" on the visa pages. Exploratory drilling. Declaration of county-level administrative status. Building a lighthouse. None of these would seem to rise to the level of *casus belli*. The worst incidents in the period in question involve ship collisions and use of water cannons.

The current issues notwithstanding, there are some points that make the South China Sea dispute not entirely intractable. First, China's interactions with other South East Asian claimants do have an institutional forum, and an international agreement, the Declaration of Conduct. Senior Chinese and ASEAN officials still meet on the subject, so diplomatic channels have not yet closed. Unlike the East China Sea, China (as of August 2017) has not declared an Air Defense Identification Zone (Xinhua 2014a). In the specific case of the clash between China and Vietnam over the HD981 oil rig, the offending structure was pulled away from the area a month before scheduled, which some analysts saw as an unspoken Chinese concession to reduce tensions (Ramzy 2014). Senior Chinese and Vietnamese leaders met in August 2014 to negotiate a maritime truce (Xinhua 2014b).

In the case of the Philippines, of course, China became much more pleasant after President Duterte downplayed the PCA ruling and visited China, allowing Filipino fishers to visit Scarborough Shoal and rescuing some during a storm (Paddock 2016: Mogato 2016).

Military intervention

The clashes and confrontations in the South China Sea notwithstanding, China did not militarily intervene in its neighbors during this period, without permission. And during the 2014 riots in Vietnam that led to violence against Chinese, there may have been a justification or rationalization to have done so on behalf of citizens, which has been seen in other regional hegemons' behavior, and which was prominently done by Russia in Crimea and eastern Ukraine at the same time. In two other instances in Southeast Asia, there were threats to Chinese nationals, as discussed below, but these did not lead to intervention. Myanmar was one of the few areas in which Chinese intervention was seriously contemplated, after the murder of Chinese crew on riverboats on the Mekong in 2011, though this involved Laos and Thailand as well (see Parello-Plesner and Duchâtel 2015: chap. 4). Chinese officials in Yunnan province continue to have a "working relationship" with the United Wa State Army (UWSA) which controls significant areas bordering China (Lintner 2015: 172–175). It should be noted that the Chinese National People's Congress in December 2015 passed a law that would allow both PLA and People's Armed Police to engage in counter-terrorism operations overseas (Duchâtel 2016: 2).

External major powers

The US role in aggravating China's diplomatic problems with its Southeast Asian neighbors has been a *leitmotif* of Chinese foreign policy statements since 2004. These statements have at times approached – but not yet come to – the point of calling for the exclusion of American forces and influence in the region. Chen Xiangyang, the deputy director of the influential China Institutes of Contemporary International Relations, wrote of the problem in 2004, pointing out US relations with the Philippines, India, and Japan all have the effect of making China's Good Neighbor Policy much more problematic, and trying to create a hegemonic presence in the region, and ". . . to clearly not allow Asian countries to manage Asian affairs" (Chen Xiangyang 2004: 290). Specifically on the South China Sea issue, China regularly criticizes the USA for its "kibitzing" in the region, and regularly calls for the United States to be "impartial" in the dispute (Xinhua 2015a, 2015b), and very specifically notes that the USA is a "non-party" to the dispute. The *Global Times* opined that "The fundamental reason for the sudden prominence of the South China Sea issue and the Diaoyu Islands dispute has been the US. Seeing the 'pivot' to Asia, the US has fomented surrounding countries into confronting China over territorial disputes, so as to disturb and check China's rise" ("Clinton must see China's territorial stance" 2012). Feng Zhongping of the China Institute of Contemporary International Relations wrote that, "It is generally believed at home and abroad that the U.S. has largely been responsible for worsening relations between China and some of its neighbors over the past two years. For example, some believe that Japan has grown tough with China because it has Washington's backing" (Feng Zhongping 2013: 53).

America's focus in the first decade of the 21st century was firmly on the Middle East and Afghanistan. The focus on American leadership was also on the domestic front from 2008–2009 as a result of the presidential election and the financial crisis. Though some remain in Afghanistan, US forces were withdrawn from Iraq at the end of 2011, when the Secretary of State, Hillary Clinton, published a provocative article "America's Pacific Century" in which she advocated the USA pivoting its power to the Asia-Pacific region (the Chinese translation is usually 重返亚太/*chongfan YaTai*). Almost immediately the term "pivot" was substituted with "Rebalance" (再平衡/*zai pingheng*), though the term *pivot* is still commonly used in Chinese and English.

As we have seen from other regional hegemons, the introduction of a new great power into the regional hegemon's space is likely to result in a conflictual relationship between the native power and the "intruder." Russia's invasion of the Crimea and the beginning of the civil war in eastern Ukraine is the most extreme example, but India's behavior toward its neighbors' connections to the USA or China, just as the USA reacted vigorously to perceived German intrusion in the Caribbean in the early 1900s and Soviet intrusion fifty years later. Yet Nigeria and Brazil's reactions have been much more muted to external powers' re-introduction in their regions. Where does China's reaction to the US pivot lie along this continuum of regional hegemonic behavior?

The initial, official reaction of the Chinese foreign ministry was muted:

> ... the US took high-profile steps to deepen its involvement in Asia-Pacific affairs. After 10 years of combatting terrorism, the United States was seeking to withdraw its troops from Afghanistan and at the same time increased input in the Asia-Pacific. The United States strengthened ties with its allies including Japan, the ROK and the Philippines, promoted relations with such regional emerging countries as India and Indonesia, expanded engagement in regional multilateral affairs, and pressed ahead with the Trans-Pacific Strategic Economic Partnership. President Obama attended the East Asia Summit for the first time.
>
> (*CFA* 2012: 4)

The next year China's foreign ministry briefly noted the term "rebalancing" (*CFA* 2013: 4). It also noted curtly that, "[t]he United States played an important part in China's disputes with neighboring countries on territorial sovereignty and maritime rights and interests" (309). The following year continued to note the "strategic rebalance" of the USA in the Asia Pacific, emphasizing at length US military and strategic cooperation with allies in the region (*CFA* 2014: 12–14).

Did China notice that America was "gone" from East Asia in the 2003–2010 period? China's previous statements about American involvement in East Asia and Sino-American relations in general have evolved during the 21st century, gradually becoming cooler. But it is also interesting to note is that the official Chinese foreign policy assessment of the USA in East Asia never characterized America as "absent" from the region prior to the "pivot" policy. The 2003 assessment of US foreign policy in the wake of the invasion of Iraq was exceptionally blunt, calling US unilateralism "trigger-happy" and questioning the US role in the world in general (*CFA* 2004: 3). Yet China's foreign ministry nevertheless said that "A stronger constructive and cooperative relationship between China and the US contributed to a healthy trend of development in Asia" (8). "Constructive and cooperative relations between China and the US continued to grow . . ." in 2004 (*CFA* 2005: 7), and the "US continued to readjust and strengthen its military posture in the Asia-Pacific region" (8). The "constructive and cooperative" Sino-American relationship tagline was also used in reference to 2005 and 2007 (*CFA* 2006: 5, 2008: 5)

However, the "constructive and cooperative" characterization dropped in 2009. The pattern continued in 2012–13, with the Chinese noting the efforts to maintain US presence in the "greater Asia-Pacific" and to strengthen ties with American allies even after President Obama was a no-show at the APEC summit (*CFA* 2014: 12–13). Thus, the view of the external great power gradually cooled during the 21st century in China's most official, most diplomatic treatment of the subject.

Other external powers began to play security roles in Southeast Asia in the 21st century, most notably Japan, Australia and India. In 2007 at the ASEAN Regional Forum meeting, the USA encouraged a meeting of these actors (and itself), though the idea receded for a while after the Bush administration. Australia has adopted what one analyst calls a "flexible alliance" approach: "Prime Minister Turnbull has built stronger security ties with regional neighbors like the Philippines and Vietnam, a trend which the US and other regional powers support as a way of preserving the rules-based regional order and reducing China's unilateral leverage in the region" (Johan 2016). Japan has offered security aid to Vietnam, including six patrol vessels and a loan of ¥120 billion (about US$1 billion), and Japanese Prime Minister Abe Shinzo visited Hanoi in January 2017 ("Abe pledges . . ." 2017). Japan (briefly) indicated its willingness to send patrols into the South China Sea, and to lend the Philippines patrol craft and surveillance aircraft (Brunnstrom 2016). India under Prime Minister Narendra Modi has also been working with Japan both economically and strategically (Baruah 2016). Within the region, there has been some symbolic cooperation between the Vietnamese and the Philippines navies (Mogato and Torode 2014).

Beyond the United States, India has begun to express its interests in the South China Sea, linking up with another power outside of the area, Japan. The relationship has been slowly warming in the 21st century, with "global partnership" announced in 2006, a "strategic and global partnership" in 2007, and following the Abe-Modi summit in September 2014, the December 2015 visit to India by Abe Shinzo upgraded relations to a "Special Global and Strategic Partnership" and discussed strategic as well as commercial ties, but the primary target was clear: China (Takenaka 2014). Small-scale naval exercises first took place in June

2012, and much larger US-India-Japan exercises including aircraft carriers were included in the annual US-India Exercise Malabar in October 2015 (Rajagopalan and Mishra 2015: 1). Japanese foreign aid in the strategically-located Indian Andaman and Nicobar Islands would help India track Chinese naval vessels' ingress to the Bay of Bengal (Barry 2016), and joint India-Japan exercises with the USA have been considered in the Philippine Sea (Miglani 2016). China has registered its objections; when the idea of a larger, more institutionalized Exercise Malabar arose in 2007, Chinese criticism prevented such an enlargement. The expansion in 2015/2016 have again led to the Chinese seeking to keep other parties out of the South China Sea issue in particular:

> No cooperation between any countries should be directed at a third party. . . . Countries from outside the area must stop pushing forward the militarization of the South China Sea, cease endangering the sovereignty and national security of littoral countries in the name of "freedom of navigation" and harming the peace and stability of the region.
>
> (reported in Rajagopalan and Sweeney 2016)

Chinese scholars and policy analysts have recognized that the rise of Chinese naval power in the region is a major component behind this cooperation, as well as US encouragement (Zhao Guojun and Zhao Chaolong 2015: 13; Liu Siwei 2015: 5–6).

Diplomatic relations with regional states

China has formal relations with all of the members of ASEAN and "partnerships" or other elevated diplomatic relationship designations with those ten countries. Despite the notable disputes, formal relations have not been suspended. The region began to divide into roughly two groups by 2009/10: those with a maritime claim in the South China Sea, and those without. The latter group has generally enjoyed better relations with China than the former, though the deterioration of relations began around 2009. By 2017, however, China's relations with two of the claimants in the South China Sea significantly improved, Philippines and Malaysia. All Southeast Asian states have also become some sort of "strategic partners" of China, a formal upgrading of strategic and diplomatic relations: Table 7.2 shows the upgrades and dates.

Thus, all states within Southeast Asia have an officially designated form of "partnership" with China, except the Philippines and Brunei, which have designated "relationships"; Singapore, just as it was the last to establish formal diplomatic relations with China in the 1990s, was also the last to agree to a partnership. Although these designations had been used earlier, Southeast Asia was one sub-region in which it was used most extensively as a diplomatic tool in which no formal treaties or alliances are formed but which represent important statements of the relationship. Although it is possible to talk about a hierarchy of these "strategic partnerships" with "Comprehensive Strategic Partnerships" at the highest level, a "comprehensive strategic cooperative partnership" which is a level down, and then a variety of

Table 7.2 China's "partners" and "strategic relations" in Southeast Asia, 2004–2014

China's "partners" and "strategic relations" in Southeast Asia, 2004–2014

State	Designation	Date
Brunei	Strategic Cooperation Relationship	2013
Cambodia	Comprehensive Relationship of Cooperation	2006
	Comprehensive Strategic Partner of Cooperation	2010
Indonesia	Strategic Partnership	2005
	Comprehensive Strategic Partnership	2013
Laos	Comprehensive Strategic Partnership	2009
Malaysia	Comprehensive Strategic Partnership	2013
Myanmar	Comprehensive Strategic Partnership	2011
Philippines	Relationship of Strategic Cooperation and Peace	2005
Singapore	Comprehensive Cooperative Partnership progressing with the times	2015
Thailand	Strategic Relations of Cooperation	2007
	Comprehensive Strategic Cooperation Partnership	2012
Vietnam	Strategic Partnership of Cooperation	2008

Source: *China's Foreign Relations* 2005–2014. Singapore: Channel News Asia 2015.

different names and ambiguous meanings. In one case, the Philippines, the term has not been used lately, and Chinese analysts concede that the term no longer has any meaning (Dai Weilai 2016: 102–104). Other countries, including the USA and India have similar designations. Empirical research on the subject shows that China's "strategic partnerships" go to ". . . regionally important countries, attractive markets, large producers of natural resources, and like-minded countries in international affairs" (Strüver 2016: 25). But as noted in Chapter 2, the term "partner" implies a transactional relationship, and a "strategic partner" implies a common strategy. By the second decade of 21st century, the term "neighbor" was being used less often in official Chinese descriptions of nearby states in Southeast Asia.

High-level visits

China has also been careful to maintain a substantial number of high-level leadership visits to the states of Southeast Asia for the past decade or more; more than a dozen State Visits to countries in Southeast Asia, even more State Visits from Southeast Asia, in addition to Premier's visits, Foreign Minister visits, visits from high-level officials of a variety of sorts, not to mention the talks held on the sidelines of the numerous Asia-Pacific international summits. Only in the case of Thailand has there not been a State Visit in either direction for the past decade or more, largely due to the poor health of the Thai King Bhumibol, who passed away in October 2016. There is little question but that in diplomatic terms, China is actively, even persistently, engaged with Southeast Asia.

China's bilateral diplomacy in the region also tends to avoid openly criticizing individual foreign leaders or regime types. China's leaders welcome democratically elected presidents and prime ministers to visit, and then just as readily welcome the military rulers who overthrew them in a coup d'état. That is not to say that China's leaders are indifferent to the domestic politics of its neighbors, and the Chinese Communist Party has established and maintained party-to-party relations both with the Communist Party of Vietnam and the Lao People's Revolutionary Party, as well as a wide variety of other parties in the region such as the (ruling) Cambodian People's Party and the royalist Funcinpec party (Tian 2012).[2] Stability, not ideology is the primary concern of China with its neighbors. One possible exception to this can be found: Benigno Aquino III, whose Presidency in the Philippines was blamed by many Chinese for inciting the crisis in Sino-Philippine bilateral relations.

Vietnam

Territorial disputes on land, the Gulf of Tonkin and most prominently the South China Sea notwithstanding, there has been periodic diplomatic progress in Sino-Vietnamese relations, though they often chill when maritime tensions rise. Trade continues to rise between China and Vietnam, and the latter's dependence on Chinese imports – over 30% of its total – make it more difficult to voice objections the way in which less trade-exposed Philippines does. Vietnam depends heavily on trade, 178% of GDP in 2015 (World Bank 2017), so its relations with one of its most important trading partners weighs heavily on its diplomatic maneuver. So, too, does tourism, also a major industry in Vietnam and one in which Chinese visitors can play a big role, or stay away, as they did in 2014 after the anti-Chinese riots in Vietnam following the oil rig dispute (Ives 2014). Finally, the two countries maintain party-to-party relations which keeps a second line of communication open, in addition to the hotline agreed to in 2008. Despite clashes in the Spratlys, the two navies conducted joint patrols of the Gulf of Tonkin in 2011, 2012, and 2013, as well as naval visits. This is not to say the two countries are particularly close, and after the oil rig incident and subsequent riots in the summer of 2014, the best that could be said is that the two were in damage-control mode. Thus, Nguyen Phu Trong, General Secretary of the Vietnamese Communist Party, visited Beijing in April 2015 as both states tried to put their relations back on a more stable, if not friendly path (Blanchard 2015b).

Not surprisingly, China has not made any arms transfers to Vietnam in the 2004–2015 period, and since the United States only lifted its arms embargo against Hanoi in the summer of 2016, the Russians completely dominate weapons transfers, with over 90% of the market (SIPRI TIV 2017).[3]

Philippines

The territorial dispute between China and the Philippines has substantially poisoned all aspects of the bilateral relationship between Beijing and Manila by 2016, yet the overall relationship begins this period very well. In 2004, Philippine President Gloria Macapagal-Arroyo made a state visit to China, reciprocated by Hu Jintao the next year, and in the official communiques of the meetings expressed "... continued commitment to peace and stability in the South China Sea and were ready to actively discuss joint exploration in the disputed area of the South China Sea" (*CFA* 2005: 262; 2006: 272). Hu's visit also saw the relationship upgraded to a "relationship of strategic cooperation for peace and development" (战略性合作关系 *zhanlüè xing hezuo guanxi*). China granted preferential credits worth $900 million to the Philippines for railway construction and President Arroyo made multiple trips to China between 2001 and 2009. In short, there was little in the official Chinese reports until 2009 to indicate a chill in the relationship. Nor was the US-Philippine alliance seemingly a problem during this period for China; the USA continued to increase its military aid to Manila and conduct joint exercises as part of the Global War on Terror (Castro 2011: 241–243).

In the 2009–11 period the relationship chilled slightly, and the Aquino Presidency saw it go into full retreat: the mutual visits grew fewer, the statements about joint development of the South China Sea disappeared after the Filipinos allowed the agreement to expire, and though the new President Benigno "Noynoy" Aquino III paid a state visit to China in August 2011, it was already clear that Sino-Philippine diplomatic relations were near a standstill even before the 2012 Scarborough Shoal Incident. Part of that was Aquino using the China issue to appear a strong contrast against his predecessor in the summer of 2011 (Zha 2015: 251).

With the June 2016 inauguration of President Rodrigo Duterte, however, the foreign policy of the Philippines has moved away from its close treaty alliance with the United States, and Duterte has stated that he had "separated" the Philippines from the USA, in addition to insulting the President of the United States after sharp criticism of extra-judicial killings in the Philippines (Liu Zhen 2016). This is probably the clearest instance of "leash-slipping" albeit an external, not a regional hegemon's leash (though the bilateral treaty has not been abrogated and the Department of Foreign Affairs maintains that the relationship is still solid). Duterte's state visit to Beijing in October also yielded $13.5 billion in trade and commercial deals, and he was prominently welcomed to China's Belt and Road Forum for International Cooperation. Foreign Minister Wang Yi hailed the progress in the relationship in June 2017 as the "golden period of fast development" (Shepherd 2017).

Cambodia

China's connections with Cambodia are close and it is a critical contact within ASEAN, as well as a long-time friend going back to the 1950s. As discussed below, Cambodia has on several occasions worked to scuttle or weaken consensus within ASEAN on issues related to the South China Sea and in particular China's claims there, most recently in July 2016. The two states upgraded their relationship from "close friendly neighbors" to "a comprehensive partnership of cooperation" in 2006, and then to a "comprehensive strategic partnership of cooperation" in

2010. King Norodom Sihamoni, who ascended the throne in 2004, made a state visit to China in August 2005, and Hu Jintao reciprocated in March 2012. Equally important and distinctive is the fact that (as noted) that the Chinese Communist Party maintains party-to-party exchanges with both Prime Minister Hun Sen's dominant Cambodian People's Party and the tiny royalist Funcinpec Party (*CFA*, 2005–2013).

China has also given economic and military aid to Cambodia, building Highway 7 to the border with Laos between 2004 and 2008, a government building, hydroelectric projects, a jointly-funded Special Economic Zone in Sihanoukville, as well as smaller projects such as small tourist buses around the Angkor Temple complex, donated by Chinese provinces. China has also transferred $114 million in military from 2004–2015, almost half of all Cambodia's arms transfers during that period (SIPRI TIV Tables 2017). Some of these transfers were donations of patrol and naval vessels (Burgos and Ear 2010: 620). The close relationship of China and Cambodia serves both Phnom Penh and Beijing well, and even western analysts concede that the affirmations of the two sides' closeness is a sincere testament to mutuality and non-interference (Burgos and Ear 2010: 638; Bader 2015).

Laos

With only about seven million people and a political system dominated by the communist Lao People's Revolution Party, Laos is squeezed between its much larger neighbors: Thailand, which dominates much of its poor but growing economy, Vietnam, which it resembles politically going back to the Cold War, and China, with which it shares a border and increasing economic ties. The two sides upgraded their bilateral relations to a "Comprehensive Strategic Partnership" in 2009. Unlike Cambodia, however, the government in Vientiane seems to pursue a strictly neutral approach to the South China Sea issue; its only statements on the subject have been in conjunction with its chairmanship of ASEAN in 2016. One analyst at Australian National University compared the approach of Laos to Cambodia on the South China Sea issue:

> ... compared to Cambodia.... Laos is in a difficult position on this issue – clearly they can't afford to completely alienate China, but they're taking a bit of a different approach than Cambodia, is my sense. Laos is still trying to argue for resolutions coming out of Asean ...
>
> (quoted in Ives 2016)

Foreign aid has been a major feature of China's relations with Laos and China has supplied youth volunteers (青年志愿者/*qingnian zhiyuan zhe*, China's equivalent to the US Peace Corps) to the country. Aid projects have also been undertaken, including hydropower plants, a stadium, a section of the Kunming-Bangkok Highway, and a drug rehabilitation center (*CFA* 2007–2008). Law enforcement cooperation has also been the focus of China's diplomacy, especially after the October 2011 murder of Chinese merchant sailors on the Mekong. China also provides scholarships for Laotians to study in Chinese universities, and has opened Chinese language schools in Vientiane (Yang 2014). Laos is also on the route for China's proposed high-speed rail link into Southeast Asia, part of the larger "One Belt, One Road" undertaking. Although negotiations have concluded with China owning 70% of the $7 billion project, construction on the Laotian side has yet to begin (Webb 2016). For a small, land-locked country such as Laos, the route is important to diversifying its options currently split between Thailand and Vietnam. Yet foreign direct investment by Chinese firms has been unpopular in some parts of Laos, as have some of the recently arrived Chinese traders and tourists (Parameswaran 2013). China also transferred $37 million in arms to Laos 2004–2015, the largest single supplier (SIPRI TIV 2017).

Thailand

Relations between China and Thailand have generally been very good in the 21st century, despite political instability in Bangkok between "red shirt" and "yellow shirt" popular movements, resulting in military coups d'état against Prime Ministers Thaksin Shinawatra in 2006 and his sister Yingluck in 2014. Both had visited China during their tenure. Nevertheless, formal relations between China and Thailand remained stable. The relationship was described as "Strategic Relations of Cooperation" in 2005, and was upgraded to "Comprehensive Strategic Cooperation Partnership" in 2012 with a detailed action plan for implementation (*CFA* 2013: 288).

The relationship between Thailand and the USA which was (and still technically is) a formal alliance was by damaged after the military coup of 2015. Thailand's government addressed this bluntly:

> As the region's oldest US ally, Thailand's role in bolstering the US position could have been augmented if not for the restrictions imposed by US laws that followed the power seizure in May 2014. In the absence of normal Thai-US interactions, several countries including China have used this unique opportunity to strengthen and upgrade strategic ties with Thailand has never seen before. Thai-Chinese defense cooperation is the biggest beneficiary.
> (Chongkittavorn et al. 2016: 11–12)

Thus, Thailand appears to have moved slightly toward China. But the Thai government is also cautious about China's behavior.

> Now ASEAN is using the same peace-oriented principles in engaging China on the South China Sea. These principles have been incorporated into the 2002 Declaration on the Conduct of Parties in the South China Sea (DoC). Unfortunately, ASEAN lacks the authority to ensure full compliance of the DoC. China is not deterred by the DoC from undertaking massive land reclamation works in disputed areas in the South China Sea in recent years. This is why ASEAN Member States want to speed up the drafting of a Code of Conduct

in the South China Sea (CoC), and to realize it at the earliest opportunity as a new legally-binding agreement with China on how to avoid tensions and manage disputes in the South China Sea. Yet, China prefers a more cautious approach, going step-by-step and working on a CoC through careful consultation and consensus. The Chinese have apparently learned to make good use of the consensus principle to their advantage.

(Chongkittavorn et al. 2016: 38–39)

China and Thailand have fostered closer military ties, despite (or perhaps because of) Bangkok's formal yet strained alliance relationship with the United States. The two sides had regular defense and security consultation meetings and held a joint Special Forces training exercise in Chiang Mai in July 2008, a joint special force anti-terror joint training in October 2010 and marine joint training exercise in November (given the murder of Chinese merchant sailors on the Mekong river in October 2011, law enforcement meetings were prominent during the period, as with Laos). China transferred $100 million in arms to Thailand 2004–2015, but had lots of competition for the market, and Singapore, Sweden, Ukraine, and the USA also moved more in total value to Bangkok in the period (SIPRI TIV Tables 2017). In April 2017, the government in Bangkok announced the purchase of a Chinese submarine for $393 million, with more to follow ("Thai junta defends buying" 2017).

Thailand is also the focus of some vague discussions of building a canal across the Kra Isthmus, bypassing the Straits of Malacca, and thus relieving the "Malacca Dilemma" noted in Chapter 5. Despite much discussion, Chinese scholars are skeptical of the project's prospects (Ren Yuanzhe 2015; Cao Wenzhen and Huang Weizi 2015).

Myanmar

China's relations with Myanmar (also known as Burma) are possibly the most complex of its Southeast Asian neighbors. On the one hand, they demonstrate the flexibility of Beijing's regional relations regardless of the domestic politics of its neighbors; the period begins with Myanmar under a military junta, isolated from the West, and apparently with only China as a friend in the world. By 2016, Myanmar was guardedly democratic; Aung Sang Suu Kyi is leading the country in all but the formal title of "President" (she is formally the Foreign Minister and State Councilor) yet China's relations with Myanmar are still stable and outwardly good. They are also a demonstration of the hard-headed orientation of the Nobel Peace Prize Winner leading that very poor nation. On the other hand, China's relations with Myanmar are also aggravated because of a long border noted for its drugs and civil warfare which spill over into China's Yunnan province. This is also one of the relationships in Southeast Asia in which there are charges that China is seeking to direct the politics of its smaller, poorer neighbor.

The period began with solid formal relations between China and the military-backed government of Myanmar, with China providing infrastructure and investment, boasting that its accumulated contractual investments there were $3.4 billion as of 2004 (*CFA* 2006: 250). The problems of drug trafficking, however, were a recurring issue during bilateral visits in the period, and China provided some rice to compensate poppy-growing farmers across the border (*CFA* 2007: 293; 2008: 215). Drug producers then switched to synthetics such as methamphetamine, which are easier to make (Lintner 2015: 176). It would also appear that issues surrounding illegal logging and mining by cross-border Chinese firms came up at meetings in 2006. Formal diplomatic relations improved in 2011, when China and Myanmar became "Comprehensive Strategic Partners," Thein Sein made a state visit to China, but already the process of gradual democratization of Myanmar was beginning. Chinese popular media were initially critical of the National League for Democracy (N.L.D.) and suspicious of Aung San Suu Kyi, seeing the Nobel Peace Prize as evidence of a Western-orientation; by 2012, she was in the parliament. Yet there is at least some evidence that the now Foreign Minister is more than willing to deal with China: "Ms. Aung San Suu Kyi, for her part, has adopted positions that are generally accommodating to China's interests, including some that seem to cut against the N.L.D.'s stated policies, such as the importance of public buy-in in major foreign projects. . . . She has praised China's 'One Belt, one Road' initiative" (Min Zin 2016).

Not all has been harmonious between China and Myanmar, however. The main issue at hand are rebels in Kachin State, Kayah State, the Karen conflict, and the Shan State conflict, many of them ethnically based and in the northern part of the country near the border with China, and the Shan State rebellion is particularly sensitive. There is also a rebellion in Rakhine State involving the ethnic Rohingyas. The government has frequently used cease-fires with one group to pressure others either to come to terms or suffer the consequences. Near the Chinese border, a 2011 government offensive led to clashes with the Kachin rebels in late 2012 and early 2013 and these were a severe problem for China. Refugees spilled across the border into China, including Chinese nationals engaged in logging and mining, and when shells also landed in Chinese territory killing four Chinese citizens, a sizeable crisis was created. The Myanmar government quickly apologized. China also helped broker a cease-fire and hosting the talks, though at the request of both sides lest it seem to be intervening (Sun 2013). Fighting resumed in April 2015, however, with the Myanmar National Democratic Alliance Army (MNDAA, the remnant of the old Burmese Communist Party, once supported by China, as discussed in Chapters 3 and 5). Once again, China was in a difficult position, since some of the MNDAA were ethnic Chinese, including its leader (Blanchard 2015a). Most recently, China has been attempting to act as a mediator between the government in Naypyidaw and the United Wa State Army and the Kokang Army, and seeking to bring the warring factions to the table (Perlez 2017).

Myanmar's international trade is relatively small but growing rapidly (about $30 billion in 2013, up from about $6 billion in 2003), and its imports are dominated by China, and its inward foreign investment even more so. By some accounts – and most reporting out of northern Myanmar must be viewed with some skepticism – Chinese projects in northern Myanmar helped aggravate tensions between the

Myanmar Army and local rebels (the Kachin Independence Army) who had been more or less observing a ceasefire (Smith 2015). The oil and gas pipeline finished in 2013 which would allow China to bypass the distance and potential interdiction at the Straits of Malacca and transport energy directly into Southwest China became a point of environmental and local compensatory controversy (Perlez and Feng 2013). Other of China's investments in Myanmar have run into local criticism, such as protests at the Letpadaung Copper Mine, a joint venture with the still-powerful Myanmar military (Blanchard 2016a). The Myitsone dam project, suspended in 2011 by the military-backed Thein Sein government, is also the focus of protests and negotiations between Foreign Minister Wang Yi and his legal counterpart, Aung San Suu Kyi (Blanchard 2016b). Few major international infrastructure projects are without controversy.

As frequently noted in the international media, China is the leading supplier of weapons to Myanmar; from 2004 to 2015 it transferred no less than US$1.478 billion to the military authorities in Yangon, with Russia coming in second with US$1.22 billion. Interestingly, and not at all noted in the international press, the Chinese supplies to the government expanded greatly *after* democratic elections there in 2012 (SIPRI TIV Tables 2017).

Finally, Myanmar may be a good test for seeing China's reaction to US involvement in countries which are adjacent to it and with which it had an almost exclusive relationship. Following Secretary of State Clinton's visit in late 2011, President Obama visited the country twice, once in November 2012 when democratization was just becoming established, and again in November 2014 during the East Asia Summit. Although Chinese popular media have shown suspicion and disdain for Aung Sang Suu Kyi, scholarly and policy-oriented Chinese analysts have been more open to the relationship, and less concerned about American influence. Liu Xinsheng, writing in 2013 pointed out that "Aung San Suu Kyi has repeatedly stressed that 'democracy in Myanmar is not directed against China,' she hopes Myanmar to seek closer cooperation with the United States while maintaining a 'friendly relations with China'" (40). Priscilla Clapp, writing for the Council on Foreign Relations in 2016 said, "As the ASEAN countries, including Myanmar, gradually democratize, they look increasingly to the United States to counter Chinese pressure. . . . The most effective defense against Chinese pressure on Myanmar will be to maximize the involvement of the United States . . ." (Clapp 2016: 17–18). This analysis points out the far greater Chinese trade, investment, and border connections that link Myanmar far more closely to China than to the USA. By the summer of 2017, moreover, reporters seemed to see Chinese focus on Myanmar far outweighing the distracted attention of American foreign policy (Perlez 2017).

Brunei Darussalam

China's diplomatic relations with the tiny oil-based Sultanate of Brunei Darussalam have growth considerably since 2004. The establishment of diplomatic relations in 1991 was followed by a very limited relationship, mainly China buying petroleum from Brunei. The relationship was characterized by China as "good-neighborly and friendly relations of cooperation" and then elevated to a "strategic cooperative relationship" in April 2013 during a state visit to China by the Sultan of Brunei, reciprocating Hu Jintao's 2005 visit (*CFA* 2006: 108, 2014: 130). China and Brunei signed a variety of cooperation agreements and memoranda of understanding, including agreements on joint oil and gas exploration and development, and the development of a large multi-purpose project at Pulau Muara Besar. It seems hardly to be a coincidence that Brunei was the chair of ASEAN during that year, which China "actively supported."

Malaysia

Sino-Malaysian relations have generally been good, with a substantial emphasis on commercial and economic relations, and some movement toward cooperation in security areas. The economic relationship between China and Malaysia is booming and the diplomatic relations remain solid, though in the last two years, Malaysians have become increasingly concerned about disputes between China and ASEAN members damaging the internal cohesion of that pact and bringing a great power conflict into the region. Thus, the security and diplomatic relationship of the two are officially friendly but somewhat formal. To be sure, the Malaysians are still grateful for the financial assistance China provided in 1997 during the crisis, and China and Malaysia have twice negotiated a bilateral currency swap mechanism, first in February 2009 for RMB 80 billion (about US$12 b) and renewed in 2012 for RMB 180 billion (about US$27b) (*CFA* 2010: 211; 2013: 215). Malaysia's Foreign Ministry very carefully notes its friendship with China, the United States, Japan, and every other country, except Israel (MOFAM 2016). In 2013 China designated Malaysia as a "Comprehensive Strategic Partner," (全面战略伙伴关系 *quanmian zhanlüe huoban guanxi*) an upgrade from its previous "traditional friendship" (*CFA* 2014: 218). Chinese and Malaysian leaders meet frequently both in bilateral meetings and in ASEAN forums, but relatively few political agreements have been realized. Xi Jinping made a state visit in October 2013, reciprocating a Malaysian Head of State visit in 2005. But key talks about joint resource development proposed in November 2004 have gone nowhere. Similarly, the deep commitment that Malaysia has to ASEAN puts a strain on Malaysia in trying to both hold the consensus of the organization together while dealing with difficult issues involving China such as the South China Sea and the agonizingly slow negotiations to implement a Code of Conduct there. In the 2015 meetings, the Malaysians hosted several of the key ASEAN meetings, and though they spoke out in favor of a stronger statement about the South China Sea issues, the statements were only slightly more direct than previous ones (Thayer 2016: 6–8). However, in the key domestic politics of Malaysia, the Malaysians, or more accurately, the Malays, remain hypersensitive to any hint of China's involvement with the ethnic Chinese minority in their country, as noted below.

In security affairs, however, Malaysia has traditionally been aligned with Western powers, especially the United Kingdom, and has made only a small purchase of $5 million worth of portable surface-to-air missiles from China in 2009, out of a total of over $4.2 billion on purchases since 2000 (SIPRI TIV 2017). It has quietly allowed US patrol aircraft to fly over Malaysian territory (Perlez 2016). The Malaysian Foreign Ministry made this equality of relations clear as late as summer 2016 when it said, "With regards to Malaysia's bilateral relations, Malaysia is renewing its focus on both China and the United States" (MOFAM 2016). This classic example of hedging seems to have been curtailed by 2016, blamed at least in part on the US Department of Justice's investigation of Malaysian Prime Minister Najib Razak's naming in its Kleptocracy Asset Recovery Initiative associated with the 1Malaysia Development Berhad (1MDB) sovereign wealth fund (Perlez 2016). Malaysia has since announced a deal to purchase Littoral Mission Ships from China (Allard and Sipalan 2016). They have also cooperated in naval exercises, and a Chinese submarine has visited Malaysia (Page and Watts 2017).

Singapore

Although Singapore has strong strategic connections to the United States, it also enjoys good relations with China. Its military connection to the United States was established first in 1990 by a Memorandum of Understanding, upgraded in 1998 to allow US naval ships to use the Changi Naval Base, and was cemented by a Strategic Framework Agreement in 2005, which places the relationship just short of a formal alliance, which runs counter to ASEAN membership and to formal "non-aligned" Singaporean policy. Nevertheless, many of the functions that had once been performed in the US Naval Base at Subic Bay in the Philippines are now performed in Singapore, for a suitable fee, of course.

Just before US-Singaporean relations improved, there was a brief but significant dispute between Singapore and China: Prime Minister Lee Hsien Loong made an "unofficial" visit to Taiwan in July 2004, and Beijing objected in vigorous terms, suspending high-level exchanges until such time that Singapore publicly expressed its opposition to Taiwanese independence, and relations warmed up again (*CFA* 2005: 286). The two sides continued high-level visits, with Lee Hsien Loong, his father and "Minister Mentor" Lee Kuan Yew and former Prime Minister Goh Chok Tong all making the visit north, and Hu Jintao and Xi Jinping making state visits in 2009 and 2015. Singapore joined with China in November 2015 as a "All-Round Cooperative Partnership Progressing With The Times," (MOFASG 2015). The two countries also had high-level military exchanges, in many ways adopting a "hedging" strategy in its relations with both the USA and China (Kuik 2008).

The majority of Singapore's people are ethnically Chinese, Mandarin is the official second language of education, and its use (as opposed to Hokkien dialect most Singaporeans grew up speaking) promoted widely along with the simplified Chinese characters used in the mainland. But the sense of attachment to the ancestral homeland has faded as the government of Singapore has vigorously pushed a policy of building a multi-ethnic nation of "Singaporeans" (Hoe 2005). The recent influx of mainland tourists and migrants has not helped the sense of connection, either (Aw Tash 2015).

The economic relations between China and Singapore are very strong, with trade and investment going both ways. Much like the rest of Southeast Asia, the trade relationship is asymmetric; China is more important to Singapore's trade than vice-versa. Unlike most of Southeast Asia, tiny Singapore has economic weight far above its small size, somewhat akin to Uruguay vis-à-vis Brazil and Botswana and South Africa. It is one of the largest investors in China, and is in China's top ten trading partners. Singapore is also an RMB clearing center, and has am RMB300 billion (about US$44b) swap line with China, making it the second-largest RMB trading center after Hong Kong (*CFA* 2014: 274).

Indonesia

China and Indonesia became "Strategic Partners" in 2005, and "Comprehensive Strategic Partners" in 2013, and their relations during this period have generally been good. The two have exchanged very frequent top-level visits, with Indonesian President Susilo Bambang Yudhoyono visiting China in 2004, 2005, 2006, 2010, and 2012, as well as side meetings at the plethora of Asia-Pacific multilateral meetings. Hu Jintao and other Chinese leaders reciprocated, with Xi Jinping in October 2013 (*CFA 2005–2014*). The trade relationship developed very quickly, as discussed below, but China has also used foreign aid as a tool of influence, concessional financing of the Surabaya-Madura Bridge and power plants, sending $25 million in relief aid after the 2004 tsunami and $2 million after a 2006 earthquake. As noted above, Indonesia is at the margin of the South China Sea dispute, and has sought to offer itself as a go-between for resolving the issues between the disputants. At the same time, Jakarta tries to maintain a friendly relationship with the United States, but will not characterize it as an effort to "balance" China (Anwar 2013: 2). Indonesia's military does have institutional relations with China's People's Liberation Army, a Navy-to-Navy Cooperation Talks, and have exchanged Defense Minister visits. The Chinese navy made a goodwill visit to Jakarta in 2010, and there have been limited training exercises between Chinese and Indonesian special forces (*CFA 2009–2014*).

The role of ethnic Chinese in Indonesia has improved since the riots in 1998, the collapse of the Suharto regime, and the rise of democracy in that nation. On the one hand, ethnic Chinese in Indonesia now enjoy far greater freedom of expression, both in speech, politics and voting, and a variety of Chinese cultural and educational activities that were once curtailed or prohibited such as Chinese language signs, surnames, and New Year's celebrations are now allowed. However, the situation continues to be difficult: the proportion of Indonesian society that is ethnic Chinese is small yet their substantial commercial and economic impact is very large (Sukma 2009: 605–606; Turner and Allen 2007). China in turn has sought to continue building its public diplomacy relationship with Indonesia, during the 2000s, both sides' publics became more comfortable in their perceptions of the other, and Indonesia's policy of trying to integrate China into the ASEAN regional framework seemed to be successful (Sukma 2009: 602–605). Indonesia agreed to allow a small number of Chinese youth volunteers to teach Chinese language in universities, and six Confucius Institutes were established in 2012 (*CFA* 2013: 185). China has transferred $244 million in arms to Indonesia in the 2004–2015 period, though that is barely 5% of Indonesia's total purchases and receipts (SIPRI TIV 2017).

Regional international organizations

Southeast Asia has a clear regional organization: ASEAN. By 1999 all current members had been admitted, and China places great emphasis on relations with ASEAN as a body, having established its relationship with the organization as a "Strategic Partnership" (战略伙伴关系 *zhanlüe huoban guanxi*) in 2003. The overlap with other regional organizations makes the Asia-Pacific and East Asia an ambiguously institutionalized region; multiple organizations exist with overlapping but not identical membership, agendas and decision-making mechanisms (see Aggarwal and Koo 2008; Emmerson 2008). Each has a reputation as being favored by some members over others. China has joined them all, and officially stands for all. In no case has China used an organization as a mechanism for establishing regional exclusivity, though it is clear that some regional actors do favor this.

The ASEAN +3 (APT) grouping comes closest to being a purely East Asian regional organization, since it encompasses Northeast and Southeast Asia (excluding North Korea, Taiwan, and Mongolia). China considers it the "main vehicle" for East Asian cooperation. In one respect, China has managed to promote its agenda through ASEAN's consensus-based decision-making mechanism. Recent ASEAN and ASEAN-Plus meetings have not issued strong statements on the issue of China's behavior in the South China Sea and the implementation of the Code of Conduct. In these initiatives, Cambodia has effectively worked as China's proxy and denied the needed consensus, such as when it chaired ASEAN in 2012 and scuttled the joint statement that year (Chheang 2012). And China's official position on issues surrounding the South China Sea territorial claims has been to deny that ASEAN as an *organization* has any role in discussions and that all such talks should be strictly bilateral. The issue came up again in the November 2015 ASEAN Defense Ministers meeting in Malaysia, but ASEAN was unable to agree to a statement on the South China Sea (Perlez 2015b). Slightly broader is the ARF, discussed in Chapter 4, which is a security-focused grouping founded in 1994 which meets in conjunction with the ASEAN meetings. With 27 members (including North Korea after 2000), it is the broadest of the Southeast Asian/East Asian organizations, which makes it problematic for reaching agreements. It has been working on the development of preventative diplomacy following the July 2010 Hanoi Plan of Action, and has a "Track Two" (unofficial) dialogue institutions and a "Track 1.5" of Experts and Eminent Persons; most statements issued from the ARF focus on terrorism, piracy, transnational crime, disaster relief and other issues that are important but not as sensitive as matters of sovereignty (DFATA 2016).

APEC has a reputation as being favored by the United States, though its remit is economics only, and it is the only regional international organization to include Taiwan as "Chinese Taipei." The importance of the organization is recognized by

China: "The Asia-Pacific Economic Cooperation (APEC) is the highest-level and most wide-ranging and influence economic cooperation mechanism in the Asia-Pacific region" (*CFA* 2014: 372). China continues to support the organization: "China values the role of APEC. It supports and actively participates in APEC cooperation at all levels and in all fields, and has made major contribution to the progress of such cooperation. China supports APEC in pressing ahead with its reform and institutional building to enhance its efficiency and effectiveness . . ." (*CFA* 2013: 362). Both the presence of the United States, and US regional allies Australia and New Zealand not to mention its economic focus makes it impossible for APEC to serve as an international organization for legalized fictions justifying Chinese regional dominance.

The East Asian Summit (EAS) is a revival of the Malaysian proposal of the East Asian Economic Grouping in the 1990s noted in Chapter 4 as a mechanism to include East Asian members but exclude Australia, New Zealand and the United States. Established as its own organization (as opposed to a caucus within APEC) in 2005, it was similar to ASEAN +3 initially, but by 2010 the USA, Russian Federation, Australia, New Zealand, and India had joined. China's official characterization of the East Asian Summit is more circumspect, at first noting that it was in its infancy, and then merely noting its membership and not taking a stand on its importance as an international organization, though Li Keqiang's speech at the 2013 summit was cautiously laudatory (*CFA* 2014: 390). Interestingly, Li's speech specifically noted the "open" nature of the organization: "[Li] acknowledged the EAS' adherence to the spirit of openness and inclusiveness in East Asian cooperation, its endeavor to reach out beyond the region and its role as an important bridge connecting East Asia and the Asia Pacific in the Past eight years since its inception." Chinese scholars have been more forthright in seeing the expanded East Asia Summit as an unwanted expansion that included the USA (Luo Yongkun 2016: 97).

Thus, despite conflicts between China and some of its neighbors, and despite issues between China and external powers, Beijing does not have control of a regional international organization through which it can dominate its Southeast Asian region, unlike the United States with the OAS during the mid-20th century, the Soviet Union with Eastern Europe, Russia with the CSTO or even Nigeria with ECOWAS and South Africa with SADC, which have taken on security functions when the regional hegemon needed legitimation. China does not control the regional organizations the way most other regional hegemons do. The "ASEAN Way" does provide China with an effective veto in some cases, though dependent on Cambodia or other partners in many ASEAN-based meetings. As will be seen below, however, China has so far been attempting to re-divide Southeast Asian states between those which have an active claim in the South China Sea (Philippines, Vietnam) and those which do not, a revival of the "hub-and-spokes" (辐辏结构 *fucou jiegou*) strategy.

Hegemon's expatriates

Ethnic Chinese communities in Southeast Asia continued to exist and prosper during the contemporary period, and compared to previous periods, they have been much less of an issue in China's relations with Southeast Asian countries. Beijing's leaders have sought to use the commercial connections to augment their political outreach to the region. Thus, in many ways, what had been a political and strategic issue – the role of ethnic Chinese in Southeast Asian states – has gradually become less that than an economic one. China continues to focus a variety of programs on reaching out to, connecting with, and recruiting overseas Chinese communities' connections, knowledge, and human and financial capital (Chang 2013).

There have been instances in which Chinese nationals have been physically threatened in Southeast Asia, however, and China has paid increasing attention to what might be called "Consular Issues" in the 21st century. Beginning in 2004, the yearbook *China's Foreign Affairs* devoted a chapter to Consular Affairs. Not surprisingly, as more and more Chinese followed the call to "go out strategy," (走出去战略 *zou chuqu zhanlüe*) beginning in 1999, those increasing numbers of entrepreneurs, laborers, students, and tourists have encountered a variety of situations in which their persons or property are threatened. This in turn has led China to begin to bend its long-standing adherence to the principle of non-interference. As more Chinese have gone abroad, there have been more incidents involving death or kidnapping that might bring about a forceful intervention by China. Parello-Plesner and Duchâtel (2015) count at least 33 serious incidents between 2004 and 2015 (28–29). Of those incidents, Africa and Pakistan stand out as particularly hazardous places for Chinese. Perhaps the most publicized incident in which China used its military forces to evacuate its nationals from a dangerous situation was in March 2015 when two frigates evacuated both Chinese and other foreign nationals from the dangerous situation in Yemen (9). The incident was non-violent and well-publicized, a source of pride for the Chinese navy. Of the incidents in which China has used its military to protect its citizens abroad, two occurred in Southeast Asia: Vietnam and Thailand/Laos. China's behavior in these incidents is worth examining, because it speaks to the degree to which the Chinese state may be resorting to interventionism.

The first incident (previously mentioned) which brought China toward the brink of unilateral intervention began on October 5, 2011 on the Mekong River in Thailand when thirteen Chinese river barge sailors were murdered (91). A variety of Chinese popular media called for action to protect Chinese citizens abroad, and the Chinese Ministry of Public Security sent patrol vessels to Thailand to escort other Chinese barges back to the Chinese section of the Mekong (Lancang in Chinese) (94–95). And though there was a report that Chinese leaders considered using a drone strike to unilaterally take out the drug lord who was behind the attack, Naw Kham, in the end Chinese authorities cooperated with Laotian, Thai, and Myanmar police to capture the suspect (95–97). Naw Kham was tried in China, however, swiftly convicted and executed.

The second major incident took place in May 2014 in Vietnam when, after a Chinese oil-drilling rig Haiyang Shiyou 981 entered waters in the South China Sea near the Paracel Islands claimed by both China and Vietnam. Popular reaction in Vietnam resulted in riots, mostly directed at Chinese- and Taiwanese-owned factories, and left several dead (Kham and Hsu 2014). Given the loss of Chinese lives and damage to Chinese property, the response of the Chinese state might have been much more demonstrative; Chinese merchant ships evacuated Chinese nationals, not naval vessels (as was the case later in Yemen), and the Chinese Foreign Ministry's response was to protest, though at a somewhat more subdued level than other incidents. By August, high-level Chinese and Vietnamese met in Beijing to resolve the conflict (interestingly, they met as Communist Party leaders, Xinhua 2014b). Neither side seemed to have an interest in letting matters get out of hand, and China's withdrawal of tourists and reduction of border trade was its primary form of economic punishment (Ives 2014, 2015).

These two incidents with China's neighbors were both opportunities for China to "flex its muscles" (as so many commentators now say), both involved the death of Chinese people, and this might have provoked a military response. Indeed, both the United States in early 20th century Caribbean and the Russian Federation in 21st-century Ukraine used attacks on citizens to at least partially justify interventions. China's restraint probably has more to do with fundamentally good relations with Thailand-Laos-Myanmar in the first case and with the quick response of the Vietnamese, but the response in both incidents could have been much more bellicose. Still, China's neighbors remain sensitive to any interference, such as Malaysia's protest over the Chinese ambassador's off-hand remarks about an ethnic Malay protest over Chinese street vendors (Hamzah 2015). The prominent arrest and trial of the ethnic Chinese mayor of Jakarta on blasphemy charges and anti-ethnic Chinese rumors in Indonesia are a test of how restrained Beijing can be (Emont 2017).

Provision of security public goods

The challenge for China to provide security public goods in Southeast Asia is the obvious one: it *is* the problem, not the solution, at least in the eyes of many of its Southeastern neighbors. But it is not the only problem; there are other disputes in Southeast Asia that do not include China, and in which China's powerful military might be a useful counterweight. Piracy and maritime armed robbery and maritime terrorism would be examples (Bateman and Chan 2014: 133–143). There are a number of other maritime functional areas in which cooperation between China and Southeast Asian littoral states would benefit all sides in the long run: prevention of smuggling, human trafficking, pollution, among others are all serious issues in one of the world's most-transited crossroads. All sides are aware of the issues, but so far little seems to be done beyond vague proposals by ASEAN and earnest work of experts (Wu and Zou 2014).

Furthermore, the South China Sea is not the only dispute in Southeast Asia. It is not even the only maritime dispute in Southeast Asia. Indonesia and Malaysia have a dispute in the Ambalat area off the coast of Borneo. Indonesia also fought a war against Malaysia's incorporation of Sabah and Sarawak into the federation in the early 1960s, the *Konfrontasi* policy. Though the war is long over, the memories are not. The Philippines has never fully accepted the Malaysian incorporation of Sabah, and a clash with Sulu activists in February 2013 resulted in scores of deaths. Cambodia still fears and resents Vietnam (Greer 2017). Cambodia and Thailand have disputed a small section of their border which includes the Preah Vihear Temple, and the two sides' militaries clashed in 2011 before cooler heads prevailed. Other minor disputes have occurred which generally fail to garner much Western media attention. It is also worth mentioning that although China is the largest actor in the region, states such as Indonesia loom very large to their neighbors. For Brunei, Malaysia is its large neighbor. For Laos, it is squeezed by three large neighbors: Vietnam, Thailand, and China. But only in the case of Cambodia does China seem to play a role of protector against potential Vietnamese intrusion. China's efforts to mediate the seemingly intractable insurgencies in Myanmar noted in 2017 may also represent not just self-interested "good offices" but a serious effort to solve a long-standing issue in an important neighbor (Perlez 2017). China also has mediated off-shore drilling disputes between Myanmar and Bangladesh.

Economic

Trade

In the 21st century, China became a free trade advocate and a trading superpower; within Southeast Asia, China has become almost every state's top bilateral trade partner. The China-ASEAN Free Trade Area Agreement (CAFTA) was signed in 2002 and came into force on 1 January 2010. Even before the formal implementation, in 2003 China reached an "early harvest program" Framework Agreement with the ten nations of ASEAN, and accepted a variety of product exclusions by poorer ASEAN states with no exclusions for itself, in a sense, accepting an inequitable trade deal for five years (Khan and Yu 2013: 95). The results have been an explosion in Sino-ASEAN trade, seen in Table 7.3.

In the space of about ten years, Sino-ASEAN trade jumped from about $105 billion annually to about $465 billion. What is particularly noteworthy is that the last four years (2012–2015), the trade deficit of ASEAN with China has grown to very substantial proportions. From 2003 to 2011, ASEAN's exports to China were between 10 and 30% lower than its imports; beginning in 2012, ASEAN exports to China leveled off while ASEAN imports from China has continued to rise rapidly. Depressed energy prices and the slowdown in the Chinese economy may have been factors. During the past decade, China has become ASEAN countries' primary trade partner, as seen in Table 7.4 below.

The following tables show an undeniable fact: Southeast Asia has become more dependent in its trade upon China, both imports and exports. All ASEAN members saw their imports from China rise both in absolute terms and as a percentage of their markets. All ASEAN members saw their exports to China rise in absolute terms and as a percentage of their markets.

China is currently pushing the Regional Comprehensive Economic Partnership (RCEP), which will broaden the existing ASEAN Free Trade agreement to include Australia, New Zealand, Japan, and India. This broader FTA is often portrayed in

Table 7.3 China: total trade with Southeast Asia, 2004–2015

China: total trade with Southeast Asia, 2004–2015 (current US$, million)

	Brunei	Cambodia	Indonesia	Laos	Malaysia	Myanmar	Philippines	Singapore	Thailand	Vietnam
2004	$299	$482	$13,470	$113	$26,248	$1,145	$13,327	$26,697	$17,338	$6,738
2005	$261	$563	$16,798	$131	$30,725	$1,209	$17,559	$33,247	$21,812	$8,189
2006	$315	$733	$19,078	$218	$37,117	$1,460	$23,414	$40,863	$27,725	$9,954
2007	$354	$932	$24,999	$262	$46,439	$2,062	$30,634	$47,200	$34,631	$15,120
2008	$212	$1,134	$31,602	$418	$53,514	$2,624	$28,596	$52,417	$41,157	$19,482
2009	$423	$941	$28,282	$713	$51,860	$2,925	$20,526	$47,826	$38,172	$21,044
2010	$1,007	$1,442	$42,733	$1,038	$74,192	$4,442	$27,763	$56,916	$52,956	$30,092
2011	$1,306	$2,504	$60,579	$1,274	$89,919	$6,502	$32,250	$63,057	$64,740	$40,196
2012	$1,608	$2,922	$66,324	$1,719	$94,772	$6,974	$36,450	$68,750	$69,679	$50,455
2013	$1,790	$3,773	$68,422	$2,741	$105,988	$10,159	$38,039	$75,473	$70,841	$65,484
2014	$1,937	$3,758	$63,662	$3,609	$102,055	$24,953	$44,506	$79,241	$72,520	$83,545
2015	$1,509	$4,436	$54,186	$2,574	$97,409	$14,626	$45,710	$79,169	$75,509	$90,169

Source: IMF DOTS (2017).

Table 7.4 Southeast Asia: trade dependency on China, 2004–2015 (part 1)

Southeast Asia: trade dependency on China, 2004–2015 (% total imports/exports)

	Brunei		Cambodia		Indonesia		Laos		Malaysia	
	Imports from China	Exports to China	Imports from China	Exports to China	Imports from China	Exports to China	Imports from China	Exports to China	Imports from China	Exports to China
2004	3.2%	5.0%	16.8%	0.5%	8.8%	6.4%	10.5%	2.1%	9.9%	6.7%
2005	3.6%	3.3%	16.6%	0.5%	10.1%	7.8%	9.1%	3.2%	11.6%	6.6%
2006	5.8%	2.8%	17.6%	0.4%	10.9%	8.3%	11.2%	3.7%	12.2%	7.2%
2007	5.6%	3.1%	17.7%	0.3%	11.5%	8.5%	9.3%	5.8%	12.9%	8.8%
2008	5.4%	0.7%	21.1%	0.3%	11.8%	8.5%	10.4%	8.5%	12.8%	9.5%
2009	6.1%	4.0%	22.6%	0.3%	14.5%	9.9%	14.3%	20.1%	14.0%	12.2%
2010	12.7%	7.0%	24.2%	1.2%	15.1%	9.9%	14.5%	23.3%	12.6%	12.5%
2011	12.7%	4.4%	28.3%	2.3%	14.8%	11.3%	11.2%	23.4%	13.2%	13.1%
2012	21.2%	2.7%	30.6%	2.3%	15.3%	11.4%	16.1%	21.5%	15.1%	12.6%
2013	21.9%	0.8%	32.6%	3.0%	16.0%	12.4%	25.7%	23.9%	16.4%	13.4%
2014	26.6%	1.8%	20.6%	4.1%	17.2%	10.0%	25.4%	34.2%	16.9%	12.0%
2015	25.2%	1.5%	22.2%	5.1%	20.6%	10.0%	18.6%	26.9%	18.8%	13.0%

Source: IMF DOTS (2017).

Table 7.4 Southeast Asia: trade dependency on China, 2004–2015 (part 2)

Southeast Asia: trade dependency on China, 2004–2015 (% total imports/exports)

	Myanmar		Philippines		Singapore		Thailand		Vietnam	
	Imports from China	Exports to China	Imports from China	Exports to China	Imports from China	Exports to China	Imports from China	Exports to China	Imports from China	Exports to China
2004	29.8%	6.0%	6.0%	6.7%	9.4%	7.7%	8.7%	7.4%	14.4%	10.9%
2005	28.9%	6.7%	6.3%	9.9%	10.3%	8.6%	9.4%	8.3%	16.0%	9.9%
2006	33.9%	5.1%	7.1%	9.8%	11.4%	9.7%	10.6%	9.0%	16.5%	8.1%
2007	33.3%	7.0%	7.2%	11.4%	12.1%	9.7%	11.6%	9.6%	20.3%	7.5%
2008	31.2%	9.3%	7.5%	11.1%	10.5%	9.2%	11.2%	9.1%	19.8%	7.7%
2009	35.4%	9.9%	8.9%	7.6%	10.6%	9.8%	12.7%	10.6%	23.5%	8.6%
2010	38.5%	13.5%	8.4%	11.1%	10.8%	10.4%	13.2%	11.1%	24.0%	10.5%
2011	38.7%	18.3%	10.1%	12.7%	10.4%	10.4%	13.3%	11.8%	23.5%	12.0%
2012	36.6%	14.3%	10.8%	11.8%	10.3%	10.8%	14.9%	11.7%	25.8%	11.2%
2013	39.5%	24.5%	13.0%	12.2%	11.7%	11.8%	15.1%	11.9%	28.6%	10.5%
2014	42.2%	63.0%	15.0%	13.0%	12.1%	12.6%	16.9%	11.0%	30.3%	10.4%
2015	42.1%	37.8%	16.2%	10.9%	14.2%	13.7%	20.3%	11.1%	34.0%	13.2%

Source: IMF DOTS (2017).

the media as a Chinese initiative, but in fact the idea was initially proposed by Japan (Aggarwal 2016: 5). The forum was formally created in November 2012 and has since seen fourteen rounds of negotiations, focusing primarily on merchandise trade, trade in services, and cross-border investment. The United States had explicitly made its own TPP free trade agreement a competitive one with China's CAFTA and RCEP. The structure of the US proposal excluded China, and the Obama administration had been forthright in saying that its passage is both a matter of economic and foreign policy leadership in the region. The Trump administration officially abandoned the deal, leaving American allies in the region adrift whether to continue to negotiate the deal without US participation, or pursue different trade strategies. Many of the Asian countries which had signed the TPP agreement in February 2016 are also hedging their trade agreement bets by also participating in the RCEP negotiations, including such traditional US partners as Australia, New Zealand, Japan, Malaysia, and Singapore.

Foreign investment

China has also become a major investor in Southeast Asia, as seen in Table 7.5.

Chinese investments in Vietnam became the target of anti-Chinese protests and riots in the Spring of 2014 following the drilling rig incident in the South China Sea (see above). China's investments in the poorer countries of Laos, Cambodia, and Myanmar are proportionally greater than their larger investments in places such as Singapore.

Tourism is a major equivalent of an export earner for several Southeast Asian countries. It is particularly noteworthy that Cambodia, Laos, and Thailand are highly dependent on tourism as a portion of their economies. China is also becoming a major source of tourists in Southeast Asia. Table 7.6 shows the enormous growth since 2004.

By 2012, over nine million Chinese tourists visited Southeast Asia, most notably Malaysia, Thailand, Singapore, and Vietnam. For those countries, the value of tourist spending was, as is often the case, somewhat discounted by odd and rude tourists' behavior. A tripling of tourists in the space of ten years, however, has left Southeast Asian cities with an increased reliance on those visits, and when China and Vietnam clashed in 2014 over the HD981 oil rig, the sudden departure of Chinese tourists from Vietnam was acutely felt, and a Chinese government travel warning against the Philippines had a similar effect (Ives 2014; Almendral 2014). Chinese tourism is expected to continue to rise in the near future, and Thailand and Vietnam are both among the top destinations (Yiu 2017).

Provision of public goods

Unlike most of Northeast Asia, where the Japanese and South Korean economies are hardly in need of large-scale public goods provision, Southeast Asian states do need economic public goods, and China has demonstrated that it is quite willing

Table 7.5 China: foreign direct investment flows in Southeast Asia, 2004–2014

China: Southeast Asia foreign direct investment, 2004–2014 (million US$)

	Brunei	Cambodia	Indonesia	Laos	Malaysia	Myanmar	Philippines	Singapore	Thailand	Vietnam
2004		$29.5	$62.0	$3.6	$8.1	$4.1	$0.1	$48.0	$23.4	$16.9
2005	$1.5	$5.2	$11.8	$20.6	$56.7	$11.5	$4.5	$20.3	$4.8	$20.8
2006		$9.8	$56.9	$48.0	$7.5	$12.6	$9.3	$132.2	$15.8	$43.5
2007	$1.2	$64.5	$99.1	$154.4	($32.8)	$92.3	$4.5	$397.7	$76.4	$110.9
2008	$1.8	$204.6	$174.0	$87.0	$34.4	$232.5	$33.7	$1,551.0	$45.5	$119.8
2009	$5.8	$215.8	$226.1	$203.2	$53.8	$376.7	$40.2	$1,414.3	$49.8	$112.4
2010	$16.5	$466.5	$201.3	$313.6	$163.5	$875.6	$244.1	$1,118.5	$699.9	$305.1
2011	$20.1	$566.0	$592.2	$458.5	$95.1	$217.8	$267.2	$3,269.0	$230.1	$189.2
2012	$1.0	$559.7	$1,361.3	$808.8	$199.0	$749.0	$74.9	$1,518.8	$478.6	$349.4
2013	$8.5	$499.3	$1,563.4	$781.5	$616.4	$475.3	$54.4	$2,032.7	$755.2	$480.5
2014	($3.3)	$438.3	$1,272.0	$1,026.9	$521.3	$343.1	$225.0	$2,813.6	$839.5	$332.9

Source: Ministry of Commerce PRC, 2011–2014.

Table 7.6 Chinese tourist arrivals in Southeast Asia, 2004–2012

Chinese tourist arrivals in Southeast Asia, 2004–2012

	2004	2005	2006	2007	2008	2009	2010	2011	2012
Brunei	5,000			28,252	27,652	15,800	24,579	32,853	27,490
Cambodia	46,325	59,153	80,540	118,417	129,626	128,210	177,636	247,197	333,894
Indonesia	50,856	112,164	147,245	230,476	337,082	395,013	469,365	574,179	686,779
Laos	33,019	39,210	50,317	54,920	105,852	128,226	161,854	150,791	199,857
Malaysia	550,241	352,089	439,294	689,293	943,787	1,015,550	1,130,261	1,245,475	1,557,960
Myanmar	17,890	19,596	24,893	29,551	30,792	36,341	46,141	62,018	70,805
Philippines	39,581	107,456	133,585	157,601	163,689	155,019	187,446	243,137	250,883
Thailand	779,070	761,904	1,033,305	1,003,141	937,358	815,708	1,132,267	1,704,800	2,761,213
Singapore	880,259	857,814	1,037,201	1,113,956	1,078,742	936,747	1,171,493	1,577,522	2,034,177
Viet Nam	778,431	717,400	516,300	574,600	643,300	518,900	905,400	1,416,800	1,428,693

Source: World Tourism Organization 2014.

to provide them. One Chinese academic was exceptionally frank: "Neighboring countries should become free riders of China's development and benefit from it" (Wu Zhicheng 2015: 64). Trade, and China's willingness to enter into formal deals in which was initially disadvantaged, has been mentioned. China has used three additional areas in the 21st century: monetary stabilization mechanisms, infrastructure provision, especially in transportation, linked in turn to development aid, loans, and investment. The 1997 Asian financial crisis represented the first time that China stepped in to help its Asian neighbors deal with foreign exchange fluctuations, and many Asian governments continue to express gratitude to China both for emergency loans made during that time and for not devaluing the Renminbi (MOFAM 2016). At that time, China's foreign exchange reserves seemed large – US$150 billion – but by the 21st century standards of US$3.9 trillion reserve now seem puny. This in turn led to the Chiang Mai initiative trying to develop mechanisms to deal with currency problems. Chinese leaders certainly did not fail to trumpet their contribution to regional stability at the time and later, but the next provision of regional financial public goods would take another twelve years.

China has entered into a number of currency swap agreements with central banks around the world, over half of them with its neighbors. Within Southeast Asia, the agreement with Indonesia was the earliest in March 2009 for RMB100 million. Subsequent deals with Singapore in March 2013 for RMB300 million, Thailand in December 2014 for RMB70 million, and Malaysia in April 2015 for RMB180 million followed (Zhu Yinhong 2015).[4] The deals represent both the internationalization of the Renminbi as a reserve currency and its willingness to swap its currency for currencies such as the baht, ringgit, and rupiah, which are not historically stable or easily convertible; in a sense, China is taking the greater risk in these deals. The other countries (counterparties) are willing to hold RMB, and both sides are willing to bypass other foreign exchange reserve currencies, most notably the US dollar.

Infrastructure provision has become the prominent aspect of China's public goods provision in the last ten years. The Asian Infrastructure Investment Bank (AIIB 亚洲基础设施投资银行 *Yazhou jichu sheshi touzi yinhang*) was one of China's most prominent economic-diplomacy triumphs of the 2010s: China assumed the role of regional organizer, a provider of regional public goods and needed infrastructure (Perlez 2015a). The United States openly opposed the proposal, Asian countries ignored the US and major American allies – most prominently Australia, New Zealand, and South Korea from the Pacific region and Germany, France, and the United Kingdom – joined anyway. Japan chose not to join. China even appeared magnanimous and offered to let the USA join the proposed bank, its opposition notwithstanding. First proposed by Xi Jinping in October 2013, a total of 57 states signed the Articles of Agreement in May 2015, and the bank is projected to capitalize at US$100 billion, almost $30 billion of which will come from China, which will have a de facto veto power (Chin 2016: 13). In the AIIB, Asian members are also allocated two-thirds of the voting shares in the bank, and the initial director is an experienced Chinese official, Jin Liqun. The Asian

Development Bank, in contrast, has a capital base of $160 billion, but is headquartered in Manila, and is traditionally headed by a Japanese. The test will come in the future, as summarized by Gregory Chin:

> China will need to be able and willing to provide a larger share of the international public goods and, at times, even be willing to sacrifice its own national interests for the greater good while forgoing random, arbitrary, or excessive use of the power it holds in the institution.
>
> (Chin 2016: 17)

The AIIB is not the only Chinese government-backed bank that is extending concessional loans for development projects in Asia and the world; the China Development Bank and the Export-Import Bank of China both engage in these activities, but the publicity surrounding the AIIB and the speed with which the institution has been set up mark it as the most prominent Chinese-led regional institution. The New Development Bank, formerly the BRICS Bank, is another such fund, and the China-ASEAN Investment Cooperation Fund was set up as a quasi-state private equity fund by China with $10 billion to invest in infrastructure, energy, and natural resource development in ASEAN. Much of the lending has been in conjunction with large infrastructure development projects, discussed below.

Transportation development in Asia has been one of the most prominent Chinese initiatives in the 21st century, and Southeast Asia in particular has been the focus of the "Maritime Silk Road" (海上丝绸之路/*haishang sichou zhi lu*) just as Central Asia is the scene of a "New Silk Road." Together, they are the "One Belt, One Road Initiative" (一带一路/*yi dai, yi lu*). Multiple corridors are being proposed (the exact routes are still vague) but would involve a major land bridge from central China through Kazakhstan and Russia and, eventually, to Western Europe (Venice is mentioned as the terminal, evoking the old route). The Maritime Silk Road would develop a network of ports linking southern China through the South China Sea to the Indian Ocean and on through the Middle East, Africa and the Mediterranean. Estimates of the cost reach $1 trillion (Hofman 2015). President Xi Jinping made the formal proposal for the New Silk Road in September 2013 for Central Asia, and a month later laid out the Maritime Silk Road in Xi's speech to the Indonesian parliament. There is little doubt but that Xi has made this a major part of China's foreign policy, and a demonstration of China's willingness to undertake the provision of a much-needed public good for land-locked Central Asian countries and infrastructure-deficient South Asian states. A "Silk Road Fund" was proposed in November 2014, with China pledging $40 billion which would ". . . provide investment and financing support for infrastructure, resources, industrial cooperation, financial cooperation and other projects in countries along the Belt and Road." As ambitious as the plan is, China rejects the analogy to the Marshall Plan that the United States used after World War II to reconstruct western Europe and bind it to the US strategic-economic system; Foreign Minister Wang Yi saying the proposal is "the product of inclusive cooperation, not a tool of geopolitics, and must not be viewed with an outdated Cold War mentality" ("Chronology of China's Belt and Road Initiative" 2015). Yet other regional hegemons have done the same: even Nigeria set up the Nigeria Trust Fund within the African Development Bank in 1976, and Russia founded the Eurasian Development Bank in 2006. The Inter-American Development Bank was largely an initiative of Brazilian President Juscelino Kubitschek, founded in 1959 and with a majority of voting power in the developing country members, though with substantial influence (and capital) of the United States.

The publicity surrounding the "One Belt One Road" initiative may be new, but Chinese support for transportation infrastructure in Southeast Asia is not. The term has been used for decades by Chinese scholars and officials in pushing the image of a benign route of interaction between China and its neighbors. Proposals for a major transportation link through Yunnan province into Myanmar can be seen in 1990 (Dao Shulin 1990: 45–51). The Trans-Asian Railway system (TAR), a pet project of the Asian Development Bank (ADB) and the UN Economic and Social Commission for Asia and the Pacific (ESCAP), as well as roadways have been strongly supported by Yunnan and Guangxi provinces. This transport link has multiple benefits for China's role in Southeast Asia. First, improved transportation links will allow for even greater commercial penetration of Southeast Asian markets by Chinese goods and raw materials flows from Southeast Asia to China's manufacturing centers. The building of regional transportation infrastructure is also a substantial public good, and by providing capital and expertise, China can help close several of the gaps in the TAR concept, most of which are in Southeast Asia (ESCAP 2013: 17). The railways in particular have been the focus of Chinese domestic and international construction, and China's high-speed passenger rail links are being touted as export product, intellectual property and Chinese soft power (Ye Tan 2014), and at the same time an opportunity to point out America's stalled progress in high-speed rail (Tao Duanfang 2014). The prospect of a high-speed passenger rail link from Kunming China to Singapore is something that captures the imagination. The rail network of Southeast Asia also have a strategic value: if China can construct port facilities in Myanmar and rail connections to those ports, it allows it to bypass the Straits of Malacca and a long shipping route that could be interdicted by the United States Navy or regional powers such as Vietnam, the "Malacca Dilemma" noted in Chapter 5 (Holslag 2010: 655–656).

One of the primary difficulties with the Trans-Asian Railway (TAR) concept is the different gauges used in Asia. China uses the Standard Gauge, 1,435 mm, and most of mainland Southeast Asia uses a narrow 1,000-mm gauge, and linking up the different widths involves cumbersome "break of gauge" systems. Nevertheless, the current TAR does not anticipate standardizing gauges between countries. Furthermore, although China has constructed rail and roadway links to its mainland Southeast Asian neighbors, progress on the other side of the border has been somewhat slower. In July 2014, China's ExIm Bank suspended infrastructure lending to Laotian infrastructure development, putting the rail link between China and Vientiane in doubt (Radio Free Asia 2014).

Notes

1 Includes the following categories from IISS's *Military Balance*: Patrol Vessel >1,000t (PSO, PSOH) and Patrol Craft Offshore (PCO). For China, this includes the China Coast Guard (organized in 2013), the Maritime Safety Administration (MSA, still in existence), the Border Defense Force (until 2013 when it merged with others to become the China Coast Guard), China Marine Surveillance (ditto), and the Fisheries Law Enforcement Command (ditto). For Indonesia, this includes Customs, Marine Police, and the KPLP (Coast and Seaward Defense Command). Japan includes the Japan Coast Guard. Malaysia includes the Malaysian Maritime Enforcement Agency (MMEA) and Customs Service. Philippines includes the Philippines Coast Guard. Vietnam includes the Coast Guard and Fisheries Surveillance Force and previously the Marine Police.
2 Australia, although not an official neighbor of China, is one instance in which China is alleged to have sought influence when Chinese-Australian citizens were recently accused of promoting Chinese interests by funding or de-funding politicians depending on their foreign policy stances toward China (Cave and Williams 2017). It should be noted that foreign donations are not illegal in Australia politics.
3 This and all other arms transfer data are calculated in SIPRI Trend Indicator Values (TIVs) expressed in US$ million at constant (1990) prices. This includes estimates for the value of the transfers even when they are at "Friendship Prices" or gifts.
4 The global total of currency swaps as of 2015 – RMB3,137 million – is about US$470 million (at RMB6.6=US$1), relatively small compared to China's total FX holdings.

Works cited

"Abe pledges fresh security-related aid to Vietnam." 2017. *Japan Times*, 16 January. <www.japantimes.co.jp/news/2017/01/16/national/politics-diplomacy/abe-jokowi-unite-south-china-sea-disputes-plan-two-plus-two-meeting/#.WH44xlzRsjx>, accessed 17 January 2017.

Acharya, Amitav. 2015. *Indonesia Matters: Emerging Democratic Power*. Singapore: World Scientific.

Aggarwal, Vinod K. 2016. Mega-FTAs and the trade-security nexus: The Trans-Pacific Partnership (TPP) and the Regional Comprehensive Economic Partnership (RCEP). *Asia Pacific Issues*, 123(March), 1–8.

Aggarwal, Vinod K., and Koo, Min Gyo, eds. 2008. *Asia's New Institutional Architecture: Evolving Structures for Managing Trade, Financial, and Security Relations*. Berlin: Springer Verlag.

Allard, Tom, and Sipalan, Joseph. 2016. Malaysia to buy navy vessels from China in blow to US. *Reuters*, 28 October. <www.reuters.com/article/us-malaysia-china-defence-idUSKCN12S0WA>, accessed 29 October 2016.

Almendral, Aurora. 2014. Philippines feels force of China travel warning. BBC News, 21 October. <www.bbc.com/news/world-asia-29684938>, accessed 22 October 2014.

Amer, Ramses. 2013. Sino-Vietnamese border disputes, in *Beijing's Power and China's Borders: Twenty Neighbors in Asia*, edited by Bruce A. Elleman, Stephen Kotkin, and Clived Schofield. Armonk, NY: M.E. Sharpe, 295–310.

Anwar, Dewi Fortuna. 2013. An Indonesian perspective on the U.S. rebalancing effort toward Asia. *National Bureau of Asian Research Commentary*, 26 February, 1–4.

APFIC. 2012. *Asia-Pacific Fishery Commission (APFIC) Regional Overview of Fisheries and Aquaculture in Asia and the Pacific 2012*, eds. Simon Funge-Smith, Matthew Briggs, and Weimin Miao. Bangkok: Food and Agriculture Organization of the United Nations Regional Office for Asia and the Pacific.

Arbitration Support Tracker. 2016. Asia maritime transparency initiative, center for strategic and international studies. <https://amti.csis.org/arbitration-support-tracker/>, accessed 14 July 2016.

Arsana, I Made Andi, and Schofield, Clive. 2013. Indonesia's "invisible" border with China, in *Beijing's Power and China's Borders: Twenty Neighbors in Asia*, edited by Bruce A. Elleman, Stephen Kotkin, and Clive Schofield. Armonk, NY: M.E. Sharpe, 61–79.

Aw Tash. 2015. Op-Ed being Chinese in Singapore. *New York Times*, 12 February. <www.nytimes.com/2015/02/13/opinion/tash-aw-being-chinese-in-singapore.html>, accessed 12 February 2015.

Bader, Julia. 2015. *China's Foreign Relations and the Survival of Autocracies*. London: Routledge/Taylor & Francis Group.

Barry, Ellen. 2016. As India collaborates with Japan on Islands, it looks to check China. *New York Times*, 11 March. <www.nytimes.com/2016/03/12/world/asia/india-japan-china-andaman-nicobar-islands.html>, accessed 11 March 2016.

Baruah, Darshana. 2016. Toward strategic economic cooperation between India and Japan. Carnegie India, 1 December. <http://carnegieindia.org/2016/12/01/toward-strategic-economic-cooperation-between-india-and-japan-pub-66326>, accessed 3 December 2016.

Bateman, Sam, and Chan, Jane. 2014. Piracy and armed robbery against ships in the South China Sea: Possible causes and solutions, in *Non-traditional Security Issues and the South China Sea: Shaping a New Framework for Cooperation*, edited by Shicun Wu and Keyuan Zou. Farnham, Surrey: Ashgate, 133–143.

Blanchard, Ben. 2015a. China protests over shelling as Myanmar battles insurgents. *Reuters*, 28 April. <www.reuters.com/article/us-china-myanmar-idUSKBN0NJ0X820150428>, accessed 28 April 2015.

Blanchard, Ben. 2015b. China, Vietnam must manage sea dispute well to keep peace: Xi. *Reuters*, 7 April. <www.reuters.com/article/us-china-vietnam-idUSKBN0MY1CK20150407>, accessed 7 April 2015.

Blanchard, Ben. 2016a. After Myanmar protests, China says companies should respect laws. *Reuters*, 9 May. <www.reuters.com/article/us-china-myanmar-mine-idUSKCN0Y00QR>, accessed 11 May 2016.

Blanchard, Ben. 2016b. China says business spats with Myanmar can be resolved. *Reuters*, 6 April. <www.reuters.com/article/us-china-myanmar-idUSKCN0X306X>, accessed 7 April 2016.

Brunnstrom, David. 2016. Japan to boost South China Sea role with training patrols with US: Minister. *Reuters*, 15 September. <www.reuters.com/article/us-southchinasea-japan-patrols-idUSKCN11L2FE>, accessed 15 September 2016.

Burgos, Sigfrido, and Ear, Sophal. 2010. China's strategic interests in Cambodia: Influence and resources. *Asian Survey*, 50(3), 615–639.

Cao Wenzhen, and Huang Weizi. 2015. Zhongguo Haiyang qiangguo zhanlue shi ye xia de Taiguo Kela yunhe xiujian shenxi [Analysis of the Thailand Kra canal project under the vision of China's "maritime power" strategy]. *YaTai anquan yu Haiyang yanjiu*, (3), 67–83.

Castro, Renato Cruz de. 2011. Balancing gambits in twenty-first century Philippines foreign policy: Gains and possible demise?, in *Southeast Asia 2011*, edited by Daljit Singh. Singapore: ISEAS-Yusof Ishak Institute, 235–253.

Cave, Damien, and Williams, Jacqueline. Australian politics is open to foreign cash, and China has much to gain. *New York Times*, 6 June. <www.nytimes.com/2017/06/06/

world/australia/china-political-influence-campaign-finance.html>, accessed 6 June 2017.

CFA [China's Foreign Affairs]. Annual. Beijing: Ministry of Foreign Affairs of the People's Republic of China. This is the official yearbook of the Ministry of Foreign Affairs of the People's Republic of China. Beginning its publication in 1987 as 中国外交概览 China's Foreign Affairs review, it is hereafter referred to as ZGWJGL, and after 1995 中国外交 it is renamed Zhongguo waijiao (ZGWJ) for the Chinese language version, and China's Foreign Affairs or CFA for the English-language version, which began publication in 2003.

Chang, Amy. 2013. *Beijing and the Chinese Diaspora in Southeast Asia: To Serve the People*. Seattle, WA: National Bureau of Asian Research Special Report 43.

Chen Xiangyang. 2004. *Zhongguo mulin waijiao: sixiang, shijian, qianzhang* [China's good-neighbour diplomacy: Though, practice, prospect]. Beijing: Shishi chubanshe.

Chheang, Vannarith. 2012. Results, expectations, and challenges for Cambodia's 2012 ASEAN chairmanship. *Asia Pacific Bulletin* (no. 183), 25 October.

Chin, Gregory T. 2016. Asian infrastructure investment bank: Governance innovation and prospects. *Global Governance*, 22(1), 11–26.

Chongkittavorn, Kavi, Termsak, Chalermpalanupap, Suthad, Setboonsarng, and Apichai, Sunchindah. 2016. *Positioning the ASEAN Community in an Emerging Asia: Thai Perspectives*. Bangkok: Department of ASEAN Affairs, Ministry of Foreign Affairs of the Kingdom of Thailand.

"Chronology of China's Belt and Road Initiative." 2015. State council of the PRC. <http://english.gov.cn/news/top_news/2015/04/20/content_281475092566326.htm>, accessed 27 May 2015.

Clapp, Priscilla A. 2016. *Securing a Democratic Future for Myanmar*. New York: Council on Foreign Relations, Center for Preventive Action, no. 75.

"Clinton must see China's territorial stance." 2012. *Global Times in People's Daily*, 5 September. <http://english.peopledaily.com.cn/90883/7936254.html>, accessed 5 September 2012.

Cochrane, Joe. 2016. China's coast guard rams fishing boat to free it from Indonesian authorities. *New York Times*, 21 March. <www.nytimes.com/2016/03/22/world/asia/indonesia-south-china-sea-fishing-boat.html>, accessed 22 March 2016.

Dai Weilai. 2016. China's strategic partnership diplomacy. *Contemporary International Relations*, 26(1), 101–116.

Dao Shulin. 1990. Chongzhen xinan silu, jiaqiang ton nanbu linguo de jingji lianxi [Restore the Southwest Silk Road, enhancing economic ties with China's southern neighboring countries]. *Xiandai guoji guanxi*, 28(4), 45–51.

DFATA [Department of Foreign Affairs and Trade of Australia]. 2016. Regional architecture: ASEAN Region Forum (ARF). Department of Foreign Affairs and Trade of Australia website. <http://dfat.gov.au/international-relations/regional-architecture/Pages/asean-regional-forum-arf.aspx>, accessed 19 July 2017.

Duchâtel, Mathieu. 2016. Terror overseas: Understanding China's evolving counter-terror strategy. *European Council on Foreign Relations Policy Brief* (no. 193), October. <ecfr.eu>, accessed 4 June 2017.

Dupont, Alan, and Baker, Christopher. 2014. East Asia's maritime disputes: Fishing in troubled waters. *Washington Quarterly*, 37(1), 79–98.

EIA [US Energy Information Agency]. 2013. Today in energy: Contested areas of South China Sea likely have few conventional oil and gas resources. US EIA website, 3 April. <www.eia.gov/todayinenergy/detail.php?id=10651>, accessed 7 August 2017.

Emmerson, Donald K., ed. 2008. *Hard Choices: Security, Democracy, and Regionalism in Southeast Asia*. Stanford: Asia Pacific Research Center.

Emont, Jon. 2017. Chinese-Indonesian governor's struggles worry some in his ethnic group. *New York Times*, 11 February. <www.nytimes.com/2017/02/11/world/asia/chinese-indonesian-governor-jakarta-basuki-purnama.html>.

ESCAP [UN Economic and Social Commission for Asia and the Pacific]. 2013. *Monograph Series on Transport Facilitation of International Railway Transport in Asia and the Pacific*, 1st ed. Bangkok: UN Economic and Social Commission for Asia and the Pacific.

FAO. 2016. *2014 FAO Yearbook: Fishery and Aquaculture Statistics*. Rome: Food and Agricultural Organization of the UN, 2016.

Feng Zhongping. 2013. Periphery strategy should focus on innovative security cooperation. *Contemporary International Relations*, 23(6), 50–53.

Ferdinando, Lisa. 2016. Carter hails "ironclad" relationship with the Philippines. *DoD News*, 15 April. <www.defense.gov/News/Article/Article/722302/carter-hails-ironclad-relationship-with-the-philippines>, accessed 1 March 2017.

Forbes, Vivian Louis. 2013. Malaysia and China: Economic growth overshadows sovereignty dispute, in *Beijing's Power and China's Borders: Twenty Neighbors in Asia*, edited by Bruce A. Elleman, Stephen Kotkin, and Clive Schofield. Armonk, NY: M.E. Sharpe, 155–167.

Greer, Tanner. 2017. Cambodia wants China as its neighborhood bully. *Foreign Policy*, 5 January. <http://foreignpolicy.com/2017/01/05/cambodia-wants-china-as-its-neighborhood-bully/>, accessed 5 January 2017.

Hamzah, Al-Zaquan Amer. 2015. Malaysia summons China envoy over comments on planned pro-Malay rally. *Reuters*, 27 September. <www.reuters.com/article/us-malaysia-china-idUSKCN0RR05920150927>, accessed 27 September 2015.

Hoe, Yow Cheun. 2005. Weakening ties with the ancestral homeland in China: The case studies of contemporary Singapore and Malaysian Chinese. *Modern Asian Studies*, 39(3), 559–597.

Hofman, Bert. 2015. China's one belt one road initiative: What we know thus far, World Bank blog: East Asia and the Pacific on the rise, 4 December. <http://blogs.worldbank.org/eastasiapacific/china-one-belt-one-road-initiative-what-we-know-thus-far>, accessed 17 August 2016.

Holslag, Jonathan. 2010. China's roads to influence. *Asian Survey*, 50(4), 641–662.

International Institute for Strategic Studies [IISS]. *Military Balance*. Annual. London: International Institute for Strategic Studies.

IMF DOTS [Direction of Trade Statistics]. 2017. IMF e-library. <data.imf.org/>, accessed 19 January 2017.

Ives, Mike. 2014. China tensions choke off tourism to Vietnam. *New York Times*, 21 July. <www.nytimes.com/2014/07/22/business/international/china-tensions-choke-off-tourism-to-vietnam.html>, accessed 31 July 2014.

Ives, Mike. 2015. When Vietnam and China bicker, traders on the border feel the bluster. *New York Times*, 25 June. <www.nytimes.com/2015/06/26/world/asia/when-vietnam-and-china-bicker-traders-on-the-border-feel-the-bluster.html>, accessed 26 June 2015.

Ives, Mike. 2016. How Laos tries to balance its powerful neighbors. *New York Times*, 6 September. <www.nytimes.com/2016/09/07/world/asia/laos-history-politics-human-rights.html>, accessed 6 September 2016.

Jesse, Neal G., Lobell, Steven E., Press-Bartnathan, Galia, and Williams, Kristen P. 2012. The leader can't lead when the followers won't follow, in *Beyond Great Powers and Hegemons: Why Secondary States Support, Follow, or Challenge*, edited by Kristen

P. Williams, Steven E. Lobell, and Neal G. Jesse. Stanford: Stanford Security Studies, 1–30.

Johan, Orrie. 2016. Australia's contentious strategy in the South China Sea. *Asia-Pacific Bulletin*, no. 358, 13 October. Washington DC: East-West Center.

Johnson, Douglas. 1997. Drawn into the fray: Indonesia's Natuna Islands meet China's long gaze south. *Asian Affairs: An American Review*, 24(Fall), 153–161.

Kham, Vu Trong, and Hsu, Jenny W. 2014. Anti-China rioting turns deadly in Vietnam. *Wall Street Journal*, 16 May. <www.wsj.com/articles/SB10001424052702304908304579562962349248496>, accessed 20 May 2014.

Khan, Shamsul, and Yu, Lei. 2013. Evolving China-ASEAN relations and CAFTA: Chinese perspectives on China's initiatives in relations to ASEAN Plus 1. *European Journal of East Asian Studies*, 12, 81–107.

Kuik, Cheng-Chwee. 2008. The essence of hedging: Malaysia and Singapore's response to a rising China. *Contemporary Southeast Asia: A Journal of International and Strategic Affairs*, 30, 159–185.

LaGrone, Sam. 2017. Former U.S. Cutter Morgenthau transferred to Vietnamese Coast Guard. *USNI News*, 17 May. <https://news.usni.org/2017/05/26/former-u-s-cutter-morgenthau-transferred-vietnamese-coast-guard>, accessed 5 August 2017.

Lintner, Bertil. 2015. *Great Game East: India, China and the Struggle for Asia's Most Volatile Frontier*. New Haven: Yale University Press.

Liu Siwei. 2015. InRi anquan hezuo ji dui YaTai diqu anquan taishi de yingxiang [India-Japan security cooperation: Implications for Asia-Pacific security situation]. *NanYa yanjiu jikan*, (160), 1–7.

Liu Xinsheng. 2013. Miandian da biange ji qi dui Zhong-Mian guanxi de yingxiang [Large change in Myanmar and its influence on China-Myanmar relations]. *Dongnanya zongheng* [Around Southeast Asia], (1), 36–40.

Liu Zhen. 2016. "We're neighbours and blood brothers": Xi tells Duterte as firebrand leader announces "separation" from US. *South China Morning Post*, 20 October. <www.scmp.com/print/news/china/diplomacy-defence/article/2038577/philippines-president-rodrigo-duterte-gets-red-carpet?edition=hong-kong>, accessed 1 March 2017.

Luo Yongkun. 2016. Changes in China's Southeast-Asia policy. *Contemporary International Relations*, 26(1), 87–100.

Martinson, Ryan D. 2015. China's second navy. *US Naval Institute Proceedings*, April, 24–29.

Miglani, Sanjeev. 2016. U.S. plans naval exercises with India and Japan in Philippine Sea. *Reuters*, 3 March. <www.reuters.com/article/india-usa-military-exercise-idUSKCN0W41UH>, accessed 3 March 2016.

Min Zin. 2016. Op-Ed: Aung San Suu Kyi, the Dragon's lady. *New York Times*, 21 January. <www.nytimes.com/2016/01/22/opinion/aung-san-suu-kyi-the-dragons-lady.html>, accessed 22 January 2016.

MOFAM [Ministry of Foreign Affairs, Malaysia]. 2016. "Malaysia's foreign policy: Bilateral relations" Ministry of Foreign Affairs, Malaysia. <www.kln.gov.my/web/guest/bilateral>, accessed 8 June 2016.

MOFASG [Ministry of Foreign Affairs of Singapore]. 2015. Joint statement between the People's Republic of China and the Republic of Singapore on the establishment of an all-round cooperative partnership progressing with the times. Press Room, Singaporean Ministry of Foreign Affairs, 7 November. <www.mfa.gov.sg/content/mfa/media_centre/press_room/pr/2015/201511/press_20151107.html>, accessed 5 August 2016.

MOFAT [Ministry of Foreign Affairs and Trade, Brunei]. 2016. Joint statement between Brunei Darussalam and the Socialist Republic of Viet Nam. Brunei Darussalam Ministry of Ministry of Foreign Affairs and Trade. <www.mofat.gov.bn/Lists/NewsHeadlines/NDispForm.aspx?ID=219&Source=/Lists/NewsHeadlines/NewsHighlights.aspx>, accessed 15 February 2017.

MOFAV [Ministry of Foreign Affairs of Vietnam]. 2016. Remarks by MOFA's Spokesperson Le Hai Binh regarding Viet Nam's reaction to the 2nd "Sansha" municipal people's congress election and the Chinese patrolling of the waters around Hoang Sa islands. <www.mofa.gov.vn/en/tt_baochi/pbnfn/ns161004083852>, accessed 15 February 2017.

Mogato, Manuel. 2016. China rescues Filipinos near disputed South China Sea shoal. *Reuters*, 2 December. <www.reuters.com/article/southchinasea-philippines-china-idUSL4N1DX1DD>, accessed 2 December 2016.

Mogato, Manuel, and Torode, Greg. 2014. Insight-Philippine, Vietnamese navies unite against China over beers and volleyball. *Reuters*, 9 April. <www.reuters.com/article/philippines-vietnam-idUSL4N0MV23620140410>, accessed 7 June 2017.

Odgaard, Liselotte. 2015. China's dangerous ambiguity in the South China Sea: Op-Ed. *New York Times*, 10 December. <www.nytimes.com/2015/12/11/opinion/chinas-dangerous-ambiguity.html>, accessed 10 December.

Paddock, Richard C. 2016. Chinese vessels leave disputed fishing grounds in South China Sea. *New York Times*, 28 October. <www.nytimes.com/2016/10/29/world/asia/south-china-sea-scarborough-shoal.html>, accessed 29 October 2016.

Page, Jeremy, and Watts, Jake Maxwell. 2017. Chinese submarine's Malaysian port call signals regional power shift. *Wall Street Journal*, 6 January. <www.wsj.com/articles/chinese-submarines-malaysian-port-call-signals-regional-power-shift-1483700183>, accessed 7 January 2017.

Parameswaran, Prashanth. 2013. China and Laos: An uneasy embrace. *China Brief*, 13(5), 7.

Parello-Plesner, Jonas, and Duchâtel, Mathieu. 2015. *China's Strong Arm: Protecting Citizens and Assets Abroad*. London: International Institute for Strategic Studies.

PCA [Permanent Court of Arbitration]. 2016. PCA case no 2013–19 in the matter of the South China Sea arbitration before an arbitral tribunal constituted under annex VII to the 1982 United Nations convention on the law of the sea between the Republic of the Philippines and the People's Republic of China: Award: Permanent Court of Arbitration, The Hague, 12 July, 1–501.

Perlez, Jane. 2015a. China creates a World Bank of its own, and the US balks. *New York Times*, 4 December. <www.nytimes.com/2015/12/05/business/international/china-creates-an-asian-bank-as-the-us-stands-aloof.html>, accessed 5 December 2015.

Perlez, Jane. 2015b. Dispute over South China Sea prompts Asian officials to cancel joint statement. *New York Times*, 4 November. <www.nytimes.com/2015/11/04/world/asia/china-wants-no-mention-of-south-sea-in-statement.html>, accessed 4 November 2015.

Perlez, Jane. 2016. Leader of Malaysia, miffed at US, visits China with a deal in mind. *New York Times*, 31 October 2016. <www.nytimes.com/2016/11/01/world/asia/malaysia-china.html>, accessed 31 October 2016.

Perlez, Jane. 2017. China showers Myanmar with attention, as Trump looks elsewhere. *New York Times*, 19 July. <www.nytimes.com/2017/07/19/world/asia/myanmar-china-us-diplomacy-trump.html>, accessed 19 July 2017.

Perlez, Jane, and Feng, Bree. 2013. China tries to improve image in a changing Myanmar. *New York Times*, 18 May. <www.nytimes.com/2013/05/19/world/asia/under-pressure-china-measures-its-impact-in-myanmar.html>, accessed 18 May 2013.

Permanent Mission of the Republic of Indonesia to the UN. 2010. Letter to Ban Ki-moon, 8 July 2010, Ref. 480/POL-703/VII/10. New York: Permanent Mission of the Republic of Indonesia to the United Nations.

Permanent Mission of the Socialist Republic of Viet Nam to the United Nations. 2009. Letter to Ban Ki-Moon, 8 May 2009. Ref. No. 86/HC-2009. New York: Permanent Mission of the Socialist Republic of Vietnam to the United Nations.

Radio Free Asia. 2014. China's Eximbank suspends loans for roads, bridges in Laos. Radio Free Asia, 22 July. <www.rfa.org/english/news/laos/investment-07222014194926.html>, accessed 4 November 2014.

Rajagopalan, Megha, and Sweeney, Pete. 2016. China warns on South China Sea as U.S., India consider patrols. *Reuters*, 11 February. <www.reuters.com/article/us-southchina-sea-china-idUSKCN0VK0WQ>, accessed 13 February 2016.

Rajagopalan, Rajeswari Pillai and Mishra, Sylvia. 2015. India-Japan-U.S. trilateral dialogue gains additional traction. *Asia Pacific Bulletin* (no. 327), 22 October.

Ramzy, Austin. 2014. A view from the sea, as China flexes muscle. *New York Times*, 9 August. <www.nytimes.com/2014/08/10/world/asia/a-view-from-the-sea-as-china-flexes-muscle.html>, accessed 14 May 2014.

Ren Yuanzhe. 2015. Kela yunhe yu Zhongguo de Haiyang anquan [Kra canal and China's maritime security]. *YaTai anquan yu Haiyang yanjiu*, (3), 84–96.

Sands, Gary. 2016. Brunei, silent claimant in the South China Sea. Foreign Policy Association Blog, 28 April. <http://foreignpolicyblogs.com/2016/04/28/brunei-silent-claimant-south-china-sea/>, accessed 29 April 2016.

Shepherd, Christian. 2017. China hails golden period in relations with Philippines. *Reuters*, 29 June. <http://www.reuters.com/article/us-china-philippines/china-hails-golden-period-in-relations-with-philippines-idUSKBN19K0T9>, accessed 29 June 2017.

SIPRI TIV. 2017. Stockholm international peace research institute arms transfers database. <www.sipri.org/databases/armstransfers>, accessed 1 May 2017.

Smith, Matthew. 2015. Op-Ed: How China fuels Myanmar's wars. *New York Times*, 4 March. <www.nytimes.com/2015/03/05/opinion/how-china-fuels-myanmars-wars.html>, accessed 4 March 2016.

Strüver, Georg. 2016. International alignment between interests and ideology: The case of China's partnership diplomacy. Hamburg: German Institute for Global and Area Studies, *GIGA Working Papers*, no. 283 (March).

Sukma, Rizal. 2009. Indonesia-China relations: The politics of re-engagement. *Asian Survey*, 49, 591–608.

Sun Yun. 2013. China's intervention in the Myanmar-Kachin peace talks. *Asia Pacific Bulletin* (no. 200), 20 February.

Takenaka Kiyoshi. 2014. Japan and India vow to boost defense ties during summit. *Reuters*, 1 September. <www.reuters.com/article/us-japan-india-idUSKBN0GW13U20140901>, accessed 1 September 2014.

Tao Duanfang. 2014. Why has the US failed to build its high-speed rail network? *People's Daily Online*, 9 September. <http://english.people.com.cn/n/2014/0909/c90000-8779893.html>, accessed 2 October 2014.

"Thai junta defends buying 'cheap' US$393 million Chinese sub." 2017. Agence France-Presse in. *South China Morning Post*, 25 April. <www.scmp.com/news/china/diplomacy-defence/article/2090410/thai-junta-defends-buying-cheap-us393-million-chinese>, accessed 25 April 2017.

Thayer, Carlyle A. 2016. Southeast Asia's regional autonomy under stress, in *Southeast Asian Affairs 2016*, edited by Malcolm Cook and Daljit Singh. Singapore: ISEAS-Yusof Ishak Institute, 3–18.

Tian Yongxiang. 2012. *International Relations of the Communist Party of China*. Beijing: China Intercontinental Press.
Tiezzi, Shannon. 2014. Why China isn't interested in a South China Sea code of conduct. *The Diplomat*, 26 February. <http://thediplomat.com/2014/02/why-china-isnt-interested-in-a-south-china-sea-code-of-conduct/>, accessed 12 July 2016.
Townsend-Gault, Ian. 2013. The China-Laos boundary: Lan Xang meets Middle Kingdom, in *Beijing's Power and China's Borders: Twenty Neighbors in Asia*, edited by Bruce Elleman, Stephen Kotkin, and Clive Schofield. Armonk, NY: M.E. Sharpe, 142–153.
Turner, Sarah, and Allen, Pamela. 2007. Chinese Indonesians in a rapidly changing nation: pressures of ethnicity and identity. *Asia Pacific Viewpoint*, 48(1), 112–127.
US State Department, Bureau of Oceans and International Environmental and Scientific Affairs. 2014. *Limits in the Seas: China: Maritime Claims in the South China Sea*. no. 143, December. Washington, DC: US State Department.
Wang Yi. 2014. China and ASEAN are fully capable of safeguarding peace and stability in the South China Sea. China Ministry of Foreign Affairs website. <www.fmprc.gov.cn/mfa_eng/zxxx_662805/t1181750.shmtl>, accessed 12 August 2014.
Webb, Simon. 2016. China, Laos say rail project to go ahead, pending environment study. *Reuters*, 29 July. <www.reuters.com/article/us-laos-china-railway-idUSKCN1091AO>, accessed 30 July 2016.
Wood, Peter. 2016. China-Indonesia relations heat up along the third "dash". *China Brief*, 16(6). <www.jamestown.org/uploads/media/_CB_16_6_1_2.pdf>, accessed 28 March 2016.
World Bank. 2017. World development indicators [Online]. 2017. <http://data.worldbank.org/data-catalog/world-development-indicators>.
World Tourism Organization. 2014. Compendium of tourism statistics dataset [Electronic], UNWTO, Madrid, data updated on 11/01/2014.
Wu, Shicun, and Zou, Keyuan, eds. 2014. *Non-Traditional Security Issues and the South China Sea: Shaping a New Framework for Cooperation*. Farnham, Surrey: Ashgate.
Wu Zhicheng. 2015. Strategic planning for its neighboring diplomacy. *Contemporary International Relations*, 25(2), 62–65.
Xinhua. 2014a. China dismisses ADIZ reports, optimistic about South China Sea situation. Xinhua News Agency, 2 February 2014. <http://news.xinhuanet.com/english/china/2014-02/02/c_126085456.htm>, accessed 25 May 2014.
Xinhua. 2014b. China, Vietnam call truce on maritime tensions. Xinhua News Agency, 27 August. In China Daily, 27 August. <www.chinadaily.com.cn/world/2014-08/27/content_18498591.htm>, accessed 27 August 2014.
Xinhua. 2015a. China urges U.S. to be impartial in South China Sea. Xinhua News Agency, 22 January. <http://news.xinhuanet.com/english/china/2015-01/22/c_133939681.htm>, accessed 7 April 2015.
Xinhua. 2015b. Commentary: America the kibitzer on South China Sea. Xinhua News Agency, 21 March. <http://eng.mod.gov.cn/Opinion/2015-03/21/content_4576041.htm>, accessed 17 April 2015.
Yang, Calvin. 2014. Young Laotians learn Chinese to improve job prospects. *New York Times*, 9 February. <www.nytimes.com/2014/02/10/world/asia/young-laotians-learn-chinese-to-improve-job-prospects.html>, accessed 9 February 2014.
Ye Tan. 2014. China's high-speed rail "goes global" based on strategy and market. *People's Daily Online*, 5 August. <http://english.peopledaily.com.cn/n/2014/0805/c90000-8765139.html>, accessed 2 October 2014.
Yiu, Enoch. 2017. Vietnam is in, France is no not, as 200 million Chinese tourists prepare to hit the road by 2020. *South China Morning Post*, 20 July. <www.scmp.com/business/companies/article/2103479/vietnam-france-so-not-200-million-chinese-tourists-prepare-hit>, accessed 20 July 2017.

ZGWG. [Zhongguo waijiao] [China's diplomacy]. Annual. Beijing: Ministry of Foreign Affairs of the People's Republic of China. This is the official yearbook of the Ministry of Foreign Affairs of the People's Republic of China. Beginning its publication in 1987 as 中国外交概览 China's Foreign Affairs review, it is hereafter referred to as ZGWJGL, and after 1995 中国外交 it is renamed Zhongguo waijiao (ZGWJ) for the Chinese language version, and China's Foreign Affairs or CFA for the English-language version, which began publication in 2003.

Zha Wen. 2015. Personalized foreign policy decision-making and economic dependence: A comparative study of Thailand and the Philippines' China policies. *Contemporary Southeast Asia*, 37(2), 242–268.

Zhao Guojun, and Zhao Chaolong. 2015. RiIn hai shang anquan hezuo zhuan xiang ji qian jin tanxi [India-Japan maritime security cooperation: Its transformation and future prospects]. *NanYa yanjiu jikan*, (no. 162), 9–16.

Zhu Yinhong. 2015. Swap agreements & China's RMB currency network. CSIS Asia Program Blog: CogitASIA, 22 May. <http://cogitasia.com/swap-agreements-chinas-rmb-currency-network/>, accessed 26 July 2017.

8 China and Central Asia in the 21st century

China's relations with its Central Asian neighbors are now in their third decade, and this region is shared with another great power, Russia. China still officially regards the five Central Asian republics (Kazakhstan, Kyrgyzstan, Tajikistan, Turkmenistan, and Uzbekistan) as neighbors, but not in the same region as China: they are officially classified as part of the "Eurasian" department of the Ministry of Foreign Affairs (MOFA), and Chinese diplomats and scholars regularly recognize Russia's interests in these places. China recognizes this as "Russia's backyard" and seeks a stable relationship with those countries and with Russia, and has generally been successful in that regard. What has changed is China's economic might. China simply has more people, money, military, and trade than Russia and its Central Asian "backyard" can muster. And with Xi Jinping's "One Belt, One Road" initiative, it has an attractive idea as well to sell in Central Asia as well.

Security

To understand China's security relations with Central Asia in the 21st century, we must first understand the situation in Xinjiang, China's far western province. Many analysts point to the role of the province in Chinese energy production – the oil fields there produce about 400,000 bbl/day, about 8.6% of total Chinese domestic production (EIA 2015). It is also the site of Lop Nur, China's former nuclear testing facility. It is domestic security, however, that is the focus of Beijing toward the Uyghur Autonomous Region of Xinjiang (新疆维吾尔自治区/*Xinjiang weiwu'er zizhiqu*, the official name of the province-level political unit) and which is core to China's relations with its Central Asian neighbors, Russia, the Shanghai Cooperation Organization, the regional international organization, and much of China's foreign relations in general. As its name implies, Xinjiang is traditionally populated by Uighurs, a Sunni Muslim Turkic-speaking people. The history of the province has been outlined in previous chapters: previous brief separatist episodes, a looming Soviet military threat, and a minority of Han Chinese in the region. By the 21st century, these conditions were changing, but their replacement was with Islamist terror strikes and the difficulty of dealing with cross-border terrorist movements. According to the START (Global Terrorism Database), out of 242 total incidents counted as "terrorism" between 1989 and 2015, 105 occurred between 2004 and 2015, with 782 fatalities and 899 injuries recorded. Many of these database incidents are not Islamist-based, and are only recorded as "unknown." However, beginning in 2005, a single Uighur attack was followed by a notable pause between 2006 and 2007. Then, in 2008, a series of attacks began in Xinjiang attributed to the East Turkistan Islamic Movement (ETIM), or more generally to "Uighur separatists." Kashgar (Kashi), Hotan (Hetian), Yarkand (Shache), Aksu (Akesu), and Luntai, among others, were also struck in a variety of attacks using explosives, incendiaries, vehicles and melee attacks. The deadliest incident was on July 5, 2009 in Urumqi when rioting led to the deaths of over 180 individuals, primarily Han Chinese, leading to the term "7/5" (鲁木齐七·五暴力事件) as a synonym for a terrorist attack comparable to "9/11" in American English. Less deadly but even more disturbing for the Chinese government have been a handful of attacks outside of Xinjiang, such as knife assaults in Guangzhou in May 2014 and March 2015 and in Kunming in March 2014, which killed 33 people, and suicide car bombings in Tiananmen Square near the Zhongnanhai leadership compound in October 2013. For a government/party which rests most of its legitimacy on the foundations of prosperity and stability, these incidents represent a serious threat.

Beijing has cast these attacks within the context of global terrorism, since the alternative would be to accept that Chinese government policies in Xinjiang are a contributing factor. Thus, China's relations with its Central Asian and South Asian neighbors are strongly affected. The role of the Regional Anti-Terrorist Structure (RATS) is discussed below. The war in Afghanistan has attracted a number of ethnic Uighurs to the fighting, and a number were captured in the fighting there in 2001–2006 (Wayne 2009: 250). The ETIM (the acronym used internationally for the organization), an off-shoot of al Qaeda, has taken responsibility for many of the attacks in China, cooperates closely with the Islamic Movement of Uzbekistan (IMU). Fortunately for China, the Central Asian republics all openly oppose this and other movements described as "the three evils: terrorism, separatism and religious extremism," and compared to the Afghan and Pakistani governments, see the threat of Islamist terrorist organizations as a serious common threat.

Territorial disputes

China settled its boundary questions with most of its newly-independent neighbors in the 1990s, the process of which led to the creation of the Shanghai Cooperation Organization. The agreements and subsequent arrangements were not always popular in the Central Asian populations and led to accusations against their governments, and became an issue that in 2005 brought down the government in Kyrgyzstan (Marat 2013: 127–128). The border with Kazakhstan was settled by treaty in 1998, and the border relationship has generally been quite good. Tajikistan still had a border issue with China that was unresolved at the beginning of this period, an area of over 1,100km^2 which had been in dispute for a very long time, and over which negotiations had begun between China and the Soviet Union in 1987, and were finally settled in 1999, but which Tajikistan did not ratify until 2011 (Gleason 2013: 283). To be sure, there are many geographers and experts in Central Asia who find the basis of these settlements to be less than satisfactory and in particular complain that the full text of the treaties have not been published, but the official government positions on the boundaries have been set (Peyrouse 2016: 224–226). Chinese sources acknowledged the concerns about the perception of a "China Threat" in Central Asia as early as 2007, but have subsequently emphasized the partnership aspects of the relations (Sun Zhuangzhi 2007: 13).

Finally, the very long Russian border treaty which had been ratified in 1992 based upon the signed but not yet ratified Sino-Soviet treaty, which then had a supplementary agreement which was reached in 2004 and concluded in a 2008 demarcation process to resolve outstanding issues. Here, too, minor protests occurred but without effect (Galeotti 2013: 258). Most of the local reaction to the border has been the recognition of opportunity for trade, tourism and investment. In general, the boundaries of China with Central Asia and Russia are not a major foreign policy issue.

Military intervention

One might expect China to intervene in its Central Asian neighbors' affairs; with instability in several of those countries, and weak governments in the border areas, a civil war in Tajikistan from 1992–97, the "Tulip Revolution" in Kyrgyzstan in 2005 (overturned by the April Uprising in 2010), and a significant Islamic insurgency in nearby Uzbekistan. More recently, a bombing of the Chinese embassy in Kyrgyzstan by a Uighur suicide bomber in August 2016 demonstrated that the region's stability remains tenuous (Nechepurenko 2016). Chinese commercial staff in Kyrgyzstan were injured in 2013 in a dispute that appears to have targeted them as Chinese (Parello-Plesner and Duchâtel 2015: 29). As noted in the previous chapter, moreover, China's National People's Congress in December 2015 passed a law that would allow both PLA and People's Armed Police to engage in counterterrorism operations overseas (Duchâtel 2016: 2).

Yet China has not openly intervened in the domestic politics of these countries, even when Beijing was clearly unhappy with events, such as the Tulip Revolution in Kyrgyzstan in 2005. China was also reluctant to see the SCO intervene in Kyrgyzstan during violence there in 2010 following the April unrest that unseated President Kurmanbek Bakiyev (who had risen five years earlier in the "Tulip Revolution"), and the subsequent violence between Kyrgyz and ethnic Uzbeks. Two reasons are fairly clear: first, the Russians are willing to provide much of the hard security in Central Asia against Islamic separatist groups, and the Chinese remain officially opposed to external intervention. The Chinese often note that the former Soviet Central Asian republics are the Russian Federation's "Backyard" – 后院/*hou yuan* (Chen Xiaoding and Ma Ru 2015: 74). The Russians maintain a military base in Tajikistan, the 201 Military Base, which is a remnant of the 1992–97 civil war there and a mechanism for maintaining a point of control in the region, particularly an eye on the Tajikistani border with Afghanistan. Russia also an airbase at Kant in northern Kyrgyzstan, under the aegis of the CSTO and negotiated an extension on its base contract ("Russia obtains . . ." 2012). Beijing has supported joint military exercises and counter-terrorism training under the auspices of the SCO, but has resisted any effort by the Russians to turn it into a formal alliance. Second, Beijing's leaders are quite aware of how sensitive both Central Asian and Russian leaders are to any such intervention.

External major powers

The year 2005 was a clear turning point in China's view of the United States involvement in Central Asia. Four years had passed since the US occupation of Afghanistan had begun, and American strategic focus was clearly centered on the war in Iraq, yet the USA showed no signs of leaving its bases in Kyrgyzstan or Uzbekistan. The "Tulip Revolution" of March 2005 in Kyrgyzstan was the primary change point; it seemed to confirm the spread of the "Color Revolutions" (Rose in Georgia in late 2003, Orange in Ukraine in late 2004) to Central Asian republics, and which China and Russia saw as having been backed by the West generally and the United States specifically (Yu Haiyang 2012: 21). Followed by protests in southern Uzbekistan which sparked a government massacre at Anjidan in May 2005, the Shanghai Cooperation Organization passed a resolution condemning the protesters, and Uzbekistan expelled Western human rights NGOs and terminated the US base agreement for Karshi-Khanabad. The organization also in July 2005 called on the USA to leave its bases in Central Asia. Additional SCO joint military exercises were held in August 2005.

One might assume that China's concern about America's democratization effort in Central Asia would have subsided after its formal withdrawal from the Manas Transit Air Center in Kyrgyzstan in June 2014 and its draw-down in Afghanistan. Most external observers see the US withdrawal from Afghanistan and bases in Central Asia to be an opportunity for China to expand its influence in the region (Weitz 2015). Yet Chinese analysts continue to see American initiatives in Central Asia, some of which seem to be directed at increasing civil society organization, as well as US public diplomacy in countries such as Kazakhstan which they see as linked to "exporting democracy" (Yang Tao 2012: 97; Yang Shu and Guo Xugang 2015: 84).

Yet, however much it would appear that great power relations in Central Asia and the SCO is a manifestation of a Russo-Chinese condominium in Central Asia to exclude American influence, the reality is more complicated, and Chinese analysts have seen Kyrgyzstan as a joint American-Russian condominium aimed at excluding Chinese influence. And since Kyrgyzstan borders China but neither Russia nor the United States, China is the more vulnerable of the three (Jia Lihong 2010: 96). Furthermore, China and Russia do not always agree about the role of the organization. Most notable was the disagreement over the position the SCO should take on the Russia-Georgia war in August 2008. During that conflict, Russia forcibly intervened in Georgia on behalf of the separatist South Ossetians and Abkhazians and sought a stamp of international approval from the SCO. All of the Central Asian republics have regions with ethnic discontent, and China in particular views any support of secessionist movements through the lens of Taiwan, Tibet, and

Xinjiang, parts of China which have seen significant break-away movements. Thus, to the Chinese, the approval of the South Ossetian republic would be the same as allowing Taiwanese independence. As one journalist summed it up, "In the tug of war between Russia's desire to secure international backing and China's fear of encouraging any separatist movements, the Chinese position apparently won out" (Stern 2008). Furthermore, Chinese attitudes toward the Central Asian republics is far less exclusionary than Russian attitudes, where the concept of the "Near Abroad" – in effect an exclusionary neighborhood concept – still dominates foreign relations. One Western analyst summarized the differences in approaches:

> While Russia seeks to be the dominating actor in the region and to reduce the presence of Western countries, China agrees that the Central Asian states have the right to form their own regional organizations. Chinese experts have asserted that, contrary to speculations, the SCO is by no means an anti-American or anti-Western alliance. According to Pan Guang, Head of the SCO Studies Center in Shanghai, China affirms the right of Central Asian states to organize and deal with other states, including Western ones, while Russia alone opposes such outreach.
>
> (Marat 2013: 135)

The "One Belt, One Road" initiative announced by Xi Jinping in Kazakhstan in 2013 in turn has been viewed with substantial suspicion by Russian diplomats who see it as an intrusion into "their" sphere:

> Russian participants only thinly disguised their concerns about the [OBOR] project, recognizing the potential damage to Russian geopolitical and economic interests if current routes transiting Russia were replaced. . . . They seemed to be saying: "wait, this is our backyard and nothing happens here without our consent.
>
> (Kirişci and Le Corre 2015)

Diplomatic relations with regional states

China has had diplomatic relations with all of the newly independent states of Central Asia, and in addition to using the SCO as a mechanism for promoting regional cooperation, China has used bilateral diplomatic mechanisms, party-to-party relations, and a modicum of "soft power" to maintain good relations. Of its Central Asian neighbors, the Russian Federation is in a class by itself. Energy-rich Kazakhstan is doubtlessly the second most important and also stable. Kyrgyzstan and Tajikistan are small, poor, and mountainous, and together with Uzbekistan, which comes close to but does not directly border China, forms a difficult swirl of ethnic, and religious tensions, accentuated by poverty and land-locked status. Turkmenistan, in contrast, is remote and unattached to the SCO, and the world for that matter. Table 8.1 shows the elevation of these former "neighbors" into "partners."

234 *China and Central Asia*

Table 8.1 China's "partners" and "strategic relations" in Central Asia, 2004–2014

State	Designation	Date
Kazakhstan	Strategic Partnership	2005
Kyrgyzstan	Strategic Partnership	2013
Russia	Comprehensive Strategic Partnership of Coordination	2011
Russia	Strategic Partnership of Coordination	1996
Russia	Constructive Partnership	1994
Tajikistan	Strategic Partnership	2013
Turkmenistan	Strategic Partnership	2013
Uzbekistan	Strategic Partnership	2012

Source: *China's Foreign Relations* 2005–2014.

Russian Federation

China's relations with Russia are extremely important, but in many ways they are part of a global relationship, as opposed to a Central Asian or an East Asian regional relationship. It is characterized as a "Comprehensive Strategic Partnership of Coordination," the only such designation in China's over-stuffed box of diplomatic honorifics. It is a relationship that is much more based upon a variety of common – but not necessarily mutual – goals and values. Not all of those goals are shared, and in particular principles of foreign policy concerning Russian promotion of separatism in areas such as South Ossetia, Abkhazia, eastern Ukraine, and the annexation of the Crimea are disturbing to China's leaders. This resulted in the Chinese abstaining on key UN and other international organizations' votes to condemn the Russian invasions. On the other hand, China and Russia are in agreement about much of world: the opposition to the expansion of liberal democracy as promoted by the West, the primacy of state sovereignty regardless of national policies, deep concern about the reach of American foreign policy, among others. All of that operates largely at the global level of activity, as denoted in Table 2.3.

At the purely regional level, China and Russia share two borders (one long, one tiny on either side of Mongolia), growing bilateral trade primarily in energy (discussed below), and a region of five former Soviet republics, over which Moscow and Beijing quietly compete for influence. After the 2014 invasion of Crimea and Western sanctions against Russia, President Vladimir Putin began to engage his own "Pivot to Asia," in the hopes of an economic relationship that would make up for the Russian losses with the EU. These efforts were generally disappointing, and in the increasingly asymmetrical economic relations, Russians have begun to worry about becoming China's "little brother," a prospect that is obviously worrying to officials in Moscow indicated by the number of times it is denied (Gabuev 2016). Yet Russian policy in East Asia is often half-hearted; Putin seldom attends the East Asian Summit and is distracted by events in Europe, the Middle East, and South Asia, which are closer to home and to core strategic areas. And in the case of the South China Sea dispute, Russia is notably quiet, since it has very good relations with Vietnam going back to the Cold War, and has sold Kilo-class submarines to Hanoi. Russia has periodically made moves toward Japan, such as the oil deal in 2001 destined for China, which was in 2003 then rerouted to Nakhodka, on the Pacific coast, and which would benefit Japan (Lee and Lukin 2016: 101). Chinese analysts have pointed out that Russia has not always supported China's positions on the Diaoyu/Senkaku dispute, Xinjiang and Taiwan, not to mention military connections with India and Vietnam (Wang Shuchun and Liu Si'en 2015: 98–100). And Putin's December 2016 visit to Tokyo briefly held out the prospect of resolving those countries' territorial dispute, which was later disappointed. Nonetheless, Russia wants to be a relevant, important, independent actor in East Asia, and though it values a good relationship with China, its leaders are fearful that too close of a partnership will reduce Russia to China's "little brother."

Kazakhstan

Larger, richer and more stable than its Central Asian neighbors, Kazakhstan has a number of advantages in its interactions with China that the other former Soviet republics lack. It was the first of the Central Asian states to be raised to the level of "Strategic Partner" in 2005, and to a "Comprehensive Strategic Partner" in 2011, which none of the other Central Asian republics have been designated as of 2014. China and Kazakhstan have had a greater number of high-level exchanges than the others, with nine state visits of Presidents Hu Jintao and Xi Jinping and Kazakhstani President Nursultan Nazarbayev between 2004 and 2014, to whom China gave the "Silk Road Peace Prize" in 2014 (*CFA* 2015: 218). Like other members of the Shanghai Cooperation Organization, many of the SCO Summits also feature bilateral "sidelines" talks between Kazakhstani leaders and their Chinese counterparts: Prime Ministers/Premiers, Foreign Ministers, and quite significantly, Defense Ministers and [internal] Security Council Secretaries which has an annual formal SCO meeting. Multiple Confucius Institutes have also been established in Kazakhstan, and a variety of cultural exchanges and lower-level visits that form the bulk of diplomacy between Astana and Beijing. Importantly, Kazakhstan ". . . consistently supported China's position on issues related to Taiwan, Tibet, and combatting East Turkistan Islamic Movement (ETIM)." China in turn supports Kazakhstan's territorial integrity and sovereignty (*CFA* 2014: 203). The latter might seem like standard diplomatic fluff, but given ethnic Russian separatist incidents in northern Kazakhstan and Russian President Vladimir Putin's 2014 statement that Kazakhstan was an "artificial state" created by Nazarbayev, the statement may have been more significant than it seems at first glance (Stronski 2016a).

Highly publicized joint economic initiatives also played a major role in the Sino-Kazakhstani relations. The oil pipeline between Atasu in Kazakhstan and

Alataw Pass in China began in September 2004, and completed the next December. A natural gas pipeline was commissioned in December 2009 as well, and a joint investment zone on the border, the Khorgos International Center for Border Cooperation inaugurated in December 2011, as well as the link up of Chinese and Kazakhstani railway (*CFA* 2012: 189). Thus, even before the One Belt One Road/New Silk Road initiative, China has been using infrastructure building as a diplomatic tool in Kazakhstan. Not surprisingly given the geography involved, Xi Jinping's speech laying out the One Belt, One Road initiative was given in the Kazakhstani capital of Astana in September 2013. And the government in Astana is keen on building on its position astride Asia, Europe and potentially the Middle East. As the Kazakhstani Prime Minister indicated in a meeting of the "Astana Club" in November 2015, ". . . their country's location is ideal for the 'connectivity' the Chinese are seeking" (Kirişci and Le Corre 2015). China also used its monetary position to help Kazakhstan in 2009 during the depths of the world recession when Kazakh banks were stressed, lending a total of $10 billion to Kazakhistani-owned firms (Perlez 2013).

Tajikistan

The second smallest and poorest of the Central Asian republics, Tajikistan and China do technically share a border, for practical purposes it is only marginally connected to China; almost all current ground traffic between the two must pass through neighboring Kyrgyzstan, the opening of a minor border port at Karasu-Kylma in 2004 notwithstanding. Nonetheless, China has a very substantial role in Tajikistan's economy, and Beijing established a "Strategic Partnership" with Dushanbe in May 2013 during Tajikistani President Emomali Rahmon's state visit to China (*CFA* 2014: 293), which Xi Jinping reciprocated the next year (*CFA* 2015: 313). Rahmon also made a state visit to China in January 2007 (*CFA* 2008: 272). In addition to the exchange of high-level visits typical of China's relations with its neighbors, China and Tajikistan have had prominent exchanges of internal security officials, such as Public Security Bureau chief Meng Jianzhu's April 2011 visit during which he ". . . reached broad consensus with political leaders of Tajikistan on a wide range of issues, including the regional counter-terrorism situation and deepening bilateral cooperation in the security field" (*CFA* 2012: 275–276). This followed a 2003 visit by Foreign Minister Li Zhaoxing which resulted in both a Treaty on Border Management and an Agreement on Cooperation in Fighting Terrorism, Separatism and Extremism (*CFA* 2004: 295).

The borders of Tajikistan with Afghanistan, however, remain largely porous, and with that the flow of smuggled goods, people, drugs and Taliban-supported insurgents into Tajikistan and on to other destinations in Central Asia – including Xinjiang – could be disturbing for China's leaders. The Tajikistani government is still under the stable and increasingly authoritarian control of Rahmon and his family, though it remains weak at best, and increasingly narrow in its political base (Stronski 2016). To make matters even more complicated for China, the relationship between Tajikistan and Uzbekistan – which has a far more powerful military – has deteriorated significantly since 2011. This puts China in a particularly difficult position; both are "Strategic Partners," both are members of the SCO, one is a major energy source for China and the other shares a border with it (Li Qi 2014: 52). The USA had a similar problem with Chile and Argentina and the Soviet Union with the Hungary-Romanian rivalry.

Infrastructure development and foreign aid are two tools that China has used in other parts of Central Asia to develop its relations, though Tajikistan's mountainous terrain makes it a difficult and expensive proposition, money the desperately poor country is challenged to repay. Tajikistan and China jointly launched the Tajik section of Line D of the China-Central Asia Natural Gas Pipeline in 2014, though the project requires cooperation with Uzbekistan (*CFA* 2015: 313). Chinese firms have also completed a coal-fired power plant in Dushanbe, the Cormazak Tunnel, the Shahriston Tunnel, power transmission lines, and roads (*CFA*, 2012–2014). China also regularly notes that it is Tajikistan's biggest investor, creditor and third largest trading partner (*CFA* 2015: 313). These exports of cheap consumer goods to Tajikistan are area in which China has succeeded in the last few years.

Kyrgyzstan

Small, poor, mountainous, and unstable, Kyrgyzstan is one of the major challenges for China's diplomacy in Central Asia. With four different governments in the past decade, two the result of "revolutions," which vary between barely democratic and fragile authoritarian, bilateral relations between Bishkek and Beijing are in a state of flux. Kyrgyzstan also borders Xinjiang, and with a notable population of Uighurs and Donggan (ethnic Chinese Muslims, called *Hui* in China;), cross-border security is a very high priority for China. Of the Central Asian borders, Kyrgyzstan's is seen by some Chinese analysts as the most important to Xinjiang security. They point out that although mountainous, the territory is not impassible, and played a role of the region in the creation of the old East Turkestan Republic in 1933 and 1944, and is a key area for contemporary Uighur separatists, supported by ISIS terrorists, and other groups. Given the instability and threat from that quarter, one Chinese analyst was unusually blunt in saying, "The situation in Kyrgyzstan has brought great harm to China, and we cannot but be alarmed" (Jia Lihong 2010: 94–96).

Despite this negative assessment and the overthrow of governments in 2005 (the "Tulip Revolution," noted above) and again in 2010, China has sought to maintain formal relations with the resulting governments. After the 2005 "Tulip Revolution," China's diplomats made sure that the new government in Bishkek did not have any new policies on key questions: "After taking office in 2005, the new Kyrgyz Government reiterated that its position on the above-mentioned questions [backing the Chinese government positions on Taiwan, Tibet, and combatting the 'East Turkestan' forces] remained unchanged." Hu Jintao met Kurmanbek Bakiev who was Acting President in July at the Astana Summit of the SCO and thereafter sent its congratulations to Bakiev after his election (*CFA* 2006: 214) and met him in June 2009. Then after he was overthrown in 2010 Hu met interim President Rosa

Otunbayeva in June 2010 (she had met the Chinese leadership previously as the interim Foreign Minister in 2005 after the overthrow of President Askar Akiev), and newly elected President Almazbek Atambayev in September 2011, mostly in conjunction with the SCO summits (*CFA,* 2010–2012). Xi Jinping paid a state visit to Bishkek in 2013, coinciding with the SCO summit meeting. China established a "Strategic Partnership" with Kyrgyzstan in 2013, upgrading from the previously "good-neighborly and friendly relations."

Foreign aid and infrastructure development are two important tools that Beijing has sought to use to cement its relations with Kyrgyzstan: the China-Uzbekistan-Kyrgyzstan highway rehabilitation project, power networks, and most importantly the Kyrgyz section of the Line D China-Central Asia Natural Gas pipeline project, a key feature in transporting Central Asian natural gas to China (*CFA, 2013–2015*). Whether this line will be fully completed remains to be seen, given Uzbekistani reluctance to complete its section of Line D and general Kyrgyzstan-Uzbekistan tensions (Quinn-Judge and Stronski 2016). China has made a number of cultural initiatives in Kyrgyzstan, and has opened three Confucius Institutes in Kyrgyzstani universities, and as the ever-optimistic *China's Foreign Relations 2014* somewhat self-complimentarily notes, "The Kyrgyz people were fascinated by Chinese traditional culture" (206). The reality may be more problematic; the Kyrgyzstani Prime Minister Temir Sariyev for forced to step down in April 2016 after allegations of bribery from a Chinese road construction corporation (Quinn-Judge and Stronski 2016).

Uzbekistan

The most populous, most militarized, and most authoritarian of the Central Asian states, Uzbekistan does not directly border China, but comes close in the Fergana Valley, where Tajikistan, Kyrgyzstan, and Uzbekistan all come together, with small enclaves of each further complicating the territorial arrangements. As noted, Uzbekistan and Kyrgyzstan in particular have a tense relationship, caused by the treatment of ethnic Uzbeks in Kyrgyzstan.

China and Uzbekistan negotiated a partnership agreement in 2004, which was implemented in 2005, and then upgraded to a "Strategic Partnership" in 2012. The two countries exchanged four state visits from 2004 to 2014, though the President of Uzbekistan Islam Karimov only visited China once in 2005. Natural gas lines have been an important focus in the Sino-Uzbekistani relationship and Line C of the China-Central Asia Gas Pipeline went into operation through Uzbekistan in 2014, though Line D is only recently under construction, and even that is now appears to be delayed (Michel 2016). A number of joint development projects aside from the natural gas pipelines exist, however, to promote relations such as the Angren-Pap railway tunnel, the Pengsheng and Jizzakh industrial parks, a soda plant, potash fertilizer plant, and power plant (*CFA* 2015: 338, 2014: 317). Two Confucius Institutes and other cultural exchanges have rounded out the bilateral exchanges.

Beijing's leaders were willing to indulge Tashkent's first family, and prominently noted the release ceremony for President's Karimov's book in 2006, entitled *Uzbek People Will Never Depend on Anyone!* (*CFA* 2007: 413). Sales figures were not immediately available, though Karimov's previous book did hit # 5,373,948 on Amazon.com). They also noted Vice Foreign Minister and Chairperson of the Forum on Culture and Arts of Uzbekistan Foundation Board of Trustees Gulnara Karimova's promotion of her fashion brand during China Fashion Week (*CFA* 2013: 313). Of course, that was before the latter had a falling out with her father, President Islam Karimov. Sales figures for the fashion brand are similarly elusive.

More important to the diplomatic relationship has been the regular security exchanges. Meng Jianzhu, and later Guo Shengkun the Public Security Minister of China, regularly visited Uzbekistan among other Central Asian countries, as well as reciprocal visits. Most of these visits were in conjunction with SCO Security Council Secretaries' meetings.

Turkmenistan

Turkmenistan may be the least populous state in Central Asia, but it does have an immense amount of natural gas and, for a while, the most bizarre leader. Saparmurat Niyazov was president from 1991 to his death in 2006, called himself "Türkmenbaşy" ("Father of the Turkmens"), and engaged in a variety of self-aggrandizing projects. China's characterization of its relations with Turkmenistan as a "close neighbor" in 2004, then as "friendly and cooperative" until 2013 when it established a "Strategic Partnership" with the government in Ashgabat. The two countries have exchanged six state visits between 2004 and 2014, and in August 2008 President Hu Jintao received the "'Saparmurat Turkmenbashi the Great, First President of Turkmenistan Medal' from President Berdymukhamedov," something Hu doubtlessly treasures, though for inexplicable reasons, it is not listed in his official biography (*CFA* 2009: 316; "Hu Jintao," China Vitae 2016). Xi Jinping received a (somewhat) more practical gift when he visited in 2014, a rare Akhal-Teke horse, a breed with a long historical association with imperial China (Feng 2014).

Turkmenistan's foreign policy makes relations with its neighbors a bit difficult, since it does not belong to the SCO, though China invited Turkmen representatives to SCO meetings in 2012 when China was hosting. Turkmenistan holds to a policy of "permanent neutrality." *China's Foreign Affairs* in 2005 officially affirmed China's support for that strategy, as well as its ". . . taking a development path compatible with its national conditions" (318). This was somewhat unusual, and subsequent statements were the more standard phrase that China ". . . supported Turkmenistan's efforts to safeguard national independence, sovereignty and territorial integrity." The Turkmens, in turn, have supported the Chinese position on Taiwan, Tibet, and the fight against "East Turkistan" forces, and in 2005 issued a statement of support for China's new Anti-Secession Law (*CFA* 2006: 332). Prominent diplomatic visits often revolved around natural gas projects, such as Niyazov's state visit to China in 2006 in which a natural gas long-term sale agreement and pipeline construction deal were reached (*CFA* 2007: 387). By 2014, China had become Turkmenistan's largest customer for natural gas.

Regional international organizations

The SCO is the primary regional organization for the Central Asian republics, China and Russia. Its origins were outlined in Chapter 4. During the 21st century it has grown and evolved, and China in particular has seen to it that its institutionalization has continued, but at the same time has sought to make sure that it does not turn into a formal politico-military alliance. As an international organization, 2004 might be marked as "the end of its beginning," and *China's Foreign Affairs* characterizes it as "In 2004, the Shanghai Cooperation Organization (SCO) completed smoothly its institutional build-up and entered a new period of comprehensive cooperation" (2005: 397). This involved the establishment of the Secretariat (in Beijing), the RATS (in Tashkent), its first Observer (Mongolia), a plan for trade and economic cooperation, as well as an anti-narcotics agreement (398). The meetings of heads of government were becoming regular, as well as the heads of state, and would lead to the ministerial-level meetings.

To be sure, China has a rival as well as a partner in the SCO: the Russian Federation. Russia in many ways is still in its own "hub-and-spokes" style of bilateralism, and seeking to ensure that its "near abroad" remains *its* neighborhood. China, on the other hand, does not have as exclusionary vision of a "neighborhood" partly because of its linguistic absence of the term and partly because the trends are so overwhelmingly in its favor. In his June 2017 speech at the SCO Summit in Astana, Xi Jinping was pointed in including "Openness and Inclusiveness" as one of his major headings (Xi Jinping 2017). One of the major differences is that the Chinese were much more in favor of institutionalizing the SCO than the Russians, who have generally preferred that it remain a weakly-instituted organization (Yuan 2010: 863). There have been variations in this theme: the Russians have supported the SCO's security function, and have pushed the idea of its becoming a military bloc, an "energy club," and an anti-terrorist organization, but China has been equally focused on promoting its economic and its social and cultural functions. The result was a deadlock of purpose that lasted "[b]etween 2006 and 2008 the SCO was widely seen as a dysfunctional organization, plagued by a protracted impasse, due to the fact that is two key members were divided over what trajectory its future development should take" (Contessi 2010: 103–106).

Beginning in 2009, a tacit compromise was struck, with Russia accepting a nominal increase in economic rhetoric (if not reality) of the SCO, and China emphasizing the anti-terrorist function, particularly the Yekaterinburg Summit in June 2009, reinforced a month later by the "7/5" attacks in Urumqi. Russian leaders continue to talk about the importance of the SCO, but they need to maintain a good relationship with China, on which it remains dependent economically and diplomatically (Blank 2016).

The SCO brought in new Observers and Dialogue-Partners: Mongolia as an observer in 2004, and Pakistan, India, and Iran as observers in June 2005 (Scheineson 2009). The issue of future expansion was another area in which China and Russia disagreed, leading to a long moratorium on new members (2006–2017), though not observers or dialogue partners. In June 2016, India and Pakistan both signed a memorandum for full membership, which occurred during the Astana Summit on June 9, 2017. India's membership was substantially pushed by Russia, and Pakistan's by China. Iran has also made it clear that they wish to join, something that China has spoken (mildly) in favor of, but which the Russians were more in favor of; yet the organization declined because of UN sanctions against Tehran. There had been speculation before the 2017 Astana Summit in which both Pakistan and India formally joined that Iran's application might be considered but there was no mention of it in the press releases.

In general, it appears that China is most concerned about expanding the organization, and would prefer to "deepen" it instead (Song 2014: 98). The other Central Asian members are also reluctant to add yet more members, let alone another big member to dilute their already small share of power, and the fear that the organization may become too large to work well (Blank 2016). Belarus became an observer in 2010, though its location in Europe and not Asia seems odd, and Afghanistan became an observer in 2012. The United States is reported to have requested observer status in 2002 and 2006 but was turned down (Hiro 2006; Fedoruk 2011). There are also a number of dialog partners. Turkmenistan, however, is not a member, though it has been often invited as a "guest."

In its annual description of the organization in *China's Foreign Affairs* usually emphasizes its ". . . cooperation in the political, security, economic and cultural fields." China wants the SCO to become an economic/cultural organization as well as a security body, though it has dropped the idea of a formal Free Trade Area which it raised in 2003 by 2007 (Contessi 2010: 107). This economic emphasis returned at the 2015 Ufa summit with the "SCO Development Strategy Towards 2025," a vague statement of economic cooperation goals. Trade was raised again by Xi Jinping in the June 2017 Astana Summit, saying that, "It is China's suggestion to gradually put in place institutional arrangements for regional economic cooperation, and we may begin with a SCO trade facilitation agreement" (Xi Jinping 2017). Unofficial Russian comments on trade proposals at Astana were much more cautious, as the Russian former Secretary-General of the SCO said, "'The establishment of a free trade zone (FTZ) requires time. We are perfectly aware that today, when competition in the world market is increasing, it is very important to find formats for interaction with each other" (Xinhua 2017). In 2009 and again in 2012, China offered $10 billion in support of bilateral and multilateral initiatives of the SCO, but quiet Russian opposition made sure the money was not loaned (Cooley 2012). The SCO development bank, food security cooperation mechanism, and e-commerce platform were among the several proposals that Chinese representatives to the various SCO meetings have raised, and despite winning "high acclaim" have not been implemented (*CFA* 2011: 401). China especially touted the 2014 "Agreement on the Facilitation of International Road Transport among the SCO Member States," since it worked well with both its economic agenda and the "One Belt, One Road" infrastructure initiative (*CFA* 2014: 391).

Chinese scholars view China's economic contributions to the SCO as part of its role in providing economic public goods to the region, while noting Russia's reluctance, and the lack of capacity in most of the Central Asian republics, Kazakhstan notwithstanding (Chen Xiaoding and Ma Ru 2015: 77). SCO-based cultural initiatives have been fairly limited.

RATS

The relative weakness of the economic and other functions of the SCO notwithstanding, the most effective element of the SCO beyond its summitry is the Regional Anti-Terrorist Structure, or RATS (上海合作组织地区反恐怖机构 *Shanghai hezuo zuzhi diqu fan kongbu jigou* in Chinese, Региональная антитеррористическая структура Шанхайской организации сотрудничества *Regional'naia antiterroristicheskaia struktura Shankhayskoy organizatsii sotrudnichestva* in Russian, the two official languages of the SCO). Since terrorism, along with separatism and extremism were designated "The Three Evils" early on in the Shanghai Five and then the SCO's existence, they are usually treated as the same phenomenon, a position that the USA and Western governments do not necessarily agree with.

The RATS had been agreed to in 1999, during the Shanghai Five period, but only in June 2002 was it designated in the SCO Treaty and even then the controversies dogged its establishment. Russia wanted the RATS headquarters to be in Bishkek, Kyrgyzstan, which China and Uzbekistan objected to, and in 2003, the headquarters was placed in Tashkent, Uzbekistan, instead. The launch of the Executive Committee was in June 2004 under an Uzbek Executive Director, with thirty employees and an initial budget of about $2 million (Plater-Zyberk and Monaghan 2014: 21–22). China and Russia provide one quarter of the funding and seven experts seconded from their security bureaucracies each (Gill and Murphy 2005: 27). An SCO Convention on Counter Terrorism was signed in 2009 at the Yekaterinburg Summit, and issued a statement supporting China after the "7/5" attack in Urumqi. The current director of the RATS is a Russian, Vevgeniy Sergeyevich Sysoyev.

The RATS has claimed to have prevented a variety of terrorist attacks, contributed to the arrest of hundreds of suspects, and acted against a number of groups. Perhaps most importantly, it is building a database of suspected terrorists and organizations based on information sharing among the member states, though the database itself is only in Chinese and Russian (Plater-Zyberk and Monaghan 2014: 23–24). Classified information is controlled by the transmitting party, according to the June 17, 2004 Agreement on Protecting Classified Information in the Framework of the Regional Anti-Terrorist Structure of the Shanghai Cooperation Organization. The Executive Committee of the RATS is also designated as the coordinating body for sharing information on border crossings, border conditions, violations, training, laws, and experiences, according to the 2015 Agreement on Cooperation and Interaction of the Member States of the Shanghai Cooperation Organization on Border Issues (SCO Secretariat 2015). The SCO in general and the RATS in particular are focused on legal issues as well, defining "terrorism," exchanging model laws, determining extradition processes, and seeking to appear to the international community to be a set of countries and an international organization that takes the rule of law – swift and sure – seriously.

The SCO has sponsored a handful of military exercises, such as the "Peace Mission 2012" exercise, the "Tianshan -2 2011" exercise, "Peace Mission 2010," and "Peace

Mission 2007" (the first in which all members participated). Joint maritime exercises between the Chinese and Russian navies occurred twice in 2016, under SCO auspices.

As noted in Chapter 2, the SCO is not the only organization in Central Asia, and Russia has its own favorite, the Collective Security Treaty Organization (CSTO – Организация Договора о Коллективной Безопасности, *Organizacija Dogovora o Kollektivnoj Bezopasnosti*) which is much more akin to a military alliance, and includes Kazakhstan, Kyrgyzstan, Tajikistan, Russia, Armenia, and Belarus, and formerly Uzbekistan which has twice withdrawn from it. Most importantly, it does not include China. The SCO and the CTSO signed a Memorandum of Understanding in 2007, but the two organizations overlap to the point that they are competitive. The CSTO also gives Moscow – where the organization is headquartered – a veto over foreign basing rights in member states, which was part of the reason Uzbekistan left. In the area of counter-insurgency/counter-terror, the CTSO sponsors annual "Rubezh" COIN joint exercises, "Kanal" anti-narcotics, "Arsenal" anti-weapons, "Proxi" anti-cyber and "Nelegal" anti-illegal migration operations with its partners (Contessi 2010: 117).

Closer to the economic sphere but still well within its broader strategy, Moscow has sought to create a new regional organization that is more closely aligned to Russian interests, the Eurasian Economic Union (EEU). Currently, the union includes Armenia, Russia, Belarus, Kazakhstan, and Kyrgyzstan and is headquartered in Moscow. The proposals and previous organizations date back to 1995, but the EEU *per se* was established by treaty in 2014, implemented in 2015. Russian president Vladimir Putin sought to establish political aspects of the organization, but its partners demurred ("Kazakhstan: the bear on the doorstep" 2014: 41). Economically, it has the benefit of a single customs union, which formally speeds trade among its members and informally reduces the potential for customs officials' graft. For Kyrgyzstan, it means that Kyrgyzstani workers can migrate to Russia and elsewhere and send remittances back, a major source of income for Kyrgyzstan, between 25 and 30% of GDP (World Bank, WDI 2017). Tajikistan is feeling pressure to join the Union because its migrant laborers do not enjoy this advantage. Interestingly, it was estimated that 8,000 Tajikistanis were working in China during the 2006–2008 period (Olimova 2008: 70).

Hegemon's expatriates

The enormous population of China compared to the vast and under-populated spaces of Central Asia inherently make countries such as Russia, Kazakhstan, Kyrgyzstan, and Tajikistan nervous; Shanghai alone has more people than any one of the Central Asian nations, and there are fourteen Chinese cities with more people than tiny Kyrgyzstan. There were few ethnic Chinese left in the Soviet Union when the USSR split up, 11,000 total, of whom only about 4,000 spoke Chinese as their native language. There were (and still are) about 60,000 Donggan (Chinese Muslims known as *Hui* within China) in Kazakhstan and Kyrgyzstan around the time of the Soviet collapse, (Pál 2007: 45).

More importantly, there are a growing number of "new Chinese migrants" (中国新移民 *Zhongguo xin yimin*) who have appeared in the former Soviet territories. In Kazakhstan, for example, it is estimated that there are now over 400,000

Chinese, though accurate figures are difficult to come by. Many are laborers, minor traders, and some are ethnic Kazakhs who are Chinese nationals but are moving back to their "motherland." And some of them are smugglers, human traffickers, criminals, terrorists and supporters of Xinjiang and Chechen independence, and other less-than-desirable elements, and Chinese scholars have begun to recognize that this has created a fear of "Sinification" of Kazakhstan (Zhang Wende and Liu Li 2016: 467–471). Kazakhstani public views of Chinese vary, but one survey in 2008 showed a mixture of indifference, with some positive (and negative) views (Syroezhkin 2009: 33). Complaints of unfair and discriminatory labor practices of Chinese construction firms, and resentment against petty Chinese traders in Kazakhstan and Kyrgyzstan have also been noted (Peyrouse 2016: 217). A Kyrgyz government estimate of the number of Chinese in Kyrgyzstan in 2008 was 60,000, and though many were ethnic Uighurs Chinese nationals, the proportion of Han Chinese was rising (Zhaparov 2008: 89). The somewhat more open political system of Kyrgyzstan makes complaints about Chinese migrants easier, and a variety of issues concerning trucking permits, unfair Chinese government subsidies for traders, unrealistic work expectations for employees and cultural conflict are common (Zhaparov 2008: 84–88). The situation in Tajikistan may be somewhat different, though hard data is difficult to find. A Tajikistani government-based estimate in 2007–08 put the number of Chinese migrants at roughly 11–13,000 people, primarily employees of Chinese companies (Olimova 2008: 71). One more recent estimate is that there are 150,000 Chinese there, a combination of workers, merchants, and investors (Goble 2016). Tajikistani attitudes toward Chinese appear to be slightly more positive than other Central Asian publics, though whether this is because of the public infrastructure being built, or the more professional (and limited) contact with migrant Chinese may be the case. It could also be related to Tajik linguistic identity: unlike the Turkic-speaking peoples of the other Central Asian republics, Tajik is a Persian-related language, limiting both information from their neighbors and sympathy for Turkic-speaking Uighurs (Olimova 2008: 70).

Agricultural development is an area of some concern, although according to Chinese FDI figures (see below) hardly the top sector of investment. Still, Chinese farmers have leased abandoned agricultural tracts in the Russian Far East, where the few remaining local Russians grudgingly respect the diligence and entrepreneurship of the Chinese while nationalists in far-off Moscow worry about encroachment (Higgins 2016a). Chinese tourists in the Russian Far East, meanwhile, casually comment about Vladivostok really "belonging" to China (Higgins 2016b). Fortunately for Sino-Russian diplomatic relations, most of these noises remain below the Kremlin's attention. Similarly, a Chinese proposal to lease unused agricultural land in Kazakhstan in 2009 ran into strident resistance even in less-than-democratic Astana (Blank 2013: 106–107). Tajikistani commentators have charged that Chinese investors are leasing the best land – that with the most water – in Tajikistan (Goble 2016). The grand plans for Xi Jinping's "One Belt, One Road" initiative would unquestionably require large numbers of Chinese engineers and laborers to help build the infrastructure involved; this in turn would continue pressure in a sensitive area, raising the specter of a "Chinese invasion" that may not go back to China when the projects are done (Zhang Wende and Liu Li 2016: 472).

Of course, these Chinese are hardly alone in the Central Asian republics; about a quarter of Kazakhstan's population are ethnic Russians, an advantage for the Russian Federation in the rivalry with China. Russians are 7.7% of Kyrgyzstan's population, 5.5% of Uzbekistan, 4% of Turkmenistan, but far less in Tajikistan. But the long-term trend has been for ethnic Russians to move to the Russian Federation, and thus the trends are not in Moscow's favor.

What is distinct and critical in evaluating the Chinese new migrants into Central Asia is that the Chinese government has not used them as a reason or excuse to engage in military or even police intervention in those countries. China has certainly noted incidents in Central Asia, such as looting of Chinese shops in Kyrgyzstan and labor disputes in Irkutsk (*CFA* 2006: 39). China and Kazakhstan have held regular consular consultations (15 as of 2014), as well as with Russia (18 as of 2014) (*CFA* 2015: 506, 508).

Economic

China needs Central Asian energy; it wants Central Asian markets. Central Asia wants to sell China energy, and have access to its ports and capital. China's economic relationship with Russia and the former Soviet Republics of Central Asia has evolved quite a bit during the 21st century, from low levels of trade to a much more complex economic relationship.

Trade

As noted in Chapter 5, Chinese petroleum demand has increased enormously in the past decade, about 5.4% annually between 2004 and 2015. And as noted in Chapter 7, China's leaders have sought to diversify their foreign sources and transport routes. As of 2015, about 15% of China's crude petroleum came from the Russian Federation or other former Soviet Republics, not nearly the 51% coming from the Middle East or even the 16% from West Africa (BP 2016). Still, these pipeline-based sources avoid sea transportation which could potentially be subject to naval interdiction, and feed into western and central China. Two major oil pipeline projects, one from Kazakhstan and one from Russia have been completed. The China National Offshore Oil Company (CNOOC) and Sinopec gained a share in the rich Kashagan oil field in Kazakhstan after having initially been rejected in 2003 by the rest of the Western consortium (Perlez and Feng 2013).

China's demand for natural gas, in particular, has risen substantially in recent years and in this sector Central Asia plays a much greater role. Estimates are that China will roughly quadruple its natural gas consumption between now and 2040, from 5.1 to 27.5 trillion cubic feet. China's natural gas consumption is thus projected to rise 6.2% per year (EIA 2015). Given the Chinese government's stated goal of reducing carbon dioxide emissions connected with global climate change, and the lower emission rate of natural gas of such greenhouse gasses – 50–60%

less – this is likely to continue to rise in the medium-term. The logical source of that growth is China's Central Asian neighbors which have substantial gas reserves. Table 8.2 shows the reserves as of 2016:

Table 8.2 Central Asian natural gas reserves, 2015

Central Asian natural gas reserves, 2015

Country	Trillion cubic feet	% world reserves
Russia	1,139.6	17.3
Turkmenistan	617.3	9.4
China	135.7	2.1
Kazakhstan	33.1	0.5
Uzbekistan	38.3	0.6

Source: BP 2016.

Thus, China's neighbors in Central Asia have over a quarter of the world's natural gas reserves. The challenge is the routing of the pipelines: Russia's main gas fields lie north of Kazakhstan in west Siberia, and thus must go through that country. Turkmenistan's gas would flow through its Central Asian neighbors, Uzbekistan, Tajikistan, and Kyrgyzstan, once a pipeline infrastructure is established. Needless to say, this also requires cooperation, stability and peaceful relations between all of these states.

Although this energy relationship would seem to imply that China is a net importer from Central Asia, the clearer picture with trade is that both sides have grown considerably between 2004 and 2015, with much of the growth in 2007 and later. Table 8.3 shows the growth since 2004:

Table 8.3 China: total trade with Central Asia, 2004–2015

China: total trade with Central Asia (current US$ million)

	Kazakhstan	Kyrgyzstan	Russia	Tajikistan	Turkmenistan	Uzbekistan
2004	$4,493.3	$602.2	$21,159.2	$68.9	$98.7	$575.2
2005	$6,801.2	$970.5	$29,097.2	$158.1	$109.4	$681.2
2006	$8,358.7	$2,225.8	$33,368.1	$323.7	$178.5	$972.0
2007	$13,866.4	$3,779.6	$48,113.5	$523.9	$351.4	$1,129.3
2008	$17,545.8	$9,335.1	$56,794.8	$1,499.9	$831.4	$1,607.8
2009	$13,981.0	$5,275.7	$38,620.5	$1,402.4	$954.4	$1,909.3
2010	$20,313.6	$4,169.0	$55,402.7	$1,431.2	$1,566.5	$2,477.3
2011	$24,889.9	$4,976.0	$77,929.1	$2,068.9	$5,478.9	$2,165.8
2012	$25,648.4	$5,161.5	$88,025.3	$1,857.0	$9,721.8	$2,875.2
2013	$28,564.1	$5,139.1	$89,172.8	$1,958.6	$10,035.0	$4,532.0
2014	$22,416.9	$5,291.0	$95,243.8	$2,516.9	$10,469.9	$4,270.9
2015	$14,266.7	$4,340.9	$67,955.0	$1,846.9	$8,641.4	$3,503.7

Source: IMF DOTS (2017).

These figures, however, do not show the asymmetry of trade. In 2004, China and Central Asia (including Russia) had imports and exports that were roughly equal, $560–$593 billion. By 2015, however, China was importing $1.6 trillion and exporting $2.2 trillion from Central Asia. Table 8.4 shows the Sino-Russian mutual dependency growing quickly in China's favor:

Table 8.4 China and Russia: mutual trade dependency, 2004–2015

China and Russia: mutual trade dependency, 2004–2015 (% total imports/exports)

	Russia		China	
	Imports from China	*Exports to China*	*Imports from Russia*	*Exports to Russia*
2004	6.9%	6.0%	2.2%	1.5%
2005	7.4%	5.5%	2.4%	1.7%
2006	9.7%	5.4%	2.2%	1.6%
2007	12.2%	4.5%	2.1%	2.3%
2008	13.0%	4.6%	2.1%	2.3%
2009	14.2%	5.6%	2.1%	1.5%
2010	18.0%	5.3%	1.9%	1.9%
2011	15.6%	6.5%	2.2%	2.0%
2012	16.3%	6.8%	2.4%	2.1%
2013	16.9%	6.8%	2.0%	2.2%
2014	17.8%	7.5%	2.1%	2.3%
2015	19.2%	8.3%	2.1%	1.5%

Source: IMF DOTS (2017).

Russia is increasingly dependent on sales to China, especially energy and other raw materials, and Chinese goods are increasingly coming into Russian markets, whereas for China, the Russian Federation represents no more than 2.3% of its imports and about the same for its exports.

Examining the trade relationships with other Central Asian over the past twenty years shows variations and fluctuations, naturally. If any theme develops, it is that Central Asian states have been gradually switching their import sources from their traditional Russian connection to China. They have also been gradually joining the WTO. Of the five Central Asian republics, Kyrgyzstan was first and joined the WTO in 1998, Tajikistan in 2013, and Kazakhstan in late 2015. Russia joined in 2012, and Uzbekistan has observer status, an intent to join. Turkmenistan is the lone hold-out.

Kazakhstan, with the biggest economy next to Russia, as well as a high per capita income, unfortunately does not fully report its trade during this period, but the overall picture is fairly clear: although Russia continues to be Kazakhstan's leading trade partner, China is catching up, especially as a source of imports, where it has over a quarter of the market. The energy effect of Kazakhstan-China relations is clear, with China constituting a growing portion of Kazakhstan's exports, growing from less than 10% of Kazakhstan's 2004 exports to 15–20% in 2011–15. As a result, Kazakhstan enjoys a balance of trade surplus with China in almost every year in question. Chinese products are also increasingly pushing Russian products out of Kazakhstani marketplaces, though Russia is still in the leading position with 33% of the market as opposed to 26% for China in 2015.

Kyrgyzstan is of course a much smaller and poorer economy, though the first Central Asian Republic to be admitted to the World Trade Organization in December 1998. WTO membership, however, has not particularly diversified Kyrgyzstan's trade profile; it is more dependent on exports (primarily gold) to Russia than it was in 1997. Kyrgyzstan's exports to China have remained fairly steady in the $40–50 million range for most of the period; the big change has been its imports of Chinese goods, leading to a very large trade deficit with China, between $4–5 billion annually since 2009. China's market dominance is impressive indeed, over 56% of Kyrgyzstani imports came from China in 2015, the highest dependency ratio seen in this study outside of the immediate postwar period when American commercial dominance over Latin America was similar. It is interesting to note that despite Chinese and Russian concerns that the "Tulip Revolution" represented an American intrusion into Central Asia, little American trade increase can be detected; indeed imports of US products declined after the Tulip Revolution from 4.7% in 2004 to less than 1% in 2009 (IMF DOTS 2017).

The small nature of Tajikistan's export economy is such that in two years (2009–2010) an aluminum deal with China boosted its share of Tajikistan's exports to over 40%. The more consistent trend, however, is the rise of Chinese imports in the Tajikistani market, which rose to over 40% of the market 2011–15, and a decline of Russian market share, and a large trade deficit with China of $1.8–$2.6 billion per year in 2011–15.

Turkmenistan is an outlier in this trade situation, as it is with almost every international issue in Central Asia. Rich in natural gas, and with extensive trade relations with neighboring Iran and even more with Turkey, Turkmenistan's gas exports to China make it the only Central Asian state with a greater export dependency on China than an import dependency, and the only one with a balance of trade surplus, $6.2 billion in 2015 alone. Turkmenistan's imports of Chinese and Russian goods are roughly equal.

Although not as dramatic as other partners, Uzbekistan's trade profile, especially its imports, have also shifted from Russia to China, to the point that the market share in 2015 was exactly even. China has a somewhat higher export share of Uzbekistan, mostly energy.

Investment

Some of the pipeline development would involve Chinese foreign direct investment in state joint ventures with Central Asian partners, such as KazMunayGas of Kazakhstan. Table 8.5 shows the Foreign Direct Investment flows of China into Central Asia from 2004 to 2014:

Table 8.5 China: foreign direct investment flows in Central Asia, 2004–2014

China: Central Asia foreign direct investment flows, 2004–2014 (current US$ million)

	Russia	Kazakhstan	Kyrgyzstan	Tajikistan	Uzbekistan	Turkmenistan
2004	$77.3	$2.3	$5.3	$5.0	$1.1	
2005	$203.3	$94.9	$13.7	$0.8	$0.1	
2006	$452.1	$46.0	$27.6	$7.0	$1.1	$(0.0)
2007	$477.6	$279.9	$15.0	$67.9	$13.2	$1.3
2008	$395.2	$496.4	$7.1	$26.6	$39.4	$86.7
2009	$348.2	$66.8	$136.9	$16.7	$4.9	$119.7
2010	$567.7	$36.0	$82.5	$15.4	$(4.6)	$450.5
2011	$715.8	$581.6	$145.1	$22.1	$88.3	$(383.0)
2012	$784.6	$2,996.0	$161.4	$234.1	$(26.8)	$12.3
2013	$1,022.3	$811.5	$203.4	$72.3	$44.2	$(32.4)
2014	$633.6	$(40.1)	$107.8	$107.2	$180.6	$195.2

Source: Ministry of Commerce, 2011–2014.

Although Chinese FDI is small compared to world FDI into Russia and Kazakhstan, which had inward world FDI positions (net cumulative FDI) in 2014 of $272 billion and $128 billion respectively, of which Chinese FDI flows calculated by the IMF were 1% and 3.1% respectively. Chinese FDI in Kyrgyz Republic and Tajikistan are quite significant. In Kyrgyzstan, China is the second leading investor after Canada at 23.1% of the world FDI of $3.2 billion in 2014 (IMF CDIS 2016). Data for tiny Tajikistan's FDI positions in 2014 were incomplete, but we do know of the $300 investment in Tajik Aluminum in 2012 by China National Building Materials Corporation (China Global Investment Tracker 2017). Turkmenistan and Uzbekistan were similarly circumspect with their FDI figures, though UNCTAD's FDI estimates that there were in 2014 annual flows of $263 million to Tajikistan, $4.1 billion to Turkmenistan, and $626 million to Uzbekistan (UNCTAD WIR 2017). The sum of all of this is to say that although we have widely discrepant figures and sources about Chinese FDI in Central Asia, China is investing there in significant amounts.

Works cited

Blank, Stephen. 2013. Kazakhstan's border relations with China, in *Beijing's Power and China's Borders: Twenty Neighbors in Asia*, edited by Bruce A. Elleman, Stephen Kotkin, and Clive Schofield. Armonk, NY: M.E. Sharpe, 96–109.

Blank, Stephen. 2016. Need for closer ties with Beijing clouds Moscow's view of the SCO. *Eurasia Daily Monitor*, 5 July. <https://jamestown.org/program/need-for-closer-ties-with-beijing-clouds-moscows-view-of-the-sco/>, accessed 5 July 2016.

BP. 2016. Statistical review of world energy 2016. <www.bp.com/en/global/corporate/energy-economics/statistical-review-of-world-energy.html>, accessed 26 November 2016.

CFA [China's Foreign Affairs]. Annual. Beijing: Ministry of Foreign Affairs of the People's Republic of China. This is the official yearbook of the Ministry of Foreign Affairs of the People's Republic of China. Beginning its publication in 1987 as 中国外交概览 China's Foreign Affairs review, it is hereafter referred to as ZGWJGL, and after 1995 中国外交 it is renamed Zhongguo waijiao (ZGWJ) for the Chinese language version, and China's Foreign Affairs or CFA for the English-language version, which began publication in 2003. See also ZGWJ.

Chen Xiaoding, and Ma Ru. 2015. Shanghai zuzhi zai sichou zhi lu jingji dai zhong de zouyong yu lujing xuanze [The role and options for the Shanghai Cooperation Organization vis-à-vis the Silk Road Economic Belt]. *Dangdai YaTai*, (6), 63–81.

China Global Investment Tracker. 2017. American Enterprise Institute, July. <www.aei.org/china-global-investment-tracker/>, accessed 25 April 2017.

Contessi, Nicola P. 2010. China, Russia and the leadership of the SCO: A tacit deal scenario. *China and Eurasia Forum Quarterly*, 8(4), 101–123.

Cooley, Alexander. 2012. Op-Ed: In Central Asia, public cooperation and private rivalry. *New York Times*, 8 June. <www.nytimes.com/2012/06/09/opinion/in-central-asia-public-cooperation-and-private-rivalry.html>, accessed 9 June 2012.

Duchâtel, Mathieu. 2016. Terror overseas: Understanding China's evolving counter-terror strategy. *European Council on Foreign Relations Policy Brief* (no. 193), October. <ecfr.eu>, accessed 4 June 2017.

EIA. 2015. China: US Energy Information Administration website, 14 May. <www.eia.gov/beta/international/analysis_includes/countries_long/China/china.pdf>, accessed 28 November 2016.

Fedoruk, Vladimir. 2011. Russia, China don't see US in SCO. *Radio the Voice of Russia*, 1 November. <http://english.ruvr.ru/2011/11/01/59706557/>, accessed 30 March 2013.

Feng, Bree. 2014. The horse at the heart of Chinese-Turkmen relations. *New York Times*, 13 May. <http://sinosphere.blogs.nytimes.com/201/04/13/the-horse-at-the-heart-of-chinese-turkmen-relations.html>, accessed 13 May 2014.

Gabuev, Alexander. 2016. Russia and China: Little brother or big sister? Carnegie Moscow Center, 5 July. <http://carnegie.ru/commentary/?fa=64006>, accessed 15 September 2016.

Galeotti, Mark. 2013. Sino-Russian border resolution, in *Beijing's Power and China's Borders: Twenty Neighbors in Asia*, edited by Bruce A. Elleman, Stephen Kotkin, and Clive Schofield. Armonk, NY: M.E. Sharpe, 250–265.

Gill, Bates, and Murphy, Melissa. 2005. China's evolving approach to counterterrorism. *Harvard Asia Quarterly*, (Winter/Spring), 21–32.

Gleason, Gregory. 2013. Tajikistan-China border normalization, in *Beijing's Power and China's Borders: Twenty Neighbors in Asia*, edited by Bruce A. Elleman, Stephen Kotkin, and Clive Schofield. Armonk, NY: M.E. Sharpe, 282–291.

Goble, Paul. 2016. China quietly displacing both Russia and US from Central Asia. *Eurasia Daily Monitor*, 13(140), 2 August. <https://jamestown.org/program/china-quietly-displacing-both-russia-and-us-from-central-asia/>, accessed 3 August 2016.

Higgins, Andrew. 2016a. Russia's acres, if not its locals, beckon Chinese farmers. *New York Times*, 31 July. <www.nytimes.com/2016/08/01/world/asia/russia-china-farmers.html>, accessed 1 August 2016.

Higgins, Andrew. 2016b. Vladivostok lures Chinese tourists (many think it's theirs). *New York Times*, 23 July. <www.nytimes.com/2016/07/24/world/asia/vladivostok-china-haishenwai-tourists.html>, accessed 24 July 2016.

Hiro, Dilip. 2006. Shanghai surprise. *The Guardian*, 16 June. <www.guardian.co.uk/commentisfree/2006/jun/16/shanghaisurprise>, accessed 30 March 2013.

"Hu Jintao." 2016. China Vitae. <www.chinavitae.com/biography/Hu_Jintao|19>, accessed 21 December 2016.
IMF CDIS [Coordinated Direct Investment Survey]. 2016. IMF e-library, <data.imf.org/CDS>, accessed September 2016.
IMF DOTS [Direction of Trade Statistics]. 2017. IMF e-library. <data.imf.org/>, accessed various dates 2013–17.
Jia Lihong. 2010. Ji'erjisitan dui Zhongguo de zhongyao xingji qi dangjin jushi dui Zhongguo de yingxiang [Kyrgyzstan's significance to China and its current influence on China]. *Xinjiang daxue xuebao (zhexue renwen shehui kexue ban)* [Journal of Xinjiang University (Philosophy, Humanities & Social Sciences)], 38(6), 92–96.
"Kazakhstan: The bear on the doorstep." 2014. *The Economist*, 21 June, 41.
Kirişci, Kemal, and Le Corre, Philippe. 2015. The great game that never ends: China and Russia fight over Kazakhstan. Order from Chaos, article. Brookings, 18 December. <www.brookings.edu/blog/order-from-chaos/2015/12/18/the-great-game-that-never-ends-china-and-russia-fight-over-kazakhstan/>, accessed 7 January 2016.
Lee, Rensselaer, and Lukin, Artyom. 2016. *Russia's Far East: New Dynamics in Asia Pacific & Beyond*. Boulder: Lynne Rienner.
Li Qi. 2014. "Lěngzhàn" yǔ kùnjìng: Wūzībiékè sītǎn yǔ tǎjíkè sītǎn guānxì zǒuxiàng ["Cold war" and the dilemma of Uzbekistan-Tajikistan relations]. *Eluosi Dongou Zhongya yanjiu* [Russia, Eastern Europe and Central Asia Research], (1), 46–54.
Marat, Erica. 2013. Kyrgyzstan: China's regional playground?, in *Beijing's Power and China's Borders: Twenty Neighbors in Asia*, edited by Bruce A. Elleman, Stephen Kotkin, and Clive Schofield. Armonk, NY: M.E. Sharpe, 126–141.
Michel, Casey. 2016. Line D of the Central Asia-China gas pipeline delayed. *The Diplomat*, 31 May. <http://thediplomat.com/2016/05/line-d-of-the-central-asia-china-gas-pipeline-delayed/>, accessed 1 June 2016.
Ministry of Commerce of the PRC. 2011–2015. *Statistical Bulletin of China's Outward Foreign Direct Investment*. Beijing: China Statistics Press. Annual.
Nechepurenko, Ivan. 2016. Suicide bomber attacks Chinese embassy in Kyrgyzstan. *New York Times*, 30 August. <www.nytimes.com/2016/08/31/world/asia/bishkek-china-embassy-kyrgyzstan.html>, accessed 30 August 2016.
Olimova, Saodat. 2008. The multifaceted Chinese presence in Tajikistan. *China and Eurasia Forum Quarterly*, 7(1), 61–77.
Pál, Nyíri. 2007. *Chinese in Eastern Europe and Russia: A Middleman Minority in a Transnational Era*. London: Routledge.
Parello-Plesner, Jonas, and Duchâtel, Mathieu. 2015. *China's Strong Arm: Protecting Citizens and Assets Abroad*. London: International Institute for Strategic Studies.
Perlez, Jane. 2013. China looks West as it bolsters regional ties. *New York Times*, 7 September. <www.nytimes.com/2013/09/08/world/asia/china-looks-west-as-it-strengthens-regional-ties.html>, accessed 8 September 2013.
Perlez, Jane, and Feng, Bree. 2013. China gains new friends in its quest for energy. *New York Times*, 23 September. <www.nytimes.com/2013/09/24/world/asia/china-gains-new-friends-in-its-quest-for-energy.html>, accessed 24 September 2013.
Peyrouse, Sebastien. 2016. China and Central Asia, in *The New Great Game: China and South and Central Asia in the Era of Reform*, edited by Thomas Fingar. Stanford: Stanford University Press, 216–239.
Plater-Zyberk, Henry, and Monaghan, Andrew. 2014. *Strategic Implications of the Evolving Shanghai Cooperation Organization*. Carlisle Barracks, PA: Strategic Studies Institute.

Quinn-Judge, Katharine, and Stronski, Paul. 2016. Kyrgyzstan at twenty-five: Treading water: The Global Think Tank, article. Carnegie Endowment for International Peace, 21 July. <http://carnegieendowment.org/2016/07/21/kyrgyzstan-at-twenty-five-treading-water-pub-64152>, accessed 22 July 2016.

"Russia obtains military base prolongation in Kyrgyzstan." 2012. Gazette of Central Asia, 18 August 2012. <http://gca.satrapia.com/russia-obtains-military-base-prolongation-in-kyrgyzstan>, accessed 14 January 2017.

Scheineson, Andrew. 2009. The Shanghai Cooperation Organization: Council on foreign relations, 24 March. <www.cfr.org/international-peace-and-security/shanghai-cooperation-organization/p10883>, accessed 30 March 2013.

Shanghai Cooperation Organization Secretariat. 2015. Agreement on cooperation and interaction of the member states of the Shanghai Cooperation Organization on border issues. SCO Secretariat website. <http://eng.sectsco.org>, accessed 2 June 2017.

Song, Weiqing. 2014. Interests, power and China's difficult game in the Shanghai Cooperation Organization (SCO). *Journal of Contemporary China*, 23(85), 85–101.

START. 2016. National consortium for the study of terrorism and responses to terrorism. Global Terrorism Database [Data file]. <www.start.umd.edu/gtd>.

Stern, David L. 2008. Security group refuses to back Russia's actions. *New York Times*, 28 August. <www.nytimes.com/2008/08/29/world/europe/29russia.html>, accessed 2 June 2017.

Stronski, Paul. 2016. Kazakhstan at twenty-five: Stable but tense. Global Think Tank, article. 4 February. Carnegie Endowment for International Peace. <carnegieendowment.org/2016/02/04/kazakhstan-at-twenty-five-stable-but-tense-pub-62642>, accessed 22 July 2016.

Sun Zhuangzhi. 2007. From neighbors to partners. *Beijing Review*, 1 February, 12–13.

Syroezhkin, Konstantin. 2009. Social perceptions of China and the Chinese: A view from Kazakhstan. *China and Eurasia Forum Quarterly*, 7(1), 29–46.

UNCTAD WIR [World Investment Report]. 2017. World Investment Report. <http://unctad.org/en/Pages/DIAE/World%20Investment%20Report/World_Investment_Report.aspx>, accessed various dates 2013–17.

Wang Shuchun, and Liu Si'en. 2015. Eluosike xin Yazhou zhanlue yi qi dui Zhong-E guanxi de xingxiang [Russia's new Asia strategy and its implication for Sino-Russia relations]. *Dangdai YaTai*, (6), 82–100.

Wayne, Martin I. 2009. Inside China's war on terrorism. *Journal of Contemporary China*, 18(59), 249–261.

Weitz, Richard. 2015. *China and Afghanistan after the NATO Withdrawal*. Washington, DC: Jamestown Foundation.

World Bank. 2017. World development indicators [Online]. 2017. <http://data.worldbank.org/data-catalog/world-development-indicators>.

Xi Jinping. 2017. Upholding solidarity, coordination, openness and inclusiveness: Building a common home of security, stability, development and prosperity: Full text of Chinese President Xi's speech at 17th SCO summit. Xinhua, 9 June. <http://news.xinhuanet.com/english/2017-06/09/c_136353884.htm>, accessed 9 June 2017.

Xinhua. 2017. Spotlight: "Historic" SCO summit to bring new opportunities for cooperation. Xinhua News Agency, 9 June. <http://news.xinhuanet.com/english/2017-06/08/c_136349429.htm>, accessed 9 June 2017.

Yang Shu, and Guo Xugang. 2015. Meiguo dui Hasakesitan gonggong waijiao shuping [Review of US public diplomacy to Kazakhstan]. *Eluosi Dongou Zhongya yanjiu*, (3), 79–88.

Yang Tao. 2012. Jiaqiang Shanghai Hezuo Zuzhi fankong hezuo mianlin de tiaozhan yu yingdui cuoshi [Strengthening the Shanghai Cooperation Organization's anti-terrorism cooperation and response measures]. *Hubei jingguan xueyuan xuebao*, (3), 96–98.

Yu Haiyang. 2012. Shang He Zuzhi shi yifu huanyao [SCO is a gradual solution]. *Zhongguo jingji zhoukan*, 6 June, 21.

Yuan, Jing-dong. 2010. China's role in establishing and building the Shanghai Cooperation Organization (SCO). *Journal of Contemporary China*, 19(67), 855–869.

ZGWJ. [Zhongguo waijiao] [China's diplomacy]. Annual. Beijing: Ministry of Foreign Affairs of the People's Republic of China. This is the official yearbook of the Ministry of Foreign Affairs of the People's Republic of China. Beginning its publication in 1987 as 中国外交概览 China's Foreign Affairs review, it is hereafter referred to as ZGWJGL, and after 1995 中国外交 it is renamed Zhongguo waijiao (ZGWJ) for the Chinese language version, and China's Foreign Affairs or CFA for the English-language version, which began publication in 2003.

Zhang Wende, and Liu Li. 2016. Hesankesitan Zhongguo xin yimin tanxi [The issue of Chinese new migrants in Kazakhstan]. *Huaiyin shifan daxue xuebao: zhexue shehui kexue ban* [Journal of Huayin Teachers College: Social Science], 38(4), 467–473.

Zhaparov, Amantur. 2008. The issue of Chinese migrants in Kyrgyzstan. *China and Eurasia Forum Quarterly*, 7(1), 79–91.

9 China and South Asia in the 21st century

India's dominant relations with the states of South Asia – Afghanistan, Pakistan, Bangladesh, Nepal, Sri Lanka, and the Maldives – have been outlined in Chapter 2. No other post-WWII regional hegemon is more dominant in its region than India is with these former colonies of Britain. And, for that reason, Pakistan especially looks across the Himalayas for Chinese protection, one of the four fundamental elements of China's relations with the region. India in turn deeply resents and seeks to counter any other power's intrusion into "its" area, an exclusionary doctrine, and which the other countries of the subcontinent resist. That is the second element of South Asia's international relations with China. The third is an unresolved territorial dispute between China and India which shows little prospect of resolution. In the 21st century, periodic efforts at improving relations between China and India raise hopes, only to see promises not kept, negotiations drag on, deals delayed indefinitely, and minor aggravations crop up. In the meanwhile, China's relations with Pakistan and Sri Lanka have improved, now pushed along by the infrastructure promises of the "Maritime Silk Road."

The fourth key element in China's relations with four of the states in South Asia – Afghanistan, Pakistan, Nepal, and India – somewhat parallel the relationship of Xinjiang and Central Asia. The issue of Afghanistan and Pakistan helping make sure that Uighur militants do not find safe refuge in those countries is similar to the other "-stans" of Central Asia. Just as China is concerned about Uighur independence, so too it is concerned with Tibetan independence. Unlike Central Asia which does not openly host any Uighur national movement, India does host the Tenzin Gyatso, the 14th Dalai Lama and the Central Tibetan Administration, a sort of government-in-exile (though India does not recognize it as such). With large Tibetan exile communities in both India (between 100,000 and 120,000) and Nepal (20–30,000), as well as in other diaspora communities, control of Tibetan ingress and egress is a paramount issue for China in its trans-Himalayan relations.

The other states of South Asia, however, often see in China a means of balancing against India, especially Pakistan. Nepal, in contrast, is highly constrained by its geographic and transportation dependence on India; Bhutan is barely allowed to have its own foreign policy, and Sikkim – invaded and annexed by India in 1975 – serves as a reminder to all of India's neighbors of the potential cost of offending New Delhi. But China's goods, investments, aid, construction projects, and diplomats continue to edge into South Asia.

Security

China's relations with South Asia share some common characteristics with Central Asia: a region that is historically defined by the imperialism of an external power whose inheritors continue to see it as "their" region. There is also an autonomous region under pressure from an ethnic group, and a Chinese fear that it may again be "split" under this pressure. The differences, however, are also significant, since none of the governments in Russia or Central Asia have any support for Uighur separatists, whereas the Dalai Lama resides in India with a large exile Tibetan community, and a great deal of foreign sympathy. Another key difference is that China strongly supports India's primary rival, Pakistan, very much as Brazil supported Chile against their common foe Argentina during the 19th and early 20th centuries. In Central Asia, China has shown no inclination to support Kazakhstan in opposition to Russia, or Ukraine against Russia. But in this respect, China does provide security public goods to Pakistan at least and to a lesser extent Sri Lanka, Bangladesh, and even Nepal as a possible balance against Indian hegemony. China is also involved in peace negotiations between the Taliban and the Afghan government, a fairly minimal provision of security public goods (Wong and Jolly 2016).

Territorial disputes

China's sole remaining significant land-based territorial dispute with its neighbors is with India. It is large, long-standing, populated, and unlikely to be resolved soon. What is in dispute are actually two areas, the Aksai Chin area, which is mountainous and sparsely populated in the northwest sector, and the other in the northeast which encompasses much of India calls the state of "Arunachal Pradesh," which prior to 1972 was called the "North-East Frontier Agency." The Chinese call it "South Tibet." About 1.3 million people call it "home." It forms an important watershed of the Brahmaputra river, and has hydroelectric potential. One of the most important towns in the region is Tawang which was attached to Tibet before 1914 and occupied by PLA troops in October-November 1962 during the border war. Some analysts believe the Chinese are increasingly strident about Tawang because it could be used by the 14th Dalai Lama to legitimize his reincarnation outside of Tibet, and outside of Chinese control (Ramachandran 2017a: 15). The Aksai Chin is high and desolate, but is a critical connection for Chinese roads between southern Xinjiang and western Tibet. As recently as April 2017, China pushed its version of "South Tibet" by publishing six place names (in Chinese, English, and Tibetan) in Indian-controlled territory, shortly after the Dalai Lama visited the area (Blanchard 2017).

The Sino-Nepalese border was negotiated in 1961, except for the places where the three borders of China, Nepal, and India come together, their trijunctions (Tiwari 2013: 205). China and Bhutan also have two tiny additional territorial disputes, one in the north in the Jakarlung and Pasamlung valleys, roughly 500 km^2 and a smaller one in the west on the Doklam Plateau along the Chumbi Valley of about 270 km^2. Of the two, Indian considers the western area critical, since its possession would expose the Siliguri corridor, or "chicken neck," the narrow part of India that wraps around Bangladesh and connects its northeastern states with the rest of India. Although China and Bhutan do not have formal diplomatic relations, they have been negotiating about these disputed areas for over thirty years, in over twenty rounds of talks, and came close to an agreement in 1996 but the Bhutanese side increased its claims (possibly at Indian instigation) and the talks broke down (Shakya 2017). One Chinese diplomat indicated in 2010 that the major issues had been largely resolved (Smith 2013: 32–33). Details have not been released, and the Indians are concerned that Bhutan is trading the Doklam Plateau for the northern valleys. It is unlikely that Bhutan will be willing to finalize these disputes until India resolves its much larger dispute with China. And that does not seem likely.

In the summer of 2017, the border issue between China and Bhutan became a major Sino-Indian problem when Indian soldiers moved into a disputed area between China and Bhutan to stop Chinese soldiers from building a road in the Doklam region, in the wedge of Tibetan territory that separates the Indian state of Sikkim from Bhutan. From the Indian perspective, the road south is a direct threat to India's territorial integrity. The Chinese see it as Indian military trespassing on Chinese territory (Shakya 2017).

There was another incident started by China in 2013 that made many analysts wonder whether the "assertiveness" seen in Beijing's South China Sea behavior was also being applied in the Sino-Indian borderlands. The incident, near Daulat Beg Oldi (Tiannan River Valley in Chinese) in the Ladakh part of the Aksai Chin sector, where the Line of Actual Control (LAC) is not defined: Chinese and Indian claims overlap, and the two sides have followed a policy in which patrols into the overlapping zones purposefully avoid one another, return to the areas that are (more) clearly under their control and do not camp. The area, a desolate wasteland above 16,300 feet/4,968 meters, is hardly a prize worth taking but in April 2013, Chinese troops on patrol pitched their tents and the Indians pitched a fit (Harris and Wong 2013). The Chinese troops stayed for almost three weeks, and local Chinese and Indian commanders did most of the negotiating, including revealing that the Chinese contended that Indian bunkers recently constructed in the area were the source of Chinese displeasure. By May 2013, both sides had once again withdrawn, and quiet diplomacy had one of its rarely publicized victories.

The tiny border between Afghanistan and China, linking the Afghan Wakhan corridor to Xinjiang, was negotiated in 1963 (Kalinovsky 2013: 12). The Chinese border with Pakistan was settled in 1963 but in the process, the Pakistani side conceded territory to China in the Karakoram mountain range that India claims; from Indians' perspective, the Pakistanis gave away their land. That these are some of the highest and most isolated areas of the world is immaterial to the claim of injustice (Tang 2013: 220–221). Further west, in the Gilgit-Baltistan area leading up to Khunjerab Pass where the Karakoram Highway crosses into China, the

Indian government continues its territorial claim. Thus, the key to the territorial claims in the area are between China and India.

Military intervention

Afghanistan and Pakistan are two very dangerous places for Chinese to go, and over a dozen Chinese were killed there since 2004 as well as kidnappings and assaults (Parello-Plesner and Duchâtel 2015: 76). Given that there are over 10,000 Chinese personnel in Pakistan working on projects there, their security has been a high priority in talks between Chinese, Afghan and Pakistani officials, often involving State Councilor Zhou Yongkang until his 2012 retirement (and subsequent disgrace) and later Meng Jianzhu, who took over the security portfolio in China. China has quietly encouraged Pakistani officials to step up security surrounding Chinese projects, and also maintaining contacts with a wide variety of political groups in these two countries, including the Afghan Taliban (Parello-Plesner and Duchâtel 2015: 82–85). Thus, despite difficult security conditions that have cost lives and property, there are no confirmed direct Chinese interventions in its South Asian neighbors during this period.[1]

External major powers

South Asia, like Central Asia, is dominated by a great power, in this case India. The United States beginning in 2001 also established a presence in Afghanistan, which necessitated reviving its relationship with Pakistan, which had been frozen in 1998 after Pakistan followed India and tested nuclear weapons. That was followed by the long and difficult war in Afghanistan, mutual recriminations about the conduct of the war, the harboring of Al Qaeda leadership across the porous Afghan-Pakistan border, the continued insurgency of Taliban forces in the region. Relations were further strained by US drone strikes and civilian casualties, and beginning in 2013 NATO forces began to withdraw from Afghanistan, but a contingent of trainers and special operations forces remains as of 2017, over six years after the USA announced it was going to "pivot" to the Asia-Pacific.

US-Indian relations have improved between 2004 and 2017, but India has been reluctant to explicitly join the USA in an anti-China coalition. Its history and reputation as a non-aligned country remains a cornerstone of New Delhi's grand strategy, and picking fights with the Chinese Navy in places such as the Spratlys and the Senkaku islands seems to be carrying the Americans' water. The lifting of the 1998 prohibition against civilian nuclear power cooperation in 2006 was a significant step toward improving US-Indian relations. By 2007 India joined the USA, Japan, and Australia in the Quadrilateral Security Dialogue, though the Indians, Japanese and Australians were circumspect about the focus of the Dialogue. President Obama's visits to India in 2010 and 2015 especially have helped bring the USA and India closer. The joint statement from that visit included the pointed phrase, "We affirm the importance of safeguarding maritime security and ensuring freedom of navigation and over flight throughout the region, especially in the

South China Sea" (White House 2015). There can be little doubt as to who that was directed against. Prime Minister Modi visited Washington in June 2017. But when the USA proposed that India join in joint Freedom of Navigation patrols in the South China Sea, India once again demurred, as did Australia and Japan. The US government has also been quiet about the Bhutan border issue in the summer of 2017, though whether that reflects a choice or foreign policy neglect is unclear.

The United States has sold over $3 billion in arms to India between 2004 and 2016, $2 billion in 2013 and 2014, largely the anti-submarine warfare P-8I Poseidon aircraft (SIPRI TIV 2017). The US Navy, Indian Navy, and Japan Maritime Self-Defense Force have jointly participated in annual Malabar naval exercises. The exercises were revived in 2002 and each year have grown in size and complexity, in some years operating in the Indian Ocean, and in some years near Okinawa. The 2007 exercises in the Bay of Bengal were the subject of Chinese discomfort, since this was the largest exercise to date, was located in the Bay of Bengal – near Myanmar and Bangladesh – and included Australian and Singaporean vessels as well as the US carriers Nimitz and Kitty Hawk. Subsequent years' exercises have waxed and waned, with Japanese participation in Malabar 2009, 2011, and 2014 when near Japan, but in 2015 Japan became a permanent partner in the exercise, and again sent ships to the Indian Ocean. Small-scale land joint exercises called "Yudh Abhyas" began in 2004 and continue today.

Finally, Russia continues to play a minor role in South Asia, largely to show that it is still a great power that must be reckoned with. Its most important role is selling weapons to its traditional ally India, $25.2 billion worth between 2004 and 2016, dwarfing China's $5.2 billion sales to Pakistan in the same period and US sales to India (SIPRI 2017 TIV tables). The deals include Su-30 multi-role fighter aircraft, helicopters, T-90S tanks, frigates, nuclear submarines, and an aircraft carrier, the INS *Vikramaditya* (ex- *Admiral Gorshkov*. Thus, both India and China have purchased and are operating left-over Soviet carriers.) The Russians also developed their own infrastructure/transportation proposal in 2002, the North-South Transport Corridor, which involves India, Iran, Azerbaijan, and Russia as a quicker bypass to the maritime route through the Suez Canal (Spector 2002). As of 2016, it was getting closer but still wasn't done (Ismailzade 2016).

Diplomatic relations with regional states

China's relations with South Asia in the 21st century have had a very significant "de-linking" in which China has sought to officially terminate the explicit link between its relations with Pakistan and its relations with India. The process began earlier, and John W. Garver dates the effort to between 1988 and Jiang Zemin's visit to India in 1996. The Bharatiya Janata Party (BJP) government in 1998 sought unsuccessfully to re-link the relationship, making any progress on Sino-Indian relations wholly dependent on China repudiating its former ally. The Chinese side at most would take a neutral view of South Asian issues such as the Kashmir dispute (Garver 2001: 221–225). This delinkage notwithstanding, China's relations with Pakistan remain an extremely sensitive issue for India's leaders.

Table 9.1 China's "partners" and "strategic relations" in South Asia, 2004–2014

State	Designation	Date
Afghanistan	Strategic and Cooperative Partnership	2013
	Comprehensive and Cooperative Partnership	2006
Bangladesh	Strategic Cooperative Partnership	2016
	Comprehensive Partnership	2005
Bhutan	(no diplomatic relations)	
India	Strategic and Cooperative Partnership for Peace and Prosperity	2005
Maldives	Comprehensive Friendly and Cooperative Partnership	2014
Nepal	Comprehensive Partnership	2009
Pakistan	All-Weather Strategic Cooperative Partnership	2005
Sri Lanka	Strategic Cooperative Partnership	2013
	Comprehensive Cooperative Partnership	2007

Source: *China's Foreign Relations* 2005–2014. Bangladesh: Paul (2016).

Pakistan

It would be no exaggeration to say that Pakistan is China's best neighbor: the relationship has been stable, useful for both sides, and has few irritants. It is, of course, it was founded on a firm basis of common adversary, India. China describes the relationship as "all-weather" (全天候/*quan tianhou*) both as an indication of how long the relationship has been positive despite the many changes of context, both in government in Pakistan and international environment, and as an implicit criticism of the fair-weather support the United States has given to Pakistan over the years. During the years, Pakistan has been consistent in backing China's core foreign policy lines: the one China policy, no Taiwanese representation in the United Nations, support for the Chinese positions on Tibet, Xinjiang, the East Turkistan Islamic Movement, and in 2012 at the ASEAN Regional Forum, the South China Sea (*China's Foreign Affairs* [hereafter *CFA*] 2013: 243). There were four formal state visits between the President of China and the President of Pakistan between 2003 and 2007. There were also three visits by Pakistani President Asif Ali Zardari in 2009 and one in 2010 that were "working visits" and, in April 2015, one from Xi Jinping. The latter visit gained attention beyond South Asia because it was one of Xi's biggest proposals for his signature "One Belt, One Road" idea.

Gwadar Sea Port is the centerpiece of China's initiative in Pakistan called the China-Pakistan Economic Corridor (CPEC), and (potentially) the key that links the 21st Century Maritime Silk Road with the Silk Road Economic Belt. It has been described as the "flagship" of the Belt and Road Initiative. The idea of a major deep-water port there goes back to the 1970s, and its geographic location could not be more favorable. China built the first phase of the project before the CPEC was formally announced, finishing it in late 2006 and formally opened it in March 2007. At the regional level, the port is near the Persian Gulf and thus could protect (or interdict) Arabian oil flows to Asia. At the local level, the port itself is on an island linked by a narrow neck of land to the city of Gwadar per se, making port security much more manageable. The 2015 deals included funding for dredging, breakwaters, an airport, fresh water treatment, a hospital, and a technical institute (Pakistan Board of Investment 2016). Conveniently, a major Pakistani naval base, the PNS Akram, is adjacent to port. Though Chinese statements about Gwadar focus solely on the commercial aspects, Pakistanis are much more open in seeing it as a possible naval base for Chinese assets. A former Pakistani naval officer went so far as to say in 2017,

> [The Gwadar port] . . . will allow the Chinese Navy to establish a robust foothold in the Indian Ocean. Pakistan's coastline is becoming a crucial staging post for China's takeoff as a naval power. . . . Pakistan's ports, which overlook some of the world's busiest oil shipping lanes, are key building blocks in a "string of pearls."
>
> (Khan 2017: 52)

The weak link in the China-Pakistan Economic Corridor is ground transportation from Gwadar up through the rest of Pakistan, and in particular through Baluchistan province, where a persistent insurgency makes construction difficult. Three different routes are anticipated, western, central, and eastern, with roads and pipelines, and each with its own political difficulties (Ramachandran 2015c). The port is not currently connected to the Pakistani rail network, and the idea of laying a major railway is currently being studied. How far north all of these would go is another issue. Linking all the way to China would pass through the Gilgit-Baltistan area which is controlled by Pakistan but is claimed by India. Proposals envision a Havelian-Kashi railway through the Khunjerab Pass and linking to the Kashgar-Hotan Railway in Xinjiang on the other side. In addition to the break-of-gauge problem (Pakistan's railways mostly use the 1,676 mm Indian gauge, instead of the 1,435 mm Standard gauge China uses), the technical challenges would be immense for a railroad, though the Karakoram Highway already traverses the Sino-Pakistan border at Khunjerab Pass. It is not open during the winter, however.

The China-Pakistan Economic Corridor projects also include "early harvest" deals such as fourteen power plants (half of them coal, half of them alternative energy) to help the strained Pakistani electric grid, and in fact these projects are over three-quarters of the total $44.4 billion in loans and aid that Xi Jinping brought to Pakistan during his April 2015 visit (Pakistan Board of Investment 2016). There have been other Chinese projects and investments in Pakistan that were not formally linked to the CPEC/One Belt One Road idea, such as the second phase of the Chashma Nuclear Power Plant, the Saindak Copper-Gold Mine, and the Haier-Ruba Economic Zone, a consumer application-production facility. Although there is mention in 2010 of a currency-swap arrangement of the kind China has provided extensively in Southeast Asia, few details were given (*CFA* 2012: 232).

For most of the period, China had to deal with Pervez Musharraf, Pakistan's leader (first PM and then President) who seized power in a 1999 coup d'état. After Musharraf stepped down (and ran away), democratic processes were restored in 2008, and China has reached out to the leaders of the major Pakistani political parties, the Muslim League, the Pakistan People's Party, and even the newly founded Tehreek-e-Insaf (PTI), the centrist party led by Imran Khan, a famous former cricket player. Nawaz Sharif, until, in August 2017, the PM and head of the Muslim League, came into office promising to improve relations with India, but there is little open evidence that this disturbed China, or that China favors particular parties in Pakistan.

China was Pakistan's largest single supplier of arms in 2004–2015, with almost $5.2 billion in sales and 47% of its market, though the United States was also a major supplier. Unlike the United States which has periodically embargoed arms sales to Pakistan, China has always been ready, willing and able to supply equipment. The Chinese-Pakistani jointly-developed JF-17 jet aircraft were a major portion of the overall sales. Frigates, corvettes, patrol vessels and submarines were also included, as well as tanks. Significantly, many of these were joint production projects, involving assembly and some of the production in Pakistan (SIPRI TIV 2017). Military exchanges between China and Pakistan are particularly frequent, with the Pakistani Chair of the Joint Chiefs of Staff Committee or branch Chiefs of Staff visiting each year from 2004 to 2014. In 2007 alone there were forty-three Chinese and Pakistani delegations who exchanged visits. The first joint naval exercises started modestly in 2003 when Pakistani ships visiting Shanghai participated in a search-and-rescue exercise; thereafter there were joint counter-terrorism exercises in 2004, the same year several Chinese were killed and kidnapped in Pakistan, and thereafter counter-terrorism and security provision for Chinese personnel in Pakistan became a frequent topic in the visits (*CFA* 2004–2014).

India

China has been seeking to improve its relations with India since the late 1980s. It is not, however, particularly sensitive to Indian concerns. Indian leaders and attentive public opinion view Chinese initiatives in the South Asian region at best as an unwelcome intrusion and at worst as an encirclement strategy. Coupled with a territorial dispute (mentioned above) and strong Chinese backing for India's traditional rival Pakistan, the Sino-Indian strategic relationship has fundamental limits, though as we will see below, remarkable commercial growth.

Several summits in the 21st century have led to hope that relations between Beijing and New Delhi are improving. Prime Minister Atal Bihari Vajpayee of the BJP visited in June 2003 and the two sides signed agreements – most notably the creation of special representatives for the border dispute – and India recognized Tibet as part of China (*CFA* 2004: 170–171). Vajpayee's government fell in 2004, and for the next ten years the new Prime Minister Manmohan Singh of the Congress Party led India. Wen Jiabao reciprocated the head of government visit in 2005 and met, and the two sides "elevated" their relationship to a "Strategic and Cooperative Partnership for Peace and Prosperity." In 2006 Hu Jintao made a state visit to India. "... President Hu Jintao pointed out that China-India relations had gone far beyond the bilateral context and acquired global significance. He emphasized that China welcomes India's development and considers that as an opportunity rather than a threat to China" (*CFA* 2007: 208). In 2010, the two sides signed a Hotline agreement, and Wen Jiabao made an official visit to India in December (*CFA* 2011: 194–196). Li Keqiang visited India in May 2013 and Singh reciprocated in October of the same year. Xi's September 2014 state visit was somewhat marred by a minor border incident (see below) but did have an agreement to reopen the border crossing at Nathula Pass for Hindu pilgrims (*CFA* 2015: 202). Modi visited Beijing in May 2015, talked mostly about trade and investment but made it clear that Chinese strategic behavior troubled India: "I stressed the need for China to reconsider its approach on some of the issues that hold us back from realizing full potential of our partnership" (quoted in Buckley and Barry 2015). The leaders also have an annual BRICS meeting at which they have often held sidelines talks, beginning in 2009 at Yekaterinburg, Russia, and the Chinese Premier has used the East Asia Summit to meet with his counterpart as well. In each of these official visits and summits there have been professions of friendship and cooperation, declarations of the "2012 Year of China-India Friendship and Cooperation," the "2011 Year of China-India Exchange," the *Shared Vision for the 21st Century of the People's Republic of China and the Republic of India* in 2008, the "2007 China-India Friendship Year Through Tourism," and the "2006 China-India Friendship Year." Et cetera.

Talks on the Sino-Indian border issue continue. They are likely to do so for a long time. Each year *China's Foreign Affairs* officially announces that "negotiations on the boundary question moved forward steadily," and each year nothing substantive happens. As late as 2004 China's official line about the dispute was that it was "... problems left over from history between the two countries" (*CFA* 2005: 173). Since then, less and less has been ascribed to "leftover history" as if the border dispute were a plate of unwanted food left behind by British imperialists. The two sides recognize the broad outlines of a likely settlement: China keeps the Aksai Chin and India retains Arunachal Pradesh, an exchange of claims that basically confirms the status quo. That idea has been around for decades. Meetings of the Joint Working Group ran in parallel with joint teams of diplomatic and military experts and had over a dozen rounds of meetings when in 2003, the two sides added another negotiations mechanism, each side appointing a Special Representative to rounds of negotiations. China was represented by Dai Bingguo and now by Yang Jiechi, State Councilors and senior foreign policy point men. Between 2005 and 2007 the Special Representatives did seem to be making progress if measured by the number of meetings (eleven) and a minor protocol on Confidence Building Measures along the Line of Actual Control in 2005. That year was also when a preliminary understanding was broached that would have avoided territorial transfers that involved areas with settled populations, a key point in Arunachal Pradesh, and in particular the town of Tawang, an important Buddhist center. According to Indian sources, China backed down from that concession in 2006. The visit of the current Dalai Lama to the monastery in April 2017 and the presence of Indian officials there led to strong protests by the Chinese side (Shepherd 2017).

Riots in Tibet in 2008 did not make Beijing confident in its hold on the region and thereafter, the Sino-Indian talks slowed, and by 2014 there have been seventeen meetings without results (*CFA* 2004–2014). Some analysts had hoped that the election of Narendra Modi in 2014 and the state visit of Xi Jinping would offer the opportunity for two leaders, solid in their domestic political positions and nationalistic bona fides, to reach a deal, with Modi playing the Indian "Nixon" who could go to Beijing, but so far the visits have not resulted in border treaties or Panda bears. Then another minor border confrontation between Chinese and Indian troops occurred in Chumar on the other side of the Aksai Chin from the previous year's incident at Daulat Beg Oldi (noted above). This time the Chinese were building a road in what Indians considered their side of the Line of Actual Control (LAC). Whether the incident had been staged by Chinese commanders seeking to ease communications with their isolated outposts, or a deliberate attempt by some in China to sabotage Xi's visit to India, the result did not help Sino-Indian border negotiations or Xi Jinping's summit, large commercial contracts notwithstanding. By 2017 the relations were chilly; Modi did not join Xi's Belt and Road Forum, the Dalai Lama visited Arunachal Pradesh, and the border stand-off continues at the time of this writing (August 2017) and shows little prospect of quiet resolution.

India's concerns are demonstrated by the increased road-building program to Arunachal Pradesh, for India the more important and vulnerable of its two disputed areas. After its defeat in the 1962 war, India pursued a policy of not developing its own road networks toward the LAC with China, with the thought that a Chinese invasion would be slowed down due to poor communications (Ramachandran 2016a: 18). That strategy was changed in 2006 and beginning in 2016 the Modi government has put almost a billion dollars into road contracts up to the border, a very difficult task (Mandhana 2017). Chinese roads on the other side in Tibet are in much better shape, something Indian analysts frequently emphasize.

Pakistan remains a persistent issue in Sino-Indian relations, and Indians see Chinese support for Islamabad as part of the reason why Pakistan seems to be willing to engage in incidents in Kashmir, along the border, and even the spectacular terrorist attacks in New Delhi in 2001 and Mumbai in 2008. Indians also see China as complicit in blocking the UN Security Council Sanctions Committee from designating Masood Azhar, the founder of Jaish-e Mohammed, the terrorist group that staged the attack on the Indian Parliament building in 2001, among other acts, as a terrorist (Pant 2017). China (along with other states) is also quietly blocking India's accession to the Nuclear Suppliers' Group, as recently as 2016 in the Seoul meeting, possibly to engineer an India-and-Pakistan dual accession, not unlike the dual accession to the SCO (Singh 2016).

Among the political parties of India, China has sought to maintain contact with the major ones, including visits by Congress Party leader Sonia Gandhi, and the leader of the Communist Party of India (M). But there is no doubt that the BJP has the most nationalist reputation in India, though much of it is internally focused on domestic Indian issues.

China has not sold military equipment to India, but regular military exchanges do occur. The two sides established a China-India Defense Dialogue in late 2007 and have met regularly, if not necessarily productively. The Indian Chief of Staff and the Chinese Chief of Staff frequently visit, and there were joint counter-terrorism joint military drills in 2007, 2008, and 2014 and naval visits on many occasions (*CFA* 2008–15). The two militaries are also considering establishing a military-to-military hotline agreement to enable the two sides to handle border security issues locally, the top-level hotline agreement having been negotiated in 2010 (Blanchard 2016a).

Bangladesh

China has a variety of interests in Bangladesh: strategic, commercial, energy, and transportation. Links between Myanmar and Bangladesh to the Chinese province of Yunnan are a core element of the "One Belt One Road" (OBOR) initiative, and the Bangladesh-China-India-Myanmar (BCIM) Economic Corridor, an idea for transportation linkages that arose in the 1990s. New Delhi regards the OBOR idea with deep suspicion, and Indian analysts often note that China's proposals for ports, roads and other infrastructure could easily be turned into naval assets with which to threaten India. India, of course, almost completely surrounds Bangladesh, and the government in Dhaka has begun a substantial arms shopping program in recent years, and China has been the primary source. China had 77% of the 2004–2015 arms transfers to Bangladesh, a total of $1.9 billion, most of which is from 2011–2015. Among the items purchased were two submarines, corvettes, frigates, patrol craft, aircraft and tanks (SIPRI TIV 2017). Military delegations from and to China have been common, and Bangladeshi military officers have received training in China.

For China, relations with Bangladesh come at a cost to its other foreign relations: clearly India is constantly concerned about Chinese activities with its neighbors. But Bangladesh has its own disputes with Myanmar, putting China in the uncomfortable position of trying to mediate between those countries. As noted in Chapter 7, in November 2008, the two countries had a naval standoff after Myanmar granted offshore licenses for oil and gas exploration in a disputed area, and China had to mediate the dispute (Sakhuja 2009: 11).

Government in Bangladesh has alternated between two women leaders over the past twenty years, Sheikh Hasina Wazed of the Awami League, and Khaleda Zia of the Bangladesh National Party (BNP). Of the two parties, the BNP developed the reputation as being more hostile to India, whereas the Awami League after 2014 has been seen as "tilting" back toward India, as well as the United States (Ramachandran 2016b: 16). China has tried to nurture relations with both parties, and has hosted party delegations from both the Awami League and the BNP. China continues to emphasize the government relationship, however, and a variety of foreign aid projects have resulted: "China-Bangladesh Friendship Bridges" 6 and 7, the Barapukuria Power Plant, the Padma Water Treatment Plant, the Shahjalal Fertilizer Plant, a 3G network, and a Confucius Institute (*CFA* 2014: 120, 2013: 116).

Sheikh Hasina visited China in 2014 and signed several agreements on aid and economic issues (*China's Foreign Affairs* 2015: 130). But China's proposal for a deepwater port at Sonadia was shelved in February 2016 in favor of a Japanese project at Matarbari (Ramachandran 2016b: 16). Indian Prime Minister Modi visited Dhaka in June 2015 and offered up a $2 billion line of credit. Undeterred, Xi Jinping saw the Indian bet and raised it $22 billion during a state visit to Bangladesh in October 2016, and went so far as to elevate Sino-Bangladeshi relations to a "Strategic Partnership of Cooperation" (Paul 2016). In April 2017, Sheikh Hasina was in India, signing more deals with Prime Minister Modi and doubtlessly enjoying the competing attention of two great power beaux (Ramachandran 2017b).

Nepal

Nepal, similar to Mongolia, is a "sandwich state" between two giants, in this case India and China, and India has clearly indicated that it is more than willing to squeeze Nepal hard if the dalliances of Kathmandu with China go too far. For China, the relationship with Nepal is intimately connected to Tibet (Zhang Yongpan 2015: 23). The Indian hosting of the Dalai Lama and a large exile Tibetan community in Dharamsala is a very large irritant in Sino-Indian relations. Nepal has also played a role, and is one of the main transit points between Tibet and Dharamsala for Tibetans pilgrims and refugees. The Nepalese government generally treated Tibetans as refugees (formally until 1998 and then informally after), moving them temporarily to a UNCHR camp near Kathmandu, and then allowing them to go on to Dharamsala in Himachal Pradesh, India, near Kashmir. Then in 2012, Nepalese border guards started actually guarding the border, thanks to Chinese training and assistance, and more vigorous Chinese patrolling. The number of Tibetans coming into Nepal dropped from 2–4,000 a year in the early 2000s to 500–600 (Wong 2013). China negotiated a series of agreements in 2012 with Nepal concerning border areas, pastures and has had regular meetings on border security issues (*CFA* 2013: 233–234). Chinese diplomats have made sure that Nepal regularly reaffirms its standard language, "Nepal continued to give firm support to China on issues related to Tibet and others and committed not to allowing any forces to engage in anti-China activities in Nepal" (*CFA* 2015: 256).

China in turn has rewarded Nepal with a number of foreign aid projects. In 2009, RMB150 million was pledged. Among the projects undertaken by China in Nepal have been a large number of road projects, including the recently finished Syafrubesi-Rasuagadi Road, renovation of the Kathmandu Ring Road, the Tatopani Dry Port, and other construction projects, such as the Civil Service Hospital (MOFAN 2010). A hydroelectric project was also pledged in 2011 estimated to be worth $1.6 billion, though it is not clear how much of this is aid as opposed to a construction contract (Wolf et al. 2013: 37). One project that could have implications for Nepal is the Chengdu-Lhasa railway, which would be a second connection into Tibet following the completion of the Golmud-Lhasa line in 2006, and its extension to Xigaze, the second-largest city in Tibet and closer to the border of Nepal. The technical difficulties and expense of the project are immense, but there is vague discussion of extending it further, to the borders of Bhutan and Nepal, though the timeline involved for the project would be sometime around 2030 ("A new railway to Tibet" 2016: 38). Even then, the prospects for Indian acceptance are probably very dim indeed.

Narendra Modi's new government in India demonstrated in 2015 that it was more than willing to use a fuel blockade to support the political demands of southern Nepalese, a blockade that China could do little to relieve ("Nepal and India" 2015: 37). China did negotiate a deal in early 2016 to allow Nepalese to use China's ports to import goods, and fuel in particular, though the actual access is by perilous roads, damaged by the April 2015 earthquake (Blanchard 2016b). Since the Nepalese purchase of anti-aircraft weaponry that led to the 1988–89 Indian economic embargo, the government in Kathmandu has received only token arms transfers from China in 2004–2015 (Armored Personnel Carriers), and India and Russia are the primary suppliers (SIPRI TIV 2017).

The problem China faces in its relations with Kathmandu is simply who is in charge there; there have been over nine governments in the last ten years and Nepalese democracy has been highly dysfunctional. After the end of the civil war in 2006 and the end of the monarchy, a plethora of fractious political parties have formed a dizzying array of unstable coalitions. China's legislature and the International Department of the Communist Party seek to keep contacts with all, though several are uncomfortably Marxist-Leninist or Maoist, reminders of how far the leadership in Beijing has strayed from that path. Equally problematic is the tendency for Nepalese political parties to gain reputations as "pro-India" or "pro-China." In the case of some parties such as the Nepali Congress Party, the reputation is deserved, and government of India and private Indians are clear in their support. China, on the other hand, has been burned in the past with political favoritism and has been careful to try to keep channels open with all partisan elements in Nepal, as difficult as that is at times (Ramachandran 2015a: 18). One of the reasons Xi Jinping has not made a state visit to Nepal was the switch from the Oli government to the Prachanda government, which nixed what had been scheduled for October 2016 (Sharma 2016).

Sri Lanka

Unlike Nepal, where after a long war the peace incorporated the rebels into the government, in Sri Lanka a much longer war resulted in the complete defeat and annihilation of the Tamil-based LTTE nationalist group by the Sinhalese majority government. A ceasefire started in early 2002 broke down in 2006 and the government prosecuted its war to a final, bitter end. China had supplied a large number of weapons to the government: China supplied 52% of Sri Lanka's arms in 2004–2015, a total of $206 million, though most of those sales were prior to May 2009 when the LTTE insurgency was crushed (SIPRI TIV Tables 2017). India's complex involvement was outlined in Chapter 2, but there are many Sri Lankans who believe that Indian support – private or surreptitious – was a key to the rebellion, and thus a tension lingers between New Delhi and Colombo. But has China in turn been advantaged by this shift? The answer is a bit more subtle than it seems: its arms sales to Sri Lanka have all but disappeared, but it has developed regular military-to-military relations with the Sri Lankan military. It has undertaken prominent aid projects, but the Sri Lankan government has been inconsistent in its approach. China's economic ties are growing as we will see below, though not as much as in Pakistan, Bangladesh, or even India.

The two sides upgraded their relationship to a "Comprehensive Cooperative Partnership" after President Mahinda Rajapaksa made a state visit to China in 2007, and another in 2013, raising the relationship to a "Strategic Cooperative Partnership" that year. Xi Jinping finally reciprocated the state visit in September 2014, a full twenty-eight years after the previous Chinese state visit (*CFA* 2015: 306). Chinese and Sri Lankan joint communiques and statements have stressed the Sri Lankan issues of sovereignty and territorial integrity (code words for staying out of Sri Lanka's civil war) and Taiwan, Tibet, and Xinjiang for the Chinese side. The formula was notably changed during the 2015 *China's Foreign Affairs* when it stated that "The two sides continued to support each other on such issues as human rights and the South China Sea" (307). The Sri Lankan government's 2009 brutal ending of the LTTE insurgency has been sharply criticized by Western human rights groups, and China's sympathies are clearly with the governments' rights to end insurrections as they wish. Military relations included the annual visits of Sri Lankan and especially Chinese military officials, and in late October 2014 a Chinese submarine and warship visited Colombo on their way to the Gulf of Aden for anti-piracy patrols, clearly making the Indian navy nervous (Aneez and Sirilal 2014).

Chinese aid projects emphasized infrastructure as usual, and included a large coal-fired power plant at Puttalam, the Galle-Matara Section of the Southern Expressway, the Hambantota Port, the Hambantota International Airport, and the National Performing Arts Theater. A Confucius Institute was established at the University of Colombo in 2014. The ports, often mentioned by Indian analysts as being part of China's "String of Pearls" idea along the Indian Ocean (the term is not used by Chinese authors), have made India worry that they might become a Chinese naval base at some time (Ramachandran 2015b). The Chinese describe these as part of the "Maritime Silk Road" idea which is part of Xi Jinping's signature "One Belt One Road" idea. The Colombo South Container Terminal, a controversial deal worth about $1.5 billion signed during Xi's September 2014 visit, came under attack by the new government of President Maithripala Sirisena and Prime Minister Ranil Wickremesinghe, who alleged corruption in the bidding process, and the government has switched its mind several times on whether to go ahead with the idea. In Sri Lankan political circles, President Mahinda Rajapaksa (2005–2015) was described as "pro-China," and his successor used that as a campaign issue, arguing for a "balanced" foreign policy. But by the Fall of 2016, the government was looking to deal with China again, selling its stake in the Hambantota Port to offset debt. The former president, now in the opposition, is using the latest Hambantota deal to criticize his successors:

> ... Rajapaksa, who used to be the member of parliament for Hambantota ... is railing 'against giving the rights of the landlord over the industrial zone

to a foreign private company' and raising concerns about 'control and sovereignty'. That is the height of hypocrisy – but it has clearly struck a nerve.

("Deep water," 2017: 33)

In July 2017, a revised deal appears to have been struck, with limits on Chinese equity and naval access (Miglani 2017).

Bhutan

Bhutan is the only neighbor of China with which it does not have formal diplomatic relations, though the two countries recognize each other and have even signed a mutual treaty. The status of Bhutan is such that India from 1949 to 2007 maintained a formal treaty role that allowed it to "guide" Bhutan's foreign and defense relations, and even today the government in Thimphu does not have formal diplomatic relations with China or any of the Permanent Five states of the UN Security Council, although it is a member of the General Assembly and many other international organizations. The 2007 revision to the Indo-Bhutan Friendship Treaty affirms the latter's independence and sovereignty, but most of its great-power relations are still conducted through India. Chinese analysts have noted this special relationship continuing even after the 2007 treaty revision (Tong Yutao 2015: 39; Liu Zhiwei and Zhu Lumin 2013: 183). In the process of negotiations about the boundary, China has proposed bundling the boundary issue with the exchange of full and formal diplomatic relations, a proposal the Bhutanese have resisted. Any breakthroughs in Sino-Bhutanese relations are thus likely to depend on a breakthrough in Sino-Indian relations.

Maldives

China began to describe the Maldives as its "close neighbor" in 2004, the 3,639 miles (5,856km) separating Beijing and Malé notwithstanding. As distant as China may be from the Maldives, in one sense it is also an existential threat to that tiny country: global climate change is threatening the very existence of the low-lying atolls and islands inhabited by some 400,000 people, and China is the largest contributor to greenhouse gases. (The cabinet of the Maldivian government received much publicity in March 2009 when the cabinet met underwater in scuba gear.) The climate issue apparently was mentioned as an area of "close cooperation" in 2013, and Xi Jinping made a state visit to the islands in September 2014 and established their "Cooperative Partnership." Although the two countries had formal ties going back to 1972, the first actual Chinese embassy was not built until November 2011. Aid projects have included building the Maldivian National Museum, a bridge, a one-thousand-unit housing project, and concessional loans were negotiated, emergency aid after the December 2004 Indian Ocean tsunami, and zero-tariff agreements (*CFA* 2015: 235–236, 2014: 219–220, 2011: 233). Chinese tourists are the Maldives' major source of foreign revenue, and in 2014, the number who flew to the islands from the eight different Chinese cities with airline links to Malé – 360,000 – almost outnumbered the entire population of that country. China has also been careful not to criticize the new government of President Abdulla Yameen, who imprisoned the former President Mohamed Nasheed in 2015, after the latter had been forced to resign in 2012 due to protests (Naish 2015). In defense matters, the Maldivian Defense Minister did visit China in 2012, but China has not provided any weapons and India's sales were limited to one patrol craft and three helicopters.

Regional international organizations

SAARC, as noted in Chapter 2, is a grouping created in 1985 by the smaller actors of South Asia with limited cooperation from India, which prefers to deal with its smaller neighbors one-on-one. The decision was made in late 2005 to accept observer states (apparently supported by the smaller SAARC members), and in August 2006, China and others were accepted. This was shortly after India and Pakistan gained observer status in the Shanghai Cooperation Organization. Now Australia, the European Union, Iran, Japan, Korea, Mauritius, Myanmar, the USA all have that same status. In 2008, the SAARC Summit decided to place a moratorium on additional observers. Russia and the Central Asian Republics are the notably excluded parties. China has sent delegations to each SAARC summit, and has organized a China-South Asia Expo in Kunming, and a China-South Asia Business Forum (*CFA* 2015: 395). But unlike ASEAN, the cooperative aspirations of SAARC are quite limited, and thus China's opportunity to use the organization as entrée are even more limited.

Hegemon's expatriates

India once had a largely Cantonese-speaking Chinese community of over 100,000 people at the time of independence in 1947, largely centered on Calcutta (now Kolkata). The 1962 war led to the internment of ethnic Chinese in India not unlike the internment of Japanese-Americans in World War II, minus the (belated) remorse, apology, and compensation. Many were expelled and many more preferred to leave, and by the 21st century there are about 4,000 left, half of them in Kolkata's Chinatown, an elderly and dying remnant ("Kings no more: Chinese Indians" 2014: 44). They have not been a major foreign policy issue in recent years.

Economic

China's security relations with New Delhi may have improved only moderately in the 21st century, but its economic relations with India and the rest of the South Asian region have shown dramatic improvement. There is little wonder that Chinese leaders love to tout grandiose ideas of mutual economic prosperity; it is an idea that attracts and has more than a kernel of truth to it. Even India, which sees itself as a country of the future, sees economic cooperation with China as a strategy to pursue, even if it is hesitant about several of the One Belt One Road

Trade

Trade has been the biggest change in China's relations with South Asia, and in particular with India. Chinese military strategists may see a rival across the Himalayas occupying "South Tibet" and hosting the "Dalai clique"; Chinese corporations, commerce and finance ministers, and a host of small merchants see over a billion potential customers. The period starts out in 2004 with China selling about US$5.9 billion worth of goods to India, heavily concentrated in chemicals and fertilizers. By 2015, that number had increased almost ten-fold, to US$58.2 billion, that is, roughly the same amount as China's exports to the United Kingdom, and includes a wider variety of products, especially consumer electronics, computers, telephones, and steel products. That number is also a greater proportion of Chinese exports, now about 2.5% and up from barely 1% in 2004. Table 9.2 shows China's trade with India and the rest of South Asia in absolute amounts:

Table 9.2 China: total trade with South Asia, 2004–2015

China: total trade with South Asia, 2004–2015 (current US$, million)

	Afghanistan	Bangladesh	Bhutan	India	Maldives	Nepal	Pakistan	Sri Lanka
2004	$58	$1,966	$1	$13,598	$8	$172	$3,060	$718
2005	$53	$2,482	$0	$18,717	$17	$196	$4,256	$978
2006	$101	$3,182	$0	$25,058	$16	$268	$5,248	$1,142
2007	$172	$3,459	$5	$38,695	$25	$400	$6,890	$1,434
2008	$155	$4,685	$8	$51,858	$33	$380	$6,998	$1,684
2009	$215	$4,583	$4	$43,407	$41	$414	$6,776	$1,640
2010	$179	$7,055	$2	$61,736	$64	$744	$8,666	$2,097
2011	$234	$8,257	$17	$73,901	$97	$1,195	$10,561	$3,141
2012	$470	$8,452	$16	$66,566	$77	$1,998	$12,420	$3,171
2013	$339	$10,311	$17	$65,492	$98	$2,253	$14,223	$3,620
2014	$411	$12,555	$11	$70,650	$104	$2,330	$16,009	$4,043
2015	$376	$14,709	$10	$71,654	$173	$851	$18,959	$4,567

Source: IMF DOTS (2017).

The two governments initially sought to set rolling trade targets in the first years of the century, setting a goal of $10 billion in mutual trade for 2005 and hitting it a year early (*CFA* 2005: 173). The next year PM Singh and Premier Wen doubled the target to $20 billion in trade in 2008, and wound up almost doubling that figure, to $39.9 billion. The next trade goal was set at $40 billion in 2010, which was met and exceeded again, to the level of $58 billion. Wen was back in India in 2010, and the two sides set a trade goal of $100 billion in 2015, but this time the goal was not met: total trade that year was $71 billion, an impressive amount nonetheless. Part of the problem lay in declining Indian exports to China, which tend to be in the primary sector (cotton, copper, iron ore) and have been adversely affected by the slowdown in the Chinese economy.

The inter-dependency of the two economies is highly asymmetrical, following the pattern seen in China's other regional trade relations: trade with China means much more to India than vice-versa, though as noted, India is a growing portion of Chinese exports, and China runs a balance of trade surplus with India.[2] Table 9.3 shows the mutual dependency of China and India:

Table 9.3 China and India: mutual trade dependency, 2004–2015

China and India: mutual trade dependency, 2004–2015 (% total imports/exports)

	India		China	
	Imports from China	Exports to China	Imports from India	Exports to India
2004	6.1%	5.5%	1.4%	1.0%
2005	7.1%	6.6%	1.5%	1.2%
2006	9.0%	6.6%	1.3%	1.5%
2007	10.5%	6.6%	1.5%	2.0%
2008	10.8%	5.4%	1.8%	2.2%
2009	11.2%	6.1%	1.4%	2.5%
2010	11.8%	7.9%	1.5%	2.6%
2011	11.9%	6.2%	1.3%	2.7%
2012	10.7%	5.0%	1.0%	2.3%
2013	11.0%	4.6%	0.9%	2.2%
2014	12.7%	4.2%	0.8%	2.3%
2015	15.7%	3.6%	0.8%	

Source: IMF DOTS (2017).

Thus, although sales of Indian goods and commodities to China have varied between about 4 and 7% of all Indian exports, the trend for India's imports is clear: Chinese products are expanding their presence in Indian shops, markets and stalls, now over 15% of all goods. For a government with fairly protectionist policies, this might be disturbing, but for Indian consumers, it means cheaper TVs. Rhetoric in 2004 and 2005 about China and India working together at the WTO to "vigorously defending the interests of the developing countries" (*CFA* 2004: 172, 2005: 174) declined, replaced with total trade goals noted above. For a while the two sides sponsored a feasibility study for a bilateral Regional Trade Arrangement, but this disappeared as well. The substantial imbalance in bilateral trade was raised by the Indians and the two sides signed an MOU on "Trade Remedy to Promote Mutual Cooperation" in 2008 (*CFA* 2009: 186).

China's trade position in the other South Asian countries has also improved. In each of the countries in South Asia (except Bhutan), China has increased its market share measured by the percentage of imports between 2004 and 2015. This is not nearly as substantial as imports of Chinese goods in Central Asia during this same period, and unlike Central Asia where the market share increase was clearly at the regional hegemon's expense, India has maintained its market share in South Asia fairly well. Unlike Southeast Asia, however, there is no overarching free trade pact in South Asia, and only India among the South Asian nations is being considered as part of the RCEP proposal. China has explored bilateral trade deals and has in some instances unilaterally offered tariff concessions to its neighbors.

Given its poverty and instability, Afghanistan is hardly a mercantile prize, and China's market share is still fairly modest compared to other neighboring countries and is the only country in South Asia where China's market share is below 10%; Afghanistan's exports flow very substantially to India, and it is one of the few places in Asia where Russia has actually gained market share (IMF DOTS 2017).

In contrast, Pakistan is a market where China has done very well, which should not be surprising. The two countries negotiated a bilateral free trade agreement which began operating in 2007. China's market share went from 8.4% to 28.3% over the period, and, in turn, China is increasingly a destination for Pakistani commodities and products, over 11% of Pakistan's export market in 2012–13, before dropping down somewhat to around 8%. It is no surprise that India's shares of Pakistan's trade are fairly low, not only because of political difficulties but also because their export profiles are fairly similar (cotton, textiles, copper), making them competitors. Pakistan also has a growing balance of trade deficit with China, growing from $1.2 billion in 2004, to $15.8 billion in 2015. Like other South Asian trade partners, Pakistan has boosted its exports to China impressively, from around $300 million in 2004 it tripled to over $900 million in 2006, and from $1.5 billion in 2010 to almost $3 billion in 2013, but in each year other than 2009 Chinese imports outpaced Pakistani exports, and in 2014–15 when Pakistani exports to China slowed somewhat, Chinese imports continued to climb (IMF DOTS 2017).

Sri Lanka has also seen Chinese market share rise, almost tripling over the period, though India remains ahead of China in both import and export dependency. China and Sri Lanka announced the beginning of negotiations for a free trade agreement in 2014 (*CFA* 2015: 307), and Chinese reports anticipate the deal being signed in May 2017 (CCTV 2017).

China overtook India's market share in Bangladesh in 2009, despite the Indian geographic and transport advantages. Neither country is a large importer of Bangladeshi exports but China is now over 2% of its exports, mostly textiles and garments. The bilateral trade imbalance grew and hit $1 billion in 2003, and was an issue in diplomatic discussions in 2005. China granted zero-tariff treatment to several Bangladeshi products under the Bangladesh under the Asia Pacific Trade Agreement (or the Bangkok Agreement), and sent a procurement delegation to Bangladesh in December 2005 in an effort to rebalance trade (*CFA* 2006: 96). It did and did not work; Bangladeshi exports to China exploded, going from $46 million in 2005 to $100 million in 2009 and then tripled to $300 million in 2011. But the trade deficit grew even faster, slowed only momentarily by the world recession in 2009. By 2010 the deficit was $4.5 billion; by 2013 it was $6.5 billion, and in 2015 it was $8.1 billion (IMF DOTS 2017). To try to deal with this issue, China in 2010 granted tariff-free access to over 4,000 Bangladeshi products (*CFA* 2011: 121), but Chinese products continue to move into the Bangladeshi market faster than the counter flow.

Nepal, despite being a sandwich state, is firmly attached to the bottom slice of bread. India remains the dominant trade partner, both in Nepalese imports and exports. China has increased its market share there, especially in 2010–2014, but it has since gone back down, at least partially because of the fuel embargo India imposed and which China could not relieve in any meaningful way. Unless and until China's transportation links to Nepal are significantly improved – most likely by rail – Nepal's economy will be dominated by India. As for tiny Bhutan, it is even more completely dominated in its trade by India than is Nepal, usually between 75 and 85% of both exports and imports go to and come from India (IMF DOTS 2017).

China also exports services and in particular construction contracting in South Asia. The line between this and aid projects is a fine one, and the Chinese Foreign Ministry regularly notes the size of construction contracting in its annual review of bilateral relations (e.g., *CFA* 2015: 201). The amounts contracted – but not necessarily completed – are very large. Between 2006 and 2015 Chinese firms contracted US$35 billion in construction contracts in Pakistan, over $12 billion in India, and about US$10 billion in Sri Lanka and Bangladesh (China Global Investment Tracker 2017).

Investment

China's trade surpluses with the nations of South Asia can at least be partially alleviated the way other Chinese trade surpluses are: by capital flows. For all of the grandeur of the One Belt One Road concept, there is a vague familiarity for those who remember US-Japan economic relations in the 1980s, when persistent Japanese trade surpluses were "recycled" in the form of direct and portfolio investments. In the case of South Asia, this involves Chinese foreign direct investment, Chinese foreign aid, Chinese loans, Chinese export buyers' credits, and, of course, Chinese tourists.

The investments that China has made in South Asia – led by Pakistan and India at over $3 billion each – would seem impressive, though they are not compared to overall world investment in those countries. The comparisons of the Chinese Ministry of Commerce FDI figures and the UNCTAD World Investment Report (WIR) data is at best questionable, since they use very different methodologies, but to give a sense of magnitude, if China has $3.7 billion in FDI stocks in Pakistan as of 2014, the world has about $30.7 billion. China lists $3.4 billion invested in India, whereas the WIR indicates India has over $252 billion in FDI stocks from around the world. Afghanistan's world FDI stock is listed by WIR as $1.69 billion,

Table 9.4 China: foreign direct investment in South Asia, 2003–2014

China: foreign direct investment flows and stocks in South Asia, 2003–2014 (current US$, million)

	Afghanistan	Bangladesh	India	Maldives	Nepal	Pakistan	Sri Lanka
2004		$0.76	$0.35		$1.68	$1.42	$0.25
2005		$0.18	$11.16		$1.35	$4.34	$0.03
2006	$0.25	$5.31	$5.61		$0.32	–$62.07	$0.25
2007	$0.10	$3.64	$22.02		$0.99	$910.63	–$1.52
2008	$113.90	$4.50	$101.88		$0.01	$265.37	$9.04
2009	$16.39	$10.75	–$24.88		$1.18	$76.75	–$1.40
2010	$1.91	$7.24	$47.61		$0.86	$331.35	$28.21
2011	$295.54	$10.32	$180.08		$8.58	$333.28	$81.23
2012	$17.61	$33.03	$276.81		$7.65	$88.93	$16.75
2013	–$1.22	$41.37	$148.57	$1.55	$36.97	$163.57	$71.77
2014	$27.92	$25.02	$317.18	$0.72	$45.04	$1,014.26	$85.11
net outward stocks, 2014	$518.49	$160.24	$3,407.21	$2.30	$138.34	$3,736.82	$363.91

Source: Ministry of Commerce. 2011–2014.

and China claims a stock of $518 million there. Thus, Chinese investors would seem to have a greater appetite for risk than others.

Outbound Chinese tourism has become a major business in the world, and parts of South Asia have benefitted greatly from it in the past decade. As destinations, India, Sri Lanka, the Maldives, Nepal, and Bhutan have large numbers of total arrivals in 2015: 539,000 in Nepal, 155,000 in Bhutan 1.8 million in Sri Lanka, 1.2 million in the Maldives, and 13.3 million in India.

World Bank data show that the Maldives, Sri Lanka, and Nepal all earn more than one-fifth of their exports thanks to international tourism. Nepal and Bhutan are also heavily dependent on tourism. Even India, the largest single tourist destination in South Asia, takes in between four and five percent of its exports as tourism receipts (World Bank WDI 2017). Chinese are the fastest-growing segment of tourism around the world, and South Asia is no exception. Table 9.5 covers 2008–12, and the numbers have gone up significantly since then.

What this means is that these parts of South Asia are benefitting in their balance of payments from Chinese going abroad. Of course, tourism may be a good revenue-generator, but it is also a notoriously skittish industry; earthquakes, tsunamis, riots and wars are among the reasons why Afghanistan, Pakistan, and Bangladesh do not have many tourists. It should be noted that Chinese tourists also tend to avoid places with recent conflicts with China, as Vietnam discovered in 2014–15.

The last major way in which China can smooth its economic relations with South Asia is the one which has been mentioned several times already: the One Belt One Road idea, and more specifically the "21st Century Maritime Silk Road."

Table 9.5 Chinese tourist arrivals in South Asia, 2008–2012

Chinese tourist arrivals in South Asia, 2008–2012 (thousand)

	Bhutan	India	Maldives	Nepal	Pakistan	Sri Lanka
2008	1,069	98,093	41,511	36,172	30,078	9,812
2009	1,143	100,209	60,666	33,487	29,996	8,550
2010	1,494	119,530	118,961	44,694	27,887	10,430
2011	2,896	142,218	198,655	64,115	42,708	16,308
2012	3,766	168,952	229,551	71,380	39,017	25,781

Source: World Tourism Organization (2014).

Technically, CPEC and the Bangladesh-China-India-Myanmar Economic Corridor (BCIMEC) are not parts of the OBOR (One Belt One Road), but even the official Chinese vision for OBOR notes that they are "closely related," and since they are among the more advanced infrastructure projects China is undertaking in South Asia, they have already been treated as if they were part of the idea (National Development and Reform Commission 2015: 4). Few would accuse the Chinese of thinking small: at a time when the West seems to be thinking small and narrow and national, China seems to be large and broad and global.

And vague. The original concept was laid out by Xi Jinping in October 2013 in Kazakhstan, and its sweep seemed immense; the National Development and Reform Commission 2015 document seems to exclude nothing, claiming, "The Belt and Road run through the continents of Asia, Europe and Africa, connecting the vibrant East Asia economic circle at one end and the developed European economic circle at the other, and encompassing countries with huge potential for economic development" (National Development and Reform Commission 2015: 4).

For a Eurasian continent with huge infrastructure needs, the list of possible projects makes for heady reading: "international trunk passageways," roads, ports, oil and gas pipelines, an "Information Silk Road," investment in industrial chains, agriculture, energy, industrial parks, and zones, yet at the same time seeking to "increase local employment, improve local livelihood, and take social responsibilities in protecting local biodiversity and eco-development" (National Development and Reform Commission 2015: 5–7). Specifics are, however, still lacking. The Belt and Road Forum for International Cooperation, Xi Jinping's major international conference in May 2017 has just begun to flesh some of this out.

But all of this requires more than just neighbors and fences; it requires *partners*, entities with a stake in the business and an interest in its success, and the success of its largest proponent and source of capability and largesse. Hence the change of terms is part of a change of attitude of China toward its adjacent states: those who are partners will benefit; those who are not will lose out. India pointedly declined Xi's invitation to take part in the Belt and Road Forum, and the Afghan, Bangladeshi, Nepalese, and Maldives governments sent lower-level delegations.

Notes

1 There is one instance of Chinese intervention which is strongly rumored, in Afghanistan, according to mainly Indian sources which photographed Chinese military or police vehicles operating in conjunction with Afghan security forces in a 50-mile stretch of their common border in early 2017 (Snow 2017). As noted in the previous chapter, moreover, China's National People's Congress in December 2015 passed a law that would allow both the PLA and People's Armed Police to engage in counter-terrorism operations overseas (Duchâtel 2016: 2).
2 The pattern of regional balance of trade surpluses reflects two key aspects of China's 21st-century trade relations: first, it has a very substantial balance of trade surplus with the entire world, over $600 billion in 2015, according to the IMF. Second, China does run a merchandise deficit with energy exporters such as Saudi Arabia, and with Germany, which is not surprising given wealthy Chinese drivers' taste for German automotive engineering.

Works cited

Aneez, Shihar, and Sirilal, Ranga. 2014. Chinese submarine docks in Sri Lanka despite Indian concerns. *Reuters*, 2 November. <www.reuters.com/article/sri-lanka-china-submarine-idUSL4N0SS0C220141102>, accessed 3 November 2014.

Blanchard, Ben. 2016a. China "positive" on India military hotline proposal. *Reuters*, 18 April. <www.reuters.com/article/us-china-india-idUSKCN0XG03Y>, accessed 19 April 2016.

Blanchard, Ben. 2016b. China to supply petroleum products to landlocked Nepal. *Reuters*, 23 March. <www.reuters.com/article/us-china-nepal-idUSKCN0WP1WV>, accessed 23 March 2016.

Blanchard, Ben. 2017. China names areas in regional disputed with India to assert claims. *Reuters*, 19 April. <www.reuters.com/article/us-china-india-idUSKBN17L19B>, accessed 19 April 2017.

Buckley, Chris, and Barry, Ellen. 2015. Modi calls on China to rethink stances that strain ties to India. *New York Times*, 15 May. <www.nytimes.com/2015/05/16/world/asia/narendra-modi-urges-china-to-rethink-policies-that-strain-ties-to-india.html>, accessed 15 May 2015.

CCTV. 2017. Sri Lanka to sign free trade agreement with China: Ambassador. *China Central Television*, 6 February. <http://english.cctv.com/2017/02/06/ARTINeMY17velxqZFnZ4ItE2170206.shtml>, accessed 25 April 2017.

CFA [China's Foreign Affairs]. Annual. Beijing: Ministry of Foreign Affairs of the People's Republic of China. This is the official yearbook of the Ministry of Foreign Affairs of the People's Republic of China. Beginning its publication in 1987 as 中国外交概览 Annual. Beijing: Ministry of Foreign Affairs of the People's Republic of China. This is the official yearbook of the Ministry of Foreign Affairs of the People's Republic of China. Beginning its publication in 1987 as 中国外交概览 China's Foreign Affairs review, it is hereafter referred to as ZGWJGL, and after 1995 中国外交 it is renamed Zhongguo waijiao (ZGWJ) for the Chinese language version, and China's Foreign Affairs or CFA for the English-language version, which began publication in 2003.

China Global Investment Tracker. 2017. American Enterprise Institute, July. <www.aei.org/china-global-investment-tracker/>, accessed 25 April 2017.

"Deep water: Anti-Chinese protests." 2017. *The Economist*, 14 January, 33.

Duchâtel, Mathieu. 2016. Terror overseas: Understanding China's evolving counter-terror strategy. European Council on Foreign Relations Policy Brief, no. 193 (October). <ecfr.eu>, accessed 4 June 2017.

Garver, John W. 2001. *Protracted Contest: Sino-Indian Rivalry in the Twentieth Century*. Seattle: University of Washington Press.

Harris, Gardner, and Wong, Edward. 2013. Where China meets India in a high-altitude desert, push comes to shove. *New York Times*, 2 May. <www.nytimes.com/2013/05/03/world/asia/where-china-meets-india-push-comes-to-shove.html>, accessed 19 March 2017.

IMF DOTS [Direction of Trade Statistics]. 2017. IMF e-library. <data.imf.org/>, accessed 19 January 2017.

Ismailzade, Fariz. 2016. The "North-South" transport corridor finally kicks off. *Central Asia-Caucasus Analyst*, 26 September. <www.cacianalyst.org/publications/analytical-articles/item/13395-the-%E2%80%9Cnorth-south%E2%80%9D-transport-corridor-finally-kicks-off.html>, accessed 21 April 2017.

Kalinovsky, Artemy M. 2013. Sino-Afghani border relations, in *Beijing's Power and China's Borders: Twenty Neighbors in Asia*, edited by Bruce A. Elleman, Stephen Kotkin, and Clive Schofield. Armonk, NY: M.E. Sharpe, 13–21.

Khan, Muhammad Azam. 2017. Pakistan's port is pivotal. *US Naval Institute Proceedings*, 143(3), 50–54.

"Kings no more: Chinese Indians." 2014. *The Economist*, 11 October, 44.

Liu Zhiwei, and Zhu Lumin. 2013. Zhongguo yu Butan guanxi de lishi, xianzhuang ji qianjing [The history, current situation and prospects of China's relations with Bhutan]. *Jintian*, (no. 306), 183.

Mandhana, Niharika. 2017. India moves mountains to build military road to China border. *Wall Street Journal*, 5 April. <www.wsj.com/articles/india-moves-mountains-to-build-military-road-to-china-border-1491384609>, accessed 5 April 2017.

Miglani, Sanjeev. 2017. Exclusive: Sri Lanka's cabinet "clears port deal" with China after concerns addressed. *Reuters*, 25 July. <www.reuters.com/article/us-sri-lanka-china-port-idUSKBN1AA0PI>, accessed 25 July 2017.

Ministry of Commerce of the PRC. 2011–2015. *Statistical Bulletin of China's Outward Foreign Direct Investment*. Beijing: China Statistics Press. Annual.

MOFAN [Ministry of Foreign Affairs of Nepal]. 2010. Nepal-China relations. Ministry of Foreign Affairs of Nepal. 12 May. <www.mofa.gov.np/bilateralRelations/Nepal-china.php>, accessed 4 September 2012.

Naish, Ahmed. 2015. "China-Maldives Friendship Bridge" project launched. *Maldives Independent*, 31 December. <http://maldivesindependent.com/business/china-maldives-friendship-bridge-project-launched-121081>, accessed 27 March 2017.

National Development and Reform Commission. 2015. *Vision and Actions on Jointly Building Silk Road Economic Belt and 21st Century Maritime Silk Road*. Beijing: National Development and Reform Commission, Ministry of Foreign Affairs, Ministry of Commerce, 28 March. <http://en.ndrc.gov.cn/newsrelease/201503/t20150330_669367.html>, accessed 25 April 2017.

"Nepal and India: Mr Oli's winter challenge." 2015. *The Economist*, 24 October.

"A new railway to Tibet: Doubling down." 2016. *The Economist*, 21 May, 37–38.

Pakistan Board of Investment. 2016. China Pakistan Economic Corridor (CPEC). Islamabad. <boi.gov.pk/ViewNews.aspx?NID=892>, accessed 17 April 2017.

Pant, Harsh V. 2017. Rekindled Sino-Indian tensions roil geopolitics in Asia. *YaleGlobal Online*, 12 January. <http://yaleglobal.yale.edu/content/rekindled-sino-indian-tensions-roil-geopolitics-asia>, accessed 17 January 2017.

Parello-Plesner, Jonas, and Duchâtel, Mathieu. 2015. *China's Strong Arm: Protecting Citizens and Assets Abroad*. London: International Institute for Strategic Studies.

Paul, Ruma. 2016. China signs deals worth billions with Bangladesh as Xi visits. *Reuters*, 14 October. <www.reuters.com/article/us-bangladesh-china-idUSKCN12D34M>, accessed 5 May 2017.

Ramachandran, Sudha. 2015a. Sino-Nepalese relations: Handshake across the Himalayas. *China Brief*, 15(22), 15–20.

Ramachandran, Sudha. 2015b. China and Sri Lanka: In choppy waters. *China Brief*, 15(10), 10–13.

Ramachandran, Sudha. 2015c. China-Pakistan economic corridor: Road to riches? *China Brief*, 15(15). <https://jamestown.org/program/china-pakistan-economic-corridor-road-to-riches/>, accessed 19 July 2016.

Ramachandran, Sudha. 2016a. China and India's border infrastructure race. *China Brief*, 16(14), 17–21.

Ramachandran, Sudha. 2016b. China's sinking port plans in Bangladesh. *China Brief*, 16(10), 15–19.

Ramachandran, Sudha. 2017a. Arunachal Pradesh: Cultural and strategic flashpoint for Sino-Indian relations. *China Brief*, 17(1), 13–17.

Ramachandran, Sudha. 2017b. India and Bangladesh: Doing deals to ward off the dragon. *Asia Times*, 4 April. <www.atimes.com/india-bangladesh-deals-fend-off-dragon/>, accessed 4 April 2017.

Sakhuja, Vijay. 2009. China-Bangladesh relations and potential for regional tensions. *China Brief*, 9(15), 10–12.

Shakya, Tsering. 2017. Bhutan can solve its border problem with China: If India lets it. *South China Morning Post*, 22 July. <www.scmp.com/week-asia/geopolitics/article/2103601/bhutan-can-solve-its-border-problem-china-if-india-lets-it>, accessed 22 July 2017.

Sharma, Gopal. 2016. Nepal looks to lessen dependence on India with China port deal. *Reuters*, 23 March. <www.reuters.com/article/us-china-nepal-trade-idUSKCN0WP2BU>, accessed 23 March 2016.

Shepherd, Christian. 2017. China says Dalai Lama "provokes" with visit to disputed border with India. *Reuters*, 12 April. <www.reuters.com/article/us-china-india-dalailama/china-says-dalai-lama-provokes-with-visit-to-disputed-border-with-india-idUSKBN17E1EZ>, accessed 12 April 2017.

Singh, Anita Inder. 2016. China's ban on India's entry into NSG highlights necessity for closer Indo-US ties- Op-Ed. *Eurasia Review*, 27 June. <www.eurasiareview.com/27062016-chinas-ban-on-indias-entry-into-nsg-highlights-necessity-for-closer-indo-us-ties-oped/>

SIPRI TIV. 2017. Stockholm international peace research institute arms transfers database. <www.sipri.org/databases/armstransfers>, accessed 1 May 2017.

Smith, Paul J. 2013. Bhutan-China border disputes and their geopolitical implications, in *Beijing's Power and China's Borders: Twenty Neighbors in Asia*, edited by Bruce Elleman, Stephen Kotkin, and Clive Schofield. Armonk, NY: M.E. Sharpe, 22–35.

Snow, Shawn. 2017. Chinese troops appear to be operating in Afghanistan, and the Pentagon is OK with it. *Military Times*, 5 March. <www.militarytimes.com/articles/Chinese-troops-afghanistan>, accessed 6 March 2017.

Spector, Regine A. 2002. The North-South transport corridor. Brookings Institution, 3 July. <www.brookings.edu/articles/the-north-south-transport-corridor/>, accessed 21 April 2017.

Tang, Christopher. 2013. The Sino-Pakistan border: Stability in an unstable region, in *Beijing's Power and China's Borders: Twenty Neighbors in Asia*, edited by Bruce A. Elleman, Stephen Kotkin, and Clive Schofield. Armonk, NY: M.E. Sharpe, 218–233.

Tiwari, Chitra K. 2013. China-Nepal border: Potential hot spot?, in *Beijing's Power and China's Borders: Twenty Neighbors in Asia*, edited by Bruce A. Elleman, Stephen Kotkin, and Clive Schofield. Armonk, NY: M.E. Sharpe, 204–217.

Tong Yutao. 2015. Indu yu Butan tezhu guanxi de fazhan jincheng [The development process of special relationship between India and Bhutan]. *Dongnan Ya Nan Ya yanjiu*, (4), 36–42.

UNCTAD WIR [World Investment Report]. 2017. World Investment Report. <http://unctad.org/en/Pages/DIAE/World%20Investment%20Report/World_Investment_Report.aspx>, accessed various dates 2013–17.

White House. 2015. US-India joint strategic vision for the Asia-Pacific and Indian Ocean region. United States Government, White House, Office of the Press Secretary, 25 January. <https://obamawhitehouse.archives.gov/the-press-office/2015/01/25/us-india-joint-strategic-vision-asia-pacific-and-indian-ocean-region>, accessed 23 April 2017.

Wolf, Charles, Jr., Wang, Xiao, and Warner, Eric. 2013. *China's Foreign Aid and Government-Sponsored Investment Activities*. Santa Monica: RAND.

Wong, Edward. 2013. China makes inroads in Nepal, and stanches Tibetan influx. *New York Times*, 13 April.<www.nytimes.com/2013/04/14/world/asia/china-makes-inroads-in-nepal-stemming-tibetan-presence.html>, accessed 17 November 2016.

Wong, Edward, and Jolly, David. 2016. China considers larger role in Afghanistan peace process. *New York Times*, 24 January. <www.nytimes.com/2016/01/25/world/asia/china-considers-larger-role-in-afghanistan-peace-process.html>, accessed 25 January 2016.

World Bank WDI [World Development Indicators]. 2017. [Online]. Available at <http://data.worldbank.org/data-catalog/world-development-indicators>.

World Tourism Organization. 2014. Compendium of tourism statistics dataset [Electronic], UNWTO, Madrid, data updated on 11/01/2014.

Zhang Yongpan. 2015. Lun Zhongguo – Nipo'er guanxi zai Xizang wending he fazhan zhong de jiazhi, yingxiang yu zhanwang [China-Nepal relations: Its significance to the stability and development of Tibet]. *Nan Ya yanjiu jikan* [South Asian Studies Quarterly], (no. 162), 23–31.

10 Conclusion

Evaluation

Is China a regional hegemon, and if so, what kind? From the standpoint of capabilities, there is no question but that China has more of what makes countries powerful than any of its neighbors: population, economic size, foreign exchange reserves, investment funds, military forces, foreign aid resources, and the like. Those margins have grown even larger in the 21st century.

What *kind* of regional hegemon is China? The media have a blithe answer of "increasingly assertive," and in some respects that is quite correct. The phrase itself implies a temporal comparison: more assertive than it used to be. Comparing temporally from 1988–2003 and 2004–2017, the point is well-founded. China's behavior in the earlier period can best be described as "active" and in the latter period shows some evidence of being hyperactive, as outlined in Table 2.3. But compared to the 1949–87 period, the latest period seems more benign.

But if we compare China's recent behavior to that of other regional hegemons seen in Chapter 2, the answer is more complex and nuanced. Let us examine the major categories of inactive/active/hyperactive behavior comparatively.

In the ideational realm, China has not announced a regional exclusion doctrine, though as Chapter 5 explored in detail, there is some evidence of movement toward that. However, when compared to the Soviet Union, the Russian Federation, India, Nigeria, and the United States before WWII, all of which had very explicit regional exclusion doctrines, China does not appear to be a hyperactive regional hegemon. Nor does China seem to try to impose political systems on its neighbors the way the Soviets and the Americans did; stability seems to be the primary criteria that China applies to the political systems of its neighbors.

In the security sphere, China does have territorial disputes, and its refusal to attend the Permanent Court of Arbitration's ruling on the Philippines' claim does seem to be a step away from legal resolution of its most prominent dispute, the South China Sea. Just as the United States refused the International Court of Justice's 1986 ruling in the Nicaraguan case, hyperactive regional hegemons do not always follow the law. The Senkaku/Diaoyu case seems similar. Although the force and intimidation being used by China in these two cases is a relatively low-level one (particularly compared to earlier periods in China's foreign relations), it is still a disturbing trend. A key question to watch for in the future will be whether China agrees to a Code of Conduct in the South China Sea in the near future; that might indicate a movement back from intimidation toward a more legal/institutional approach. Along the Sino-Indian border, minor incidents notwithstanding, China has not used force. Both sides are negotiating though it is highly doubtful that a resolution will occur any time soon.

Military intervention, however, is one aspect of regional hegemonic behavior in which China is clearly not behaving in a hyperactive manner. Unlike the Soviets, Russians, Americans, Indians, and South Africans (both pre- and post-apartheid), China has not militarily intervened in the domestic affairs of its neighbors in any appreciable way since the 1980s. In that respect, they are closer to the Brazilians and Nigerians, the latter having generally only intervened in the context of a multi-lateral effort. Even in the recent instances where citizens are threatened such as with Vietnam in 2014, multiple times in Pakistan and Central Asia, and in Myanmar, when one might expect a regional hegemon to put troops into the situation, China has not.

Diplomatically, China has managed its neighboring relations very well: it has established relations with all but one neighbor, has regular summits, state visits, official visits, and sideline meetings with its neighbors, even those with whom it does not particularly warm relations, such as Japan. China also participates in a wide variety of regional international organizations, ASEAN +3, APEC, and the SCO. Although we might expect the formation of rival counter-organizations, such as the GUAM in former Soviet Union against the Russians' organizations, or the subtle competition of South and Latin American organizations between Brazil's favorite MERCOSUL and others, China has joined all organizations, including the East Asian Summit, for which it is clearly unenthusiastic. Within Southeast Asia, no formal anti-Chinese coalition has formed, indicative of that region's hedging behavior.

At the same time, China does not provide security public goods the way other regional hegemons have, though definitional problems make it a difficult issue to resolve. In arms sales, China does sell weapons to its neighbors, but unlike India which reacts badly when neighbors such as Nepal purchase from other countries, or the Soviets/Russians or United States which want their friends and allies to purchase from alliance sources only, China does not appear to have any troubles with countries such as Pakistan having multiple sources of arms.

The expatriate issue is one which has seen great change for China and its relations with Southeast Asia in particular; suspicions and controversies that once were serious impediments to relations in the 1949–87 period had largely disappeared by the 21st century. In contrast, the Russian Federation in particular is loath to see its citizens and Russian-speaking citizens of neighboring countries as anything other than the "Near Abroad," and has demonstrated a willingness to use massive force to protect them.

In the economic sphere, China has shown unmistakable aspects of active hegemonic behavior: it has very high levels of trade with its neighbors, has negotiated regional trade agreements, shown high levels of inward foreign investment, and in recent years, outward investment in its neighbors. Xi Jinping's 2017 Davos speech

282 *Conclusion*

advocating for free trade would have been unthinkable twenty years ago, but now at least in rhetoric, China is a champion of free trade. It has provided bilateral aid and multilateral aid to its neighbors, and has started multi-lateral development banks, such as the AIIB and the New Development Bank. In some ways in its economic relations, China seems to be leaving its regional focus and moving into the global phase, something that Brazil was doing until 2007.

But China has also demonstrated a willingness to use its economic tools for policy ends as well. Japan, South Korea, the Philippines and Vietnam have all suffered economic retaliation from China over serious policy disagreements. Whether embargoes, boycotts, and tourists not coming, this can be a significant coercive tool, just as trade and investment are also rewards. Sometimes this is the result of the Chinese public seizing a *cause célèbre*, but there is almost always Chinese government backing. As China's neighbors grow more and more asymmetrically dependent on trade with China, this is a policy tool that China may increasingly turn to, just as many other regional hegemons we have examined have done so. This has not yet come close to the level of Russia's 2009 gas embargo, or India's petroleum embargoes against Nepal, but it is certainly a tool that China has shown to be willing to use.

But in one respect, the diplomatic initiatives and the elevation of other countries to "partner" status carries with it an implication that is difficult to parse from the idea of "neighbor": to call another person or country a "neighbor" is to accept them and their condition as they are. With a "partner," there is an expectation of interaction, of a mutual project, of a transaction. Whether that represents an active or hyperactive phase of regional hegemonic relations is hard to say; although other regional hegemons (most notably the USA) have used the term in a regional context, it has not been commonly used by other regional hegemons in the past.

Altogether then, China still seems to be in an active but not wholly hyperactive regional hegemon. And it is important to remember that as "assertive" as China may appear – and it appears even more so because of the asymmetry with its neighbors – its behavior must be evaluated both comprehensively and comparatively. Comprehensively, China has twenty-eight neighbors. Table 10.1 lists those and the author assigns an impressionistic rating of -2 (poor) to 2 (good) and their short-term prospects (positive or negative) for those neighbors as of the time of writing, August 2017:

Table 10.1 Summary of China's neighboring relations, 2017

Summary of China's neighboring relations, 2017

Country	Rating (2 = good, – 2 = poor)	Prospect (↑ = improving ↓ = deteriorating)
Japan	–1	↑
South Korea	0	↓
North Korea	–1	↓

Summary of China's neighboring relations, 2017

Country	Rating (2 = good, −2 = poor)	Prospect (↑ = improving ↓ = deteriorating)
Mongolia	0	
Russia	2	↑
Kazakhstan	2	↑
Kyrgyzstan	1	
Uzbekistan	1	
Tajikistan	2	
Turkmenistan	1	
Afghanistan	0	
Pakistan	2	↑
India	−2	↓
Maldives	1	↑
Sri Lanka	2	
Bangladesh	2	↑
Bhutan	0	
Nepal	0	
Myanmar	2	↓
Thailand	1	↑
Malaysia	1	↑
Brunei	1	↑
Philippines	0	↑
Cambodia	2	↑
Laos	1	↑
Vietnam	−1	↑
Indonesia	1	↓
Singapore	1	↓

Source: Author's estimation.

Other scholars may quibble with the individual evaluations. But the need to evaluate China's neighboring relations comprehensively necessitates dealing with twenty-eight relationships. If we look at all twenty-eight, then the average of the admittedly impressionistic numbers is 0.75, so positive as measured for all neighbors, not just the ones that grab the headlines or which we might personally or politically prefer.

Comparatively, China's behavior has aspects of hyperactivity. An unwillingness to work multilaterally to resolve territorial disputes is particularly noteworthy. Building islands and bumping coast guard boats is disturbing. Using economic means to punish neighbors whose policies are adverse is petty. But it is not unusual. We must compare China's "hyperactive" behavior to other regional hegemons: bumping boats and building islands in a disputed sea is not the same thing as invading one's neighbor, annexing a large portion of its internationally-recognized territory, and starting a war that has killed over 10,000 people so far. China is not Russia. Some American officials have stated that the behavior is the same (Brunnstrom 2015), but this author strongly disagrees with the equivalency. China is not what the United States was both at the turn of the 20th century and as recently as the 1980s when American forces invaded both Grenada and Panama and replaced their governments.

But China is also not Brazil, which has been an active and fairly benign regional hegemon, or post-Apartheid South Africa. It can do better. For each instance of inspirational rhetoric of ideas such as the One Belt One Road, China's self-righteous claims to the entire South China Sea or all of Arunachal Pradesh make it seem like other regional hegemons: big, bullying and unapologetic.

Causes

We return to the question that has vexed analysts of China's foreign relations in the 21st century: why does China seem to be increasingly assertive toward some of its East Asian neighbors in the past decade? Why is this behavior less seen in its South and Central Asian relationships? Here we will look at internal, regional and extra-regional factors.

Internal

The first, and perhaps most obvious reason for China's changed behavior in the past few years is a simple answer: "Because they can." The rise of Chinese capabilities, fueled by an economy that continues to grow very rapidly has given China tools both of coercion and of bribery that it lacked in the 1990s and early 2000s. No longer forced to keep a low profile, a full generation has passed since Deng Xiaoping's famous dictum was issued. This explanation would hold that the desire for historical and territorial revision in East and Southeast Asia were held previously, but Chinese capabilities could not enforce them. The incidents surrounding the Diaoyu/Senkaku and South China Sea stretching back to the 1970s might be seen as evidence that the desire was long-standing but until the Chinese maritime forces developed greater capacity, it was unlikely to be more than a few minor skirmishes. By the 2010s, however, China has not only greater overall capacity to enforce its maritime claims, it has forces capable of a nuanced approach: a Coast Guard with a navy backing it up, and a logistical component that can allow Chinese patrols to linger in areas that it once had only briefly visited.

A second internal factor that may be impelling Chinese behavior into the hyperactive phase is one that is at least partially of the regime's own making, yet has a life of its own: nationalism and a deep-seated sense of national grievance toward a variety of foreign actors, but most notably Japan. There is little question that the government in Beijing has encouraged a strong sense of nationalism and grievance, but there are also independent groups in Taiwan and Hong Kong that push the same agenda, especially in the Diaoyu/Senkaku issue. Thus, Beijing's confrontational posture has at least a partial external spur to it, groups that are just as Chinese as the central government but which can and have pushed further by landing individual protesters on the disputed islands. In the case of the Spratlys, Taiwanese forces occupy the largest of the islands (Itu Aba/Taiping) and the expansive Chinese claim to the South China Sea dates from the Republic of China nine-dashed map, and the mainland forces have certainly not sought to expel them, even though they could claim it to be a purely "internal affair."

Regional

Within the region, it is difficult to detect any changes that would impel China toward hyperactive behavior, other than perhaps a lack of change in a positive direction. One of the core interests that has been the source of belligerent behavior in the past has been Taiwanese independence, yet the May 2008 election of the KMT's Ma Ying-jeou at least temporarily removed this prospect, given his mainland-friendly policy, and so far, Tsai Ing-wen has not shown the kind of risk behavior that Ma's predecessor Chen Shui-bian (2000–08) did. At the same time, for a country with deep-seated grievances against Japan especially, that country has not changed: despite changes in leadership and ruling political parties, Japan remains committed to its alliance with the United States and to Chinese eyes is unwilling to go beyond pro-forma apologies for wartime aggression, even going so far as to question even that. Changes in the interpretation of the Japanese constitution in 2014 allowing the sale of weapons abroad and the upgrading of the Defense Agency to Ministry status have only reinforced the image in Chinese eyes of an unrepentant militarism lying just below the surface of Japanese politics.

In at least one area, however, there has been minor movement to which China is extremely sensitive: human rights. Although Japan has generally been at best low-key in its approach to human rights issues in foreign policy in the past, that has changed in the past decade with a much more prominent articulation of human rights and democracy as an issue by Abe Shinzo. Some analysts see this as a selective criticism of North Korea, but Japan's support of the International Criminal Court (ICC) points toward that has gone beyond American foreign policy and has also changed its constitutional law to accede to the ICC by allowing greater international participation, though in a way that seemed to soften the anti-war Article 9 of its constitution (Dukalskis and Johansen 2013: 15–17). For China, Japan's implicit or explicit criticism of its human rights and their role in East Asian international relations is hardly a major issue, and seen as historical amnesia at best. But other Asian nations have adopted the issue as well. ASEAN began to raise human rights issues to a new level in 2009 when it established the ASEAN Intergovernmental Commission on Human Rights (Southwick 2013). This led to the ASEAN Declaration of Human Rights (ADHR) in late 2012, a long list of rights with a notable number of exceptions and caveats; it does, however, raise the issue of human rights in the Asian context, and though China does not belong to ASEAN, it is nonetheless another point of public pressure on Beijing's stance that such issues are purely internal. Some Chinese analysts, however, have interpreted ASEAN's concern for human rights to be the product of Western pressure in the post-Cold War era (Yu Zhen 2011).

China's relations with Vietnam and the Philippines are perhaps more difficult to parse; neither has done much in the past 25 years to offend China, other than their continued insistence on maintaining their territorial claims in the South China Sea against China's historically based claims. Whether this is a matter of offense to the Chinese sense of historical rights and contemporary greatness or both, the increasing use of "Great Power"/大国 (daguo) seems to point toward a renewal of a sense of international hierarchy. The contrast of China's fleet of gleaming new coast guard vessels arrayed against the pathetically weak Filipino forces is exemplified by the standoff at Ayungin Shoal (Second Thomas Shoal), where the Filipinos maintain a handful of sailors on a rusting WWII-era ship that was run aground as their "claim" (Himmelman and Gilbertson 2013). The naval and coast guard forces of Vietnam are marginally larger and better maintained than the Filipinos, but small nonetheless. Both are irritants, and most importantly, neither has backed down from their claims, whereas the Malaysians and Bruneians have remained relatively quiet and non-confrontational. Aside from the lack of change, however, there seems to be little in the broad brush behavior of China's neighbors *by themselves* that would seem to provoke the sharp responses in the Diaoyu/Senkaku and South China Sea disputes in the 2010s.

If we interpret the "increasing assertiveness" as something that is primarily directed at those countries with whom China has claims and with whom China has recently had confrontations, then we might expect the issue to be as China claims: a series of bilateral issues which can and should be resolved diplomatically. But one of the difficulties that Chinese leaders have is in seeing themselves as the world sees them, especially their smaller neighbors. In this regard, China pushing around the Philippines or Vietnam has a demonstration effect, certainly in public opinion and in the quiet councils of Asian capitals. The former can be seen in the Pew Research Center's Spring 2015 opinion survey, in which they asked if people were concerned about the territorial disputes between China and its neighbors. Table 10.2 shows the results:

Table 10.2 Asia public concern over China's territorial disputes

Asia public concern over China's territorial disputes				
Country	Very concerned	Somewhat concerned	Not too concerned	Not at all concerned
Australia	17	46	25	6
India	38	24	6	3
Indonesia	11	30	25	11
Japan	52	31	10	4
Malaysia	12	33	30	14
Pakistan	18	27	10	7
Philippines	56	35	7	1
South Korea	31	47	18	2
Vietnam	60	23	5	4
average	32.8	32.9	15.1	5.8
combined	65.7		20.9	

Source: Stokes (2015). Numbers do not add to 100 because of omission of DK/Refused.

The correlation of having both a territorial dispute with China and recent disturbances and "very concerned" public opinion is very high: Vietnam, the Philippines, and Japan are all above 50% public opinion saying they are "very concerned." India, which had a minor incident in 2013 at the time of the survey, comes next with 38%. The further away from China, the less likelihood of the public being "very concerned." It is the overall combined averages of "very concerned" and "somewhat concerned" that the demonstration effect can be best seen: fully two-thirds of Asian publics show some level of concern about China's territorial claims.

Extra-regional

Finally, we turn to the US Role in East Asia as a factor in China's apparent move from active toward a hyperactive neighborhood policy. As seen in Chapter 2, the introduction or re-introduction of external major power actors to a region often provokes regional hegemons to a sharp response, and depending on available resources, moving policy toward the hyperactive. In short, did the US "Pivot" provoke?

A growing theme that may point in the direction of an exclusionary regional security doctrine has been the criticism of the United States role in East Asia. Li Xiangyang, a Director at Chinese Academy of Social Sciences, wrote in the October 2013 round table that, "Safe to say, most nearby conflicts or problems China confronts are closely entangled with American pressure and influence . . ." (Li Xiangyang 2013: 72). The Obama administration's October 2011 announcement of a "pivot to the Asia-Pacific" has been cited by both Chinese government officials and scholars with concern bordering on offense. One scholar put the matter bluntly when claiming that the many in China and elsewhere believe that the USA has been largely

> . . . responsible for worsening relations between China and some of its neighbors over the past two years . . . some believe that China's relations to Japan and the Philippines has given the U.S. an 'excuse' to return to East Asia, and this has exacerbated the conflicts between China and those countries.
> (Feng Zhongping 2013: 53)

Some Chinese scholars have looked at the US role in the region as one that is likely to decline and that of China improve. Zhao Xiaochun of the University of International Relations stated that the states in the region ". . . still need to safeguard their own economic and security interests and so they will not blindly follow the U.S. and make an enemy of China. China is still pursuing its 'good neighbor' policy, and has the ability to handle conflict with its neighbors" (Zhao Xiaochun 2013: 48).

Works cited

Brunnstrom, David. 2015. U.S. compares China's South China Sea moves to Russia's in Ukraine. *Reuters*, 26 June. <www.reuters.com/article/us-usa-china-blinken-idUSK-BN0P62O120150627>, accessed 2 July 2015.

Dukalskis, Alexander, and Johansen, Robert C. 2013. Measuring acceptance of international enforcement of human rights: The United States, Asia, and the International Criminal Court. *Human Rights Quarterly*, 35(3), 569–597.

Feng Zhongping. 2013. Periphery strategy should focus on innovative security cooperation. *Contemporary International Relations*, 23(6), 50–53.

Himmelman, Jeff, and Gilbertson, Ashley. 2013. A game of shark and minnow. *New York Times Magazine*, 24 October. <www.nytimes.com/newsgraphics/2013/10/27/south-china-sea>, accessed 30 September 2014.

Li Xiangyang. 2013. China's neighboring strategy goals and challenges. *Contemporary International Relations*, 23(6), 71–75.

Southwick, Katherine G. 2013. Bumpy road to the ASEAN human rights declaration. *Asia Pacific Bulletin* (no. 197), 22 January.

Stokes, Bruce. 2015. How Asia-Pacific publics see each other and their national leaders. Pew Research Center, 2 September. <www.pewglobal.org/2015/09/02/how-asia-pacific-publics-see-each-other-and-their-national-leaders/>, accessed 19 April 2017.

Yu Zhen. 2011. Lengzhan hou DongMeng dui Xifang renquan yali de fanying ji qi yingxiang [Post Cold-War responses by ASEAN to Western human rights pressure and its effects]. *Dongnanya yanjiu*, 2011(1), 52–60.

Zhao Xiaochun. 2013. Solving challenges to China's periphery diplomacy. *Contemporary International Relations*, 23(6), 46–49.

Index

Abkhazia 31
Afghanistan 7, 84, 118, 124, 127, 129, 193, 232, 254, 257
agricultural development 244
"Akinyemi Doctrine" 39
Alliance for the Peoples of Our Americas (ALBA) 51
Andean Community of Nations (CAN) 56
Angola 37, 46
Argentina 40, 47
Armenia 33, 53
Asia-Pacific Economic Cooperation (APEC) 98, 110, 130, 193, 206–207
Association of Southeast Asian Nations (ASEAN) 1, 12, 35, 110–112, 130, 185, 187, 269; Plus One 110; Plus Three 16, 98, 110–111, 206–207; Regional Forum 98, 193; trade agreements 210–214
Australia 10

Bangladesh 8, 48, 53–54, 126, 128–129, 264–265
Bay of Pigs invasion 41–42
Belarus 33, 53
Benin 47
Bhutan 8, 73, 127, 255–256, 268
Botswana 36, 37
Brazil: Cisplatine War 40; economic and organizational behavior of 55–57; inactive phase 25; interventionist doctrines 42–43; Monroe Doctrine 40; no exclusionary doctrine 40–42; Platine War 40; policy changes 57–59; radical phase 59; regional hegemon of 15; relations with neighbors 25, 47; Roosevelt Corollary 40; territorial disputes 48; US support for 1964 coup d'état 30
Brezhnev Doctrine 30, 44–45
Brunei Darussalam 8, 78, 188, 202–203
Burma *see* Myanmar

Cambodia 8, 72, 80, 84, 104, 109, 197–198, 210
Cameroon 39
Canada 48
Caribbean 29–30, 49, 52, 60
Central America 23, 30, 49, 52, 60
Central Asia: diplomatic relations with regional states 119–120, 233–242; economics 245–249; expatriates and co-ethnics 121–122, 243–245; foreign direct investment 248–249; military intervention 118; provision of public goods 122; Regional Anti-Terrorist Structure 242–243; regional international organizations 120–121; relations with China 83–84, 116–123, 229–249; relations with external major powers 118–119; relations with USSR/Russia 118, 120; role of United States 124; security issues 116–119, 229–233; territorial disputes 117–118; trade 122–123, 131, 245–248
Chad 25
Chile 47, 55, 98
China: Angolan Civil War 46; border management with North Korea 93; border with Tsarist Russia 70; boundaries with Korea 71; "Chinese Dream" policy 141; "Chinese Monroe Doctrine" 26; as cooperative partner in war on terror 104–105; currency swap agreements 175, 217; diplomatic visits in foreign countries 88–89; economic growth 100; energy supply vulnerability 140; engagement in Middle East 142; exclusion doctrines 150–151; expatriates and co-ethnics 130–131; extra-regional factors guiding foreign relations 132, 287; Five Principles of Peaceful Co-existence 84, 90–91, 103; foreign policy behavior 2–5; Good Neighbor

Policy 7, 58, 88–132, 141; high-level visits 195–196; hyperactive phase 75–85; ideology 89–90; inactive phase 69–75; infrastructure provision 217; internal factors guiding foreign relations 131, 284–285; investments in Central Asia 248–249; investments in Northeast Asia 172–175; investments in South Asia 273–276; investments in Southeast Asia 214; Korean War 77; imperial relations with neighbors 69–73; overseas Chinese during the imperial era 73–75; lending of hard currency 50; maritime boundary between Japan and 71; maritime disputes 93; military intervention 94, 103–104, 118, 124, 130, 167, 191; neighboring regions and neighbors 10–12, 142–143; Nixon's opening to 78; One Belt One Road initiative 2, 122, 145, 152, 175, 199, 218–219, 244–245, 269, 273; partners 8–9, 142–143; policy changes 57–59; Regional Anti-Terrorist Structure 121, 242–243; regional factors guiding foreign relations 131, 285–287; regional hegemon of 17–20; relations with Afghanistan 127; relations with Bangladesh 126, 264–265; relations with Bhutan 127, 255–256, 268; relations with Brunei Darussalam 188, 202–203; relations with Cambodia 78–79, 109, 197–198; relations with Central Asia 83–84; relations with Central Asia 229–249; relations with external major powers 94–95, 104–105, 118–119, 124, 159, 191–194; relations with India 76, 84, 125, 128, 254, 261–264; relations with Indonesia 81–82, 106–107, 188–191, 205–206; relations with Japan 77, 95–96, 100–101, 157–158, 160–163, 170–171; relations with Kazakhstan 230, 235–236; relations with Kyrgyzstan 231, 237–238, 247–248; relations with Laos 108–109, 198–199; relations with Malaysia 78, 81, 83, 109, 187–188, 203–204; relations with Maldives 127, 268–269; relations with Mongolia 77–78, 165–167, 172, 175; relations with Myanmar 78, 82–83, 107, 200–202; relations with Nepal 126, 265–266; relations with Northeast Asia 76–78, 157–175; relations with North Korea 96–97, 101, 163–165, 171–172, 174; relations with Pakistan 84–85, 124, 125–126, 128, 256–257, 259–261; relations with Philippines 78, 81, 108, 186–187, 196–197; relations with Singapore 110, 204–205; relations with South Asia 84–85, 254–275; relations with Southeast Asia 72–73, 78–79, 182–219; relations with South Korea 92, 96, 100–101, 158–159, 163–165, 171, 174–175; relations with Sri Lanka 127, 266–268; relations with Tajikistan 230–231, 236–237, 248; relations with Thailand 78, 81, 107–108, 199–200; relations with Turkmenistan 239, 248; relations with United States 3; relations with USSR/Russia 76, 83, 230–231, 234–235, 240–241, 247–248; relations with Uzbekistan 238–239; relations with Vietnam 1–2, 71–72, 78, 79–81, 89, 105–106, 186, 196; resources in foreign direct investment 140; role of United States 147–152; security issues 92–95, 101–105, 124, 182–194, 229–233; Senkaku/Diaoyu Island dispute 94; Sino-French War 72; Sino-Japanese War 71; Sino-Nepalese border negotiations 255; territorial disputes 80–81, 92–94, 101–103, 117–118, 124, 129–130, 157–159, 182–191, 230–231; trade with Central Asia 122–123; trade with Northeast Asia 100–101, 168–172; trade with South Asia 128–129, 270–273; trade with Southeast Asia 113–115, 131, 210–214; Trans-Asian Railway (TAR) 219; transportation development 218–219; Treaty of Amity and Cooperation (TAC) 112; Treaty of Kiakhta 70; Treaty of Nerchinsk 70

China-ASEAN Free Trade Area Agreement (CAFTA) 210
Code of Conduct (COC) 185
co-ethnics 49, 99, 112–113, 121–122, 130–131, 168, 207–209, 243–245, 269
Collective Security Treaty Organization (CSTO) 53, 243
Colombia 30, 47
Commonwealth of Independent States (CIS) 16, 53
Community of Latin American and Caribbean States (CELAC) 51
Côte d'Ivoire 46
Council for Mutual Economic Assistance (CMEA/COMECON) 52
Crimea 31
Cuba 23, 30, 41–42, 43, 51, 56, 162
Czechoslovakia 32–33

Declaration on the Conduct of Parties in the South China Sea (DOC) 102, 185
Diaoyu/Senkaku dispute 182–183, 235
diplomatic relations as measure of regional hegemony 49
Dominican Republic 30, 52

East Asian Summit (EAS) 207
East Berlin 32
East China Sea 162–163, 185
Economic Community of West African States (ECOWAS) 16, 39, 55, 207
Egypt 76
Estonia 31
Eurasian Economic Union (EEU) 53
Eurasian Union 53
exclusion doctrines 26–28, 30–32, 61, 150–151
Exclusive Economic Zone (EEZ) 93, 183, 186, 188–189
expatriates 49, 99, 112–113, 121–122, 130–131, 168, 207–209, 243–245, 269

fisheries 185
foreign direct investment (FDI) 50, 140–141, 172–174, 214, 248–249, 273–275
France 25, 39, 60, 72
Free Trade Area of the Americas (FTAA) 51, 56

Gabon 46
Georgia 31, 33, 49
German Democratic Republic 53
Germany 29–30, 59
Good Neighbor Policy 7, 43–44
Great Britain 29
"Greater East Asia Co-Prosperity Sphere" 73, 150
Grenada 30
Guatemala 30
Guinea 40, 47, 60
Guinea-Bissau 46
Gujral Doctrine 45
Guyana 29

Haiti 28, 30, 52
Hungary 32

India: economic and organizational behavior of 53–54; exclusion doctrines 33–35; expatriates 269; "Extended Neighborhood" policy 34–35; Gujral Doctrine 45; inactive phase 24; Indira Doctrine 34–35, 59; interests in South China Sea 193; interventionist doctrines 35–36; as neighbor of China 8; regional hegemon of 15; relations with China 76, 84, 88, 125, 254, 261–264; relations with neighbors 47; relations with United States 257–258; small-scale naval exercises 193–194, 258; territorial disputes 124
Indira Doctrine 34–35, 59
Indonesia 8, 50, 73, 76, 81–82, 88, 106–107, 188–191, 205–206, 209–210
interventionist doctrines 28–30, 32–43
Iran 241

Jakarta 82
Japan 8, 17, 19, 70–71, 77, 88, 95–96, 99, 150, 157–158, 160–163, 170–171, 173, 194, 258

Kazakhstan 8, 31, 53, 117, 129, 230, 235–236, 243–245, 255
Kenya 36
Kyrgyzstan 8, 33, 53, 118–119, 129, 231–232, 237–238, 243–245, 247–248

Laos 8, 72, 78, 88, 102, 108–109, 129, 198–199, 210
Latin America 23–24, 42, 51, 58, 141
Latin American Integration Association (ALADI) 51
Latvia 31
Lesotho 36
limited sovereignty doctrine 30–31

Malawi 54
Malaysia 8, 50, 73, 78, 81, 83, 88, 109, 112–113, 203–204, 209–210, 214
Maldives 8, 10, 35, 127, 268
Mandela/Mbeki Doctrine 36, 38
Mercosul ("Mercosur") 56
Mexico 23, 28, 30, 48, 52, 56, 58, 98
Middle East 142, 193
migrants 73–75
Mongolia 8, 10, 17, 69–70, 77–78, 92–94, 97–98, 99, 101, 117, 129, 165–167, 172–173, 175, 240
Monroe Doctrine 23, 26–30, 40, 146, 150–151
Mozambique 36, 37, 46
Myanmar 8, 10, 72–73, 76, 78, 82–83, 103, 107, 151, 200–202

Namibia 36, 46
Natuna Islands 186, 188–191
natural gas 245–246
neighbors: China's idea of 7–8; concept of 5–7
Nepal 8, 34, 35, 53–54, 56, 126, 129, 254, 255, 265–266
Nicaragua 30, 44, 58
Niger 47
Nigeria: "Akinyemi Doctrine" 39; continental jurisdiction 38–40, 59; economic and organizational behavior of 55, 56; economic growth 19; foreign policy 25, 39–40, 46–47; inactive phase 25; interventionist doctrines 40; interventions in Chad 25; *Pax-Nigeriana* 38–40; policy changes 57–59; regional hegemon of 15; relations with neighbors 25; territorial disputes 48
"Nine Dashed Line Map" 148, 183–184, 188–189, 190
North American Free Trade Agreement (NAFTA) 51
Northeast Asia: diplomatic relations with regional states 95–98, 159–167; economics 100; expatriates and co-ethnics 99, 168; military intervention 94, 167; provision of economic public goods 174–175; provision of public goods 99; provision of security public goods 168; regional international organizations 98, 167; relations with China 76–78, 92–101, 157–175; relations with external major powers 94–95, 159; security issues 92–95; territorial disputes 92–94, 157–159; trade 100–101, 131, 168–172
North Korea 8, 17, 77, 88, 92–93, 96–97, 99, 101, 163–165, 171–172, 174

Organization of American States (OAS) 16, 50–51, 207

Pakistan 8, 34–35, 47, 48, 54, 84, 88, 124, 125–126, 254, 259–261
Panama 30, 48
Papua New Guinea 98
Paraguay 42, 56
partners 8–9, 142–143
Pax-Nigeriana 38–40
Peru 98
Philippines 8, 78, 81, 88, 103, 108, 186, 196–197, 209
Poland 32, 53
public goods 21–22, 99, 115–116, 129, 174–175, 214–219

Regional Anti-Terrorist Structure (RATS) 121, 242–243
Regional Comprehensive Economic Partnership (RCEP) 210
Regional Counter-Terrorism Structure (RCTS) See Regional Anti-Terrorist Structure
regional hegemons: active phase 21; asymmetric capabilities of 20–21, 61; behavior 20–23; definition of 14–23; diplomatic relations 49; economic and organizational behavior of 49–57; exclusion doctrines 26–28, 30–32, 61; expatriates and co-ethnics 49; "globalist" phase 21–23; hyperactive phase 21, 25–26, 61–62; ideational and security foundations of 23–57; inactive phase 21, 23–25; international institutions and 62; interventionist doctrines 28–30, 32–43; policy changes 57–60, 61; resistance 62; security behavior of 47–49; territorial disputes 48–49
regional international organizations 98, 110–112, 120–121, 127–128, 167, 206–207
Regional Trade Agreements (RTAs) 51
resistance 62
Rhodesia 36, 37, 46
Roosevelt [Theodore] Corollary 29–30, 40, 44, 58
Russia *see* USSR/Russia

security public goods 113, 122, 168, 209–210
Shanghai Cooperation Organization (SCO) 16, 116, 119, 120–121, 130, 230–232, 240–241
Siam 72
Sikkim 10, 35, 48, 84, 254
Singapore 8, 78, 88, 110, 204–205, 214
South Africa: Angolan Civil War 46; apartheid policy 36–37; economic and organizational behavior of 54–55, 56; economic growth 19; inactive phase 25; interventionist doctrines 37–38, 59, 60; Mandela/Mbeki Doctrine 36, 38; outward policy and "détente" 46; policy changes 57–59; regional hegemon of 15; relations with Nigeria 40; territorial disputes 48
South Asia: diplomatic relations with regional states 125, 258–269; economics 128, 269–275; expatriates and co-ethnics 269; foreign direct investment 273–275; military intervention 124; provision of public goods 129; regional international organizations 127–128, 269; relations with China 84–85, 123–129, 254–275; relations with external major powers 124; security issues 124, 255–258; territorial disputes 124; trade 128–129, 270–273

South Asian Association for Regional Cooperation (SAARC) 12, 16, 45, 53–54, 127, 269
South Asian Free Trade Area (SAFTA) 54
South China Sea 102–103, 129–130, 182–185, 189–190, 193–194, 209
Southeast Asia: diplomatic relations with regional states 105–110, 194–206; economics 113; expatriates and co-ethnics 112–113, 207–209; foreign direct investment 214; high-level visits 195–196; military intervention 103–104, 191; provision of public goods 115–116; provision of security public goods 113; regional international organizations 110–112, 206–207; relations with China 72–73, 78–79, 101–116, 182–219; relations with external major powers 104–105, 191–194; security issues 101–105, 182–194; territorial disputes 101–103, 182–191; trade 113–115, 131, 210–214
Southern African Customs Union (SACU) 54
South Korea 8, 17, 19, 77, 93, 96, 99, 158–159, 163–165, 171, 174
South Ossetia 31
Spain 28
Spanish-American War 30
Sri Lanka 34, 35, 58, 88, 127, 129, 266–268
Swaziland 36

Taiwan 71, 98, 103–104, 232
Tajikistan 8, 33, 117, 129, 230, 236–237, 243–245, 248
Tanzania 46
"Ten Dashed Line Map" 148, 186
territorial disputes: Central Asia 230–231; Northeast Asia 92–94, 157–159; regional hegemons 48–49; South Asia 124; Southeast Asia 101–103, 182–191, 209–210
Thailand 8, 50, 72, 78, 81, 88, 107–108, 113, 199–200, 210, 214
Tibet 69, 73, 84, 232, 255
Timor Leste 8, 10
trade: Central Asia 122–123, 131, 245–248; Northeast Asia 100–101, 131, 168–172; South Asia 128–129; Southeast Asia 113–115, 131, 210–214
Trans-Asian Railway (TAR) 219
Trans-Atlantic Trade and Investment Partnership (TTIP) 52
Trans-Pacific Partnership (TPP) 52
Turkmenistan 8, 239, 248

"U-Dashed Line" 183
Ukraine 31, 33, 56, 49, 59, 255
Union of South American Nations (UNASUR) 56
United Nations Conference on Law of the Sea 48
United States: agreement with Kyrgyzstan 118, 232; Angolan Civil War 46; armed intervention in Caribbean 29–30; Bay of Pigs invasion 41–42, 58; as cooperative partner in war on terror 104–105; economic and organizational behavior of 50–52, 56; expatriates and co-ethnics 49; Good Neighbor Policy 43–44, 50, 58, 147; hyperactive phase 58; inactive phase 23–24; interventionist doctrines 29–30; Mexican-American War 48; Monroe Doctrine 23, 26–30; policy changes 57–59; regional hegemon of 15; relations with China 94; relations with India 257–258; relations with Northeast Asia 94; role in Central Asia 124; role in Southeast Asia 191–194; Roosevelt Corollary 29–30, 40, 44; small-scale naval exercises 193–194, 258; US-Japan Security Treaty 159
Uruguay 40, 56
USSR/Russia: border with China 70; Brezhnev Doctrine 30, 44–45; connections with non-communist countries 76; doctrine of limited sovereignty 30–31; economic and organizational behavior of 52–53, 56; exclusion doctrines 30–32; inactive phase 24; interventionist doctrines 32–33, 59; member of Asia-Pacific Economic Cooperation 98; Monroe Doctrine 28; as neighbor of China 8; penetration of Mongolia 69–70; perception of Western influence in former territories 31, 59–60; policy changes 57–59; policy toward newly-independent states 31–32, 33; regional hegemon of 15; relations with Central Asia 120; relations with China 76, 83, 230–231, 234–235, 240–241, 247–248; relations with Northeast Asia 94–95; relations with Southeast Asia 104; renunciation of Brezhnev Doctrine 44–45; territorial disputes 48–49, 117; Treaty of Kiakhta 70; Treaty of Nerchinsk 70; withdrawal from Afghanistan 124
Uzbekistan 8, 119, 238–239, 245

Venezuela 28, 29, 43, 51
Vietnam: as neighbor of China 8; relations with China 1–2, 71–72, 78, 79–81, 89; relations with China 105–106; relations with China 186, 196; territorial disputes 80–81, 102, 129–130, 186, 210; tourist spending 214

War of the Triple Alliance 40
Warsaw Pact 16, 53, 76
Warsaw Treaty Organization 33, 53

Zaire 46
Zambia 46
Zimbabwe 37